Gendering Labor History

ALICE KESSLER-HARRIS

Gendering
Labor History

UNIVERSITY OF ILLINOIS PRESS

Urbana and Chicago

Library of Congress Cataloging-in-Publication Data
Kessler-Harris, Alice.
Gendering labor history / Alice Kessler-Harris.
p. cm. — (The working class in American history)
Includes bibliographical references (p.) and index.
ISBN-13: 978-0-252-03149-6 (cloth : alk. paper)
ISBN-10: 0-252-03149-0 (cloth : alk. paper)
ISBN-13: 978-0-252-07393-9 (pbk. : alk. paper)
ISBN-10: 0-252-07393-2 (pbk. : alk. paper)
1. Women—Employment—United States—History.
2. Women labor union members—United States—History.
3. Working class women-United States—History.
4. Women—Employment—Government policy United States—History.
5. Sex role in the work environment—United States—History.
I. Title.
HD6095.K4487   2007
331.4'70973—dc22   2006020764

For Rhoda Dorsey,
who introduced me to American history,
Charles Budd "Pete" Forcey,
who taught me its language,
and for Bert, *sine qua non.*

Contents

Gendering Labor History

Conflicts in a Gendered Labor History

When I remember that I've been a historian for forty years, I sometimes feel an overwhelming sense of continuity and pride at being part of a long and distinguished line of labor historians. Sometimes I feel only despair, a sense that we have accomplished so little after so long. The tension between achievement and despair has me in its grip as I sit down to write the introduction to this volume. In this essay, I seek, finally, to reconcile two competing parts of my intellectual life. I imagine myself as a historian of labor in the United States and beyond, and at the same time I proudly call myself a historian of women. Along with a connection to the centrality of class in labor history, I feel a deep commitment to the political project of feminism in my historical work and in my daily life. Though these two fields ought to meld gracefully into an analytic whole, we students of U.S. history who inhabit both fields continue to find ourselves subject to one label or another even as we imagine ourselves to be engaged in an integrated enterprise. Perhaps because I was lucky enough to become a historian at a moment when both fields were in creative ferment, my work reflects some of the issues that divided them and some that bridged the gaps. I've arranged the essays in this collection to speak to the historical challenges to feminism posed by the field of labor history and to class by women's history as they emerged at different moments. Read together, they tell a story of evolution and change. Read separately, I hope they reveal some of the rich possibilities of a gendered labor history.

None of these essays emerged from a vacuum. They are located, like all my work, in a powerful burst of creative energy that followed the politics of the

With grateful appreciation to the Feminist Reading Group at Columbia; to Ilene DeVault and David Montgomery for sensitive readings; and to audiences at Cornell University's School of Industrial and Labor Relations and the City University of New York's Herbert G. Gutman Lecture series.

1960s, which excavated the histories of women in industry, in rural life, in the office, and in the marketplace.[1] This creative outburst melded the history of women, households, family life, and the workplace.[2] It uncovered an array of materials on black women, Latinas, and women in trade unions.[3] It featured the achievements of individual women whose lives had long been forgotten or whose achievements had been obscured.[4] And it culminated in Ava Baron's forceful 1991 call to recognize that gender is "embedded in social relationships, institutions, processes." Baron's call for explorations of how gender ideology was imported into production—how it developed, maintained, and changed as the labor process was transformed—turned the conversation within the discipline to the role of male identity as it impacted on female workers.[5]

When I entered the field in 1962, none of this had happened. "Women's history" did not exist as such, and a newly revised "labor history" was only beginning to emerge from the grip of economic historians. Our bible was not E. P. Thompson's *Making of the English Working Class* but Edward Hallett Carr's *What Is History?* Carr is perhaps best known for his pungent metaphor about facts and fish: "The facts are really not at all like fish on the fishmonger's slab, they are like fish swimming about in a vast and sometimes inaccessible ocean."[6] Carr argued that what the historian catches depends largely on what part of the ocean he or she chooses to fish in and where his or her net is cast: choices made by historians who cannot help but be influenced by their own circumstances. The best history, he argued, represents a historian's dialogue not merely with the present but with the future: "Great history is written precisely when the historian's vision of the past is illuminated by insights into the problems of the present."[7] Towards the end of *What Is History?* Carr extends his earlier plea to link past and present to suggest that he should have described history as "a dialogue between the events of the past and progressively emerging future ends."[8] By way of illustration, he notes that if the main goal of a particular generation were organizing constitutional liberties and political rights, its historians would tend to interrogate the past in constitutional and political terms.

What were the main goals of our generation? We entered graduate school when racism and the civil rights movement of the 1960s occupied the newspaper headlines; when the war in Vietnam demanded explorations of the nature of American imperialism; when a new cultural revolution raised questions about the meaning of a consumer society and its impact on the family. Our mentors rose to the challenges; William Appleman Williams, Merle Curti, Edward Pessen, and John Higham were our heroes. The times shaped the questions we asked. Herb Gutman's provocative volume on *The Black Family in Slavery and Freedom* is only one example of this phenomenon. Beginning as a response to Daniel Patrick Moynihan's assertions about the responsibility of the black community for its own poverty, *The Black Family* became a carefully researched analysis of the transformations wrought by economic and social pressure on family life. Like many of the vanguard books of "New Left" historians, it began with questions fostered by the challenging events of the day. Historians could not avoid the interpretive gauntlets thrown down by American forays into the world, the rise of welfare activism, and the apparent failures of utopian dreams. The new labor history came out of those challenges, and I became a historian in the exhilarating days of the early second wave of feminism.

I watched from the sidelines as the labor movement tried to deal with demands for racial justice, as it sponsored Medicare and fostered Medicaid, and as it split over which side to take in a rising antiwar movement. But I also protested the blows of the "hard-hats" who attacked longhaired kids marching for peace and resisting authority. Not much later, I witnessed the turf battles that led union members to oppose affirmative action in an effort to protect their jobs against new claimants. Our history was reinvented in the light of Vietnam, the civil rights movement, and the rise of the New Left.

I have shared in the renaissance of a field once dominated by economists and social theorists, and I have experienced the tensions of its efforts to draw inspiration from the labor movement. If labor history arose in the 1960s, with a generation of young people who hoped that a revitalized labor movement would support the reassertion of social momentum (by the poor for welfare rights; by women for equal opportunity in education and jobs; by families for health care and economic security), it foundered on our disillusionment with labor's visions of itself. In those days, we thought organized labor could point the way to solidarity—to a revived sense of unity among working-class people who would learn to resist the abuses of capitalism. We searched for a history that would illuminate a path into the future. For better or for worse, we asked questions and wrote in dialogue with a vibrant present, filled with hope and alternative possibilities.

But we neither understood nor came to terms with the transformation of class and culture all around us. As the labor movement succumbed to the government and corporate assaults of the 1970s and 1980s; as a shifting occupational structure eliminated traditional manufacturing and removed desirable jobs beyond the reach of many; as skilled workers came to participate in middle-class lifestyles and to understand increasing consumption as the American way, activism became bogged down in debilitating divisions among working people and a deep skepticism about the viability of class consciousness as a source of social and political change. These changes led many labor historians to question the relevance of traditional conceptions of class conflict, to argue that the notion needed to be enriched and perhaps redefined to incorporate the complexities of race and racism, ethnic identity, religious commitment, tradition, and culture.

My experience parallels that of my generation. I use it as a touchstone, calling on the injunction of my mentor, Warren Susman, who used to say, "Every history is an autobiography." I didn't believe this until I saw it in my own case. I chose to write a dissertation on Jewish immigrant workers in New York City in the 1890s. I wanted to explore the American dream in the life of the minds of immigrant workers. At the time, the dissertation seemed to me a way of understanding America, a topic I thought I had chosen despite, not because of, my own immigrant childhood. It ended up, as so many of our products do, being far more autobiographical than I could have imagined.

On the face of it, my topic was quite distant: I was writing about the turn of the century; reading in a learned language (Yiddish); exploring a religion and culture that my refugee parents once shared but had resolutely denied their children. I had spent my childhood in England, though we spoke Hungarian and German at home. We lived in Leicester, in those early years, in a houseful of refugees that included one of my mother's three sisters and her three children. Most of the refugees were Jews, like my parents, but several, including my aunt's husband, my uncle Yup, were not. He had been imprisoned at Sachsenhausen, outside Berlin, for political rather than religious reasons. It didn't matter. We were all strangers—politics, not religion, was our common bond; German, not English, our lingua franca. Then the war ended, and when some of the refugees found they could go "home," my parents discovered they could not. My brothers and I learned English after the war's end made it clear that there was no "home" in Prague or Budapest for us to go to. Only then did my parents pick up their three children and move to South Wales to start a new life.

My life's story has few parallels with the Jewish immigrants who inhabited New York in the 1890s. And yet, in retrospect it is clear that in their story, I searched for the past I wished I had, the past I imagined might have been mine: a past of immigrant community, of radical conversation, of utopian dreams, of political struggle. That was the past I wanted to have. Immigrant that I was, I wrote the story reflected in my own life: a story of hierarchical power dominated by those who could speak the language well, of futile efforts at assimilation, of masculine ascendancy in a world of male unions. It was then that I recognized, with some surprise, that I could no longer avoid my own past.

Only in retrospect did I realize that I had produced a partial story. That dissertation, for which I learned to read Yiddish in order to access microfilmed newspapers, led me to the handwritten letters and autobiographies of new immigrants and to the records of the *landsmanschaften* they established. As I worked through the material, I systematically discarded everything to do with women. This, after all, was a dissertation about labor and the labor movement.

At a time when the iconography of work was writ male, when class activity was most effectively figured in collective action, women seemed hardly relevant. If I came across them, and I sometimes did, they quickly became romantic icons to be admired and then forgotten.[9] I think now that I simply could not see beyond the normative male image: "worker" was a male term, and labor unions were, in my limited experience, male organizations.

In 1968, when I defended the dissertation, I raised my head from the typewriter to discover the incipient women's movement. Furious with myself for overlooking the women whose voices I was now ready to hear, I set the dissertation aside and went back to work again. Where were all the women workers? I asked. Why were women excluded from unions? What roles did female workers play during strikes and at meetings? These became the subjects of the first articles I published, "'Where are the Organized Women Workers?'" and "Organizing the Unorganizable."

But the emergence of a women's movement was only one factor that drew my attention to the lost women. I could turn to them in the early 1970s because by then I had met Herb Gutman. Charles Budd (Pete) Forcey, my adviser, and Warren Susman, who had mentored me at Rutgers after Pete left to go to Binghamton, were both friends and former Wisconsin classmates of Herb's. While I was working on the dissertation, they repeatedly urged me to call Herb. But I wanted the dissertation done and over. I was shy, insecure, young, harried (already the mother of a four-year-old daughter), and intimidated by an unsupportive husband. And Herb Gutman? Who was he then? Still an unknown assistant professor, tucked away at Fairleigh Dickinson, fearful that his own radical past would be discovered.

I finally encountered Herb in 1969, at what I think was the first of the Socialist Scholars' Conferences. He encouraged me to send him the dissertation. A few weeks later, Herb was in town for a few days, and we met for lunch at an East Side coffee shop. He had read the dissertation, and he wanted to talk. Lunch leached into the afternoon, and a very long conversation. Later I knew I had made a dreadful mistake in not calling him earlier. It was an "interesting" dissertation, Herb told me in his warm and candid way, but I had got it all wrong. I knew he was right.

The message he transmitted in those hours—a message that became familiar to students of labor history everywhere—was about the importance of understanding what he called the "self-experience" of immigrants and workers. It was, after all, Herb who (in the 1960s and 1970s) pushed us to explore the rich troves of workers' psychology and culture. In contrast to Selig Perlman's economistic job consciousness (rooted in a collective solidarity born of job scarcity), Herb encouraged us to see the consciousness and identity of workers as products of rich ethnic and racial family and community lives. Following E. P. Thompson, he focused less on the internal dynamics of the trade-union movement and more on relations within families and among workers. His notion of "workers' culture" melded the community and family lives of workers with workplace resistance, political struggles, and aspirations for social change, enriching the idea of class even as it turned to "culture" to explain the persistence of idiosyncratic notions of fairness. And if attention to the lived experience of working people fostered a recognition of race and ethnicity as participants in the production of consciousness or identity, it also made room for gender.

Against all expectations, the turn from class to anthropological notions of culture (culture as lived experience) exerted a profound force. Class faded from the political vocabulary. As it appeared increasingly irrelevant to the lives of workers, it lost its power to explain social cohesion, its capacity to persuade us that it had functioned in the past as the engine of social movements and demands for change. And yet, as Herb was among the first to recognize, as class faded, so did our capacity to explicate power relations, particularly between workers and employers. By the early 1980s (towards the end of his sadly short life), he was troubled by the ways that attention to ethnicity and race fragmented our view of the working class. He struggled to explain how culture could function as more than a descriptive concept—how it might be conceived in a way that illuminates power relationships. Useful as they were, he feared that cultural approaches would highlight differences rather than commonalities, emphasizing the romantic or colorful detail rather than explaining processes of change.[10]

In a provocative 1984 conference organized at Northern Illinois University to discuss these issues, I turned my attention to some of them. For if our neglect of changing class relations had left us devoid of adequate explanations for the behavior of working people, as everyone at the conference seemed to insist, how would we draw lessons about the direction of the labor movement? While some scholars sought explanation in the emergence of mass culture, in rising standards of living, or in the development of a homogenizing media, others took their cues from prevailing efforts to promote ethnic bonding, whiteness, or maleness. For me, however, the process of gender seemed to provide the clearest illustration of how culture might influence class relations. I tried to articulate some of these thoughts in the essay that became "A New Agenda for Labor History," written after the conference's end. There I moved from the ideological concerns that had informed my views of relations between male and female workers (in "Stratifying by Sex" and "Independence and Virtue in the Lives of Wage-Earning Women") to more material perspectives. Gender, I argued, has acted most persistently to divide the working class against itself and, in the end, has served the interests of employers. Gender also participates in class formation by setting normative standards for appropriate behavior, education, and aspirations in ways that further influence class relations, structures, and values.

That essay probably wouldn't have been possible had feminist historians not kept the notion of class alive. In 1973, I joined with a small group of women historians in New York to form a Marxist-feminist study group. Our initial purpose was to read Marx together to try to understand how *Capital* deals with women and households. The word "gender" was not yet part of our ordinary vocabulary. Discouraged at first by the virtual exclusion of women except as producers of household goods and agents of social reproduction of the next generation of labor, we quickly turned our attention to how women seem invisibly to have shaped the processes of capital accumulation and distribution. In the early days, we thought of women as a "sex-class" silently accommodating and strengthening a class structure based on a man's position in the mode of production, while simultaneously benefitting from its advantages or suffering its indignities.[11] But in the end, Marxist-feminism revealed the central importance of locating women within the paradigm of class power relations (as agents of social reproduction, maintainers of households, income extenders, and wage earners) and illuminating their positions with relation to class structure.

The distinguished Renaissance historian Joan Kelly was part of this little group at the time she was thinking about the piece that would become "The Social Relation of the Sexes," which I often think of as the intellectual progenitor of Joan Scott's famous piece, "Gender: A Useful Category of Historical Analysis."[12] Joan Kelly's work and our conversations during the several years we met together opened up the meaning of class for analysis of systemic change, setting the stage to challenge the traditional ways in which labor historians had used the notion of class. The subtle ways in which gender reshaped our notions of class by introducing the power of social reproduction, of sexuality, of consumption, and of ideologies that emerged not from the places of workers in production but from the location of men and women in households would, I came to believe, immeasurably enrich the notion of class. Joan Kelly died in 1982—the year I published *Out to Work: A History of Wage-Earning Women in the United States*—and I don't think I've ever fully acknowledged my intellectual debt to her. It is reflected in many of the essays of the early 1980s, but it emerges most powerfully in "Treating the Male as Other."

Marxist-feminism precipitated my own turn to gender as an explanatory device. I came to gender not out of an effort to reject class but as an attempt to understand it in its full complexity. The identification and celebration of female labor leaders now seemed less important than finding out how gender has worked within the labor movement, how the play of gender could help to explain why labor leaders act in apparently idiosyncratic ways. These were the themes of two essays: "Problems of Coalition Building" and "Rose Schneiderman." I began to think as well about how nineteenth-century ideals of masculinity, and particularly the idea of "free labor," influenced the shape of the proto-industrial and industrial household and reified male breadwinners as privileged political citizens. Building on new work on masculinity as a regulatory device, I tried to unravel the implications of male/female relationships (at work and in the home) for the behavior and consciousness of workers.[13] For me the moment of epiphany came when I imagined gender not as an organizational category but as a normative device that influences conceptions of appropriate work and regulates the aspirations and goals of women and men. Like Thompson's notion of class, gender began to look more like a process— protean enough to be shaped by historical circumstance, and yet powerful enough to influence structures and institutions. My work, through the years, to understand protective labor legislation as it applied to women grew out of this insight. "The Paradox of Motherhood" reflects this stage of thought. The social movements that pressured legal changes appear in this essay as contests over male and female domestic expectations and as mechanisms for organizing the labor market.

Like many of my generation, I had tried to combine activism with scholarship. For several years in the early 1970s, the women's movement seemed the way for me to do so. But in 1974, shortly after our Marxist-feminist group formed, I had the opportunity to participate in creating a new labor college— one that joined the resources of a trade union (the Distributive Workers of America, District 65) with those of a university (Hofstra) to produce a college degree program that provided a free education to union members who would get release time from work to attend classes. I met Alice Cook at a labor education conference. As were many others, I was immediately taken by the uniqueness of this woman who could look beyond the fierce loyalty demanded by the labor movement into the real problems of women's lives. Her pamphlet on *The Working Mother* appeared in 1975, just before I met her in 1976 and while I was still working with District 65.

I was particularly interested in Cook's work because I had just begun to think about the historical roots of protective labor legislation in a comparative context and was, at the same time, busily protesting the limits on opportunity placed on wage-earning women in general and mothers in particular. My own conclusions, quite unlike Cook's, emphasized the costs of labor legislation to women's opportunities in a market-driven society. Later, working with a dozen European women from as many different countries, I discovered that the circumstances surrounding the passage of legislation made all the difference. We concluded that while every country had passed some form of labor legislation limiting the hours of women's work and the kind of work they could do, each had done so from its own particular motives.[14] In Austria the movement was led by Roman Catholics who wanted to insure that women remain obedient to the authority of their husbands; in France it was led by Catholics concerned about women's capacity to be attentive mothers. In the United States, trade unionists rallied in support of a mentality that imagined jobs as male turf and women as the necessary comfort of working men. In Denmark, politicians insisted that it was "uncivilized" to allow women to work at night. In Britain, reformers claimed a maternal interest in women's childbearing and child-rearing activities. And in Sweden, socialists objected to "women only" legislation except when it was conceived as a first step to legislation for all workers. The result was a variety of different sorts of legislation that sometimes eased the lives of wage-earning women and sometimes imposed new burdens on them. All of these represent efforts to sustain the patriarchal family—to refigure what we came to call the "gender order" in the interests of maintaining male power.

It took us a while to see how effectively the industrialization process made use of protective labor legislation: to recognize that laws justified as part of a broad effort to ameliorate the condition of women in the working class served, in practice, to sustain family life. It was another leap to understanding how the maintenance of "gender order" participates in shaping power relations by facilitating capital accumulation and flow, regulating and organizing the labor force, and channeling labor migrations and opportunities. These lessons became central to the debate over "difference and equality" that occupied historians of working-class women in the 1980s. The historical questions directly impacted on social policies then under consideration. If women were treated "as women" in the labor force, what impact would this have on their prospects for occupational success? If they were treated "like men," how would they cope with pregnancy, child rearing, and family life? Where does justice lie? "The Just Price, the Free Market, and the Value of Women" and "The Debate over Equality for Women in the Workplace" address these questions. And, not incidentally, my involvement as an expert witness in one famous case of the 1980s, *The Equal Employment Opportunity Commission v. Sears Roebuck and Co.*, suggested the significance of paying more attention to the relationship of social policy to occupational structure and institutional change.

By then the field of women's history was booming. A growing cohort of scholars had begun to ask and answer questions first about women, then about abstract notions of gender, and finally about how ideologies of gender matter in daily decision making.[15] I had thought before about how prevailing ideas about what men and women "should be" informed their behavior and politics, but in the 1990s, notions of gender as relational, and as process, led me to wonder whether in the social policies of the twentieth century I might find an integrative view of gender. I wanted to see how gender participated in the shaping of social visions of the good life by examining how it influenced such things as unemployment and old-age insurance. I wanted to understand how ideas of manliness and the male breadwinner, femininity, and respectability appeared in laws and institutions. If I could find the language with which ordinary people in the past imagined themselves constrained or released by conscious and unconscious gendered injunctions, I could go some distance towards framing one of the key dynamics that led to a reciprocally confirming set of institutional structures. "Gendered Interventions" was my first effort to do this.

These questions brought me back full-circle to the problem of how gender functions as a set of ideas that move people to act in particular ways. A generation of young scholars in the United States and outside is beginning to answer questions that plumb the depths of ideology as it regulates relationships between wage work and notions of manhood and womanhood; between the politics of consumption and incentives to labor; between state labor regulations and family lives.[16] Answers to these questions require excavating the analytic assumptions that have enabled historians of women and labor to constitute two camps.

For labor historians, the field remains rooted in traditional notions of class derived from a worker's position in production. For all the very good work in the field, and perhaps despite it, the notion of labor history retains its male framework; the language of "work" and "workers" still conjures up male images. But the image of class is called into question by the changing character of work, the new identities it constructs, and particularly by the mobilization of women as wage earners. If class (still, I think, the best way to understand power relations) is to remain the central analytic tool for understanding work, the consciousness of working people, and the sources of social action, then labor history must incorporate such cultural constructs as gender into its parameters. Just as appeals to class solidarity barred the door to full female participation in the labor movement for generations, intellectual adherence to traditional notions of class now inhibit the full flowering of gendered insights. The inverse is also true. Gendered analysis calls for a greater, not lesser, attention to class dimensions. The thriving subfield called "women's labor history," which draws much of its intellectual strengths and political inspiration from women's history and the women's movement, has permitted "labor history" to retain its male coloration, to continue its institutional bias, and to remain vested in traditional notions of class.

The result is that gender differences still appear to some scholars to run parallel with, rather than to be constitutive of, class. Unlike class, gender differences are said to be culturally, if not biologically, ordained, and thus to permeate class boundaries. To most people, the absence of satisfactory answers to the question, "Who will take care of the children?" renders gender differences in the labor force essential to its orderly maintenance.[17] And for all the practical contemporary attention to restructuring the labor force, gender appears to some historians of the working class not to be analytically useful. As Eric Hobsbawm bluntly declared, "[P]atriarchy is not a historical category."[18] Labor historians routinely reject the language of discourse and agency used by feminist theorists and historians of women to access consciousness. They hold family and tradition separate from and secondary to production as a source of meaning. And though some now agree that gender (masculinity) is produced in the workplace, most insist that gender is merely an "identity"—its political ramifications past and present limited to a destructive "identity politics," a subversion rather than an enrichment of class.

Negating the salience of gender has two contradictory effects. On the one hand, it continues to encourage the development of a thriving subfield of "women's labor history." On the other hand, it has allowed eminent labor historians (many of them male) to relegate the empirical work of a generation of serious scholars to the margins. It lends itself to the notion that women's history and labor history may be two different fields with incompatible political agendas.[19] One result is a kind of stubborn failure to "see" that impoverishes the field, inhibiting scholars from coming to terms with the changing meaning and the growing complexity of class.

The speed with which we are traveling lends urgency to resolving the tension between class and gender. As we consider the increasing force of technology in reshaping old notions of class and class loyalty, and as we watch the globalization of the world around us and ponder the divisive forces of ethnic practice, even the diehards among us must stop and ask if traditional notions of class are still useful. Our most pressing issues—escalating migration across national borders, shifting labor-market structures, competing interests of family and wage work, and sustaining civil liberties and protecting human rights—are far more susceptible to gender than to class analysis. Gender provides an intuitive entry point to understanding the changes through which shifts in authority, manliness, and power are played out in the multinational corporation. The bodies of women are sometimes called on to rationalize war (as when the United States declared its intention to bomb Afghanistan in order to free the women); at other times they are the cheap labor that constitutes the incentives for capital flows.[20] Unless we all take on the gendered dimensions of labor history, not only will our field quickly become irrelevant, but our world will become less and less comprehensible.

I puzzle over how gender got caught in this conundrum. Among American historians, parallel efforts to historicize race and ethnicity are now widely accepted. No one any longer doubts that race is not natural. Most of us argue, in the argot of the day, that it is "socially constructed," that its meaning changes over time and place in response to historical circumstance. Nor does anyone question that, like ethnicity, racial constructs are consistent with and often defined within the realm of class analysis. So, for example, "race" has sometimes been attributed to the color of skin, or conflated with the shape of the head, the proportions of the body, or even the size of the genitalia. It has just as often been used to signify class position. The single black mother still conjures up the negative image of "welfare"; the white mother without a male partner is more likely to generate images of choice in the shape of a professional woman or as part of a lesbian couple. Ethnic attribution can evoke more than one meaning at the same time. The Nazis' use of the word "Jew," for example, sometimes produced an image of a conspiratorial international financier, and sometimes of a "subhuman" beast who deserved to die. These images have historical resonance, as David Roediger famously demonstrated when he showed that the major asset of many nineteenth-century U.S. workers lay in their claim to "whiteness."[21]

But the idea that gender carries the equivalent of the "wages of whiteness," or what the Australian sociologist R. W. Connell calls a "patriarchal dividend," has never had the same persuasive power.[22] Why not? The historical record leaves little doubt that though the places of men and women in production have been differently organized, they have almost everywhere privileged men over women.[23] We see this in law and custom, in trade-union practice, in rituals of workplace initiation, and in the displaced anger against women that results in sexual harassment. We understand that in many places "maleness" still constitutes a form of human capital that can be traded in the labor market, while "femaleness" is associated with restricted workplace choices, a barrier to be overcome. Yet even as we recognize the fundamental importance of gender in shaping the workforce, many scholars still overlook or dismiss the salience of gender in the construction of class.[24]

I suspect that this is because to recognize the reciprocal interaction between class and gender would require historians to come to terms with what Connell describes as frequent disruptions in the "world gender order" that have characterized the past several centuries. In Connell's view, "[T]he structure of relationships that connect the gender regimes of institutions and the gender order of local society on a world scale" has been seriously disrupted. At first this occurred in consequence of the expansion of European trade in the fifteenth century; it continued in the wake of the colonization and empire-building process that followed; and it persists as a by-product and participant in what we sometimes call transnationalism but more generally describe as globalization.

Unprecedented migrations of labor and capital across borders, flexible labor markets, spreading technological opportunities, and failing welfare states have all, in Connell's judgment, shifted the gender composition of the global workforce and magnified gender competition. They have forced families to accommodate to new economic realities, subverted the male-breadwinner ideology (which was for decades the goal of class politics), and challenged workplaces to develop new rules to meet a dramatically different labor force. They have, according to Connell, produced an "ascendant masculinity." Put another way, Connell believes a gendered order is embedded in the imaginations of western culture, and he measures its ascendancy by the more or less successful efforts of western states and cultures to regulate and maintain control over nonwestern cultures by imposing particular views of masculinity and domesticity on them.

For labor historians who have generally thought about globalization in terms of the movement of capital, Connell's view seems idiosyncratic at best. And yet it is sustained by mountains of empirical evidence. In the last several years we have learned, often from historians of Asia, Africa, and Latin America, something of how powerful ideologies of gender shape the behavior of ordinary people—how ideas that privilege codes of masculinity are embedded within perceived options and expectations. We have learned how states routinely use gender (often racially defined) to naturalize and enforce hierarchies of power and privilege. For example, colonial regimes helped to create a new labor force in colonial Africa by convincing men to leave their village homes for urban or mine work, while retaining women in "domestic" income-producing tasks.[25] We understand how British colonials harnessed Sikh conceptions of manliness (vested in military prowess) to maintain control over vast stretches of India, and how they used the bureaucratic skills of "effeminate Bengalis" to organize government services.[26] We've learned that 1950s industrialists intent on manufacturing clothing in the Puerto Rican garment industry conducted an extensive sterilization program to create a reliable supply of labor, and that women who found relatively good jobs in *maquilladoras* on the Mexican border and in Philippine electronics factories challenged their families to renegotiate deeply rooted gender roles.[27]

Under conditions where intersecting issues of family and work manifest themselves across the globe, the logic of refocusing on gender questions seems irrefutable. Daily we see their impact: battles conducted by people of goodwill in the United States against child labor in India face opposition from poor Indian families who cannot imagine survival without the income of their children. The advance of computer technology, which once encouraged male migration to postindustrial countries, now shifts jobs to the same men in their own homelands. But the demands of professional women in industrialized countries pull wives and mothers across oceans to replace female domestic labor. Unemployment, reemployment, and the sexual division of labor affects family living standards, intrafamilial relations, and values passed on to children. And while class is often too muddy to define over geographical boundaries, and race/ethnicity is too diverse to compare, gender remains a fundamental category, its presence everywhere felt and its impact on policies around it immediate.

Considering the geopolitics of new technology and economic transformation provides new frameworks for our current questions. I try to pose some of these in the essays in the final section of this volume. Yet in the end, they suggest little more than ways of thinking about the impact of our new knowledge on large questions like the meaning of citizenship or the consistency of gendered roles across national borders. Among other questions to which we still need to turn our attention, I would propose two. First, we might ask about the relationship between large-scale economic transformations and gender relations. We would want to return to questions like the sources and consequences of the commercial revolution, marketization, and industrialization on the lives of men and women. We would want to closely examine the lives of ordinary women and men in different times and places to find out how they have participated in economic activity and to explore the constraints and incentives for their choices. We might want to pay attention to shifts in gender ideology and the gendered imagination as they emerge from changes in prescribed gender roles; to the changing cultures of masculinity and femininity, including conceptions of honor, service to the family, and fealty to lords; and the varied demands that a gendered political citizenship exacts of wage work.

A second kind of question might explore the shaping impact of gender relations on the organization of production, on the changing nature of the world economy, on the transformation of local economies to national economies, and on their adaptation to a global marketplace. It would encourage us to explore how the social organization of households and their belief systems have influenced the shape of the workplace, limiting or expanding aspirations and expectations of men and women in particular ways. For example, nations where families routinely sequester women seem far slower to industrialize than those where women freely enter into industrial labor.[28] Paying attention to the religions and ideologies that shape how ordinary women and men live promises to reveal how the shape of their daily lives and cultures informs economic decisions on local, national, and even global levels.

I conclude these essays by wondering, once again, about the impact of subjectivity as it informs all of our writing, but particularly as it has informed my own engagement with the field. In my own lifetime, the dramatic transformation in women's relationship to paid work all over the world has transformed the relations of men, women, and children, reshaped notions of social rights, and challenged patterns of social justice based on family models. These shifts suggest some of the ways gender has functioned historically: in the formation of class, in the creation and maintenance of a labor force, in the cohesion or disintegration of community, and within the labor movement itself. They pose difficult questions for labor historians, fostering a search for answers within and beyond the labor movement, in and outside the tensions between collective action and individual opportunity. To answer them, I believe that we must refuse a separate "women's labor history" in favor of a healthy and vigorous labor history that conceives gender as part and parcel of the cultural experience—and which therefore can neither marginalize women nor neutralize gender. If we do that, we may yet recover some of the exultant energy of the labor history of the 1960s. For if the vitality of the labor history of the 1960s and 1970s emerged from our desire to speak to the challenges of equality and social justice faced in those decades, our challenges come from the effort to deal with the twenty-first-century flows of capital and the globalization of labor. If in the 1960s our visions of social justice were framed within national borders, we must now draw our questions from a larger, global sphere. Our inspiration can no longer come from a romanticized ideal of family life, rooted in outdated models of jobs, patriarchy, and sexuality. Nor can it come primarily from a declining labor movement, whose deep splits reflect confusion over the changing composition and values of the working class itself. Rather, it must be drawn from the search for new forms of global cooperation and justice in human rights. Gender and class are integral to that search. To engage them, let us insert gender, as we have learned to insert race, into the center of our understanding of the shaping of a labor force. A thriving labor history, a creative labor history, will be a gendered labor history.

PART I

Women and the Labor Movement

At the beginning of the 1970s, as historians of women began to excavate the meaning of public and private spheres, they raised questions about whether these arenas could be conceived of separately. While from a political perspective, the barriers between men and women could still be clearly defined, from that of economics they quickly crumbled. Many historians returned to neglected work by scholars like Julia Spruill, Helen Sumner, and Edith Abbott to document the active participation of women in the labor force and to challenge definitions of work as limited to wage-earning jobs.

Still, it appeared to many that women's roles in the American labor movement had been sharply constricted. In "'Where Are the Organized Women Workers?'" I ask what accounts for the absence of women labor leaders at the turn of the century. The answer to that question, which lay largely in the sexual division of the labor force, sparked a series of essays on some of the women leaders I had already encountered. "Organizing the Unorganizable" was one of the earliest essays to insist on the relevance of the cultural commitment and personal lives of female organizers to their union activity. I pursued this insight in a piece on Rose Schneiderman that suggests that her transition from trade-union activist to the president of the Women's Trade Union League to participant in the implementation of New Deal policy reflected her conviction that better conditions for women workers could be achieved in a variety of ways outside the trade-union movement as well as within it. "Problems of Coalition Building" expanded this effort to seek out the effects of the different experiences of men and women in the labor movement. Evoking notions of honor and dignity and arguing that these emerge from gender as well as class locations, it notes the ways that these conceptions might account for the hostility of men to women and speak to the decline of trade-union influence in the challenging period of the 1920s.

1

"Where Are the
Organized Women Workers?"

“T he organization of women," wrote Fannia Cohn, an officer of the International Ladies' Garment Workers' Union (ILGWU), to William Green, the newly elected president of the American Federation of Labor (AFL), "is not merely a moral question, but also an economic one. Men will never be certain with their conditions unless the conditions of the millions of women are improved.”[1] Her letter touched a home truth and yet in 1925, the year in which the letter was written, the AFL, after nearly forty years of organizing, remained profoundly ambivalent about the fate of more than eight million wage-earning women.

During these four decades of industrial growth, the women who worked in the industrial labor force had not passively waited to be organized. Yet their best efforts had been tinged with failure. Figures for union members are notoriously unreliable, and estimates fluctuate widely. But something like 3.3 percent of the women who were engaged in industrial occupations in 1900 were organized into trade unions. As low as that figure was, it was to decline even further. Around 1902 and 1903 trade-union membership among women began to decrease, reaching a low of 1.5 percent in 1910. Then, a surge of organization among garment workers lifted it upwards. A reasonable estimate might put 6.6 percent of wage-earning women into trade unions by 1920. In a decade that saw little change in the relative proportion of female and male workers, the proportion of women who were trade-union members quadrupled, increasing at more than twice the rate for trade-union members in general. Even so, the relative numbers of wage-earning women who were trade-union members

The Louis M. Rabinowitz Foundation and the American Philosophical Society provided essential financial support to write this essay, and Jan Shinpoch ably aided in the research. It is reprinted from *Feminist Studies* 3 (Fall 1975), by permission of the publisher, Feminist Studies, Inc.

remained tiny. One in every five men in the industrial workforce belonged to a union, compared to one in every fifteen women. Although more than 20 percent of the labor force was female, less than 8 percent of organized workers were women. And five years later, when Fannia Cohn was urging William Green to pay attention to female workers, these startling gains had already been eroded.[2]

Figures like these have led historians of the working class to join turn-of-the-century labor organizers in lamenting the difficulty of unionizing female workers. Typically, historians argue that the traditional place of women in families, as well as their position in the workforce, inhibited trade unionism. Statistical overviews support these arguments. At the turn of the century, most wage-earning women were young, temporary workers who looked to marriage as a way to escape the shop or factory; 85 percent of these women were unmarried, and nearly half were under twenty-five years old. Most women worked at traditionally hard-to-organize unskilled jobs: a third were domestic servants, and almost one quarter worked in the garment and textile industries. The remainder were scattered in a variety of industrial and service jobs, including the tobacco and boot and shoe industries, department stores, and laundries. Wage-earning women often came from groups without a union tradition: about half of all working women were immigrants or their daughters who shared rural backgrounds. In the cities, that figure sometimes climbed to 90 percent.[3]

For all these reasons, women in the labor force unionized with difficulty. Yet dramatic fluctuations in the proportions of organized working women testify to their potential for organization. And the large numbers of unions in which the proportion of women enrolled exceeded their numbers in the industry urge us to seek further explanations for the small proportions of women who actually became union members.[4]

No apparent change either in the type of women who worked or in the occupational structure explains the post-1902 decline in the proportion of unionized women. On the contrary, several trends suggest the potential for a rise in their numbers. The decline began at the point when union membership was increasing dramatically after the devastating depression of 1893–97. The proportion of first-generation immigrant women who were working dropped after the turn of the century, only to be matched by an increase in the proportion of their Americanized daughters who worked. Married women entered the labor force in larger numbers, suggesting at once a more permanent commitment to jobs and greater need for the security unions could provide. Large declines in the proportion of domestic workers reduced the numbers of women in these isolated, low-paying, and traditionally hard-to-organize jobs. At the same time, increases in office and clerical workers, department-store clerks, and factory operatives offered fertile areas for promoting unionization among women. Strenuous organizing campaigns by and among women in all these areas achieved few results.

Although cultural background, traditional roles, and social expectations hindered some unionizing efforts, they were clearly not insurmountable barriers. Given a chance, women were devoted and successful union members, convinced that unionism would serve them as it seemed to be serving their brothers. In the words of a seventeen-year-old textile worker, "We all work hard for a mean living. Our boys belong to the miners' union so their wages are better than ours. So I figured that girls must have a union. Women must act like men, ain't?"[5] In the garment workers' union, where the majority of members were women, they often served as shop "chairladies" and reached positions of minor importance in the union structure. Faigele Shapiro recalled how her union activity began at the insistence of a business agent but quickly became an absorbing interest. In these unions, women arrested on picket lines thought highly enough of the union to try to save it bail money by offering to spend the night in jail before they returned to the line in the morning.[6]

In mixed unions, women often led men in militant actions. Iowa cigar makers reported in 1899 that some striking men had resumed work, while the women were standing pat.[7] Boot and shoe workers in Massachusetts were reported in 1905 to be tough bargainers. "'It is harder to induce women to compromise,'" said their president. "'They are more likely to hold out to the bitter end . . . to obtain exactly what they want.'"[8] The great uprising of 1909, in which twenty thousand women walked out of New York's garment shops, occurred over the objections of the male leadership, striking terror into the hearts of Jewish men afraid "of the security of their jobs."[9] Polish "spool girls" protesting a rate cut in the textile mills of Chicopee, Massachusetts, refused their union's suggestion that they arbitrate and won a resounding victory. Swedish women enrolled in a Chicago Custom Clothing Makers local lost a battle against their bosses' attempts to subdivide and speed up the sewing process when the largely male United Garment Workers union agreed to the bosses' conditions. The bosses promptly locked out the women, forcing many to come to terms and others to seek new jobs.[10] At the turn of the century, female garment workers in San Francisco and tobacco strippers, overall makers and sheepskin workers, and telephone operators in Boston ran highly successful sex-segregated unions.[11]

If traditional explanations for women's failure to organize extensively in this period are not satisfying, they nevertheless offer clues to understanding the unionization process among women. They reveal the superficiality of the question frequently asked by male organizers and historians alike: Why don't women organize? And they encourage us to adopt the economist Theresa Wolfson's more sensitive formulation: "Where are the organized women workers?"[12] When we stop asking why women have not organized themselves, we are led to ask how women were, and are, kept out of unions.

The key to this question lies in looking at the role that wage-earning women have historically played in the capitalist mode of production. Most women entered the labor force out of economic necessity. They were encouraged by expanding technology and the continuing division of labor, which in the last half of the nineteenth century reduced the need for skilled workers and increased the demand for cheap labor. Like many immigrants and African Americans today, women formed a large reservoir of unskilled workers. But they offered employers additional advantages. They were often at the mercy of whatever jobs happened to be available in the towns where their husbands or fathers worked, and they willingly took jobs that offered no access to upward mobility. Their extraordinarily low pay and exploitative working conditions enabled employers to speed up the process of capital accumulation. Women's labor was critical to industrial expansion, yet they were expected to have few job-related aspirations and to look forward instead to eventual marriage. Under these circumstances, employers had a special incentive to resist unionization among women. As John Andrews put it in the 1911 *Report on the Condition of Women and Child Wage Earners:* "[T]he moment she organizes a union and seeks by organization to secure better wages she diminishes or destroys what is to the employer her chief value."[13]

If the rising numbers of working women are any gauge, women for the most part nicely fulfilled the expectations of employers. Traditional social roles and the submissive behavior expected of women with primary attachments to home and family precisely complemented the needs of their bosses. Unionization came more easily to those women whose old-world or American-family norms encouraged more aggressive and worldly behavior—Russian Jews, for example. Yet, for the most part, women fought on two fronts: against the weight of tradition and expectation, and against employers. If that were not enough, there was yet a third battlefront.

Unionists, if they thought about it at all, were well aware of women's special economic role. Samuel Gompers, the head of the AFL, editorialized in 1911 that some companies had "taken on women not so much to give them work as to make dividends fatter."[14] In a competitive labor market, unionists tended to be suspicious of women who worked for wages and to regard them as potentially threatening to men's jobs. "Every woman employed," wrote an editor in the AFL journal *American Federationist,* "displaces a man and adds one more to the idle contingent that are fixing wages at the lowest limit."[15]

Since employers clearly had important economic incentives for hiring women, male trade unionists felt that they had either to eliminate that incentive or to offer noneconomic reasons for restricting women's labor-force participation. In the early 1900s they tried to do both. To reduce the economic threat, organized labor repeatedly affirmed a commitment to unionize women wage earners and to extract equal pay for them. Yet trade unionists simultaneously argued that women's contributions to the home and their duties as mothers were so valuable that women ought not to be in the labor force at all. Their use of the home-and-motherhood argument had two negative effects: it sustained the self-image on which the particular exploitation of women rested, and it provided employers with a weapon to turn against the working class as a whole.

Buttressed by the grim realities of exploitative working conditions and the difficulties of caring for children while working ten or more hours a day and supported by well-intentioned social reformers, the argument to eliminate women from the workforce held sway. It was, of course, impossible to achieve, so the AFL continued to organize women and to demand equal pay for equal work. But genuine ambivalence tempered its efforts. The end result was to divide the working class firmly along gender lines and to confirm women's position as a permanently threatening underclass of workers who finally resorted to the protection of middle-class reformers and legislators to ameliorate intolerable working conditions. The pattern offers us some lessons about what happens to the workforce when one part of it attacks another.

The published sources of the AFL reveal some of the attitudes underlying its actions, and I have focused attention on these because I want to illustrate not only how open and prevalent the argument was, but because the AFL's affiliated unions together constituted the largest body of collective working-class opinion. We have amassed enough evidence by now to know that the AFL was a conservative force whose relatively privileged members sacrificed the larger issues of working-class solidarity for a piece of the capitalist pie. In the creation of what the labor economist Selig Perlman called "a joint partnership of organized labor and organized capital," the Federation cooperated extensively with corporation-dominated government agencies, sought to exclude immigrants, and supported an imperialist foreign policy.[16] Its mechanisms for dealing with the huge numbers of women entering the labor force are still unclear. Yet they are an integral part of the puzzle surrounding the interaction of ideological and economic forces in regulating labor-market participation.

In the period from 1897 to 1920, the AFL underwent dramatic expansion. It consolidated and confirmed its leadership over a number of independent unions, including the dying Knights of Labor. Membership increased from about 265,000 members in 1897 to more than four million by 1920 and included four-fifths of all organized workers. In the same period, the proportion of women working in the industrial labor force climbed quickly. Rapid and heady expansion offered a golden opportunity for organizers. That they didn't take advantage of it is one of the most important facts in the history of labor organizing in America.

Union leaders were sure that women did not belong in the workforce. Anxious about losing jobs to these low-paid workers, they tried to drive women out of the labor force. "It is the so-called competition of the unorganized defenseless woman worker, the girl and the wife, that often tends to reduce the wages of the father and husband," proclaimed Samuel Gompers.[17] The *American Federationist* was filled with tales of men displaced by women and children. "One house in St. Louis now pays $4 per week to women where men got $16," snapped the journal in 1896. "A local typewriter company has placed 200 women to take the place of unorganized men," announced an organizer in 1903.[18]

The Federation's fears had some basis. In the late nineteenth and early twentieth centuries, new technology and techniques of efficiency pioneered by Frederick Taylor eroded the control and the jobs of skilled workmen, replacing them with managerial experts and the unskilled and semiskilled. Skilled members of the AFL who might appropriately have directed their anger at the way technology was being manipulated lashed out instead at women who dared to work. Gompers offers a good example of this. In an article published in 1904, he declared, "The ingenuity of man to produce the world's wealth easier than ever before, is utilized as a means to pauperize the worker, to supplant the man by the woman and the woman by the child."[19] Some of the least appropriate bitterness was expressed by Thomas O'Donnell, the secretary of the National Spinners Union, whose constituency, once largely female, had been replaced by men after the Civil War. The advent of simple electric-powered machinery caused him to complain that "the manufacturers have been trying for years to discourage us by dispensing with the spinning mule and substituting female and child labor for that of the old time skilled spinners."[20]

Real anxieties about competition from women stimulated and supported rationalizations about woman's role as wife and mother. Working men had argued even before the Civil War that women belonged at home, and the harsh conditions of labor and the demands of rearing a family supported their contention. But the women who worked for wages in the early 1900s were overwhelmingly single and often supported widowed mothers and younger siblings with their meager pay. An argument that could have been used to improve conditions for all workers was directed at eliminating women from the workforce entirely. By the early 1900s it had become an irrepressible chorus. "The great principle for which we fight," said the AFL's treasurer in 1905, "is opposed to taking . . . the women from their homes to put them in the factory and the sweatshop."[21] "We stand for the principle," said another AFL member, "that it is wrong to permit any of the female sex of our country to be forced to work, as we believe that the man should be provided with a fair wage in order to keep his female relatives from going to work. The man is the provider and should receive enough for his labor to give his family a respectable living."[22] And yet a third proclaimed, "Respect for women is apt to decrease when they are compelled to work in the factory or the store. . . . More respect for women brings less degeneration and more marriages . . . if women labor in factories and similar institutions they bring forth weak children who are not educated to become strong and good citizens."[23] No language was too forceful or too dramatic. "The demand for female labor," wrote an official of the Boston Central Labor Union in 1897, is "an insidious assault upon the home . . . it is the knife of the assassin, aimed at the family circle."[24] The *American Federationist* romanticized the role of women's jobs at home, extolling the virtues of refined and moral mothers, of good cooking, and even of beautiful needlework and embroidery.[25]

These sentiments did not entirely prevent the AFL from attempting to unionize women. Gompers editorialized on the subject in 1904: "We . . . shall bend every energy for our fellow workmen to organize and unite in trade unions; to federate their effort without regard to . . . sex."[26] Yet the limited commitment implied by the wish that women would get out of the workforce altogether was tinged with the conviction and perhaps the hope that women would fail in the end. The Federation's first female organizer, Mary Kenney, had been appointed as early as 1892. But the AFL had supported her only halfheartedly and allowed her position to expire when she gave up the job to marry. It was 1908 before the organization appointed another woman, Annie Fitzgerald, as a full-time organizer. While Gompers and others conceded the "full and free opportunity for women to work whenever and wherever necessity requires," Gompers did not address the problem of how to determine which women were admissible by these standards, and his actions revealed that he thought their numbers relatively few.[27] The AFL repeatedly called for an end to discriminatory pay for women and men: "Equal compensation for equal service performed."[28] The demand was a double-edged sword. While it presumably protected all workers from cheap labor, in the context of the early 1900s labor market it often functioned to deprive women of jobs. The Boston Typographical Union, noted one observer, saw "its only safety in maintaining the principle of equal pay for men and women."[29] Officials must have been aware that equal compensation for women often meant that employers would as soon replace them with men. It was no anomaly, then, for an AFL organizer to say of his daughters in 1919 that though he had "two girls at work [he] . . . wouldn't think of having them belong to a labor organization."[30]

When the AFL did organize women, its major incentive was often the need to protect the earning power of men. Women were admitted to unions after men recognized them as competitors better controlled from within than allowed to compete from without. "It has been the policy of my associates and myself," wrote Gompers in 1906, "to throw open wide the doors of our organization and invite the working girls and working women to membership for their and our common protection."[31] *American Federationist* articles that began with pleas for women to stay out of the workforce concluded with equally impassioned pleas to organize those who were already in it. Alice Woodbridge, writing in 1894, concluded an argument that women who worked for wages were neglecting their duties to their "fellow creatures" with the following statement: "It is to the interest of both sexes that women should organize . . . until we are well organized there is little hope of success among organizations of men."[32] The AFL officially acknowledged competition as a primary motivation for organizing women in 1923. "Unorganized they constitute a menace to standards established through collective action. Not only for their protection, but for the protection of men . . . there should be organization of all women."[33]

These were not, of course, the only circumstances in which men suspended their hostility toward women's unions. Occasionally in small towns female and male unions in different industries supported each other against the hostile attacks of employers. Miners in Minersville, Pennsylvania, for example, physically ousted railroad detectives who tried to break up a meeting of female textile workers.[34] The women in this case were the daughters, sisters, and sweethearts of miners. Far from competing with men for jobs, women were helping to support the same families as the miners. Similarly, women and men in newly established industries could cooperate more effectively in unionizing together. The garment industry saw parallel but equally effective organization among its various branches. Though female organizers complained bitterly of the way they were treated, male leadership depended on the numerical majority of female workers to bargain successfully with employers and did not deny women admission. Yet, even here, union leadership successfully eliminated "home work" without offering to the grossly underpaid and often needy female workers who did it a way of recouping their financial losses.

Occasional exceptions notwithstanding, the general consequence of union attitudes toward women was to isolate them from the male workforce. Repeatedly, women who organized themselves into unions applied for entry to the appropriate parent body only to be turned down or simply ignored. Pauline Newman, who had organized and collected dues from a group of candy makers in Philadelphia, in 1910 offered to continue to work with them if the Bakery and Confectionery Workers International Union would issue a charter. The international stalled and put them off until the employers began to discharge the leaders and the group disintegrated.[35] Waitresses in Norfolk, Virginia, suffered a similar fate. Mildred Rankin, who requested a charter for a group of fifteen, was assured by the local AFL organizer that she was wasting her time. "The girls were all getting too much money to be interested," was his comment on denying the request.[36] New York's International Typographical Union (ITU) refused to issue female copyholders a charter on the grounds that they were insufficiently skilled. When the group applied to the parent AFL for recognition, they were refused on the grounds that they were within the ITU's jurisdiction. The Women's Trade Union League (WTUL) got little satisfaction when it raised this issue with the AFL Executive Council the following year. Though the Federation had agreed to issue charters to black male workers excluded from all-white unions, it refused to accord the same privilege to women. The parent body agreed only to "take up the subject with the trade unions and to endeavor to reach an understanding" as far as women were concerned.[37]

A strong union could simply cut women out of the kinds of jobs held by unionized men. This form of segmenting the labor market ran parallel to and sometimes contradicted the interests of employers who would have preferred cheap labor. A Binghamton, New York, printing establishment, for example, could not hire women linotype operators because "the men's union would not allow it."[38] The technique was as useful for excluding racial minorities as it was for restricting white women.[39] Like appeals to racism, arguments based on the natural weakness of women worked well as a rationale, as the following examples indicate. Mary Dreier, then president of the New York chapter of the WTUL, recalled a union of tobacco workers whose leaders refused to admit women because "they could only do poor sort of work, . . . because women had no colour discrimination."[40] A Boston metal polishers union refused to admit women. "We don't want them," an official told a Women's Bureau interviewer. "Women can only do one kind of work while men can polish anything from iron to gold and frame the smallest part to the largest"; and besides, he added, "metal polishing is bad for the health."[41]

Women were often excluded from unions in less direct but equally effective ways. The International Retail Clerks Union charged an initiation fee of three dollars and dues of fifty cents a month. Hilda Svenson, a local organizer in 1914, complained that she had been unable to negotiate a compromise with the international. "We want to be affiliated with them," she commented, "but on account of the dues and initiation fee we feel it is too high at the present time, for the salaries that the girls in New York are getting."[42] Sometimes union pay scales were set so high that the employer would not pay the appropriate wage to women. Joining the union could mean that a female printer would lose her job, so women simply refused to join.

Though the AFL supported its few female organizers only halfheartedly, male organizers complained of the difficulty of organizing women. Social propriety hindered them from talking to women in private or about moral or sanitary issues. Women felt keenly the absence of aid. When the Pennsylvania State Federation of Labor offered to finance the Philadelphia WTUL's program for organizing women, its secretary pleaded with Rose Schneiderman to take the job: "We have never had a wise head to advise, or an experienced worker."[43]

But even membership in a union led by men guaranteed little to women. Such well-known tactics as locating meetings in saloons, scheduling them at late hours, and ridiculing women who dared to speak deprived women of full participation. And unions often deliberately sabotaged their female members. Fifteen hundred female street-railway conductors and ticket agents, dues-paying members of New York City's Amalgamated Streetcar Workers Union, complained in 1919 that their brother union members had supported a reformers' bill to deprive them of their jobs. When the women discovered they had been betrayed, they resigned from the union and formed their own organization, sending women from throughout the state to Albany "to show them that they . . . were able to take care of their own health and morals"—to no avail. Eight hundred of the fifteen hundred women lost their jobs, and the remaining seven hundred continued to work only at reduced hours.[44] Supporting union men was not likely to benefit women either. Mary Anderson, the newly appointed head of the Women's Bureau, got a frantic telegram from a WTUL organizer in Joliet, Illinois, early in 1919. The women in a Joliet steel plant who, in return for the promise of protection, had supported unionized men in a recent strike were fighting desperately for jobs that the union now insisted they give up. The company wanted to retain the women, but union men argued that the work was too heavy for them.[45]

As the idea of home and motherhood was used to exclude women from unions, so it enabled unionized workers to join legislatures and middle-class reformers in restricting women's hours and regulating their working conditions through protective labor legislation. The issue for the Federation's skilled and elite corps of male workers was clearly competition. Their wives did not work for wages, and most could afford to keep their daughters outside the marketplace. In an effort to preserve limited opportunity, they attacked fellow workers who were women, attempting to deny them access to certain kinds of jobs. Abused by employers who valued women primarily for their "cheap labor," women were isolated by male workers who were afraid their wages and jobs would fall victim to the competition. Arguments used by male workers may have undercut their own positions, confirming the existence of a permanent underclass of workers and locking men psychologically and economically into positions of sole economic responsibility for their families. Appeals to morality and the duties of motherhood obscured the economic issues involved, encouraging women and men alike to see women as impermanent workers whose major commitment would be to families and not to wage earning. Women would therefore require the special protection of the state for their presumably limited wage-earning lives.

The argument reached back at least as far as the 1880s, and it was firmly rooted in the idea that the well-being of the state depended on the health of future mothers. But the line between the interests of the state and those of working men was finely drawn, and occasionally a protagonist demonstrated confusion about the issue. A few examples will illustrate the point. The cigar maker Adolph Strasser, testifying before a congressional committee in 1882, concluded a diatribe against the number of women entering the trade with a plea to restrict them. "Why?" asked his questioner. "Because," replied Strasser, "I claim that it is the duty of the government to protect the weak and the females are considered among the weak in society."[46] Nearly forty years later, a Women's Bureau investigator reported that the secretary of the Amalgamated Clothing Workers Union, fearful that women were taking jobs from men, had argued that women were "going into industry so fast that home life is very much in danger, not to mention the propagation of the race."[47] As the idea spread, it took on new forms, leading a Boston streetcar-union secretary to acknowledge that "he would not care to see [women] employed as conductors. ... It coarsened [them] to handle rough crowds on cars."[48] But in more sophisticated form, the argument for protective legislation appeared as a patriotic appeal to enlightened national self-interest. "Women may be adults," argued one AFL columnist in 1900, "and why should we class them as children? Because it is to the interest of all of us that female labor should be limited so as not to injure the motherhood and family life of a nation."[49] Sometimes pleas were more dramatic. In a piece entitled "The Kingdom of God and Modern Industry," Ira Howerth, a sociologist writing for the *American Federationist*, asserted:

> The highest courts in some of our states declare that a law limiting the hours of labor for these women is unconstitutional. It may be so, but if it is so, so much the worse for the state. The state or nation that permits its women to stunt their bodies and dwarf their minds by over-exertion in unsanitary stores and mills and factories is thereby signing its own death warrant. For the degeneracy of women is the degeneracy of the race. A people can never be any better than its mothers.[50]

Gompers, as well as other AFL officials, at first opposed the idea of legislation. But in the period following World War I, their attitudes changed, perhaps as a result of what seemed like an enormous increase in the number of women in the industrial labor force. The AFL encouraged the Department of Labor to set up a Women's Bureau to defend the interests of wage-earning women.[51] The bureau, on investigation, found that many union officials viewed unionization and protective legislation as alternate means to the same goal: better working conditions. Sara Conboy, a United Textile Workers official and a WTUL activist, told a Women's Bureau interviewer that she believed in "legislation to limit long hours of work for women where and when the union [was] not strong enough to limit hours."[52] Some unionized workers thought legislation surer and faster or remarked that it was more dependable than possibly untrustworthy union leaders. A. J. Muste, secretary of the Amalgamated Textile Workers Union of America, perferred unionization but was said to have believed that legislation did not hinder organization and might be essential in industries with many women and minors.[53] But some women union leaders were not so sanguine. Fannia Cohn of the ILGWU only reluctantly acquiesced to the need for protective legislation. "I did not think the problem of working women could be solved in any other way than the problem of working men and that is through trade union organization," she wrote in 1927, "but considering that very few women are as yet organized into trade unions, it would be folly to agitate against protective legislation."[54] Cohn laid the problems of female workers on the absence of organization.

In any event, exclusion from unions merely confirmed many women's discomfort about participating in meetings. Italian and southern families disliked their daughters going out in the evenings. Married and self-supporting women and widows had household duties at which they spent after-work hours. Women who attended meetings often participated reluctantly. They found the long discussions dull and were often intimidated by the preponderance of men. Men, for their part, resented the indifference of the women and further excluded them from leadership roles, thereby discouraging more women from attending. Even fines failed to spark attendance; some women preferred to pay them rather than to go to the meetings.[55]

Self-images that derived from a paternalistic society joined ethnic ties in hindering unionization. Wage-earning women, anxious to marry, were sometimes reluctant to join unions for what they believed would be a temporary period. Occasionally, another role conflict was expressed: "No nice girl would belong to one," said one young woman.[56] An ILGWU organizer commented that most women who did not want to join a union claimed that "the boss is good to us and we have nothing to complain about and we don't want to join the union."[57] A woman who resisted unionization told an organizer that she knew "that $6 a week is not enough pay but the Lord helps me out. He always provides . . . I won't ever join a union. The Lord doesn't want me to."[58] A recent convert to unionism apologized for her former reticence. She had always scabbed because church people disapproved of unions. Moreover, she told an organizer, she and her sister had only with difficulty overcome their fear of the Italian men who were organizing their factory.[59]

Exceptions to this pattern occurred most often among women whose ethnic backgrounds encouraged wage labor and a high level of social consciousness, as in the American Jewish community, for example. Young Jewish women constituted the bulk of the membership of the ILGWU in the period from 1910 to 1920. Their rapid organization and faithful tenure is responsible for at least one quarter of the increased number of unionized women in the second decade of the twentieth century. They were unskilled and semiskilled workers, employed in small, scattered shops, and theoretically among the least organizable workers. Yet these women, unionized at their own initiative, formed the backbone of the ILGWU, which had originally been directed toward organizing the skilled, male cutters in the trade.

As it became clear to many laboring women that unionists would offer them little help, many women turned to such middle-class allies as the Women's Trade Union League. Established in 1905, the WTUL, an organization founded by female unionists and upper-middle-class reformers, offered needed financial and moral support for militant activity. Its paternalistic and benevolent style was not unfamiliar to women, and those who came from immigrant families seemed particularly impressed with its Americanizing aspects. Young immigrant girls spoke with awe of the "fine ladies" of the WTUL and did not object to the folk-dancing classes that were part of the Chicago League's program.[60] But help from these non-wage-earning women came at a price. Working women who became involved in the WTUL moved quickly from working-class militance to the search for individual social mobility through vocational training, legislation, and the social refinements that provided access to better-paying and rapidly increasing clerical and secretarial jobs. Rose Schneiderman illustrates this syndrome well. Beginning as a fiery organizer of the hat- and capmakers, she moved through the WTUL to become secretary of the New York State Department of Labor. Like the WTUL, which had begun by organizing women into trade unions, she began in the 1920s to devote herself to attaining protective legislation, even borrowing some of the arguments used by men who did not wish women to compete with them.

By this time, many working women were moving in the direction of legislative solutions to exploitative working conditions. It seemed to be the most accessible solution to the problems of exploitation. Female workers interviewed by the Women's Bureau at first felt that women and men should be included in any legislation. Later, they asked that office workers be exempted.[61] Other women acquiesced reluctantly. "I have always been afraid," wrote a supervisor in a Virginia silk mill, "that if laws were made discriminating for women, it would work a hardship upon them." By 1923 she had changed her mind: "'[I]t would in time raise the entire standard rather than make it hard for women.'"[62] As women came to accept the necessity for legislation, they, like men, saw it as an alternative to unionization and rationalized its function in terms of their female "roles." A Women's Bureau agent noted of the reactions to a forty-eight-hour law passed in Massachusetts that "the girls felt that legislation establishing a 48–hour week was more 'dignified' and permanent than one obtained through the union as it was not so likely to be taken away."[63] By the mid-1920s only business and professional women remained staunchly opposed to protective legislation.

Within this framework of trade-union ambivalence and the real need of wage-earning women for some form of protection, employers who were particularly anxious that women not unionize pressed their advantage. Using crude techniques, rationalized by the home-and-motherhood argument, they contributed more than their share toward keeping women out of unions. In the small businesses in which women most often worked, employers used a variety of techniques to discourage organization, some of them familiar to men. Department-store employees whose union membership became known were commonly fired. Many stores had spy systems so that employees could not trust their co-workers. Blacklists were common. A representative of the year-old retail clerks union testifying before a congressional committee in 1914 was afraid even to reveal the number of members in her union. Owners of New York's garment shops, fighting a losing battle by 1910, nevertheless frequently discharged employees who were thought to be active organizers or union members.

Other tactics were no more subtle. Employers often played on ethnic and racial tensions in their effort to prevent women from unionizing. Rose Schneiderman, who formed the Hat and Cap Makers Union in 1903, fought against bosses who urged immigrant workers to stick to the "American shop"—a euphemism for an antiunion shop. Jewish owners sometimes hired only Italian workers, who were thought to be less prone to unionization than Jews.[64] Others hired "landsmen" from the same old-country comunity, hoping that fraternal instincts might keep them from striking. Blacks were played off against whites. Waitresses picketing Knab's restaurant in Chicago were met with counterpickets paid by the employers. A representative of the waitresses' union reported indignantly that the employer "placed colored pickets on the street, colored women who wore signs like this, 'Gee, I ain't mad at nobody and nobody ain't mad at Knab.'" When the non-union pickets attracted a crowd, police moved in and arrested the union members. The women were further discouraged by trials engineered by employers who had previously given "every policeman a turkey free."[65]

Police routinely broke up picket lines and outdoor union meetings. Women who were accused of obstructing traffic or were incited into slapping provocateurs were arrested. More importantly, women who might have been interested in unionization were intimidated by police who surrounded open-air meetings or by department-store detectives who mingled obtrusively with potential recruits. Department-store owners diverted workers from street meetings by locking all but one set of doors or sending trucks, horns honking full blast, to parade up and down the street in which a meeting was scheduled.[66]

Small employers formed mutual assistance associations to help them resist their employees' attempts to unionize. The Chicago Restaurant Keepers Association, for example, denied membership to any "person, firm, or corporation . . . having signed agreements with any labor organization."[67] Garment manufacturers in New York and Chicago created protective associations to combat what they called "the spreading evil of unionism."[68] In small towns, the power of town officials was called into play. Ann Washington Craton, organizing textile workers in Minersville, Pennsylvania, was warned by the town burgess: "You are to let our girls alone . . . Mr. Demsky will shut the factory down rather than have a union. . . . The town council brought this factory here to provide work for worthy widows and poor girls. We don't intend to have any trouble about it."[69]

Employers justified continued refusal to promote women or to offer them access to good jobs on the grounds that women's major contribution was to home and family. When they were challenged with the argument that bad working conditions were detrimental to that end, they responded slowly with paternalistic amelioration of the worst conditions and finally by acquiescing to protective labor legislation. Often concessions to workers were an effort to undercut mounting union strength, as, for example, when department-store owners voluntarily closed their shops one evening a week. Some employers introduced welfare work in their factories, providing social workers or other women to help smooth relationships between them and their female employees. Mutual benefit associations, sometimes resembling company unions, were a more familiar tactic. Though they were presumably cooperative and designed to incorporate input from workers, membership in these associations was compulsory, and dues of ten to twenty-five cents per month were deducted from wages. In return, employees got sickness and health benefits of varying amounts, but only after several months of continuous employment. A 1925 investigation of one widely publicized cooperative association operated by Filene's department store in Boston revealed that in all its twelve years, only store executives had ever served on its board of directors.[70]

Manufacturers seemed to prefer legislation regulating the hours and conditions of women's work to seeing their workers join unions. One, for example, told the Women's Bureau of the Department of Labor that a uniform forty-eight-hour week for women would equalize competition and would, in any event, only confirm existing conditions in some shops. Some went even further, hoping for federal legislation that would provide uniform standards nationwide.[71]

When occasionally employers found it in their interests to encourage unionism, they did so in return for certain specific advantages. One of these was the union label. In the garment industry, the label on overalls assured higher sales in certain parts of the country. To acquire the right to use it, some employers rushed into contracts with the United Garment Workers and quite deliberately urged their workers into the union. New York garment manufacturers negotiated a preferential union shop, higher wages, and shorter hours with the ILGWU, in return for which the union agreed to discipline its members and to protect employers against strikes. The garment manufacturers' protective association urged employers to "make every effort to increase the membership in the union so that its officers may have complete control of the workers and be enabled to discipline them when necessary."[72] Southern textile-mill owners, otherwise violently opposed to unions, were similarly interested in the disciplinary function of unionism. They would, an observer reported, modify their opposition "if the purposes of the union were to improve the educational, moral, and social conditions of the workers."[73]

In general, however, employers made strenuous attempts to keep women out of unions. The paternalism, benevolence, and welfare they offered in compensation were supported by other sectors of their society, including the trade unions. Middle-class reformers and government investigators had long viewed the harsh conditions under which women worked as detrimental to the preservation of home and family, and government regulation or voluntary employer programs seemed to many an adequate alternative. Unions played into this competitive structure, adopting the home-and-motherhood argument to restrict women's labor-force participation. In the process they encouraged women to see their interests apart from those of male workers.

Limited labor-force opportunities, protective labor legislation, and virtual exclusion from labor unions institutionalized women's isolation from the mainstream of labor. Not accidentally, these tendencies confirmed traditional women's roles, already nurtured by many ethnic groups and sustained by prevailing American norms. Together they translated into special behavior on the part of female workers that isolated them still further from male workers and added up to special treatment as members of the labor force.

In acquiescing, women perhaps bowed to the inevitable, seeking for themselves the goals of employers who preferred not to see them in unions, of male workers who hoped thereby to limit competition and to share in the advantages gained, and of middle-class reformers who felt they were helping to preserve home and motherhood. Echoing labor-union arguments of twenty years earlier, the head of the Women's Bureau, Mary Anderson, defended protective legislation in 1925 on the grounds that such laws were necessary to conserve the health of the nation's women.[74]

As a final consequence, women were led to search for jobs in non-sex-stereotyped sectors of the labor market. Employers' needs in the rapidly expanding white-collar sector led women increasingly toward secretarial and clerical work. Vocational education to train women for office jobs, teaching, and social work expanded rapidly in the early twentieth century. Working women rationalized these jobs as steps up the occupational ladder; state and local governments and employers provided financial aid; and middle-class women launched a campaign to encourage women to accept vocational training.[75] It took an astute union woman like Fannia Cohn to see what was happening. She drew a sharp line between her own function as educational director of the ILGWU and the functions of the new schools. Her hope was to train women to be better union members, not to get them out of the working class.

The parallel development of protective legislation and vocational education confirmed for many working women their marginal positions in the labor force, positions they continued to rationalize with obeisance to marriage and the family. As Alice Henry said of an earlier group of female wage earners, "[T]hey did not realize that women were within the scope of the labor movement."[76] Fannia Cohn understood what that meant. That hardheaded and clear-sighted official of the ILGWU prefaced a call for a revolution in society's view of women with a plea for an end to competition between working women and men. Because it was destructive for all workers, she argued, "this competition must be abolished once and for all, not because it is immoral, yes inhuman, but because it is impractical, it does not pay."[77] But in the first two decades of the twentieth century, the moral arguments prevailed—releasing some women from some of the misery of toil, but simultaneously confirming their places in those jobs most conducive to exploitation.

2

Organizing the Unorganizable: Three Jewish Women and Their Union

Women who were actively engaged in the labor struggles of the first part of the twentieth century faced a continual dilemma. They were caught between a trade-union movement that was hostile to women in the workforce and a women's movement whose participants did not work for wages. To improve working conditions for the increasing numbers of women entering the paid labor force, organizers painstakingly solicited support from labor unions that should have been their natural allies. At the same time, they got sympathetic aid from well-intentioned women with whom they otherwise had little in common. The wage-earning women who undertook the difficult task of organizing their co-workers also faced another problem: they had to reconcile active involvement in labor unionism with community traditions that often discouraged worldly roles.

Understanding how women who were union organizers experienced these tensions tells us much about the relationships of men and women within unions and throws into relief some of the central problems unionization posed for many working women. It also reveals something of what feminism meant for immigrant women. Evidence of conscious experience, frequently hard to come by, exists in the papers of three women who organized for the International Ladies' Garment Workers' Union (ILGWU): Pauline Newman, Fannia Cohn, and Rose Pesotta. They were Jews working for a predominately Jewish organization, and their careers span the first half of the twentieth century. Taken together, their lives reveal a persistent conflict between their experiences as women and their tasks as union officers. Their shared Jewish heritage offers

This essay was originally presented at the Conference on Class and Ethnicity in Women's History, State University of New York at Binghamton, September 21–22, 1974. It was written with the generous support of the Louis H. Rabinowitz foundation and appeared in *Labor History* 17 (Winter 1976).

insight into the ways in which women tried to adapt familiar cultural tradition to the needs of a new world.

Like most of the women they represented, Newman, Cohn, and Pesotta were born in Eastern Europe. Newman emigrated as a child before the turn of the century; Cohn arrived as a nineteen-year-old in 1904; Pesotta came as a teenager in 1913. In the United States, Cohn refused the support of her middle-class family, while poverty drove Newman and Pesotta to the East Side's garment shops, where they worked in the dress and waist industry, a rapidly expanding trade in which Jewish workers predominated until the 1930s and women made up the bulk of the workforce.[1]

Their experience was in many ways typical. Among immigrant Jews in New York, Philadelphia, Boston, and other large cities, only the exceptional unmarried woman did not operate a sewing machine in a garment factory for part of her young-adult life.[2] In the old country, where jobs were scarce, daughters were married off as quickly as possible. In America they were expected to work, for the family counted on their contributions. Many young girls emigrated as teenagers to go to an uncle or older sister who would help them find a job so that a part of their wages could be sent back to Europe.[3] The wages of others helped to pay the rent, to buy food and clothing, to bring relatives to America, and to keep brothers in school. An eldest daughter's first job might mean a larger apartment for the family—"a dream of heaven itself accomplished."[4] When they married, young women generally stopped working in the garment shops. As in the old country, they were still expected to contribute to family income. Married women often took in boarders, helped in their husbands' businesses, or ran small shops.

A combination of factory work before marriage and the expectation of a different kind of paid labor afterwards presented problems for Jewish women like Newman, Cohn, and Pesotta, who wanted to take advantage of the new world's possibilities. Women who earned wages could dream of self-sufficiency.[5] Adolescents hoped that the transition to America would bring about a previously unknown independence and offer them new and different roles. Rose Pesotta (the name had been changed from Peisoty) arrived in America in 1913 at age seventeen. She had left Russia, she said, because she could "see no future for [herself] except to marry some young man . . . and be a housewife. That [was] not enough. . . . In America a decent middle class girl [could] work without disgrace."[6]

Expectations of independent self-assertion were frustrated when marriage intervened and women were confined to more restricted roles. But aspirations towards upward mobility may have provided the death blow. The legendary rapidity of Jewish economic success perhaps did women a disservice by encouraging husbands to deprive their wives of the limited economic roles marriage permitted—contributing, incidentally, to the American version of the "Jewish mother." Yet the hard physical labor required of women who worked for wages at the turn of the century led them to escape from the workforce as soon as possible. A folksong, reportedly first sung in Eastern Europe at the turn of the century and later heard in New York's sweatshops, records one woman's wish for a husband:

> Day the same as night, night the same as day.
> And all I do is sew and sew and sew.
> May God help me and my love come soon
> That I may leave this work and go.[7]

Women who hoped they would soon marry and leave the shops joined trade unions only reluctantly, and male union leaders thought them poor candidates for membership.[8]

It must have been extraordinarily difficult to choose a militant and active future among a people who valued marriage and the family as much as most Eastern European Jews did.[9] Women who chose to be continuously active in the labor movement knew consciously or unconsciously that they were rejecting traditional marriage. In her autobiography, Rose Schneiderman, just beginning a career in the Women's Trade Union League (WTUL), recalls her mother warning her she'd never get married because she was so busy.[10] One woman organizer who did marry made the following comment to an interviewer who asked her about children: "I wouldn't know what to do with them. First of all I never ... we were very active, both of us, and then the unions. I don't think I ... there were always meetings ... so we had no time to have children. I am sorry now."[11] Even after so many years, her discomfort at talking about her unusual choice is apparent. Despite difficulties, many in the first generation of immigrants, Newman and Cohn among them, did not marry, and there are numerous examples of women whose marriages did not survive the urge to independence. Rose Pesotta divorced two husbands, and the anarchist Emma Goldman and the novelist Anzia Yezierska divorced one each before they sought satisfying lives outside marriage.

These women were not entirely outside the pale, for while American-Jewish culture urged women into marriage, that culture's injunction to self-sufficiency encouraged extraordinary militancy. In this respect Jewish women may have been luckier than most. They came from a class-conscious background in which competitive individualism and the desire to make it in America was only one facet. A well-developed ethic of social justice was equally important and played its part in producing perhaps the most politically aware of all immigrant groups. Socialist newspapers predominated in the Yiddish-speaking Lower East Side. Jews were well represented in the Socialist party at the turn of the century and were among the best organized of semiskilled immigrants.[12] On the Lower East Side, as in Europe, women absorbed much of their community's concern for social justice.[13] A popular lullabye provides a clue to the extent to which women experienced a prevailing class consciousness:

Sleep, my child, sleep,
I'll sing you a lullabye.
When my little baby's grown
He'll know the difference and why,

When my little baby's grown
You'll soon see which is which,
Like the rest of us, you'll know
The difference between poor and rich.

The largest mansions, finest homes,
The poor man builds them on the hill.
But do you know who'll live in them?
Why, of course, the rich man will!

The poor man lives in a cellar,
The walls are wet with damp,
He gets pain in his arms and legs
And a rheumatic cramp.[14]

There is no way of knowing whether Cohn, Newman, or Pesotta knew that song, but it is likely that women in the shop sang the following tune:

No sooner in my bed
Than I must up again
To drag my weary limbs
Off to work again.

To God will I cry
With a great outcry!
Why was I born
To be a seamstress, why?

Should I once come late
'Tis a long way,
They dock me straight off
A full half-day!

The machines are old,
The needles they break,
My bleeding fingers—
Oh, how they ache!

I've nothing to eat,
I'm hungry all the day.
They tell me: forget it
When I ask for pay![15]

Like the women who sang them, the songs had traveled to America, steerage class. In the garment shops of the Lower East Side, they could sometimes be heard over the noise of the machines, reflecting always the conscious desire of working women not only to get out of the shops but to make life in them better.

Faced with the exploitative working conditions characteristic of the early twentieth-century United States, many women turned naturally to unionism. The ILGWU, founded and nurtured by socialist Jews from New York's Lower East Side, offered an appropriate organizing agency, and early expressions of enthusiasm indicate something of its romantic appeal. "I think the union is like a mother and father to its children. I'd give my whole life for the union," said one young woman in 1913.[16] Half a century after she joined the union in 1908, an eighty-year-old woman wrote to David Dubinsky, the ILGWU's president, "And I still have my membership book of that year. And I will keep it with reverence until the end of my days."[17] Another recalled her experience on the picket line: "I felt as if I were in a holy fight when I ran after a scab."[18]

It could be said of the early 1900s that Jewish women courted the unions that should have been courting them. Rose Schneiderman solicited the signatures of twenty-five capmakers before the union would acknowledge them or provide aid.[19] Her friend, Pauline Newman, recalled that when she and her friends "organized a group, we immediately called the union . . . so that they could take the members in and naturally treat them as they would treat any member who joined the union. Our job was to attract women which men were not willing . . . to do."[20] But unions did not treat women evenhandedly. During a capmakers strike, for example, when married men got strike benefits amounting to six dollars per week, women, even those who supported widowed mothers and young siblings, got nothing.[21]

Women who had had to struggle to create and enter trade unions, who were baited, beaten, and arrested on picket lines, and who had already rejected traditional roles sought help from other women, identifying their problems as different from those of male workers. Large numbers indicated their need for organization by participating in spontaneous strikes. Workers on women's clothing (largely female) tended to strike without union support more than half again as many times as workers on men's clothing (largely male).[22] In the early years of organizing, attacks against other women often elicited support from co-workers. Clara Lemlich, whose proposal to strike sparked the 1909 uprising of twenty thousand in the dress and waist trade, had been badly beaten by thugs. A woman who had participated in the Chicago garment strike of 1911 recalled that violent attacks against other female strikers had persuaded her not to return to work until the strike was won. As she and her fellow workers were negotiating with their employer to call a halt to the strike, they heard a terrific noise. "We all rushed to the windows, and there we [saw] the police beating the strikers—clubbing them on our account, and when we saw that we went out."[23] A sense of female solidarity joined the oppressed together. A 1913 striker who said she was "in good" at her job refused to work without a union "for the sake of those that didn't have it good."[24] In jail, women strikers passively resisted when their captors tried to separate them.[25]

Yet solidarity among women was limited by ethnic and class antagonisms that persistently interfered with the best efforts of organizers and of which the organizers themselves were often guilty. Organizers repeatedly complained that their work was hampered by ethnic conflict among women. Jewish women thought they were superior unionists. They treated non-Jews in the garment shops with suspicion, complaining, for example, that Polish women would listen to their speeches quietly and then report them to the boss.[26] Italian women were believed to be unreliable allies, and fear that they would not join in a strike sometimes hindered other garment workers from going out.[27] In the 1909 uprising, Italian and Jewish women, divided by language barriers, met separately. The ILGWU, without an Italian-speaking organizer, selected women to harangue the Italians in English daily until the Italians agreed not to desert the strike.[28] Julia Poyntz, the ILGWU's first educational director, used the pages of *Justice,* its official journal, to argue in 1919 that "our Italian sisters who are still suffering from the age-long seclusion of women in the home need a long and serious education to enable them to function intelligently as members of the working class in the shop and in the political field."[29]

"American" women, as the organizers persistently called them, were the most challenging for Jewish women to unionize. It was a necessary assignment to prevent some shops from undercutting the wages of others, enabling them to charge lower prices for finished goods. But it was dreaded by Jewish organizers, who saw "shickses" as at best indifferent to unionism and more often as strikebreakers and scabs.[30] Success at organizing "Americans" evoked unconcealed glee. Pauline Newman wrote to Rose Schneiderman from Massachusetts that they had "at last succeeded in organizing an English-speaking branch of the waist makers union. And my dear not with ten or eleven members—but with a good sturdy membership of forty. Now what will you say to that!"[31] Long after most Jewish women were comfortable within unions, Rose Pesotta complained that she was having a "hell of a job" with the Seattle workers she had been sent to organize. They were, she said, the "100 percent American white daughters of the sturdy pioneers. They are all members of bridge clubs, card clubs, lodges, etc. Class consciousness is as remote from their thoughts as any idea that smacks with radicalism."[32] Women from such an ethnic background could severely inhibit the success of an organization drive. Pesotta complained that she could not call a strike, as women would not picket. "No one will stand in front of the shop . . . as they will be ashamed. Not even the promise of getting regular strike benefits moved them."[33]

Isolated from the mainstream of the labor movement and divided from other working women who came from less class-conscious backgrounds, Jewish women gratefully accepted help from middle-class groups like the WTUL. But the financial and moral support of the WTUL came at a price. Jewish women had been nurtured in the cradle of socialism, and for them, alliances with other women were largely ways of achieving a more just society. Many middle-class members of the WTUL, in contrast, held that political, social, and biological oppression of women was the major problem. They saw labor organization among women as a way of transcending class lines in the service of feminist interests.

Contemporary testimony and filtered memory agree that the WTUL provided enormously valuable organizing help.[34] Yet the tensions were not easily suppressed. Rose Schneiderman, working for the WTUL in 1911, needed reassurance from a friend: "You need not chide yourself for not being able to be more active in the Socialist Party. You are doing a much needed and splendid work."[35] And it was always clear to those who continued to work for the union that the women of the WTUL had only limited access to and limited understanding of the Jewish labor movement. "Remember, Rose," wrote Pauline, "that no matter how much you are with the Jewish people, you are still more with the people of the League."[36] And again, Pauline comforted her friend: "They don't understand the difference between the Jewish girl and the gentile girl."[37]

Neither the trade union nor solidarity from other women offered adequate support to the exceptional women who devoted themselves to organizing. How did they choose between the two? And at what cost? They worked in a lonely and isolated world, weighing the elements of their success against the conflict and tension of their lives. They were not typical of rank-and-file union women, nor symbolic of others' lives. The three female ILGWU organizers I have selected chose not to conform to traditional patterns and to pursue what for women was an extraordinary lifestyle. Their particular struggles crystallize the tensions other women faced and more easily resolved in the service of a familiar destiny. As their relationship to the union is filled with conflict, so their attitudes towards women reflect the way feminism is experienced by working women. Their lives illustrate a continuing uncertainty over the sources of their oppression.

Pauline Newman became the ILGWU's first female organizer in the aftermath of the Great Uprising of 1909. She had a stormy relationship with the union until she settled down in 1913 to work for the Joint Board of Sanitary Control—a combined trade union and manufacturers unit designed to establish standards for maintaining sanitary conditions in the shops. Fannia Cohn worked for the union from 1919 to the end of her life. For most of that time she was educational director, though she also served as an executive secretary and briefly as a vice president. Rose Pesotta (ten years younger than the other two) became a full-time organizer in 1933 and a vice president of the union in 1934. She remained active until 1944, when she returned to work in the shops.

Their lifestyles varied. Pauline Newman, warm, open, and impulsive, had a successful long-term relationship with Frieda Miller. Together, they raised the baby Miller adopted in 1923. Fannia Cohn lived alone—a sensitive, slightly irritable woman, concerned with her ability to make and retain friends. Rose Pesotta married twice and afterwards fell in love with first one married man and then another. Cohn and Newman called themselves socialists; Pesotta was an anarchist. No easy generalization captures their positions on women or their relationships to the union, but they all felt some conflict surrounding the two issues.

From 1909 to 1912, just before she went to work for the Joint Board, Newman vacillated between the union and the middle-class women of the WTUL. Frequently unhappy with a union that often treated her shabbily, she nevertheless continued to work for them throughout her life. "I cannot leave them," she wrote in 1911, "as long as they don't want to accept my resignation." "Besides," she rationalized a few months later, "they are beginning to realize . . . women can do more effective work than men, especially where girls are involved."[38] Yet later that year she angrily severed her connection with the ILGWU, for which she had been organizing in Cleveland. "They wanted me to work for *less* than the other organizers get," she wrote angrily to her friend Rose Schneiderman, "and while it was not a question of the few dol[lars] a week with me, I felt that I would lower myself before the others were I to go out on the price offered to me." Her anger increased as the letter continued to describe the women selected by John Dyche, the union's executive secretary, to replace her: "Well they too are not bad looking, and one is rather liberal with her body. That is more than enough for Dyche."[39] Two months later she was still angry: "The International does not give a hang whether a local lives or dies," she wrote to Rose.[40] And several weeks after that: "I for one would not advise you to work for any Jewish organization."[41] But within a few months she was back at work again for the ILGWU.

She had little choice. Though she disliked the union's attitude towards women, she had equal difficulty relating to the middle-class women who were potential non-union allies. Not that she disagreed with them on the women's issues; she was more than sympathetic. An ardent supporter of the ballot for women, she could not, she said later, recall any woman (save for Mother Jones) "in any of our organizations who was not in favor of getting the vote." Like her friends, she was convinced that the ballot would "add greatly to our effectiveness for lobbying or sponsoring labor legislation."[42] Moreover, she not only willingly accepted aid and support from women who were not workers, she actively solicited it, even quoting Christ to induce church women to help garment workers.[43] To gather support for striking corset workers in Kalamazoo, Michigan, in 1912, she visited women's clubs. When local officials and the mayor were unable to help resolve the strike, she "decided that the best thing to do would be to ask the ladies who wear corsets not to buy that particular brand."[44]

Yet the task of reconciling class and feminist interests exhausted her. "My work is horrible," she complained from Detroit a few months before the Kalamazoo strike. "The keeping sweet all the time and pleading for aid from the 'dear ladies' and the ministers is simply sickening."[45] Her greatest praise went to the St. Louis WTUL. It was, she said, "a strictly working class organization in spirit as well as in action." When she submitted an article praising it to the WTUL journal, *Life and Labor,* Margaret Dreier Robins suppressed it.[46] Newman explored her feelings about the effect of the WTUL on women workers in a remarkable letter to Rose Schneiderman in 1911. Robins, she noted, "has made all the girls of the League think her way and as a consequence they do not use their own mind and do not act the way they feel but the way Mrs. R. wants them to." She frowned at the league's Saturday-afternoon teas (which served "a glass Russian Tea") and disapproved of giving the girls folk-dancing lessons. "It is of course very nice of her," conceded Newman, "but that is the instinct of charity rather than of unionism."[47]

Her disagreements were not simply over matters of style. She was more than willing to give way when she thought a well-spoken woman could influence a stubborn manufacturer. But she thought it bad strategy to raise issues of morality when they threatened to interfere with negotiations over wages and hours. It may have been true, she argued, that a factory owner's son and his superintendent had taken liberties with female employees: "There is not a factory today where the same immoral conditions [do] not exist. . . . This to my mind can be done away with by educating the girls instead of attacking the company."[48]

Caught between the union and middle-class allies, Newman called for help—a pattern repeated by other women involved in the labor movement. Her letters to Schneiderman are filled with longing ("[A]ll evening I kept saying if only Rose were here . . .") and with loneliness ("No matter how good the people are to me, they do not know me as yet").[49] At times one can only guess at the toll her job took. She wrote repeatedly of trying to "get away from the blues" and complained, "I am just thrown like a wave from one city to another. When will it end?"[50] Respite came at last in the form of a position with the Joint Board of Sanitary Control. With the struggles to organize behind her, she could spend her energies improving working conditions for women in the factories.

Feelings of displacement and the need for support may have preceded the drive by women members of ILGWU's Local 25 to create first an educational department and then a vacation retreat. The men in the union had no patience with the demands at first. One active woman recalled the men's snickers: "What do the girls know—instead of a union they want to dance."[51] But the women persisted, insisting that the union would be better if the members danced with each other. The women proved to be right. By 1919 Unity House, as the vacation home was called, had moved to quarters capable of sleeping nine hundred people, and two years later Local 25 turned it over to a grateful International.

Unity House may have symbolized a growing solidarity among working-class Jewish women. In any event, the feminism of ILGWU members seems to have become a problem, for just at the peak of its success, *Justice,* the union's official journal, began to attack middle-class women. Could it have been that some union leaders feared that working women were seeking alliances with others of their sex and would eventually cease to identify their interests with those of working men? "Women who work," an editorial intoned early in 1919, are not like "that type of woman, who to her shame be it said, is less a person than a thing."[52] Increasingly, *Justice*'s writers argued that working women had it in their own power to defend themselves. When female pickets faced attacks by gangsters, *Justice* insisted that the solution was in the hands of the strikers themselves. It urged women to "take a little trip down to City Hall and get the vote that will put these fellows out of business."[53] Julia Poyntz, *Justice*'s writer on women's affairs, was adamant that middle-class women no longer interfere with their sisters. "The interests of the women of the working classes are diametrically opposed to those of the middle classes."[54] A month later, she attacked a Women's International League for Peace and Freedom conference for virtually excluding working women and their problems.[55] Although the journal continued to solicit support for the WTUL, and the ILGWU continued to send women to the Bryn Mawr Summer School, attacks did not cease. A 1923 article protested the absence of working women at a conference on women in industry: "The ladies who employ domestics came to Washington to speak about higher wages, shorter hours, and better working conditions for their help. The domestics, of course, or their representatives were not invited."[56]

It was in this period that Fannia Cohn climbed to a position of authority in the ILGWU. In many ways she was fully aware of women's issues. In 1919, in the aftermath of a successful shirtwaist strike, she pleaded for tolerance from male union members. Recalling the militancy of the young female strikers, she wrote: "Our brother workers in the past regarded with suspicion the masses of women who were entering the trades. They did everything to halt the 'hostile army' whose competition they feared."[57] Wasn't it time, she asked, finally to accept fully the women strikers who had so often been jailed and beaten? An ardent supporter of the Bryn Mawr Summer School and a regular contributor to the WTUL, Cohn had friendly relations with many of its officers.[58] In 1926 she protested the absence of women's names on a list of antiwar petition signatures, and later she was to fire off a rapid telegram insisting that Anne Muste (the wife of the well-known activist A. J. Muste) be included in a tribute offered to her husband.[59] Her experiences strike familiar chords. She complained of the difficulty of holding independent views from the men she worked with, but noted, "It is still more painful to have women, too, assume a similar attitude toward their sex."[60] She laughed with a friend whose husband was called by his wife's surname ("let men have the sensation of changing their lifelong name for a new one") and supported Mary Beard's proposed world center to preserve a record of women's achievements.[61]

Cohn's strong empathy for women's feelings surely derived from her own uncomfortable experiences in the ILGWU. Theresa Wolfson, later to become a well-known economist and an expert on the problem of working women, glimpsed this suffering in 1923. "Never have I realized with such poignancy of feeling," she wrote to Cohn, "what it means to be a woman among men in a fighting organization as last Monday when I heard your outcry and realized the stress under which you were working."[62] In a letter she hesitated at first to mail, Cohn shared some of her angry frustration with a woman who taught at Brookwood Labor College. Cohn had urgently requested the college's faculty to make two studies of union women for her. The faculty had repeatedly postponed the request. "I wonder whether they would treat in the same manner, a 'man' who would find himself in a similar position," she wrote. "The labor movement is guilty of not realizing the importance of placing the interest of women on the same basis as of men and until they will accept this, I am afraid the movement will be much hampered in its progress."[63]

Despite the anguish caused by her male colleagues and her strong sympathy with women's causes, Cohn came down on the side of the labor movement when a choice had to be made. She rejected a request to segregate men and women workers in evening classes: "I am a great believer that men and women working together in the labor movement or in the classroom have much to gain from each other."[64] In 1925 she appealed to William Green, the AFL's president, "not as an officer speaking for her organization [but as] a woman trade unionist" protesting conferences called by ladies. "When the deplorable conditions of the unorganized working woman are to be considered," she objected, "a conference is called by many ladies' organization who have no connection with the labor movement and they are the ones to decide 'how to improve the conditions of the poor working woman.'"[65] A year and a half later, she regretfully refused an invitation to attend a WTUL conference on working women, cautioning the delegates to "bear in mind that it is very difficult nowadays to even organize men and they should remember that in proportion there are not enough men organized in our country as yet."[66] On the question of protective legislation for women, Cohn only reluctantly sided with the middle-class reformers who favored it: "I did not think the problem of working women could be solved in any other way than the problem of working men, and that is through trade union organization, but considering that very few women are as yet organized into trade unions, it would be folly to agitate against protective legislation."[67]

These contradictory positions were not taken without inner struggle. Cohn knew well the sacrifice she was making to stay in the labor movement. "Did you ever think of the inner pain, worry, and spiritual humiliation?" she lamented in 1922.[68] Her remedy, like Newman's, was close friendship. "You know that I . . . must be in constant touch with my friends," she wrote. "If I can't have personal contact then the medium of letters can be employed."[69] Or again, "To satisfy my own inner self, I must be surrounded by true friends . . . [who] never for a moment doubt my motives and always understand me thoroughly."[70] Cohn found refuge in the education department of the ILGWU, where she could continue the battle and yet remain sheltered from the worst of the storm.

Rose Pesotta took no shelter and asked no quarter. By 1933, when she began full-time organizing for the ILGWU, it had become clear to many that women, married and unmarried, were in the workforce to stay, and the ILGWU willingly committed money and resources to organizing them.[71] Membership campaigns no longer focused on the East Coast cities. In the garment centers of the Far West and in places like Buffalo and Montreal, Jews took second place to Mexican, Italian, and "American" women. But Pesotta was a Russian Jew who worked for a still-Jewish union and, like her predecessors, she suffered the turmoil of being a woman in ambivalent territory. Sent by the ILGWU to Los Angeles in 1933, she moved from there to organize women in San Francisco, Seattle, Portland, Puerto Rico, Buffalo, and Montreal before she became involved with war mobilization.

None could question her awareness of women's particular problems. Persuaded by the argument that there were no women on the union's General Executive Board, she accepted a much-dreaded nomination for vice president. "I feel as if I lost my independence," she confided to her diary.[72] She often berated the union leadership for its neglect of women: "[O]ur union, due to the fact that it has a WOMAN leader is supposed to do everything, organizing, speechmaking, etc., etc."[73] She was not shy about asking for courtesies that men might have had trouble obtaining. Women who earned meager wages could not be expected to pay even modest union-initiation fees, she suggested at one point. At another, she demanded that the ILGWU pay not only the expenses but make up the lost income of a Spanish woman elected to attend the biennial ILGWU convention.[74] And she knew the advantages of solidarity among women, making personal sacrifices to "win the support of the ladies who might some day be of great help to the girls."[75]

Repeatedly, however, Pesotta and her fellow West Coast organizers sacrificed feminist issues in the interests of generating an enthusiastic and loyal membership. To keep striking women happy, they agreed to double strike benefits before Easter Sunday "for the girls to buy something."[76] When newly organized women brought their husbands to discussion meetings, the men were made welcome.[77] In 1933, Pesotta compromised to the extent of abandoning the negotiating process to men and confining her own activities to organizing women because "our late President Schlesinger once told your humble servant to stop this kind of business and go home and get married. I hate to hear that from an employer."[78] Her perspectives were not always those of other women. While WTUL officials were praising the National Recovery Administration (NRA) codes, Rose Pesotta condemned them. Organizing in Seattle and witness to how badly the codes were abused, she complained, "the women are satisfied that the NRA gave them 35 hours and better wages, why pay dues to a union that does nothing for the workers?"[79]

Pesotta carried the scars of the woman organizer. "A flitting happy little whirlwind," her friends called her. It was an image that did not fit. "Nobody knows how many cheerless, sleepless nights I have spent crying in my loneliness," she confided to her diary.[80] Unlike Newman and Cohn, she sought solace in men, and depriving herself of close women friends exacerbated her isolation. Tormented by the gossip of her female colleagues she struggled with her self-image. Occasionally she confessed, "I feel so futile," or sorrowed, "[E]verybody has a private life. I have none."[81] In an effort to avoid entangling herself with a married man, she exiled herself to Montreal in 1936. It was no use. She wrote from there to her lover: "Why must I find happiness always slipping out of my hand? ... I'm sinking now and who knows where I will land."[82] For ten years, Rose Pesotta battled against police alongside her union colleagues. Then she returned to the comparative peace of the garment shop from which she had come.

By the mid-1930s, with unionism apparently secure and the ILGWU's membership expanding rapidly, it looked as though women might at last begin to raise issues peculiar to them within the confines of the union. Fannia Cohn wrote a play in 1935 that raised critical issues Intended for presentation at union meetings, it described a husband and his "intellectually superior" wife. Both worked, but because the wife had to devote her evenings to caring for the home, the husband rapidly developed more interests and became increasingly discontented with his spouse. The wife, wrote Cohn, brought with her the resentment and "the protest of a woman worker, wife, and mother against an economic condition that compels her to work days in the shop and evenings at home."[83] Chivalry, Rose Schneiderman had said, "is thrown away" when a girl enters the factory or store: "Women have to work and then are thrown on the dust heap the same as working men."[84] Working men were by no means chivalrous in 1935, but enough women had been organized in the ILGWU that the union, no longer afraid of imminent disintegration and collapse, could lend an ear to the women's issues. Perhaps in consequence, the solidarity of women within the unions diminished.

Those who came before walked an uneasy tightrope, slipping first to one side and then to the other. Tempted sometimes by the money and support of middle-class women, at others by the militance of a changing labor union leadership; alternately repelled by "ladies," and repeatedly hurt by their union's male leadership, women who tried to organize their sisters were in a precarious position. They were not feminist—they did not put the social and political rights of women before all else. They did draw strength and support from the solidarity of women inside unions and outside them. Their lives illustrate the critical importance of "female bonding" and of female friendship networks. Newman and Cohn, who had particularly strong relationships with women and who managed to find relatively comfortable roles within the union, maintained their relationship with the ILGWU far longer than Pesotta, who relied on men for support and who stayed in the front lines of battle. All were class-conscious, insisting that the class struggle was preeminent. When their class consciousness and their identification as women conflicted, they bowed to tradition and threw in their lot with the working class.

3

Problems of Coalition Building: Women and Trade Unions in the 1920s

How do we, who are feminists and committed to the labor movement, come to terms with the shortcomings of organized labor with regard to women? How do we explain the persistent failure of women to make their way to positions of power inside trade unions? In a path-breaking essay, Ruth Milkman has argued that contemporary feminists who neglect the labor movement (with all its faults) risk perpetual weakness, just as a labor movement that fails to come to terms with wage-earning women risks continuing stagnation.[1] In the end, Milkman lays the absence of common goals at the door of an exclusionary and male-oriented trade-union movement and pleads with feminists not to turn their backs on it. But her description of organized labor's years of neglect of women and their concerns yields no source for optimism, and her argument offers few hints of any possibility of change. Whether the trade-union movement can ever become a vehicle for nonsexist activity on behalf of all its members is still a major question for women. The need to develop a strategy in that direction remains one of the pressing issues of the contemporary period.

This essay addresses the unresolved tension between trade unions and women from the perspective of the past. Drawing upon a relatively brief moment in their relationship, it attempts to make sense of seemingly paradoxical behavior on both sides. It does so around two central questions: What can we say about the nature of trade unions that will help us to understand how organized labor treats its female members? And what can we say about women's culture (especially the culture of wage-earning women) that will help us to understand women's sense of themselves inside the trade-union movement?[2]

Originally published in Ruth Milkman, ed., *Women, Work, and Protest: A Century of U.S. Women's Labor History* (Boston: Routledge and Kegan Paul, 1985).

I want to focus on the quality of relationships between men and women inside trade unions—on the sources of tension and agreement. This approach tends to emphasize the problems or paradoxes in coalition building at the expense of illustrations of harmony. But because it juxtaposes women's needs against the purposes of trade unions, it holds the promise of some useful political lessons for the present.

Tensions between women and men in trade unions were not new in the 1920s. A hundred years earlier, organized men had complained that wage-earning women deprived breadwinners of jobs, reduced wages, and lowered standards. Repeatedly in the nineteenth century, they debated the efficacy of organizing women as opposed to excluding them from their trades, and they appealed to the state to regulate women's work lest their own efforts to raise standards be hindered.[3] But I have chosen the 1920s as the focus for exploration and illustration for several reasons. It was a decade when issues posed by the spread of waged work, especially for married women, were the subject of national debate.[4] Trade unions not only participated in the debate but accepted women for the first time as a permanent factor in the labor force. Women had, after all, just won the vote—a circumstance many thought would move them quickly toward economic equality. Moreover, the decade followed a period of rapid and heady organization by women, such that in 1920 nearly four hundred thousand women (6.6 percent of all nonagricultural wage-earning women, and 18 percent of all women in industry) belonged to trade unions.[5] Although these figures may seem tiny by present standards, they reflect a quintupling of the absolute numbers of women in trade unions over the preceding ten years, and that alone should have laid to rest prevailing skepticism about the possibility of organizing wage-earning women. Indeed, one can argue that by this time most trade unionists involved in female-employing industries had stopped asking whether to organize women and started wondering which women to organize. Given the corporate assault on trade unions in general and an unsympathetic national mood, the possibility for a successful coalition between men and women existed. That this did not occur certainly contributed to (though it by no means explains) declining trade-union membership nationwide and the labor movement's relative weakness throughout the decade.

Despite incentives, male trade-union leaders failed to create fruitful alliances with the women in their organizations. In an embattled period, one expects little effective organizing activity on the part of men or women, but the record shows a pattern of treatment of women that can be described at best as an uneasy truce. Trade-union leaders paid little attention to the methods needed to organize or service their female members. The labor movement as a whole (the rhetoric of American Federation of Labor [AFL] presidents Gompers and Green notwithstanding) welcomed women no more than in the period before they had demonstrated their effectiveness. Even in the face of the great garment and textile strikes, with their militant demonstrations of female commitment and leadership, women remained on the periphery of trade-union structures. They were recruited, sometimes reluctantly, as dues-paying members, tolerated as shop-level leaders, and occasionally advanced to become business agents and local and international officers. But incentives or inducements designed to create a loyal and effective female membership hardly existed in the early 1920s.[6]

Instead, we find the opposite. Where it could have fostered harmony, cooperation, and a sense of belonging, the trade-union movement persistently mistrusted its female members. It created friction, resentment, and defensiveness among them, reducing their value and undermining their ability to do good work. Why would a labor movement aware of and articulate about the problems posed by female members consciously perpetuate divisions between these workers and others?

Let us begin with an initial discussion of how women entered the trade-union movement in the second decade of the twentieth century. In 1920, about 40 percent of unionized women (169,000) were garment-workers in the International Ladies' Garment Workers' Union (ILGWU), the Amalgamated Clothing Workers of America (ACWA), and the United Garment Workers (UGW). Eighty percent of these women had been recruited since 1910 and, given the high turnover rate in the garment industry, probably less than 5 percent had been union members for ten years. Another 15 percent of the nation's unionized women were textile workers, close to 90 percent of whom were new recruits. About thirty thousand shoe workers were organized into three unions. Most of the remaining unionized women were railway clerks, food workers, printers, department-store clerks, and school teachers.[7] The weight of numbers makes it necessary to speak primarily of garment workers, though I think the conclusions are valid generally.

Everything we know about trade-union organizing between 1910 and 1920 points to the fervor with which women entered the process. From the 1909–10 garment strike, in which the "spirit" of the "girl" strikers captured the heart of the public and formed the backbone of the ILGWU, down to battles against discrimination on the job fought by telephone operators, railway clerks, and printers in 1920, women appealed to the community's sense of morality.[8] Observers described them as idealistic, self-sacrificing, willing to suffer, and committed. Bread-and-butter issues were never unimportant, but as James Oppenheimer successfully conveyed in his 1912 poem about the Lawrence strike, they were accompanied by a demand for "roses" as well. Dignity, honor, right, and justice had their place. The strength of these battles lay in the appeal wage-earning women made to the discrepancy between their wages and conditions at work and their ability to be virtuous and pure—potential mothers of the race. From the perspective of wage-earning women themselves, this rhetoric is probably best understood as a demand for time to attend to family and personal needs: to launder, to cook, to help out at home, to go to night school; and for sufficient wages to live decently, without dependence on family or men. In contrast to the perceptions of skilled male workers, dignity involved not so much the practice of one's craft as the capacity to retain one's sense of place while earning a living. Mary Anderson put it this way in 1911: "If the women who labor could only realize that the union movement . . . means better wages and shorter hours. Better wages means a home—a real home, and shorter hours mean family life, a life where father, mother and children have time to be with one another and learn together and play together."[9] Around this set of perceptions, wage-earning women allied with middle-class women prepared to legitimize and give voice to their struggle.

Lacking economic power or political voice and with meager trade-union support, wage-earning women relied on tactics of moral suasion to achieve their goals. In contrast to the 1930s, the big women's battles of twenty years before were won not so much by denying employers needed services or by exerting economic pressure as by relying on public support, indignation, and protest. Resort to moral suasion created a sense of what the anthropologist Victor Turner calls "communitas."[10] Women drew together out of a need for companionship, for bonding, in their effort to attain a larger goal. Without developed leadership or a formal organizational structure, women's shared sense of violation of accepted norms provided the warmth behind cross-class alliances and sustained them. As women organizers were fond of pointing out, individual women remained in the labor force only briefly, and when they struggled, they fought for the women who would follow them.[11]

The tactics of struggle reflected the knowledge that moral outrage, not economic pressure, was their trump card. Women repeatedly put themselves in positions where they forced the authorities to violate convention, as when they were beaten up or thrown into jail with prostitutes, or when a pregnant striker at Lawrence, Massachusetts, was shot by city police. In such extreme circumstances, women dramatized the injustices of their daily treatment in the shop and factory. Addressing a nation committed to the rhetoric of chivalry, motherhood, and the ideal of "the weaker sex," they demonstrated the brutal treatment that daily violated ideas about womanhood, inside as well as outside the workplace. Their actions called attention to the discrepancy between what society thought women ought to be and what working life made possible for them. They affirmed the reality of women's accusations of shop-floor abuse, lending legitimacy to their demands for decent pay, shorter hours, and reasonable sanitation.

Such demonstrations rested squarely on the notion that women were different from men: not that they were unequal, but that their actual or potential motherhood gave them special claims to a woman's sphere. Wage-earning women, like their middle-class allies, accepted and relied upon their special place as the moral basis of their demands for better workplace conditions. As Agnes Nestor, a lining-maker and organizer for the International Glove Workers' Union, wrote of her trade union struggles in 1902, "[W]e shall keep our womanly dignity through it all."[12]

Male trade-union leaders, at first skeptical of this mode of organization, soon recognized its advantages and began admitting women to their organizations as weaker members in need of protection. Thus, John Mitchell, president of the United Mine Workers, told a garment-workers' convention in 1913 that there was "no one more anxious that women should be queen of the home than the working man." He would, he added, "be happy indeed if our industrial conditions were such that every woman in America could have the protection of a home."[13] Since that was not possible, Mitchell conceded that "chivalry" ought to be carried into the factory, where organized women could be protected by organized men. Expectations became practice. Women entered unions with lower initiation fees and dues that, as the economist Theresa Wolfson eloquently pointed out in 1926, justified paying them lower strike, sickness, and death benefits, as well as paying less attention to their wage negotiations. "In many instances," Wolfson noted, leaders "naively explained the difference in wages by the fact that women's dues in the union were less than men's." The lesser commitment represented by the lower dues placed each woman in the continuing "status of an apprentice."[14]

After World War I, a series of events undermined assurances about the differences between men and women and reduced the effect of appeals to women's sphere in the public mind. Unions therefore lost some of their incentive to admit women as a matter of chivalry or protection. Probably most important among these developments in the 1920s was women's new sense of place, including the public perception that many women worked out of choice, not necessity—a perception reinforced by the image of the flapper. The newly acquired vote was thought to offer political options to women, providing them with the same possibilities as men to redress grievances and opening to them formerly closed paths to labor-force equality. This idea was buttressed by the creation of a Women's Bureau within the Department of Labor—an agency meant to provide a voice for all wage-earning women. As political structures opened to women, middle-class allies who had been drawn by the appeal of community drifted away from providing organizing aid and publicity and moved instead into the battle to maintain protective labor legislation—a battle that would utilize women's new political clout even as it preserved their traditional place. A startling number of female trade-union activists moved into government jobs and paid administrative positions, where they hovered around the edges of legislative action. Mary Anderson, Elizabeth Christman, Emma Steghagen, and Rose Schneiderman are among them.

As the political realm altered, women's relationships to trade unions changed. Women had won the protective arm of organized labor on the grounds that they were different. Primarily out of self-interested fear of female competition, reinforced by their perception of the male role, trade-union leaders had taken advantage of women's need for protection. Now women threatened to take jobs away from organized men. Bitter postwar struggles by women to defend places they had earned during the war effort raised questions about whether women would utilize trade unions to serve their own ends in ways that violated societal norms. In an environment in which political access had reduced the value of moral arguments, leaving economic clout as the only viable weapon to win strikes and improve the position of workers, how were trade unions to treat women? From the male trade-union perspective, the demands of women for continued protection as future mothers seeemed irreconcilable with their insistence on equality in the competition for jobs. The editor of *Advance,* the official journal of the ACWA, put it this way: "[T]he social inferiority of women ... is a sequence of tens of thousands of years of recorded history and development. In a world based upon fierce individual competition, ... there is no escape from the truth that if women want an improvement of their status, *they must fight for the improvement of their status, not appeal to men.*"[15] In the new environment of the 1920s, protection would come from legislation, while trade unions would reduce competition for jobs by organizing those women who competed directly with their male members. Women inside unions would continue to be treated as "different," but now not because they required protection but because they lacked economic power.

From the perspective of the female trade unionist, in contrast, membership was an invitation to struggle for equal pay and access to good jobs. Believing that their new political voice could be translated into economic power, women expected to participate fully in union activities. They abandoned the tactics of moral suasion as well as the security of their own "communitas," hoping to join trade-union structures as full-fledged political participants. Yet the continuing belief in women's special place, coupled with the realities of discrimination, led trade-union women to resist attempts to dismantle the hard-won privileges of legislative protection—a solution that yielded divided loyalties. Where wage-earning women were concerned, the trade union was only one avenue for increasing well-being. The other, which was heir to the higher morality of the prewar period, was protective labor legislation. Ambiguity about the relationship between equality and difference left women who were inside the trade-union movement vulnerable in struggles for power and, because ambiguity provided an alternative means for regulating job competition, encouraged male trade unionists to treat women as "outsiders."

Women's own perceptions of the work experience explain how easily that happened. I want here to adopt what some anthropologists have called an emic stance—to ask how the female wage earner, and especially the female trade-union member, saw herself in the period before and after World War I. The work of the economist Charles F. Sabel is helpful. In *Work and Politics*, Sabel suggests that different groups of workers enter the workplace with different worldviews, which condition their notions of "ambition," "dignity," or "social honor" as well as their ideas about "which jobs are disgraces and which are accomplishments."[16] We recognize this phenomenon in American history in the so-called bird of passage—the immigrant who came to the United States to make his fortune, hoping to return home with sufficient funds to buy land and marry. Such a person was willing to work at jobs other workers would not take, under conditions that would have created revolt among his fellows. His "dignity" or "honor" were not tied to the job so much as to the potential rewards his sacrifice would provide when he returned to the old world. Since every worker lives in a family, comes out of a tradition or culture, and is at a particular place in his or her life-cycle, workers have a variety of (sometimes competing) worldviews and act on those that are dominant at a given moment. Herbert Gutman offers a parallel notion when he argues that to understand how immigrants from different racial/ethnic groups and rural/urban traditions approach their jobs, we need to examine their traditional values and customs.[17]

Social scientists have only begun to develop the notion of culture to understand women's special place. Instead of a pattern imposed by a dominant male society, women's culture is now understood as the way women perceive and impose social order, construct family relationships, act out their own roles, socialize one another, and acknowledge meaning in their lives.[18] In this context, we need to ask questions about how women approach the world of work: how they create what Sabel calls "careers at work." I want to argue that women as a group bring to the work experience a socialization, a set of values, and roots in home and family—in short, a *culture* that shares class, ethnic, and racial characteristics with their menfolk but that differs in terms of gender. While workers with similar traditions and roots share many work values, the "cultural baggage" associated with gender enters into a woman's sense of "dignity" or "honor" at work, ordering her perceptions of what she is willing to tolerate and what violates her sense of dignity. How women acted on that sense of honor or dignity accounts for much of the strength of their organizing campaigns between 1910 and 1920 and the power of moral suasion in that decade. Their failure to pay attention to these aspects of difference accounts for women's relative weakness in the labor movement of the 1920s. For just as allegiance to trade-union discipline among men addresses the cultural factors unique to them, so organizing among women and maintaining their loyalty to the trade union require special attention to the cultural factors unique to wage-earning women.

In the period before World War I, wage-earning women supported by an expanding women's movement successfully incorporated their perspective into the labor movement. To organized labor they brought notions of self-sacrifice for the future, a recognition of women's particular needs, and special attention to sanitation and cleanliness as well as traditional demands for higher wages and shorter hours. These perspectives are captured in the unique ways in which women related to their unions in this period: ILGWU officials called it "spirit," and women organizers developed it by meeting the social needs of young women through dances, social hours, education, and entertainments. Fannia Cohn put it this way: "'I do not see how we can get girls to sacrifice themselves unless we discuss something besides trade matters. . . . There must be something more than the economic question, there must be idealism.'"[19] Mary Anderson spoke of undertaking the burden of additional preparation and cleanup in order to create a "homelike atmosphere and a social get-together now and then for shoe workers."[20] Together, these issues add up to what we earlier called "communitas" and what some contemporaries referred to as "soul." They seem to have been as effective at galvanizing loyalty and discipline among women as appeals to bread-and-butter issues were among men.

But while such tactics had the advantage of developing unity and strength among women, they carried new risks. To represent a female constituency effectively—to draw on women's own sense of honor—required women to stimulate and lead the kinds of activities that male unionists labeled irrelevant in periods of quiescence and perceived as a challenge to their leadership when they felt threatened. Allegiance to women and their modes of organization could be of itself subversive because it risked creating dual loyalties. And in reducing the strength of a militant organization, it could undermine the trade union itself.

The assertion of a separate culture that served women so well in organizational campaigns of 1910–20 ran afoul of the internal politics of the trade-union movement in the 1920s, which adopted a more pessimistic outlook and perceived a heightened need for loyalty. Best captured by Robert Michels's notion of an embattled group, loyalty to which transcends its members' original idealistic purposes, the trade-union movement had already developed oligarchic characteristics by 1910. Craft-oriented, protective of special interests, concerned more for its membership than for the whole class of workers, by 1910 the AFL (with which 80 percent of all organized workers were affiliated) had developed a primary commitment to job security and bread-and-butter gains. With the dismemberment of the Industrial Workers of the World during World War I and the intense divisions within the American Left that resulted from the Russian Revolution, unions with a social agenda found themselves operating defensively. In 1910, only 20 percent of U.S. industrial workers belonged to trade unions, and that number was declining. Survival of the institution was key. Battling communism on one side and the "American system" on the other side, the AFL and its international affiliates drew the wagons into a tight circle.

By 1910, most U.S. trade unionists had become what they have remained since: agents of "social closure," to use Frank Parkin's felicitous phrase. Seeing their major task as preserving or extending the socioeconomic position of their members, they operated primarily to increase (or usurp) authority and social place from those above them. Any union's capacity to provide increasing benefits depended on the loyalty of its members, and membership loyalty, conversely, rested on the degree to which leadership came through for them. Leaders had to insure that they could control a job and had the economic resources to sustain lengthy strikes. Weak or potentially weak members were unwelcome, except when leaving such people out might increase labor-market competition and lead to the loss of job control. Then, when closing the doors to membership threatened the possibilities for increased usurpation, trade unions accepted new recruits.[21] Parkin calls this phenomenon "dual closure." The trade union's primary gain comes from utilizing the economic power of a strong and united constituency to win more benefits for its members. A secondary gain derives from keeping out those whose presence would tend to weaken the organization's bargaining power—that is, those who are readily replaceable in the workforce.

Applied to male-dominated trade unions in the 1920s, the concept of dual closure illuminates the persistent tension between the labor movement and wage-earning women. To engage in activities calculated to usurp, the trade-union movement required a tight political structure and loyalty on which it could rely. But women as wage earners were perceived as different—a perception of which women themselves had taken advantage in the past, and which they were still reluctant to abandon. Could they then be relied upon for the solidarity necessary for successful usurpationary activities? In industries where jobs were largely male-defined, unions preferred simply to exclude them. In other industries, where women competed directly with male members for jobs, unions admitted them to membership and then protected usurpationary struggles by relegating women to special places justified in the same language of difference that women used to protect themselves. To rally women to membership in such female-employing industries as those manufacturing garments, textiles, and shoes, unions appealed to shared notions of social justice. In male-dominated industries and crafts, these appeals were unnecessary, and unions sought solidarity through exclusion. The conception of woman as outsider served both kinds of unions well. AFL president William Green testified to its continuing value in a 1929 *American Federationist* editorial: "When there were hand industries in the home, women were definitely a part of production undertakings. But when industries left homes to go into factories, men were the first to follow. They made the factory their job before women entered to any appreciable extent."[22]

If male trade unionists, fearing that women would reduce internal strength or loyalty, could divest themselves of the responsibility of chivalry, they could not so easily shed the burden of a potentially competitive female labor force. The notion of dual closure illuminates some of the discrepancies between the rhetoric of the AFL regarding women and the actions of its constituent members. For while an exclusionary demand relies on the integrity of the group as it already exists, usurpation often involves appeals to some higher authority and morality, such as to the principle of justice or the right to a living wage.[23] Exclusion calls for internal unity and cohesion against an unwitting Trojan Horse; usurpation requires solidarity in the cause of right and must appear at least to represent all workers. The AFL, representing the labor movement as a whole, could and did take strong moral positions in favor of organizing and integrating women. Not to do so would drive away the support of friendly social-reform groups such as the League of Women Voters, the National Consumers' League, and the Women's Trade Union League. Introduction and passage of the AFL's well-known resolution and program for organizing women in 1925 must be seen in this light. Cognizant of competition, as well as of the permanent place of women in industry, the AFL asked its affiliates to support an extensive organizing campaign among them. But the campaign foundered, scuttled by local resistance. For, as Theresa Wolfson noted in her classic volume on women workers in the trade unions, the AFL "has had a far more liberal and far-sighted official attitude than the unions which it depended on for carrying into operation its official attitude."[24]

The constituent members responsible for carrying out the program had their own protective interests in mind. In their capacity as agents of exclusion, unions in such male-dominated industries as iron molding continued to refuse to admit women to membership, using legalistic tactics whenever possible and reverting to moral arguments about propriety and a woman's place when it was not. When employers tried to substitute women for male workers, unions too weak to resist the change were forced to confront the issue of solidarity. The Journeymen Barbers' International Union provides a good example. Young women began to "bob" their hair after the war, and barber shops added women to their staff. The union refused to admit "lady barbers" under a constitutional provision that denied females the right to membership. As shop after shop became "open" and then moved out of union hands altogether, the union realized it had a problem. Theresa Wolfson records the 1924 convention debate that ranged from questions about whether women's sense of honor from a pecuniary standpoint "would be as strong as a man's" to whether the presence of several "ladies in a shop of ten or twelve chairs would be conducive to good discipline." But the nub of the matter seems to have been whether an attractive woman would "not have a tendency to create discord among the men, who, up to the time of her admittance to membership, were real working brothers." Women, in other words, would disrupt the solidarity of male members, interfering with the smooth running of the organization to become, in the end, "nothing but a blithering liability."[25] The Brotherhood of Electrical Workers solved this problem by isolating a strong union of female telephone operators into a separate local, where the women were relegated to second-class status. Other internationals relied on their ability to control access to the job or, like the railway clerks and printers, appealed directly to the state to declare their jobs off limits to women.

One notes in passing that such instances of exclusion often relied on state legislatures to do the job that the unions could not themselves undertake.[26] Appeals to the state were rationalized by male trade unionists on the grounds that women's potential motherhood required protection; within the labor movement, recourse to the state was justified by trade unionism's self-perception as an embattled force that would inevitably be weakened by the admission of workers who could not be counted upon. There was enough truth in both perceptions in the 1920s to legitimize them.

More complicated issues arose within female-dominated industries, where women were of necessity inside the unions. There, the same sense of women's place that excluded women from other unions blinded labor leaders, eager to close ranks in the service of a militant fighting force, to the desirability of community for women. Indeed, they often insisted that women accede to the prevailing male methods and goals and interpreted women's attempts to find new paths to loyalty and participation as subversive. The ILGWU leadership offers repeated examples. Its women leaders insisted, and some of its male vice presidents recognized, that who organized and the manner of organization had consequences.

But the union's General Executive Board persisted in attributing failure and success to the character of women, rather than to union policy. So, for example, in 1911, the board decided to suspend "out of town organization work in the waist and dress industry" because "to attempt to organize largely gentile girls in the small towns would, under the present conditions, be a waste of money and energy."[27] This sort of sexism could inhibit a union's growth, for, as one vice president who successfully organized gentile girls reported, "Most of them are married which makes them independent and full of fighting spirit. The girls in the little cities, it seems, are the best element."[28] In 1917, President Benjamin Schlesinger recommended reducing the union's involvement in Toronto because the majority of workers in the industry there were "women, and largely Gentile, and consequently not an organizable element."[29] Not everyone agreed with him. When the predictable stagnation happened, the leaders of three Toronto locals chastised the General Executive Board. They asked for an English-speaking woman organizer, because "men organizers appointed by the union failed to achieve satisfactory results . . . and only women organizers can have access to this unorganized element."[30] Repeatedly, the ILGWU ignored requests such as the one for "a girl organizer" to go to St. Louis; or, in one case, for fifteen unemployed Philadelphia union girls to go to Baltimore, where the organizer Hortense Powdermaker was sure they could successfully recruit the most difficult American-born women.[31]

ILGWU policies came not out of a failure to understand the need to recruit women for the union's own protection but rather out of a conviction that women did not constitute a "fighting force." Incredibly, this view persisted despite the ILGWU's own history of militant female activity. Seven short years after "inexperienced" girl strikers successfully rebuilt the union in 1909, a vice president commented on a hard-fought Chicago strike: "I must say here that I never expected that the girls, being out for the first time on strike would understand and be so devoted and active and ready to sacrifice and to listen and take orders and do everything and more than we could possibly expect from strikers."[32] Another vice president recalled the willingness with which a group of young anarchist women responded to union requests. "When the union asked them to be on the picket line at 7 o'clock in the morning, they were there. . . . Every morning I saw the girls there." And yet he insisted that these women were so argumentative and divided that they "needed the men to keep peace between them."[33]

Suspicion and doubt about female commitment to unionization undermined women's efforts to make their own demands. It meant that women would spend enormous energies simply convincing men that they belonged in a common struggle. Men resented what Ann Washington Craton called women's "optimism, and freshness, as well as the way they upset traditional routines."[34] And even their successes required apology. Fannia Cohn, reporting to the ILGWU membership on a victorious strike of women, noted that "they never were willing to accept better conditions unless their brothers who were working with them were also included. Our women members realized long ago, as did the International, that there must be no such thing as sex division in the trade unions."[35]

Being part of, and yet not part of—this was the dilemma of the woman trade unionist of the 1920s. In 1924, at the ILGWU's biennial convention, Cohn introduced a motion instructing the union's delegates to the forthcoming AFL meeting to "introduce resolutions and work for the adoption [of] . . . a plan of organization of workingwomen that shall include an educational campaign among women directly and through organized men indirectly." The committee to which the resolution was referred rejected it reprovingly. "It can be stated without contradiction," the committee noted, "that as yet no successful methods of organizing women workers have been found." It went on to argue that the union's delegates "possess a quite satisfactory acquaintance with the principles, policies, and methods of our International Union and can be fully relied upon to carry out such policies during conventions of the AFL without any specific instructions to do so."[36]

Female rank-and-filers who failed to support women leaders implicitly acknowledged the real power structure and simultaneously protected their own interests. Women who supported male leadership faced fewer accusations of disloyalty. And since female trade-union officials did not speak for women or to their particular issues and had minimal voice in the union as whole, women members reasonably felt that they deserved better representation than that offered by women. This explains the seeming paradox of Jennie Silverman. An ILGWU business agent, she was rejected by a women's shop as its representative. A manager of the local recalled that the shop refused to be persuaded by the argument that "you are all women. Jennie is a woman. . . . She and you will work together." The workers simply replied, "[N]ever mind this, we want a man."[37] Here, workers acknowledged the power of the formal political structure, as they did in a similar instance recorded by the *New York World* in 1922. Before women got the vote, a Massachusetts shoe-workers' local had consistently selected a woman to be their manager. Afterward, they repeatedly chose men. A woman stitcher explained why: "'The business man is getting so he doesn't pay as much attention to the requests of women as he did before we were given the franchise.'"[38]

The practical manifestation of this set of dilemmas was the extraordinarily awkward place in which women in the labor movement found themselves. After leaving her position as organizer with the ACWA, Ann Washington Craton despaired of the situation. In an article for *The Nation* in 1927, she noted that to maintain even minor official positions in the trade-union movement, women "have discreetly learned to play the union game as men play it. . . . On the theory that a poor union is better than no union, they steadily refused to embarrass labor officials by a vigorous protest at the discriminations and inequalities to which women have been subjected in the unions." As a result, she correctly observed, "they have been unable to achieve any outstanding leadership among the rank and file of trade-union women."[39]

Perhaps no single union so successfully illustrates the way a woman's worldview could translate into disloyalty as Local 25, the waist- and dressmakers' local of the ILGWU, in the immediate postwar period. Familiarly known as "the girls' local," its size and strength had come from the great organizing strikes of the 1909–12 period. Though it had gone through ups and downs since its organization, by 1919 Local 25 had thirty thousand members and was by far the largest single local in the ILGWU, with nearly 25 percent of the international's total membership. Shop chairladies were virtually all female; local officers were all male. Despite political disputes among the leadership, which ranged from anarchist and socialist to "American-born gentiles," the local managed to maintain a loyal and active membership as the result of its unique educational program started in 1915 by the Barnard instructor Juliet Stuart Poyntz. With the support of a core of young women, including Fannia Cohn, Pauline Newman, and Rose Schneiderman, Poyntz initiated a program that touched the spirit of Local 25's members. Classes in history, politics, physical fitness, and art, as well as concerts, plays, and discussion groups, appealed to the idealism of rank-and-filers and drew them in huge numbers into borrowed school buildings known as Unity Centers. The local went on to purchase a large country house where members could take vacations together. In 1919, it counted ten thousand members in its various classes and an additional seven thousand in attendance at concerts and plays. Other women's locals in Philadelphia and Chicago followed the example of Local 25. Unorthodox activity produced traditional results. Despite a membership that turned over entirely every three years, members managed to achieve some of the best wage and hour gains among semiskilled workers. In a lengthy and spirited 1919 strike, the waist- and dressmakers won a forty-four-hour week.[40]

By 1919, fired by the idealism the local had nurtured, young women began to agitate for a greater voice in union affairs. The shop-delegate system they proposed threatened the international's General Executive Board, whose sole female member—Fannia Cohn—retreated under the attack. Sometime after 1920, shop delegates organized into leagues that seem to have been taken over by communists, providing added incentive to the male leadership's decision to break them up. This they did, first splitting Local 25 into three constituent locals, under the supervision of a Dress and Waistmakers' Joint Board, and then combining that board with one of male cloakmakers. Simultaneously, the General Executive Board passed a rule denying anyone with less than two years' membership in the union the right to hold office.

The result was as devastating for the ILGWU as for Local 25. In vain, women protested the two-year rule, declaring they would find no one eligible for office. In a period when membership was declining because shops were shifting from urban areas to small towns and from north to south, and the trade was changing in character, female membership dropped disproportionately—falling from 75 percent of the total in 1920 to 38.7 percent in 1924.[41] Women, as the organizer Jennie Matyas recalls, simply "'ran away. If I couldn't go with these idiots and I couldn't fight them, I would just go to school. And a lot of my colleagues who felt as I did went out. Some got married, some went into some or another little business. They couldn't stay in the union and not be on one side.'"[42]

Without debating the justice of the international's post-1921 acts, it seems clear that a union that could meet the needs of female members could expect to hold and keep their loyalty to the organization. Moreover, the ILGWU accepted their activity until women, building on their own sense of priorities, began to demand democratic participation, or insider status. At that point, as early as 1919, before any discussion of communist infiltration, and while the local was engaged in what the General Executive Board acknowledged to be an "energetic campaign" to recruit dressmakers in which "thousands of new members enrolled," the ILGWU began to accuse Local 25 of inefficiency and of not paying attention to union business.[43] In 1919, an outsider was hired to take over Local 25's educational program, and in 1920, the international appointed a supervisor for education who would work with the vice presidents.

Fannia Cohn got caught on the firing line. Having initially supported— indeed, having helped to create—Local 25's activism, she did not quickly abandon the young women when they came under attack. But she moved away, turning back to her primary interest in education and insisting that, under trade-union control, education made good unionists. She did not move quickly enough. Her loyalty remained in question, leading Israel Weinzweig to warn Cohn's friend Theresa Wolfson in the spring of 1922 about the strong possibility of Cohn "being dropped by the administration forces as a candidate for vice president." She had not, according to Weinzweig, been among the "deserving followers" who had participated effectively "in the attack on the left wingers."[44] With her capacity for creative activity on behalf of women crippled, and lacking the female support that had sustained her spirit as well as theirs, Cohn retained her precarious and sometimes humiliating position until she was removed from the vice presidency in 1926 and denied even the directorship of the education program she had created.[45]

But neither Cohn nor the ILGWU women who withdrew from the struggle fully understood that in moving from tactics that relied on a spirit of social unity to develop strength, they had also moved from expressions of solidarity to alter the union in their image. Local 25's representatives to the 1922 convention recorded their goals quite clearly. The movement for a shop-delegate sys-

tem "aimed to weld together all workers of an industry into a strongly organized representative unit with many workers participating in the making of
decisions rather than leaving it to officers, executive boards, and a small group
of active members who are responsible to no one but themselves."[46] Their plea
that this process had "stimulated thought and awakened a healthy progressive
interest in our union," as well as winning "the support of a number of our
local officers," produced an entirely negative reaction. In challenging leadership, they subjected themselves to the full fury of an embattled and oligarchic
political machine, opposition to which was described by President Schlesinger
in a *Justice* editorial as a "veritable treason."[47]

While trade-union leaders insisted on what the ILGWU male leadership
called "unity, discipline, faithfulness,"[48] the female rank and file searched for
community, idealism, and spirit. But when spirit brought loyalty into question, it became too costly for the male leadership to risk. Labeling women
leftists and communists was not so much an indication of their political position (although some were surely communists) as an acknowledgment of their
potential power and a fear that oppositional politics of whatever kind would
breed disloyalty in a fighting organization. To toe the line, as Cohn did, however, was to neglect the needs of women members in the interests of organizational loyalty. Cohn watched helplessly as Local 25 was first split asunder and
then shriveled into what one vice president described "as a very small local
with little influence to do any extensive organizing work and to build up a
strong union."[49] Although she still clung to the notion that education would
unify members and revive their spirit, she ran into a leadership determined in
the 1920s to direct education to its own ends. She never again had charge of
education for the ILGWU.

Conflict in organizational and leadership styles also appeared in the ACWA,
the second-largest concentration of unionized women in the 1920s. There, as
in the ILGWU, women raised the issue of how they wanted to participate in
their union. In the fall of 1926, the female leaders of a women's local in Chicago challenged the male leadership to acknowledge the separate needs of
women. The Executive Board of Local 275 asked, in a letter to *Advance*, "What
means do our leaders employ to combat the idea that women are not tem-
porarily in industry? What methods do our officials use to promote greater
activities among women workers since they have become a permanent factor
in industry? What has become of the Women's Bureau for which the women
have so long struggled?" The editor responded predictably that it was up to the
women to rectify their complaints:

> Leadership in the union is a prize to those who know how to win it. Leaders of
> unions are not likely to leave their positions of vantage in favor of women, any

more than women would in favor of men. The battle for mastery is a human trait, a very human trait too. The nature of this battle remains the same regardless of whether men or women are found on one side of the fence or the other. It is up to women to fight their way to the front.[50]

A member from Rochester replied almost immediately:

> No, Mr. Editor, it is not leadership or power that we want, but special attention given our women so that they may have an opportunity to develop as intelligent members. You will probably say, "Why special attention . . . why not adopt the same methods as the men?" No thank you, Mr. Editor, we will not take your advice. We hope that we'll never learn to adopt the same methods as some of the men use to come to the front.[51]

There followed an exchange of letters over several months, most of them charging the ACWA with failure to offer adequate support to its female members. But the editor would not budge. "Do we," he asked, "want to build up a 'solid South' of women or anti-women in the Amalgamated?" Instead of criticizing the union, he repeated, women should ally with men to organize other women. "Those who want to climb the stairs which lead to the top must first come down to what is the basis of distinction—strength. They will have to match power with power, and prove that they are stronger."[52]

The difficulty with following this advice and accepting the ACWA's invitation to become like men was that female unionists felt themselves to be different. As one member wrote, "I'm sure you will agree with me that, historically, woman is a product of the kitchen. Though she has been coming out of it in the last twenty-five years, mentally she is still in the kitchen and hopes to remain there."[53] For the ACWA women, this difference was a strength upon which they hoped their union would build. For Cohn, by 1927, it had become a weakness: "Just as soon as women can reasonably dissociate their personal feelings from the job they must do, just as soon as they can deliberate coolly and decide a case on its merits and not on the prejudices aroused by their excessive emotions, so soon will they find that they have very much in common with men."[54]

If struggling for difference within unions invited defeat, women would have to accept the challenge to become like men. Cohn suggested that women could contribute "persistence, endurance, devotion, and all of the other traits women have developed as the mothers of the race" to the trade-union movement. They could add "their enthusiasm, freshness, and vigor" and thus "exert a great influence on men in the movement and on the movement itself, from the infusion of their qualities into the work." She did not suggest that these qualities would enable women to become leaders. But they would allow women to function within the trade-union movement in ways that provided satisfaction and material gains while they sporadically protested the evident discrimination against them. Women who continued to see themselves as a community would have to be satisfied with only a peripheral relationship to power in the larger organization.

Activities that continued to develop community, such as women's summer schools, women's locals, the Women's Bureau, and the Women's Trade Union League, persisted on the edge of the trade-union structure. As a way of channeling women's aims, they worked well. As a way of "catching up" with men, women's locals seemed to many the ideal alternative. Agnes Nestor put it this way: "[W]here the women have locals of their own, greater interest is shown because they have full responsibility for their own affairs. In these unions, women leaders have developed because they were forced to assume responsibilities and develop leadership."[55] Women in one New Jersey local decided to organize separate monthly meetings because "they felt that the men were further advanced in organization work and were rather timid about speaking." The result was a "friendly spirit, which has drawn the girls together and kept them in touch with one another's working conditions."[56] A hosiery-worker noted that her "girls' meetings" had taught "[us to] conduct our own business, get women speakers, and try to solve our own problems." Like its New Jersey counterpart, this local engaged extensively in social activities—forming a basketball team, sending children to summer camp, and sponsoring parties, picnics, banquets, and dances, all of which united members into "one big family and that's what we want."[57] Here was community without a threat to power.

Ironically, the struggle against the 1923 Equal Rights Amendment (ERA)—called "the Blanket Amendment" by trade-union women—provides the most successful example of the resuscitation of the spirit of community that prevailed in the prewar period. The labor movement's unmitigated antagonism to this first ERA illustrates the remaining strength of moral suasion. For here was an amendment that proclaimed the equality of men and women—an equality that trade-union women knew had no economic reality but which, if it were asserted, would threaten even their limited organizational position. Eager to affirm their sense that women still required the special protection offered by labor laws, women labor leaders joined with middle-class allies and the Women's Bureau to renew once again the spirit of struggle. Acting now as a community of women seeking not to usurp the prerogatives of men but to acknowledge their own special place, they drew on trade-union support to bring the ERA to a standstill.

Male trade-union leaders, of course, understood protective labor legislation as a way of restraining women's demands for admission into their organization and opposed the amendment all too willingly. Self-definition as outsiders and the development of a notion of community without a politics of its own enabled individual women to continue to function within the trade-union movement, extracting some benefits from it. Those who became spokespeople won more social and economic mobility for themselves than most working women could hope to achieve. With the Women's Bureau as their vehicle, they were able to bring public attention to many of the problems facing women wage earners, and they succeeded in gaining the tacit support of the male-dominated trade unions for issues that concerned women. But the trade-union movement offered women no access to the power structure and insisted that women in its ranks accept male assumptions about their role and place. It thus undermined whatever female leadership developed within the movement, leaving women like Rose Pesotta, who rebelled, without support (labeled "unstable"), and those like Cohn, Newman, and O'Connor, who conformed, without power.

What then of the power of difference? The material presented here suggests that two intersecting factors have to be acknowledged if we are to understand the past and present relationships of women to trade unions. Between 1910 and 1920, a sense of women's culture was joined with the more open stance of some trade unions to create successful alliances. By the 1920s, the alliance had broken down on two fronts. Some elements of the feminist coalition looked to a new equality with men to transcend women's confined place. And the labor movement, no longer convinced that appeals to women's place worked as well as economic struggle, and itself battling to survive, perceived women as a source of weakness better taken care of by the state. Ambivalent about an equality that seemed illusory, and now without the organized feminist support that had sustained the struggle for difference, trade-union women floundered or, as Jennie Matyas put it, "ran away."

Failure was not so much a result of bad faith as of conflicting perceptions. For women to come to terms with the changing social values of the 1920s, to integrate their worldview with the decade's new realities, was a difficult task. To do so in the context of a defensive and harassed trade-union movement might have been impossible. At the same time, to expect an embattled trade-union movement to recognize women's cultural space seems equally unlikely. But such were the conflicts of the 1920s.

They give us cause to hope that the dual purposes of feminism and trade unionism are not irreconcilable. In the contemporary period, when socioeconomic forces have confronted wage-earning women with profound challenges to their perceptions of themselves as wage earners, and when trade unions are beginning to recognize the workforce shifts that demand organization of new groups of women workers, the culture of women might yet find a place in the politics of unions.

4

Rose Schneiderman
and the Limits of
Women's Trade Unionism

I n April 1943, to celebrate the twenty-fifth anniversary of Rose Schneiderman's accession to the presidency of the New York branch of the Women's Trade Union League, Dorothy Canfield Fisher wrote in a brief biography: "[B]y 29 [Schneiderman was] a figure of towering influence in the labor world, a terror to conscienceless employers, a pillar of light to underpaid women factory workers. ... Here is a magnificent graphline of ascending power." Fisher's hyperbole did not stop there. This "little and red-headed warm hearted" woman was described as "a valiant crusader ... full of vitality, righteous wrath, and hearty kindness, ... magnetic," and with "great organizing ability." She achieved such recognition that "we as Americans feel almost as proud of her record, as we women are proud of the proof she gives that women are valuable citizens." Schneiderman, reading a draft of this tribute, objected only to the clause that described her as "a terror to conscienceless employers." "I have always," she wrote, "been a rather mild human being and have depended on my abilities to interpret and persuade people in order to get results."

The interchange offers an essential insight into Schneiderman's lifelong devotion to improving the working conditions of women. She thought of herself not as a "terror" but as an arbitrator, not as one who waged war but as a peacemaker. In doing so, she accepted one reality of women's work situation. Like most people who thought about the issue at all in the early twentieth century, she believed that women joined the labor force as foot soldiers—in transit between childhood and commitment to their own families. Wage-earning women, in Schneiderman's view, accepted this description of themselves and acquiesced in the relative powerlessness that followed from it. Any strategy for change had to accommodate to this essentially conventional self-perception.

But this set of assumptions created a dilemma for the woman labor leader. To improve women's work lives by this logic required the intervention of those with greater power and influence than working women themselves possessed. Soliciting such support required compromise; how and with whom to compromise proved to be less troublesome for Schneiderman than resolving the question of what such support would mean for working women themselves. The two sets of logical partners both posed problems. Reliance on union men meant adapting women's behavior to the world of working men, and reliance on benevolent women meant accepting the constraints of twentieth-century womanhood while battling to stretch the boundaries of women's lives. Either strategy required skill, patience, and flexibility in order not to alienate those with power. Together they demanded staunch allies among nonworking women and a supportive atmosphere among working men.

Not all women labor leaders agreed with Schneiderman's assumptions. Other women of her generation (Julia O'Connor Parker, Dorothy Jacobs Bellanca, Fannia Cohn, and Agnes Nestor among them) chose to work inside the labor movement, where they attempted to represent women's interest as part of the working class. But there were many, including Elizabeth Christman, Leonora O'Reilly, and Mary Anderson, who like Schneiderman began their careers as wage earners and union officers, only to decide that working women required the kind of help that could best be obtained by exercising leverage against an organized labor movement they supported but did not fully trust. Sooner or later, these women, often in the name of their commitment to organizing, sought either to circumvent or to work parallel to the established trade-union movement. In doing so, they tried to encourage the labor movement to respond to too-often neglected needs of women workers. Why and how these choices were posed, their implications for wage-earning women, and the insight they provide into gender differences around political strategy constitute some of the larger lessons of Schneiderman's life.

The poverty and struggle of Schneiderman's youth mirrors that of many of the young women whose cause she later championed. Born in Poland in 1882, she came to the United States at the age of eight with her parents and two younger brothers. Little more than a year after the family settled in New York's Jewish Lower East Side, her father, a tailor, died, and her mother, pregnant and destitute, put first one child and then another into orphanages. Schneiderman spent about a year in an institution before her mother, her resources once more gathered, came to fetch her.

At first Rose cared for her younger sister, attending school only sporadically and yet completing nine grades in the space of four years. At age thirteen, she found a job as a cash girl in a department store for the munificent sum of $2.16 per week. The sixteen cents was for laundering uniforms. It was not long before she became impatient with such low wages and over her mother's objections about its lack of gentility turned instead to factory work. By the time she was eighteen, she had found a relatively secure place sewing linings in a cap factory. With the help of a neighbor, she began to learn the skills of a sample maker. As a more skilled worker, she would be less subject to layoffs and perhaps marginally better paid as well. Now she earned six dollars per week and instead of dutifully turning the whole sum over to her mother for household use, she kept a dollar a week for her own expenses. All this time she wore homemade or hand-me-down garments. It took Rose until she was twenty, by which time the family's economic situation had improved, before she retained enough of her slowly increasing pay to buy some ready-made clothing. Around the same time she became involved in the labor movement.

For her, as for many poor garment makers, that was a natural step, for the small unions that dotted New York's Lower East Side at the turn of the century were part of the landscape. There, where the major industry was in making one or another form of clothing, where the boss was almost always an immigrant like oneself, and where shops were small and vulnerable, unions sprang up and flowered or withered as their trade picked up and declined. Organized largely into an umbrella organization called the United Hebrew Trades, they reflected the weakness of a labor movement rooted in an industry of poorly paid workers and undercapitalized ventures. But in moments of crisis, unions benefited from being part of a community with a strong tradition of social justice. They shared at least the rough-hewn socialism articulated by the Lower East Side's largest Yiddish-language newspaper, *The Forverts*, and practiced in its early years by the International Ladies' Garment Workers' Union (ILGWU)—the union with which Schneiderman was in closest contact for most of her life. The Lower East Side was by no means entirely rebellious. But it did nurture a militant and diffuse radicalism that came from the desire to turn the American dream into reality. Where the peddler and the contractor were nourished by the prospect of social mobility, the socialist and trade unionist drew sustenance from the potential of a democracy that offered workers the capacity to change the world.

For Schneiderman, these experiences coalesced into a coherent desire to influence conditions around her during a fortuitous year that she spent in Montreal, where her mother moved to be near a sister. There Schneiderman became the protégé of a socialist family whose books and arguments confirmed her belief in the political promise of a socialist vision. She returned to New York, now twenty-one and open to the possibilities of trade-union organization. In her autobiography, she recalls how she and three women friends, angry at such persistent injustices as paying for their own machines and thread and aware of the differences between their own treatment and that of the organized men in their shop, approached the United Cloth Hat and Cap Makers Union in 1903 to seek help in organizing their co-workers. In the context of the Lower East Side, the success of this quartet in gathering the signatures of twenty-five women who agreed to join is unremarkable except for the speed and determination with which they accomplished the task. Within a few days, they were the proud recipients of the first charter for women in the union.

In this early period, the organization of workers seemed to Schneiderman to be the most effective way to raise wages and ameliorate working conditions. Like Samuel Gompers and the craft-oriented unions of the American Federation of Labor (AFL), she believed that workers had to rely on their united strength to achieve greater bargaining power with employers. So she threw herself into the struggle. She was rewarded with a meteoric rise. For three years, while she continued to earn her living in the factory as a capmaker and milliner, she organized for the capmakers. In 1904 she became a member of the union's General Executive Board, and in 1905 she played a leading role in the first successful industrywide strike of capmakers. It was then that she first encountered the Women's Trade Union League (WTUL).

Her efforts in the 1905 strike ran afoul of a series of problems commonly encountered by those who organized women. Their long hours of work, and responsibility for some household chores as well, made women's active participation in unions difficult. Marriage- and family-oriented, women believed their tenure in the labor force would be short, and a commitment to unionization seemed unnecessary, as well as outside the context of their future lives. Because most women were only minimally skilled, their strikes could be easily broken. These problems were exacerbated by the reluctance of labor leaders, anxious to stretch limited resources, to invest in such poor candidates for organization. The success of the 1905 capmakers' strike was assured only when the WTUL donated money and organizational skills to the effort. Hoping to find in their support better and faster ways of reaching women workers, Schneiderman joined the fledgling organization in 1906.

The coalition of women trade unionists and affluent social reformers (called "allies") who had founded the WTUL in 1903 shared with the AFL the conviction that organization would benefit women as much as men. But whereas the Federation talked about the expense of organizing the unskilled and the difficulty of appealing to women whose hearts were in leaving the labor force, the WTUL suggested that women workers would respond to tactics different from those used for men. The financial resources, political contacts, and public sympathy offered by the wealthy in conjunction with the skills and knowledge of men and women in the trade-union movement could form a partnership that would enhance possibilities for organizing women. Traditional craft unions welcomed the WTUL's initiative as a solution to one pressing problem. Although reluctant to take on the task of organizing women, trade unionists nevertheless believed that their low pay and poor conditions mitigated against working women being good wives and future mothers. They also believed that women's low pay drove down the wages of less-skilled men, leaving them without the resources to raise a family decently. Not because they cared so much about women's working conditions but because they feared the negative impact of those conditions on the family, the AFL and its affiliates welcomed the WTUL.

Schneiderman, who joined the New York branch, seemed to many WTUL activists a valuable asset. Already at twenty-four an experienced organizer, she could speak for the trade-union movement whose cooperation the league so eagerly sought. And since Yiddish was her mother tongue, she felt utterly at home with that group of women workers who were among the league's major targets. While Schneiderman needed and wanted help in organizing women, she approached the league with some skepticism. Like her lifelong friend Pauline Newman, she wondered what "allies" understood of working women. Were they simply do-gooders in the progressive vein, quick to sympathize with the plight of the poor working girl but equally quick to impose their own solutions? Would they encourage trade-union women to participate in making policy? Skepticism retreated a bit in 1907 when, only several months after she became a member, she was elected vice president of the New York branch. It faded even further when a wealthy ally donated a year's wages to the league to enable Schneiderman to quit her factory job so that she could attend school and become a part-time organizer for the WTUL. She became a full-time organizer in 1909.

By now she was the essential liaison between the league and the intensive organizing activities of the Lower East Side. As a kind of roving agent, she led a successful white-goods workers strike in 1909, organized the union that later became Local 22—the dressmakers local of the ILGWU—and participated in the famous shirtwaist-makers strike of 1909–10. To achieve some communication among the variety of groups active in enhancing the welfare of garment workers, she led the WTUL in developing a conference group to discuss industry policies. And she served as a troubleshooter, rushing home from a vacation in 1910 when the WTUL encountered a developing problem in the shirtwaist-makers union "which none of us can manage but you." Deftly she negotiated the difficult terrain that lay between skilled and organized male cutters and the semiskilled female sewing-machine operators who worked with them. When the cutters bargained for four paid holidays—which would leave operators without work or pay on those days—she persuaded the men to help organize the women in return.

Seeking new ways to bring women into unions, Schneiderman suggested a variety of techniques to appeal especially to women. We "have not considered seriously enough," she wrote in her organizer's report for 1908–9, "the joyless life of the working woman and that perhaps we have not done all that is necessary to give the labor organization a social as well as an economic attraction." The same year she proposed that the WTUL organize women into a separate federation rather than into trade unions led by men. The league, unwilling to offend the AFL, rejected the notion. Repeatedly she spoke in public and to allies about "the foreign girls," attempting to describe their culture and to discuss their conditions of work and need to organize. And always, as one of her correspondents wrote to her, she gave evidence of her "trade union class consciousness."

The years before 1911 exhibited a kind of unity that must have been very satisfying to Schneiderman. Working as an organizer in the garment trades for the New York branch of the WTUL, she was free to give herself to the cause she thought most important. At times, as in the waistmakers' strike of 1909–10, the ILGWU and the WTUL worked so closely together that her experience seemed of a piece. She remained a committed socialist, though she sometimes regretted her lack of activity in the Socialist party. Still, she wrote occasionally for *The Call,* attended party meetings, and consulted with members of the women's committee about appropriate speakers who were good trade unionists and socialists. Briefly in 1911 she considered running for alderman on the Socialist party ticket. As if this were not enough, the women of the league introduced a new dimension into her life. The warm friends she made among the affluent women who still funded and guided the WTUL led her into feminism. She began speaking for suffrage in 1910. Not yet thirty, she had already earned recognition as a moving orator and an effective organizer. After listening to her appeal for votes for women, one observer commented: "No one has ever touched the hearts of the masses like Miss Rose Schneiderman. . . . Strong men sat with the tears rolling down their cheeks. Her pathos and earnestness held the audiences spellbound."

But Schneiderman's attachment to the WTUL rested on its willingness to organize poor garment workers, and when that commitment came into question in the winter of 1911–12, she began to differ with other league members. The dispute touched the heart of Schneiderman's commitment to the organization. In its crowning success to date, the WTUL had provided money, pickets, and publicity for the 1909–10 strike of more than twenty thousand young women waistmakers. ILGWU Local 25, the waistmakers' local, had entered the strike weak and with diminishing numbers. It emerged whole and hearty.

In acknowledgment of their aid, the waistmakers offered the WTUL a seat on their executive board. This seat Schneiderman occupied. But shortly after the strike's end, membership began to decline once again, and the ILGWU and the WTUL blamed each other for the dwindling numbers. The union, happy to accept money and support at moments of crisis, wondered about the value of external advice on how to conduct its day-to-day affairs. For their part, Schneiderman and the WTUL proposed tactics addressed to women's specific needs that male local officers in the male-dominated union rejected out of hand. A shrinking membership merely confirmed their sense of women as ephemeral trade unionists.

Disquieted, the league leadership accepted what seemed a plausible explanation offered by one of its number. Melinda Scott, a league vice president and a highly skilled and well-paid hat trimmer, persuaded the WTUL that more skilled and disciplined American-born women made better candidates for unionization. Membership loss, Scott argued, was the fault of the "Jewish girl," whom she described as too difficult to organize and as an unstable union member. She also pointedly questioned Schneiderman's organizing abilities and socialist politics.

In the spring of 1911, the league withdrew Schneiderman from the waistmakers' executive board, provoking a bitter split in the leadership of the New York branch that surfaced in the winter of 1911–12. One faction, led by Melinda Scott and supported by the executive secretary, Helen Marot, insisted that WTUL energy and funds should go to organizing American-born workers. Another, led by Schneiderman, aghast that the big victories of 1909–10 in New York and those that followed in Philadelphia and Chicago should be so easily squandered, vehemently opposed abandoning foreign-born workers.

Torn by the debate and stung by the newly perceived notion that her socialism was a cause for alarm, Schneiderman gave up her job as an organizer and, as she describes it, offered her services to Anna Howard Shaw in the cause of women's suffrage. "I wasn't going to parade under false colors," she wrote in her autobiography, "so I told her that I was a socialist and a trade unionist who looked upon the ballot as a tool in the hands of working women with which through legislation, they would correct the terrible conditions existing in industry."

Now in her thirties, the unity of her life disrupted, Schneiderman weighed her commitments against each other. For nearly two years, she worked for the campaign for women's suffrage in Ohio and New York and between trips organized white-goods workers. At the end of 1914, she withdrew from the league and went to work for the ILGWU as an organizer. She returned briefly to the suffrage campaign early in 1917 and, finally, in 1918 went back to the New York WTUL as its president and general organizer. In these years, the contrasting pushes and pulls of the suffrage and labor movements helped her to develop the approach that was to be the hallmark of her long life. She would be loyal to the labor movement but remain independent of it: she would support organization among women, although realism bade her not to count on it. And above all, she would commit herself to obtaining legislative relief for the most pressing problems of wage-earning women.

The suffrage campaign resolved whatever residual distrust she had of affluent women, for it provided evidence of the mutual dependence of wage-earning and more prosperous women on each other. In her early experience with the WTUL, she had had to rely on the goodwill of well-connected women whose money and influence sustained the organization and provided its political strength. The suffrage campaign, in contrast, taught her not only that women needed each other but that she could offer her better-off sisters something they desperately needed—access to working-class men. It enabled her, as well, to work out a position that assured her own importance in the battles that would follow a victory at the polls.

The National American Women's Suffrage Association (NAWSA) commonly argued that women ought to have the vote in order to bring to the electorate a sensibility different from that of men and more likely to induce morality and virtue in politics. Schneiderman, in contrast, harked back to the old Elizabeth Cady Stanton argument that women had a natural right to participate in government, derived from their common humanity, not from their special capacities. What differentiated her from more radical feminists organized in the Congressional Union is that, like NAWSA and unlike Stanton, she framed her arguments not on the grounds of self-evident justice but on those of future ends. "Political democracy," Schneiderman argued, "will not do us much good unless we have industrial democracy, and industrial democracy can only come through intelligent workers participating in the business of which they are a part and working out the best methods for all." Her campaign speeches picked up themes on which she was later to act. The vote, she argued, would do even affluent women no good at all unless they understood and could develop a program to deal with the conditions under which most women lived and worked. Wage-earning women who daily encountered the abuses of the workplace had already begun to develop the capacity to deal with repeated affronts through their organizations. The middle class, which had so far been protected, would soon be left behind. For their own sake and so that they could vote intelligently when the time came, affluent women ought to recognize the "distinct contribution" of the organized worker and be ready "to stand by her in her heavily handicapped struggle to better her conditions." Without cross-class cooperation, the women's vote would be, as she put it, "a blunt hammer." With it women could, together, humanize industry.

Optimistic possibilities inherent in women's suffrage contrasted sharply with Schneiderman's discouraging experiences with the trade-union movement. Returning to the ILGWU as a general organizer in late 1914, she encountered once again the difficulties women faced within this male-dominated organization. That is not to say she did not do useful work, participating in a strike settlement here or an organizing campaign there. Some of these settlements revealed the still-primitive condition of women's work situations. In 1915, for example, a Springfield, Massachusetts, corset company agreed to a forty-eight-hour week, as well as to abolish payments for needles and ironing wax and to eliminate the scrubbing of floors by operatives. But frequently she felt undermined. The international moved her from place to place, pulling her out of difficult campaigns just as she had begun to make progress or assigning her to new areas for periods so short that she felt unable to do anything. One day before a planned strike of a Boston group with which she'd been working for months, the international sent a man who knew nothing of the situation to direct the strike. At the end of 1916, she submitted a letter of resignation. "For the last several months," she wrote, "I have been working in an atmosphere of ... distrust which, to say the least, is not conducive to putting forth one's best efforts." Although these events show her weakened faith in the ILGWU, her loyalty to trade unionism in general remained untouched. She hoped, she said in her letter, to retain her "spirit and interest ... for the sake of a cause which is bigger than any organization." When the ILGWU refused her resignation, she hung on in the hope of compromise for several more months, before she returned once again to become the chair of the 1917 women's suffrage party campaign in New York State.

Her experience with the ILGWU demonstrated, and later events affirmed, that the labor movement was not a reliable partner as far as women were concerned. Schneiderman never abandoned her sense of herself as a trade unionist. But she had already become impatient with the agonizingly slow path to change it offered to women. Coming at the same time as her positive experiences in the suffrage campaign, that recognition moved her towards the decision that labor legislation for women was the only way to assure that barbaric industrial conditions would not continue to exist.

In a sense she had already traveled some distance down this road before she realized where she was going. In the aftermath of the 1908 Supreme Court decision in *Muller v. Oregon,* which upheld a state's right to restrict working hours for women but not for men, many industrial states had moved to regulate women's working days. Agreeing with the famous Brandeis brief, the court held the state's interest in women as future mothers to outweigh women's own right to freedom of contract. Schneiderman and the New York branch of the WTUL fought unsuccessfully in 1910 for a bill limiting women's working hours to fifty-four in a week and ten in a day. They attributed their failure to women's lack of political power. Without the vote, legislators would not listen to them.

A year later, the Triangle fire turned public interest toward such legislation as well as toward factory conditions in general. That Saturday afternoon in March 1911, when 146 people, mostly women and young girls, ended their lives by plunging onto the sidewalks of lower Manhattan or crushing each other against locked exit doors, turned everyone's attention to state regulation. Schneiderman's bitter speech at the funeral service rejected attempts of "good people" to help. Workers, she insisted, would solve their own problems. But as social reformers used the tragedy of the fire to create commissions to investigate factory conditions and pressure for legislative action mounted, Schneiderman participated more and more in attempts to win such battles. She committed herself once again to the fifty-four-hour bill, taking credit for fighting it through the New York Senate and Assembly in the spring of 1912; and she began to believe that if a senator "could be shown . . . that long hours and factory work [are] demoralizing to women and the race he would cast money and business to the winds and vote to benefit womankind." She testified before the commission formed to investigate the Triangle fire and to enact a new industrial code to abolish fire and health hazards in factories. And she worked closely with Pauline Goldmark's state committee on sanitation and comfort to establish standards of cleanliness for workrooms and factories and for drinking water, washrooms, dressing rooms, and toilets. She insisted that achieving the ballot would enhance women's ability to win such legislation. The effort moved her firmly, and this time permanently, into the ranks of social reformers committed to this goal. In 1918 she returned to the WTUL.

In some sense, Schneiderman had already made a choice about the future direction of her life. Yet the next few years were to solidify her assumptions about women and affirm the validity of the course she had chosen. Up to this point, she retained her radical vision, continuing to describe herself as a socialist until well after World War I. Early in the 1920s, her vision narrowed as she accepted a more conventional portrait of women's sense of self. In public she began to talk and to write about women's own failures to unionize or to take on leadership positions. A mass-circulation newspaper quoted her on the difficulty of "prodding the working girl to a realization that she should be organized." In a mid-1920s radio broadcast, she complained of women's failures to provide themselves with intelligent, informed leadership. The theme persisted for the rest of her career. It emerged, for example, in a 1935 speech in which she reproached the AFL for its failure to give adequate representation to women and then added, "[O]ne feels that a good deal of the blame lies with the women themselves." She repeated this idea twenty years later when, commenting that there was not a single woman on the executive councils of either the AFL or the Congress for Industrial Organizations (CIO), she wrote: "[T]o be fair, however, I must say that a good deal of this is the fault of the women themselves."

This vision of women provided justification and explanation for the direction into which she now moved. It explains how she could simultaneously berate the labor movement for its self-evident failures and yet remain loyal to it. It provides rationalization for the rigidity with which she held onto the idea of legislation even when it proved to be divisive. And it was affirmed by the recognition she received from important friends such as Raymond and Margaret Dreier Robins and the Roosevelts. In the aftermath of the victory over the ballot, she slowly abandoned her socialist dreams, turning instead to Democratic party politics that promised immediate, if more limited, results. Her move was sustained by the way in which the WTUL, the labor movement, and the women's movement intersected with each other in the 1920s.

After she became president of the New York WTUL in 1918, Schneiderman's strong antipathy towards upper-class leadership created divisions that were exacerbated when she attempted to bring trade-union women into positions of influence within the organization. "It is most important that the majority of our delegates be trade unionists," she wrote to East Coast members of the league before the 1922 convention. Simultaneously she altered the personnel of the league to ensure that its leading figures were products of trade-union experience and the factory floor rather than graduates of college. The strategy succeeded in enhancing the league's legitimacy as a representative of working women, and it pushed the wealthy women who sustained its day-to-day activities into less active roles than they had previously occupied. Within four years she would use the support she got from the New York league to promote the candidacy of Maude Swartz, a trade unionist, for national president, and in 1926, when Swartz resigned the job, Schneiderman moved smoothly into leading both the national organization and its strongest chapter.

The work of the National WTUL as well as that of the New York WTUL now became largely routinized. Concerned with creating a generation of female leaders and still convinced that organization would enhance women's lives, Schneiderman supplemented the league's small training school by devoting effort and energy to the Bryn Mawr Summer School for women workers. An effective fund raiser, she successfully garnered enough money for the New York WTUL to purchase its own clubhouse in 1922. Once established, maintaining, organizing, and supervising the place as well as raising the money to keep it going occupied substantial chunks of her time. She had to "give the cafeteria a lot of time," she wrote to Mary Dreier in 1922. Repeatedly her secretary, apologizing for delays in answering letters, offered explanations such as, "she is frightfully busy with the rummage sale."

Relative tranquility, however, was a product of having come to terms with the labor movement, not of being at peace with it. From the league's perspective, organized labor continued to evade its responsibilities towards wage-earning women. League offers of aid as well as requests for local unions to support its work with financial assistance met only suspicion. In the city and state of New York, labor leaders objected to the potential of divided loyalty among their female members and disliked the two classes of members the WTUL created. So the league's attempts to convince local unions to organize women often met with failure. Tensions grew in 1918 when the national president, Margaret Dreier Robins, tried to convince the AFL to persuade its affiliates to organize women. Gompers, not wanting to create friction, offered to place women who fell outside the jurisdiction of the craft unions into a federal or catch-all union. He refused to intervene on behalf of women who worked at jobs where the international affiliates that held jurisdiction simply did not wish to admit women to membership. Robins protested vigorously, to no avail.

Attempts to demonstrate loyalty to the AFL proved equally ineffective. The WTUL, which had sent Schneiderman as a delegate to the First International Conference of Working Women in Vienna and hosted a second conference in 1920 in Washington, D.C., withdrew from the International Federation of Working Women when the latter decided to affiliate with the existing International Federation of Trade Unions, of which the AFL was not a member. Instead of acknowledging such loyalty, the AFL tried to undermine the WTUL further. In a sharp slap at the WTUL, which considered itself the Federation's organizing arm for women, the AFL proposed in 1924 to create its own Women's Bureau. Had the measure passed, many feared that the new bureau would make the league redundant.

Although the national WTUL still continued to think of itself as a major force for organizing women, its activities languished. The league published a 1921 pamphlet called "Case for Trade Unions" and followed with a broadside letter that argued, "We could not win political independence until women were organized for it and working women will never get equal pay for equal work and justice and fair play in industry if they are not organized as working men and as employers are organized." But its efforts to pressure the AFL into paying more attention to organizing women ended in stalemate. The AFL executive council did not deal with the question until 1924, and the increased organization of women it then called for produced virtually no response from its affiliates

Schneiderman's problems in New York mirrored the national arena. The New York league attempted and failed to convince local unions to set up a joint organization council to "promote an intensive campaign among unorganized women." In the fall of 1921, Schneiderman sent a letter to all the upstate

New York central bodies and unions offering the league's services in organizing women. Only one—a local of Binghamton machinists—responded. They would be delighted to have the WTUL's help in principle, they said, but in view of the depressed state of their industry, it would not be of much use just then. Still the league persisted. For a while it organized feather-boa workers and fancy-leather-goods workers. By 1922 even these activities dwindled. Schneiderman refused to extend the leave of absence of a league organizer because, she said, "for the past two years very little organization work has been called for." And not long after that, Schneiderman commented of the WTUL's services in support of a strike of milkmen: "It seems as though at this time there is nothing else to do but to organize the wives of strikers."

Still nominally a socialist, Schneiderman's residual radicalism seems to have exacerbated the tension. She ran afoul of James Holland, the president of the New York Federation of Labor. Labeling her the "red rose of anarchy," he denounced her before New York State's Lusk Committee, called to investigate subversion. Ironically, Schneiderman had by now abandoned socialism as a political strategy. In the light of women's suffrage, she began to devote her attention to the kinds of lobbying that would achieve tangible results. But attempts at conciliation failed. In 1922 she resigned from New York City's Central Trade and Labor Council. She was, she said, "rather tired and disgusted with the machine and [I] have decided not to waste any more time on them." For the rest of the 1920s, the state federation of labor remained obstinately hostile.

Curiously, Schneiderman's commitment to labor legislation blinded her to the contemporary failures of the labor movement in regard to women. For while she viewed the strength wielded by organization as an important asset in winning legislation acceptable to working women, the legislative direction released her from dependence on organized labor. On this basis she appealed to the trade-union movement for help in lobbying for legislation that unions often saw as less threatening than admitting women to membership. As one of several paths women could take, and as an instrument that would strengthen their hand, trade unions remained more than desirable in her eyes. But they were no longer absolutely necessary. Her relationship to the WTUL became clearer too. Less wedded to its organizing function, she acquiesced in the circumstances that deemphasized this role, guiding the WTUL into educational activities and honing it into an effective lobbying organization on behalf of working women.

If the prevailing antipathy of organized labor to women members pushed Schneiderman and the WTUL toward protective labor legislation, the fervor with which the WTUL embraced that position created divisions among working women themselves. Many in the rank and file had benefited from the wartime (1917–18) opportunities for women and had hoped to hold on to their new jobs when the war ended. As a result, they chafed under provisions of New York State's six-day-week and night-work limits on women that had been passed in 1915 with the full support of the WTUL. Railway clerks, newspaper reporters, writers, and printers petitioned the state for exceptions. Although the legislature revoked restrictions on writers and reporters in 1919 and on printers in 1921, the WTUL vigorously opposed these petitions until 1921. Railway clerks whose unions opposed modifying the law on their behalf lost their jobs. The WTUL's rigidity alienated trade-union women who found their individual rights restricted by protective legislation.

Such incidents alerted more militant feminists to the dangers of protective legislation and led them to begin discussions about an Equal Rights Amendment, which they introduced into Congress for the first time in 1923. Fearful that such an amendment, which they called the Blanket Amendment, would threaten the legislative gains of two decades, most social reform advocates vigorously opposed it.

Schneiderman took on the issue directly in October 1922, when Harriot Stanton Blatch, an American Labor party candidate for the New York State Assembly with whom she had worked closely for suffrage and whose opinion she very much trusted, made a speech opposing labor legislation. Shaken, Schneiderman wrote to the party asking for an explanation. She got little satisfaction. Julius Gerber, the party chair, noted organized labor's shortcomings in regard to women and asked Schneiderman whether she didn't want to change her mind: "While Gompers and the AF of L are opposed to a minimum wage law or a law fixing the maximum hours in a day's work on the ground that it can be accomplished by the union, the AF of L favors these measures for women and children. Don't you see where the inconsistency comes in, and even you will object to being placed in the same class with children." Blatch pointed to the WTUL's lack of consistency on the issues. "You must not forget we saw the welfare workers bitterly fighting the women printers many sessions, at last admitting its mistake, allowing the amendment on night work to go through at Albany. If your long opposition was right, then your yielding was wrong, and if the final yielding was right, then the opposition was wrong."

The confrontation pushed Schneiderman into a weak defense but stiffened her spine. Like other WTUL leaders, she had always argued for protective legislation on economic and social grounds. Women's commitment to families, their lower skill levels, employers' eagerness to use them as replacements for male labor, their lesser bargaining power: these disadvantages would be tempered or corrected either by unionization or by legislation. Legislation was simply faster. But in the face of the accusation of inconsistency, she reverted to the argument used in the Brandeis brief and a favorite of women reformers. "We have got to see to it," she wrote to Blatch, that woman is "safeguarded from selling her labor at a starvation wage and that her hours of work are not too exhausting so that the child to come may inherit the strength and vitality which is rightly due to it." If women were to be protected because they were the "mothers of the race," then the state had an interest in their well-being that transcended the individual rights of any woman. It was not merely their inability to compete effectively at the moment, a balancing of the scales of justice, that required legislative intervention, but women's ongoing biological and social roles.

An issue of equality had become one of morality; the concern with women's right to compete effectively in the labor force had become the concern with preserving their capacity to perform their present and future home-related tasks effectively. The labor movement had espoused the motherhood argument from the time it initially turned to labor legislation for women and children in the first two decades of the century. On the basis of this interpretation, Schneiderman and the WTUL reforged an uneasy alliance with the AFL. They could and did convince the Amalgamated Clothing Workers Union to adopt a consistent anti-ERA stance. And they successfully persuaded the AFL and its constituent unions to adopt an anti-ERA position for three decades.

In the meantime, the league's lobbying activities intensified. Centered now on legislation, Schneiderman organized efforts to achieve a forty-eight-hour week in New York, minimum-wage legislation, state-funded unemployment insurance, and old-age pensions. The New York league housed a service to help women file claims under the state's accident compensation laws. It supported friendly legislators for reelection and worked to defeat those whose records it disliked. Schneiderman actively supported the national league's call to outlaw war as well as its campaign to ratify the federal child-labor amendment.

Into this policy-oriented, reform organization, Eleanor Roosevelt entered. Roosevelt first met Schneiderman and Maude Swartz at a tea in 1920 and was apparently quite taken with them. After 1922, when Roosevelt joined the league, the friendship developed rapidly. Roosevelt invited Schneiderman and Swartz to visit her at Campobello and at Hyde Park. Increasingly she relied on them for advice about the labor movement and passed on what she learned to Franklin Delano Roosevelt. But it is hard to know who influenced whom more in the relationship between the Roosevelts and Rose Schneiderman, for Schneiderman was clearly taken with the Roosevelts as well. She bestowed on Eleanor an exuberant and affectionate gratitude for her contributions to the WTUL, addressing her in letters as "Dearest Eleanor" or "My dearest darling." Roosevelt seems to have earned these accolades. In addition to her considerable financial contributions to the league, she sponsored an annual Christmas party, contributing toys and clothing to poor children, and she could be counted upon to provide patrons for the league's benefit dinners and concerts without intervening in the league's policy-making functions at all. By the time the Roosevelts entered the White House, Schneiderman had become a trusted friend subject to Eleanor's chiding if she failed to visit her on occasional trips to Washington. Trying to persuade her to follow the pattern of other presidents' wives and donate a portrait of herself to the nation, Schneiderman wrote to Roosevelt, "Never before have we had a first lady who has been so genuinely interested in the public good. Never before has a wife of the president had the social vision and the desire to bring about a decent life for the majority of the people."

How much her feelings for the Roosevelts influenced her enthusiastic response to New Deal policy is hard to say. By the late 1920s she had committed herself sufficiently to the necessity of legislation to welcome an administration that supported these goals. She had worked for FDR's election to the governorship, soliciting the support of labor leaders on his behalf and offering him legitimacy in labor's eyes. She worked again for his election to the presidency. And she was utterly delighted, if not completely surprised, when the secretary of labor, Frances Perkins, suggested, and FDR approved, her appointment to the National Recovery Administration's (NRA) labor advisory board. It was a perfect job for her. Always a good administrator, she would be one of five labor representatives charged with supervising the NRA codes as they affected workers; she would have special responsibility for women. She described it as the high point in her life. "Imagine setting standards for millions of women and girls," she wrote to Margaret Bondfield, Britain's minister of labor. "The codes are the Magna Charta of the working woman," she declared later, "a revolution . . . the most thrilling thing that has happened in my lifetime."

Eagerly she plunged into the job. She watched over codes in the textile and garment industries, paying special attention to the pleas of labor leaders and delighting at the role reversal involved in having men such as David Dubinsky look up to her. In the spring, she was sent to Puerto Rico on a special mission to investigate the extraordinarily low wages paid there and the impact of home work on those wages; Eleanor Roosevelt joined her briefly to add weight to the mission. Schneiderman counted the code she drew up there as one of the great achievements of her life. As she became a more public and political figure, she took on a series of regular radio programs in which she placed the great changes in the labor movement of the 1930s into the context of past struggles. She returned to New York when the NRA ended in 1935. But the fever had struck, and when, on Maude Swartz's death in 1937, the job of secretary to the New York State Department of Labor fell vacant, she snatched at the chance to move into public service once more. As the second ranking official in the State Department of Labor, she was in a good position to continue her efforts on behalf of women. Now she turned her attention to bringing household employees under minimum-wage provisions and to including domestic workers in the workmen's compensation laws, as well as to enforcing a new wages-and-hours bill.

In her absence, the WTUL floundered. She retained her jobs as president of the national and New York State chapters during her tenure with the NRA and afterwards with the New York State Department of Labor. Despite the resentment this caused, she turned over only the day-to-day administrative tasks to Elizabeth Christman, the national secretary. Schneiderman argued that her visibility spoke well for the league, bringing it into public view. But in her absence, and without alternative leadership, no new initiatives emerged. Her assertions that the most effective codes were those where the workers were organized and therefore well represented did not resonate in the league, which took little part in the rising tide of organization that marked the 1930s. It was peripherally involved in campaigns to organize hotel chambermaids and laundry workers and supportive of department-store workers, but its role was always on the sidelines. Instead, the league lobbied for inclusion of household workers in new social security laws, for eight-hour days for all New York State employees, and against home work.

By 1941 Schneiderman had stopped defining the league in terms of its original aims. Rather, she described its "education" programs as its proudest accomplishment. The WTUL, she wrote to Eleanor Roosevelt, gives to minimum-wage boards, industrial committees, and legislative hearings "a forthright exposition by labor representatives of the economic and human factors in their industries." It equips women workers, she continued, with the capacity "to discuss their individual problems intelligently before public boards." Eleanor Roosevelt picked up the theme beautifully. "The basis of all good organizing," she wrote to Schneiderman, is "education, and I think the WTUL has contributed in a remarkable way to the increased knowledge of working women of today."

This approach enabled Schneiderman to handle the league's big challenge of the 1930s with equanimity. When the Committee for Industrial Organizations split from the AFL to create the Congress of Industrial Organizations, the WTUL confronted a dilemma. For all the tensions between the two organizations, the WTUL had remained loyal to the AFL for the twenty-three years of its existence. Yet the CIO's commitment to organizing plantwide and industrywide offered the promise of overcoming the WTUL's greatest frustration—its inability to convince the AFL to spend time and money organizing women into unions. Moreover, most of the constituent unions of the WTUL, because they represented women, were sympathetic to the CIO, and some had moved into its ranks. At its 1937 meeting, the WTUL debated whether to stick by the AFL. The result was unambiguous. The executive board agreed that "the League must be true to its purpose and act accordingly to the principles it has always followed. . . . When the organization of women becomes impossible within the framework of the A.F. of L., . . . the local leagues are free to extend their activities and to aid in the organization of women workers wherever opportunity offers."

But Schneiderman dragged her feet, adopting a passive-aggressive response to the CIO. She acceded to the AFL when its top leaders refused to attend a WTUL banquet in the presence of CIO leadership, invited AFL but not CIO leaders to conventions, and discouraged Eleanor Roosevelt from speaking to striking CIO women, while orchestrating appearances of the president's wife before members of AFL unions. Several factors could account for this, none more compelling than Schneiderman's reluctance to challenge her own convictions about the strategy she had adopted early in the 1920s. For if women could and would organize in the CIO, then her characterizations of them as unwilling candidates for unionization came into question. And if women would willingly fight outside the bounds of propriety, then protecting them might have been less necessary. All this remained unspoken. Rather, Schneiderman expressed her discomfort with the CIO's radical leadership—discomfort exacerbated in the end of the 1930s by John Lewis's outspoken criticism of the Roosevelt administration. She became something of Eleanor Roosevelt's conscience in this regard, advising her as to which organizations were safe and which were tainted by communist affiliation, and assuring her in 1941 that she had asked that her own name "be dropped from at least two organizations . . . because I find that the communists are using perfectly fine and public spirited people for their own ends." She was so offended when a political commentator, reviving the label that haunted her in the early 1920s, called her "the red rose of anarchy" that she threatened to sue for libel until he redacted.

These tactics contributed to the continuing decline of the WTUL, for their upshot was that the league removed itself even further from labor-movement activism. Together the CIO and the AFL had nearly tripled union membership in the 1930s, and of the new members, fully 20 percent were women. The unionization of the mass-production industries, which accounted for most of the increase, bypassed the league entirely. Its education activities dwindled, too, as the trade-union movement, faced with a variety of regulatory agencies and new laws, developed its own training schools and institutes. More important, New Deal labor legislation blanketed nearly all workers with a protective coat, and although significant groups of women, including domestic workers and agricultural workers, were excluded, many felt it was only a matter of time before they would be covered too. And, in any event, the Women's Bureau continued to lobby for their protection. The league began to debate its future existence.

In an effort to rekindle labor support, Schneiderman once again turned her attention to the labor movement. Early in 1943, in one of the superb ironies of her long career, she persuaded Eleanor Roosevelt to send invitations out on her letterhead inviting leaders of forty trade unions to meet with her at the

Cosmopolitan Club in New York City to consider the relationship between the WTUL and the labor movement. The meeting, nominally a success, prompted William Green to send a letter to AFL affiliates asking for financial help for the league. But it failed to spark any further interest among labor's leaders. Later that year, on the occasion of the league's fortieth anniversary, Schneiderman followed up with an address to the AFL annual meeting. She offered an incentive to the assembled leadership. "The League," she said, "has served the labor movement by interpretations of its principles and problems to the people outside our movement. . . . We hope to expand the work this year by undertaking an effective public relations job in the women's field designed to offset some of the untoward and downright false publicity directed against all labor." Nonbelligerent as ever, she thanked the AFL for encouragement and offered the league's services at the Federation's pleasure.

Coming when it did, the address must have cost Schneiderman something, for by now she and other league officers understood that the WTUL was in serious trouble. As debts increased and tensions mounted, Schneiderman's administrative assistant, Cora Cook, resigned in the spring of 1942 with a bitter letter in which she asked whether Schneiderman did not recognize that "the league may be coming to the end of its usefulness and must face the possibility of a gradual liquidation of its activities." Schneiderman acknowledged the reality, "[B]ut before that time," she answered, "I want to make a last desperate attempt to revive it." A few months later, however, she asked Eleanor Roosevelt to give her a few minutes to discuss a decision she had made. "I have decided not to stand for reelection next Spring. I can no longer stand the strain and worry it takes to keep the League going and feel that we need new young blood."

But she did not resign for six years more. The best guess as to the cause of this delay comes from the role the league played in sustaining her self-image. The year 1943 marked the twenty-fifth anniversary of her accession to the presidency of the New York branch. In celebration, members chose to give a party for her, which Eleanor Roosevelt hosted at Hyde Park. The skit performed on that occasion reveals something of why Schneiderman could not yet leave. Read as a Greek chorus, with people speaking sometimes in unison and sometimes individually, it recalled the history of the WTUL and the great work it had done for working women over the years. At its center was Rose Schneiderman. Speakers began by recalling the ghosts of the past:

No light in the factories
No rest rooms
No water
Low wages
These were the evils which Rose dared to fight
In darkness of ignorance in darkness of night
These were the death hands at working girls' feasts

That wanted to turn them from humans to beasts.
But Rose dared to organize
And Rose dared to fight
Rose was so little
But Rose had great might

They concluded, many tributes later, by proclaiming:

Rose, Rose, Rose, dearest president
Hail, Hail to you
Rose, Rose, you have been heaven sent
We honor you.

How was Rose Schneiderman, an orphaned, immigrant child of New York's Lower East Side, just resigned from her New York State Department of Labor job, to walk away from such adulation? And what does this remarkable expression of sentiment tell us about the WTUL, its leaders, and its members? It speaks of a community of women with boundless admiration and love for each other who stood together to oppose the forces of evil. No working-class identification here—only the ring of frail women bonding against elements that would deprive them of their humanity. The sentiments confirmed her sense of self as a tireless defender of the weak and the powerless. Not until 1949, aged sixty-seven and tired at last, did she decide to retire. Then she voted to dismantle the National Women's Trade Union League, while she turned over the presidency of the New York branch to a younger woman.

Looking back from retirement, Schneiderman re-created the connection between labor legislation and organizing in the following way: "We only began to stress legislative activities when we discovered, almost accidentally, a stepping stone cause and effect relationship in the American labor movement. If we organized even a handful of girls, and then managed to put through legislation which made into law the advantages they had gained, other girls would be more likely to join a union and reap further benefits for themselves." The memory here speaks less to what actually happened than to Schneiderman's wishes about what might have happened. But it does confirm one of Schneiderman's favorite theories: that strong organization would encourage effective legislative enforcement. And in that aspect, it resolves one of the basic dilemmas of the woman labor organizer in the years before the New Deal. The discovery that for women legislation could provide many of the benefits of unionization, that it could be more efficiently achieved, and that it would touch wider numbers of women workers surely made it the more desirable alternative. And yet the labor leader that Schneiderman remained in her self-image had to reconcile the danger that Gompers and others in the early AFL most feared. Supporting legislation meant that the labor movement weakened its own appeal in the attempt to benefit unorganized workers. Absent such direct political influence as could be exerted by European labor parties, the American labor movement sought strength in service to its own members.

In urging legislation, Schneiderman came perilously close to having to acknowledge women's outsider position. She repeatedly and insistently affirmed her loyalty to the AFL in order to avoid that pitfall. So she claimed that organized women could most effectively influence the law's content, enforce its provisions, and ensure equality in its application. Those who were organized, she argued in her NRA years, profited more by the codes than "unorganized girls." Yet the dilemma persisted until the 1930s, at which time a new social compact affirmed labor's right to exist and a newly validated labor movement threw itself behind legislative restrictions for all workers. Not accidentally, the special role of legislation for women diminished as the new industrial unions offered the promise of membership to them. The WTUL's influence waned at the same moment.

But before this happened, the central concern of Schneiderman's life was how to obtain legislation for women without alienating them from the labor movement. The path to solving this problem broke down some of her class identifications, leaving her with a profound respect for the powers of the state and a growing dependence on its agencies for reform. It thus undermined her earlier radical analysis at the same time that it disengaged her from a labor movement that had proven so unwilling a partner. But it left her as dependent on the state as she had once been on the labor movement.

Schneiderman's life represents one way in which a woman labor leader could serve her constituency. Freeing herself from the rigid and sometimes restrictive confines of a labor movement uncomfortable with female leadership, she nevertheless remained loyal to its principles and supportive of its goals. Eager to ease women's work lives and unable to conceive of them as a fighting force, she turned instead to the kind of protection the law could offer. And she salved her conscience by using the WTUL to educate the nation at large and women in particular as to labor's virtues. In the end, she was right when she denied that she was a terror to employers. For that would have violated the limits she imposed on her conception of womanhood.

Bibliographic Notes

Many of the manuscript sources for Rose Schneiderman are now available in the microfilm edition of the Papers of the Women's Trade Union League and its Principal Leaders. These include the papers of the New York Women's Trade Union League, housed in the New York State Department of Labor Library in New York City; the papers of the National Women's Trade Union League, located at the Library of Congress; the Rose Schneiderman collection from the Tamiment Library, New York University; and two useful collections from the Schlesinger Library in the history of women, Cambridge, Mass.: the papers of Leonora O'Reilly and Mary Anderson. The Eleanor Roosevelt Papers at Hyde Park contain a number of Schneiderman letters, written mostly in the 1930s. The Pauline Newman Papers, housed at the Schlesinger Library, opened to researchers after this essay first appeared.

Although not a prolific writer, Schneiderman produced a number of pieces that capture her changing orientation. "A Cap Maker's Story," *The Independent* 58 (April 27, 1905): 930–40, and "The Shirtwaist Makers' Strike," *Survey* 23 (January 15, 1910): 505–6, reflect the militancy of her early years. "Is Woman Suffrage Failing?" *The Woman Citizen* 8 (March 22, 1924): 730, reveals her continuing faith in women's political role; "Women's Role in Labor Legislation," *Industrial Bulletin* 25 (January 1956): 4–6, indicates that even at this late date she had not abandoned her interest in legislative solutions. Schneiderman's autobiography, written with Lucy Goldthwaite, *All for One* (New York: Paul Erickson, 1967), reduces many of her conflicts to platitudes.

Annelise Orleck, *Common Sense and a Little Fire: Women and Working-Class Politics in the United States, 1900–65* (Chapel Hill: University of North Carolinia Press, 1995), contains the best discussion of Schneiderman. The only full-length biography is Gary Edward Endelman, *Solidarity Forever: Rose Schneiderman and the Women's Trade Union League* (New York: Arno Press, 1982). Endelman sees Schneiderman as a social reformer committed to "the power of political action" and convinced that only big government could solve the problems of wage-earning women. In contrast, Nancy Schrom Dye, *As Equals as Sisters: Feminism, Unionism, and the Women's Trade Union League of New York* (Columbia: University of Missouri Press, 1980), places Schneiderman within the context of women's collective action. See also Robin Miller Jacoby, "The Women's Trade Union League and American Feminism," *Feminist Studies* 3 (Fall 1975): 126–40, for the feminist context. Ellen Lagemann, *A Generation of Women: Education in the Lives of Progressive Reformers* (Cambridge, Mass.: Harvard University Press, 1979), suggests that Schneiderman's life is best understood as an attempt to retrieve the educational opportunities she was denied as a child and to create them for other women. For the broader context of the WTUL, see Allen F. Davis, "The Women's Trade Union League: Origins and Organization," *Labor History* 5 (Winter 1964): 3–17; and Gladys Boone, *The Women's Trade Union League in Great Britain and the United States of America* (New York: Columbia University Press, 1942). In the absence of a good critical history of the ILGWU, consult Louis Levine, *The Women's Garment Workers: A History of the International Ladies' Garment Workers' Union* (New York: B. W. Heubsch, 1924); and Benjamin Stolberg, *Tailor's Progress: The Story of a Famous Union and the Men Who Made It* (New York: Doubleday, 1944).

PART II

Gender and Class

Very early on in my explorations of women's wage work, I turned to ideology to explain women's persistently disadvantaged positions in the labor market. There seemed no other way to account for why the vast majority of women never got the training or the education to pursue good jobs or careers. While structural and family explanations could account for the relative absence of married women in traditional wage labor, they could not account for the low pay women received when they pursued work at home. Nor could they account for the brutally poor conditions of the vast majority of sweatshop and factory workers, or domestic servants and seamstresses, many of whom were in short supply. Wherever I turned, explanations seemed to come back to a deeply rooted set of expectations about how men and women should behave and what roles they ought to perform.

In "Stratifying by Sex"—an early effort to provide a synthetic framework for women's work—I adopted a notion briefly popular among radical economists who argued that labor-market segmentation accounts for persistent differences. In my view, the segmented labor market (which could be traced to opportunities for schooling and job training) is governed by gender as well as by race. Ideas about men's and women's roles determine who has access to training of different kinds. The other essays in this section all take advantage of this basic insight to explore how ideology shapes the expectations and aspirations of male and female workers differently. "Independence and Virtue" opened up the issue around the question of whether work has historically meant the same thing to women as to men. A product of its times, it dealt with ideas of virtue as they emerged from the literature on white working-class women. Some recent literature has since affirmed that though black women faced very different economic pressures, their conceptions of virtue took similar forms.

"A New Agenda for Labor History" was written in the aftermath of a 1984 conference of labor historians in which issues of culture and class were extensively debated, but gender hardly figured in the making of the working class. Gender, I argue here, is a significant component of our cultural understanding, and not to see it as such is to miss an important way of understanding how class relations were formed. The perspective of masculinity, I argue in "Treating the Male as Other," constitutes an important way of seeing how gender operates. The piece suggests that only when we make visible the kinds of privileges that accrue to masculinity in the labor market will we be able to see how powerful a force gender remains. "Measures for Masculinity," the final piece in this section, tries to do just that. It is a case study of how men and women in a large industrial plant in the late 1920s viewed their relationships to wage labor and to the home. At the same time, it provides evidence that managers and employers contributed to sustaining traditional views by utilizing paternalist techniques that affirmed gendered belief systems.

5

Stratifying by Sex:
Understanding the History
of Working Women

The sexual division of labor is one of the most pervasive and effective bases on which the labor market is segmented. Its success rests on the use of ideological arguments to justify sex roles and to resist efforts to change them. This essay will attempt to make explicit the assumptions that surround sexual roles in the labor market. It will explore the various ways in which sexual stratification has occurred over time in the United States and demonstrate how effectively ideas have simultaneously sustained and obscured discrimination against working women. Because ideological constraints and limits on aspiration regulate the participation of all workers and influence the entire operation of the labor market, exploring the boundaries of women's workforce participation should tell us something about the subtle nature of segmentation mechanisms.

The relationship between changing ideas about women and divisions in the workforce involves several important elements. First, the segmentation process, as it affects women, reflects the economic interdependence of individuals within the family and the ideological and economic relationship of the family to the surrounding culture. Most recent literature acknowledges that inducements for women to work are mitigated by their primary relationships to the family but stops short of asking about the family's changing relationship to the political economy.[1] In a brilliant essay, Eli Zaretsky addresses this fundamental problem. He explores the consequences of changing economic needs for individuals within families, concluding that the family can only be understood as part of the surrounding economic structure.[2] In capitalist society,

Originally published in Richard Edwards, Michael Reich, and David Gordon, eds., *Labor Market Segmentation* (Lexington, Mass.: D. C. Heath, 1975). This piece was reprinted in slightly altered form as "Women, Work, and the Social Order" in *Liberating Women's History,* ed. Berenice Carroll (Urbana: University of Illinois Press, 1976). Rereading this, after thirty years, I note how much has changed in the structure of the labor market—as well as what has remained the same.

where families have served as stabilizing agencies, transmitting the particular values necessary to sustain the economic system, women have played special roles. Their child-rearing and socializing functions as well as their household maintenance have been critical. As long as most work took place within the home, few women felt any tension between their work and family roles. The growth of industry in the eighteenth and nineteenth centuries encouraged many employers to seek ways to use potentially profitable female labor power in their factories. To do this without undermining women's primary allegiance to family ties remained a continuing problem of employing women in the labor force. The struggle to contain the tension between the need for certain kinds of labor power, on the one hand, and perceived women's roles in a changing family, on the other hand, is a recurring theme of this essay. It provides a dynamic explanation for the variety of ways women have been integrated into the labor force and their varying consequences for women of different classes and ethnic groups.

A second element in women's paid labor-force participation has been the way in which socialization and culture influence perceptions of roles so that they appear to be inevitable and unchangeable. Since even in the best of times women were expected to function in quasi-subservient ways, to restrict their aspirations, and to possess certain nurturing qualities, these became the boundaries of their job opportunities. Only exceptional women could consciously resist the psychological and cultural attributes into which they were overwhelmingly socialized. And though it happened, not infrequently, that poor working women demanded better pay and working conditions, only rarely did they question the family structure that was the instrument of their oppression.[3] Widespread convictions that women's proper work was within the family explain their particularly poor position in the labor force throughout the nineteenth and twentieth centuries. Until the present, only financial necessity has driven most women into the paid labor force, but as with men, class differences have to some extent determined job opportunities, and values derived from traditional immigrant families often influenced perceptions of job possibilities.

A third theme in the problem of sexual stratification is rooted in the changing economic needs of employers. These operated in a dialectical relationship that comprehended the function of ideology in sustaining societal goals as well as changes in family-centered social values and economic structure. The use of technology to increase labor productivity and the changing organization of work have been critical variables in inducing women of different strata to enter or leave the labor force. The changing demands of the labor market explain much of the slow accommodation of educational institutions and family patterns to the demands of women.

The pattern of women's historical participation in the workforce is rooted in all these factors. It is, in part, a function of the ideology of the family, and therefore of the roles that women, like men, are convinced they must play. That ideology emerges from the objective needs of families and from a complex of societal goals that derive from a changing political economy. Women are used in the workforce in ways that relate the ideological justifications of a whole society to its immediate labor-force needs. These together provide part of the complex reality that translates back into class divisions among working and nonworking women and into specific policies that affect women workers. What follows is an attempt to sketch out these changing relationships in the United States, to break through the mystification process, and to explore the social realities of the millions of women who have always worked.

Regulating Respectability

The family had been a keystone of social order in Puritan New England. The Massachusetts Bay Colony self-consciously encouraged families to be "little cells of righteousness where the mother and father disciplined not only their children, but also their servants and any boarders they might take in."[4] Unmarried men and women were required to place themselves in the home of a family in order to be guided by them. Family members were encouraged to supervise one another in order to guard the morals of the community as a whole. John Demos sums up his study of the Plymouth colony by noting that the family functioned as a business, a school, a training institution, a church, and often as a welfare institution. "Family and community," he concludes, "... formed part of the same moral equation. The one supported the other, and they became in a sense indistinguishable."[5] The middle and southern colonies did not differ markedly.[6]

While the functions of the family changed toward the end of the eighteenth century, certain assumptions remained. A preindustrial society assumed that, except among the privileged few, all family members would work as a matter of course. So widely accepted was this practice that colonial widows often took over businesses left by their deceased husbands, and in at least one instance an innkeeper, deprived of the services of a wife, recently buried, was denied permission to operate his tavern.[7] Widows and orphans with no other means of support were set to work by the community. In her pioneering work on women in industry, Edith Abbott notes that "court orders, laws, and public subscriptions were resorted to in order that poor women might be saved from the sin of idleness and taught to be self-supporting."[8] But work for women was so closely identified with home and family that when Alexander Hamilton in his famous report on manufactures suggested putting women and children to work in incipient manufacturing enterprises, his idea was scorned. The curse of idleness was insufficiently threatening to justify removing women from their homes.

The heavy burden of household production and the interdependency of family life and economic survival encouraged little revolt against these roles. Family and work were bound together in an integrated and stable whole. But as the agrarian society of the eighteenth century moved into the early industrialization of the nineteenth century, new economic conditions produced a need to reaffirm and articulate "proper" places for women. At first, mills took over the spinning, and the fiber was handed out to women to weave in their homes. When weaving machinery became more complex, both processes were moved to the factory. It seemed natural that women should follow. The new mill owners sought their labor supply among widows and children who needed to work, sometimes hiring whole families. Removing women from their homes did not prove appealing to a largely agrarian population with a coherent conception of women's roles, and independent farmers were reluctant to adapt to the discipline of the factory. Mill owners complained constantly of the difficulties of finding an adequate labor supply.[9]

The unmarried daughters of New England farmers seemed to be the only alternative. Could one reconcile the moral imperative of the home with the use of these young women in factories? It was the genius of Francis Cabot Lowell to conceive of a way of doing so. He appealed to the young single daughters of farm families to fulfill their family responsibilities by engaging in hard work away from home. For the mill that finally opened in Lowell, Massachusetts, in 1821, he proposed carefully supervised boardinghouses for women who would spend a few years before marriage at the mills, and offered salaries that were to be saved for their trousseaux, to help pay off mortgages, or to send a brother through college. At the same time, parents were assured that their daughters would experience the hard work and discipline that would make them into better wives and mothers. The mills at Lowell and elsewhere in New England attracted a reliable labor force that was easily disciplined in industrial routines and cheaper than male labor. In return, they offered a training ground in morality.

The mill owners' need coincided with their conviction that they were providing a service for the nation. Mill owners repeatedly stated "that one of their prime purposes in launching the textile industry was to give employment to respectable women to save them from poverty and idleness."[10] They argued that they were preserving republican virtues of hard work and raising the moral and intellectual tone of the country.[11] The mill women themselves, at least in the early years, determined to preserve their own respectability in the eyes of the public. In a manner reminiscent of the early Puritans, they "supervised" one another, ostracizing those whose morals were in question.[12]

But the need to maintain high wages and good working conditions proved too much for employers to bear. Within a few years, Lowell women complained of excessively long hours, wage cuts, and extra work. Occasional strikes and rumblings of discontent became audible from Pawtucket, Rhode Island, to Paterson, New Jersey, and Philadelphia, Pennsylvania. In 1828, factory women in Dover, New Hampshire, "turned out" for the first time, marching through the streets to the ridicule of onlookers.[13] Repeated complaints in the 1830s received no response. When Lowell workers organized themselves into the Female Labor Reform Association in 1845, the mill owners abandoned their moral stance. Taking advantage of increasing Irish immigration, they rapidly eliminated the old workforce. In 1845, only 7 percent of the employees in the eight Lowell mills were Irish. By 1852, more than half of the workforce was foreign-born. The pattern was repeated in Holyoke, Massachusetts, in New Hampshire, and in Connecticut. The protected New England mill woman swiftly disappeared.

The pages of the *Lowell Offering*, a factory-supported paper, reveal how completely an alternative cheap labor supply took precedence over the employers' oft pronounced morality. Some operators continued to believe as late as 1849 that corporation owners would raise wages so as "to attract once more the sort of girl who had made the industry what it was."[14] Skeptics felt that the mills had lost the respect of the community because standards of morality and the old spirit of mutual surveillance had declined. Caroline Ware, a historian of the textile industry, assesses the position of the employers: "Necessity had forced them to gain and hold the respect of the community in order to attract the requisite workers and they were only too eager to be relieved of that necessity by the advent of a class of labor which had no standing in the community and no prejudice against mill-work."[15] Native-born females simply stopped applying for jobs. One Massachusetts paper remarked in 1852 of the Chicopee mills that "'foreign girls have been employed in such numbers that what American girls are employed there experience considerable difficulty in finding society among their workmates congenial to their tastes and feelings.'"[16]

Although only about 10 percent of all women worked in the paid labor force, the mills depended on their labor. In the mid-1840s, about one-half of the factory population was female. In textiles, shoes, and hats their numbers were even higher. From 80 to 90 percent of the operatives in some mills throughout New England were women.[17] As the numbers of working women rose, the proportions who came from nonimmigrant families declined. In part this was the result of the development and institutionalization of a new regulating device: the domestic code, which established proper roles for women and towards which poor and immigrant women could only aspire.

The source of this major ideological transition remains imperfectly understood, but its elements are fairly clear. The growth of industry, a developing laissez-faire ideology, and a concurrent redefinition of the home and family required more constricted women's roles and resulted in sharper divisions in the self-concept of middle- and working-class women. Industrialization and urbanization slowly increased the number of men who worked in impersonal factories beyond the immediate surroundings of home and community. Because men were removed from contact with children during the lengthy and exhausting day, women assumed responsibility for training children to fill future labor-force needs. Simultaneously, the old Puritan ethic, which stressed morality, hard work, and community, gave way to laissez-faire economic policies that emphasized individualism, success, and competition. Men who worked hard and strove for success required wives who were emotionally supportive and who could competently supervise the household.

Ideas about what women should do conformed to these new societal requirements. Their clearest expression occurred first among the prosperous and growing urban middle class. In what the historian Bernard Wishy calls a reappraisal of family life that took place after 1830, motherhood rose to new heights, and children became the focus of womanly activity. Mothers were asked to give up wealth, frivolity, and fashion to prepare themselves for a great calling. "The mother was the obvious source of everything that would save or damn the child; the historical and spiritual destiny of America lay in her hands."[18] Simultaneously, the woman became a lady. Meek and passive, modest and silent, women were expected to submerge their wills into those of their husbands and fathers. Piety, purity, and submissiveness became the ideals. The art of homemaking reached professional proportions, with some educators arguing that women must be trained to that end. There could be no higher calling.[19]

The public schools that multiplied in the 1830s and 1840s admitted girls readily. Discipline, respect for authority, adherence to routine, and the rudiments of reading, writing, and arithmetic were as essential to their future lives at home as to the lives of men.[20] Most children left school before they had completed the fourth grade. But girls often stayed on. They were not, after all, expected to go out into the world to make their living, and schooling beyond the initial socialization process was not seen as vocational preparation. With occasional exceptions, colleges, even the lyceums that offered community lectures, remained adamantly closed to females until the 1860s, when the pressure of feminism opened them.

In its most dramatic form, the developing ideology described the female as functioning only within her crucial sphere. Aileen Kraditor notes, "[I]t was not that social order required the subordination of women, rather . . . it required a family structure that involved the subordination of women."[21] One popular nineteenth-century schoolbook argued, "'When a woman quits her own department . . . she departs from that sphere which is assigned to her in

the order of society, because she neglects her duty and leaves her own department vacant.'"[22] Though many strong voices objected to the constraints, they
received little support from the majority of middle-class women, who were
persuaded that they were functioning usefully. In return for an ideology that
glorified their roles and perhaps offered some power within the family, women
were denied a broad range of social and economic options. By the mid-1850s,
the sanctioned occupations for women included teaching, printmaking, and,
when genteel poverty struck the homes of the respectable, dressmaking.

As ideas about "proper roles" for women became institutionalized in the
first part of the nineteenth century, they had severe consequences for the vast
numbers who could not meet their rigid prescription. By defining the role
at home as the measure of respectability, the domestic code sharpened class
differences. In this period of early industrialization, more women than ever
before could aspire to display the perquisites of the "lady"—elegant dress,
servants, and the absence of an economic contribution to household maintenance. These requirements excluded from respectability most women who had
to work in the paid labor force and created for them a set of perhaps unattain-
able aspirations centered on the family. Factory work and domestic service
slid rapidly down the scale of status. Immigrants, black women, and the destitute who toiled at necessary jobs found no focus for their aspirations at work
and no protection from exploitation in an ideology that excluded them from
respectability. Yet their presence in the labor force had a number of tangible
benefits for employers.

First, the existence of the middle-class feminine ideal of domesticity provided employers with a docile group of women who, convinced that marriage
and work were incompatible and that their real calling lay in marriage and
child rearing, had only a transient interest in their jobs. The desire for respectability provided working women with a set of aspirations (equivalent to
upward mobility for men) that mitigated class consciousness and complaints
about present exploitation. A Knights of Labor organizer, Leonora M. Barry,
summed up the problem in 1887: "[I]f there is one cause more than another
that fastens the chains on ... working women it is their foolish pride, they
deeming it a disgrace to have it known that they are engaged in honest toil."[23]

Second, the belief that women belonged at home permitted employers
to exploit working women by treating them as though their earnings were
merely supplemental. Until the end of the nineteenth century, women cus-
tomarily received about one-third to one-half of the prevailing wages for men,
a sum seldom sufficient even for a single woman to support herself.[24] John
Commons estimated that while a living wage for a single person was defined
as eight dollars per week in 1914, only 25 percent of all female wage earners
earned that much, and half took home less than six dollars per week. A 20

percent unemployment rate further reduced these wages.[25] The assumption that women belonged at home occasionally led employers to ask that the help received by women living at home be taken into account in calculating "living wages." Department-store managers pointedly refused to hire sales clerks who did not live in families for fear that financial need would drive them to the streets.[26] The same assumption led employers to refuse to train women to perform skilled jobs, exacerbating their poverty and offering them no choice but to remain unskilled laborers.

Third, employers benefited by competition between men and women. Working men argued that women workers held wages down. Repeatedly in the 1830s, and with growing stridency thereafter, they insisted that wages paid to them would be higher if women were excluded from the workforce. In 1836, a National Trades Union Committee urged that female labor be excluded from factories. After explaining that women's natural responsibility and moral sensibility best suited them to domesticity, the report argued that female labor produced "ruinous competition ... to male labor," the final end of which would be that "the workman is discharged or reduced to a corresponding rate of wages with the female operative." The report continued:

> One thing ... must be apparent to every reflecting female, that all her exertions are scarce sufficient to keep her alive; that the price of her labor each year is reduced; and that she in a measure stands in the way of the male when attempting to raise his prices or equalize his labor, and that her efforts to sustain herself and family, are actually the same as tying a stone around the neck of her natural protector, Man, and destroying him with the weight he has brought to his assistance. This is the true and natural consequence of female labor when carried beyond the family.[27]

The president of the Philadelphia Trades Association advised women to withdraw altogether from the workforce: "[T]he less you do, the more there will be for the men to do and the better they will be paid for doing it, ultimately you will be what you ought to be, free from the performance of that kind of labor which was designed for man alone to perform."[28]

Male fears of displacement or reduced wages seemed justified. While men and women normally did not compete for the same jobs, employers often substituted one for the other in response to changing technology and labor-market conditions. New England textile factories, whose workers were 90 percent female in 1828, were only 69 percent female in 1848.[29] The proportion of Massachusetts teachers who were male had dropped from about 50 percent in 1840 to 14 percent in 1865.[30] By 1865, the labor press was complaining of "'a persistent effort on the part of capitalists and employers to introduce females into its various departments of labor heretofore filled by the opposite sex.'"[31] The feared consequence would be a drop in the price of labor "to the female standard, which is generally less than one half the sum paid to men." Employers sometimes trained women to act as strikebreakers. According to a Senate report, a Chicago newspaper publisher "placed materials in remote rooms of the city and secretly instructed girls to set type and kept them there until they became sufficiently proficient to enter the office."[32] Silk manufacturers testified in 1910 that "as long as there are women horizontal warpers, . . . [the manufacturers have] a strong defense against the demands of the men."[33]

A fourth effect of attributing proper roles to women was to keep women out of unions. Since many felt their work life to be temporary, women had little incentive to join in a struggle for better conditions. Leonora Barry complained in 1889 that in the absence of immediate discomfort, the expectation of marriage blinded many women to the long-range advantages of unions.[34] But the hostility of employers and of male co-workers may have been decisive. Because unions would negate the advantages of low wages and docility, employers would not tolerate them. A government report issued in 1910 noted that the moment a woman organized a union, "she diminishes or destroys what is to the employer her chief value. Hence the marked objection of employers to unions among women."[35]

Men's attitudes toward organizing women varied with their particular circumstances. Sensitive to the competition engendered by employers who used women as strikebreakers or to undercut wages, workers frequently saw clearly the economic role women in fact played in the nineteenth-century labor market. But they rarely repudiated conventional ideas about the social role that women were expected to play. Male trade unionists offered support to women attempting to unionize about as often as they struck to protest the hiring of females. In the 1830s Baltimore's journeymen tailors, New York's bookbinders, and Massachusetts's cordwainers all encouraged their female counterparts to unite for better working conditions.[36] The National Labor Union in the late 1860s persistently urged women to organize, and the Knights of Labor, in its halcyon period in the early 1880s, organized about fifty thousand women into units.[37] Yet these instances can be measured against examples of many craft unions that well into the twentieth century had constitutions calling for suspending members who trained, or worked with, women.

Women who repeatedly, and often successfully, organized themselves throughout the nineteenth and early twentieth centuries still faced the problem of securing recognition for their unionizing efforts. As union structures developed nationally at the turn of the century, their brother trade unionists often refused to admit them to national membership. Philadelphia candy workers, Norfolk waitresses, and New York printers pleaded in vain for admission to their respective national unions. If the men did not reject them outright, they procrastinated until the women succumbed to pressure from their employers.[38] A consistent pattern appears only toward the end of the century with the emergence of arguments that since women were working anyway, it was safer to have them in unions than outside them. The International Typographers admitted women under duress in 1869, and the Cigar Makers began to admit them when competition threatened their own jobs.[39]

Finally, the "cult of true womanhood" glorified the family structure and contributed to a stability that encouraged and even coerced the male head to work harder to support his family and provide for his wife. For one's wife to be working meant that the husband had failed. The need to secure the wife's position on the proverbial pedestal helped to isolate men in an endless search for upward mobility and financial success. The idea that women should be able to stay at home—the better to mother their children—justified hard work, long hours, economic exploitation, and a host of other evils for male workers. A *New York Post* writer in 1829 accurately summed up a prevailing attitude when he asserted that the only way to make husbands sober and industrious was to keep women dependent by means of insufficient wages.[40]

The moral imperative that confined women to their homes served many purposes. It maintained social order by providing stable families. It kept most married women out of the labor force, confining them to supportive roles in relation to the male workforce. It helped to ensure that those women who did work would stay in the labor force only briefly, remaining primarily committed to their families and satisfied with low-paid jobs. The special position of women as the least-paid and least-skilled members of the work-force induced hostility from unskilled male labor. Afraid that women might take their jobs, some workingmen might have been afraid to demand justice from intransigent employers.[41]

Overflowing Tensions

For most of the nineteenth century, notions about the proper roles of women effectively contained the tension between the need for labor and the need for stable families. If those who worked on farms are excluded, less than 20 percent of all women worked in the paid labor force before 1900. Of these, 70 percent were domestic servants in 1870, and 24 percent worked in textile mills and the developing garment industry. Together with tobacco making, these areas comprised most of women's participation in the nonagricultural workforce before 1900. Within these trades, women were the lowest-paid workers and performed the least-skilled jobs. Poor rewards and unpleasant working conditions discouraged all but the poorest from working. Their entry into the labor market was thus naturally regulated, and many left the workplace with relief when marriage and motherhood offered an acceptable escape.

Towards the end of the century, changes in the structure of work and the economy began to alter this seemingly harmonious balance, encouraging women to enter the labor force in ways that directly challenged their family roles. Increasing numbers of women in the labor force and the deteriorating conditions under which some women worked reflected the failure of ideas about women's proper roles to keep them out of the workforce in the face of labor-market demands. At the same time, a mature industrial society encouraged changes in the nature of families that led affluent women to become dissatisfied with constrained roles and to seek new outlets. The resulting tension called forth new definitions of social roles and new compromises in the ways that women could be employed.

The nature of the compromise emerged from the transition from competitive to monopoly capitalism, whose greatest thrust was concentrated in the years from 1890 to around 1920. Its outlines are by now familiar. Small competitive businesses dependent on local markets and a local labor supply gave way to the giant impersonal corporation, whose markets were national and whose workers were increasingly drawn from rural towns and villages to large industrial centers. As the size of plants expanded, impersonal relations replaced the old paternalism; jobs became increasingly specialized, and the number of workers employed in skilled labor declined. Control over workers, which had formerly been a result of community sanctions and loyalty, was achieved by a developing hierarchy of employees and reinforced by the persistent availability of a large surplus of labor. Workers responded to the denigration of their skills, to economic insecurity, and to the pressures of steadily worsening work conditions by forming labor unions. The period around the turn of the century witnessed bloody strikes in railroads, coal, steel, and the garment industries. They were decades in which it seemed, to some, plausible to unite all "producers" to resist corporate encroachment on humane relationships in the name of profits. In the end, economic rationalization and corporate efficiency won the day. The early twentieth century witnessed a modification of laissez-faire policies in favor of government regulation in a corporate state.

Accelerating job specialization in the factory, which raised the demand for unskilled and semiskilled labor, increased employment opportunities for women. In addition, the developing bureaucratic hierarchy and corporate structure demanded increasing numbers of office workers who had limited skills and few job-related aspirations. The proportion of women in the nonagricultural labor force rose dramatically. In 1880, 12.8 percent of all women had worked in nonagricultural jobs. By 1900, the figure had climbed to 17.3 percent, and by 1910 to 20.7 percent. There the figure stabilized.[42] By 1910, one of every five gainfully employed workers was female. Except among African Americans, within the ranks of working women, the proportions working as domestics decreased steadily. More than 60 percent of all working women and 90 percent of African

American women (including farm workers) were so employed in 1870. By 1910, only a little more than one-quarter of all employed women worked as servants, and by 1920 the figure had dropped to 18.2 percent. The proportion of African American women in these jobs remained stable. In contrast, the percentage of women who worked in factories—still largely white—increased from 17.6 percent in 1870 to 20.3 percent in 1890 and 23.8 percent in 1920. The proportion who worked in offices climbed from little more than 5 percent to more than one-quarter of all working women in 1920.[43] Some industries depended heavily on unskilled and semiskilled female labor. Fully 40 percent of the vast complex of textile workers, for example, was female in 1910.[44]

Less dependent in post–Civil War America on skilled workers, employers took advantage of the plentiful labor supply offered by immigration to reduce wages and to coerce hard work out of vulnerable employees. As trade unions sprang up and strikes spread, public attention was drawn to their grievances. Newspaper exposés and government investigations noted the injurious effects on all workers, but especially on women, of harsh working conditions and of wages insufficient to keep body and soul together. Investigators worried incessantly about the morality of working women. Some pointed to spreading prostitution as one consequence of low industrial wages. Others insisted that it was their business to determine "in what particulars . . . employment exerted pressure upon the feminine character."[45] Still others argued that stunted and warped young women endangered the health of unborn children and that working mothers were forced to leave children to roam the streets all day with "latchkeys" strung about their necks. Pressure for legislation to protect these women began to build up.

Simultaneously, it became apparent to the investigators and to male workers that women were finding it increasingly necessary to work. Sickness, accident, and death rates among industrial workers reached all-time heights between 1903 and 1907. Unemployment fluctuated cyclically. Despite rises in real wages after 1897, they remained too low to meet normal family needs. Perhaps as a consequence, the proportion of married women in the nonagricultural workforce almost doubled between 1890 and 1920.[46] Workingmen now voiced new fears that women would undermine the wage standards and work opportunities of the male labor force. While occasional trade unions, especially in industries where women were heavily concentrated, made sporadic attempts to organize them into trade unions, most supported legislation that would effectively limit women's opportunities to work by raising their wages, regulating their hours, and prescribing the kinds of jobs in which they could be employed. Adolph Strasser, the secretary of the Cigar Makers Union in 1879, was only a few years ahead of his time when he said, "[W]e cannot drive the females out of the trade but we can restrict their daily quota of labor through factory laws."[47]

The changing nature of the immigrant population adds another dimension in explaining women's increasing participation in the workforce and the continuing breakdown in prescribed social roles. Primarily Southern and Eastern European, Catholic and Jewish, new immigrants were channeled into the bursting ghettos of expanding cities. Anxious to help their families achieve economic security, women from preindustrial origins who had not been socialized into nineteenth-century America and whose traditions incorporated strong family loyalty and strong work orientations regularly contributed to family incomes. Married women took in boarders or sewing at home. Unmarried women worked as dressmakers and in factories as well as in other people's houses. Among gainfully employed women, the proportion who were immigrants or their daughters increased steadily until 1910, when it began to drop.[48] Aware of the threat to stable family life, reformers undertook movements to "Americanize" immigrants. Beginning in the 1890s and continuing through the 1920s, they were especially concerned with the health and domestic aptitude of present and future mothers. The social settlement, for example, tried with some success to resocialize immigrant women through classes in the arts of homemaking, bathing and caring for children, sewing, and cooking. Although they also made enormous efforts to improve factory conditions, many settlement residents were convinced that mothers belonged at home.

But the tension between the desire to keep women in families and the disruptive consequences of the need for labor was equally apparent among some middle-class women. While social values dictated leisure and an absence of work for women, enforced idleness bred a challenge to social order. For the wealthy married woman, affluence, servants, and a decline in the birthrate all added up to boredom. Some middle-class women developed symptoms of hysteria in response; others insisted on an education or threw themselves into charitable activities.[49] Excess energies spent themselves in ways that often had consequences for working women. Those who sought suffrage allied themselves with white working women, breaking down momentarily the class barriers that had consistently divided them. Affluent women who became involved in the trade-union movement not only contributed to the success of women attempting to organize themselves but revealed the common disabilities that linked the two groups. Those who became reformers and social-settlement residents investigated and exposed abuses against children and women in factories, publicizing, in consequence, the conditions on which their own leisure rested.[50]

A third group crossed class lines more dramatically. Attracted by new jobs opening in offices, they chose to work. Large numbers of women who came from groups not previously employed began to search for jobs. In 1890 only 35.3 percent of all women who worked were native-born daughters of native parents. By 1920 this figure had soared to almost 44 percent, while the proportion of native-born daughters in the population had increased only slightly.[51] The dramatic increase in the proportion of native daughters accompanied enormous shifts to the clerical sectors of the workforce.[52] The needs of employers for people who were, at one and the same time, relatively well educated and relatively poorly paid seems to have created a new labor market. In part, this was met by rising educational levels among immigrant daughters who had traditionally worked, but in part it was met by native white women entering the labor market for the first time.

The expansion of acceptable jobs for white women between 1900 and 1920 and the spread of gainful employment beyond the very poor contributed to attacks on conceptions of "proper roles." Leading feminists, like Charlotte Perkins Gilman, questioned women's economic dependence; the suffrage campaign mounted in intensity and solicited support among industrial workers of both sexes; and unskilled women in factories and department stores redoubled their efforts towards unionization.[53] The interests of white working women and their middle-class sisters joined in groups like the proliferating working girls' clubs, the Consumers Leagues, and the Women's Trade Union League. Their goals coalesced around the desire of working women for better conditions, shorter hours, and fair pay—and the concern of the more affluent that work not detract from the health and morality of their working sisters and thus undermine the still-essential family. The groups united under the banner of protective legislation.

Protective legislation acknowledged the increasing place of women in the workforce while attempting to control implicit changes in women's social roles.[54] It recognized that women had two jobs, one of which had to be limited if the other were to be performed adequately. Yet legislation institutionalized the primary role of social reproduction by denying that women were full-fledged members of the working class. It extended an ideology of "proper roles" to working-class people while loosening the bonds of propriety from the arms of some middle-class women. Protective legislation thus provided a device for dividing workers along gender lines and stratifying the workforce in a period when homogeneity in levels of skill threatened to lead to developing class consciousness and to give rise to class conflict.[55]

The new body of laws was rooted in the potentials inherent in an expanding technology and increasingly productive labor force. Large-scale corporate enterprise and the rapid expansion of capital led many corporations to seek new ways to invest their economic surplus and to stimulate the consumption of the goods they produced. This had two opposing consequences for women. On the one hand, slowly rising wages and better working conditions for some workers encouraged wives to remain at home. On the other hand, expanding labor productivity influenced the structure of the family. As society became more urban, households began to produce less of their food and clothing and to rely more heavily on consumer goods. Declining work for women in the household encouraged those whose husbands did not earn sufficient income to consider paid labor as a realistic alternative. Specialization and the division of labor meant that children were frequently trained outside the home, altering further the functions of women within the household. On balance, the early twentieth century witnessed a steadily rising proportion of women in the nonagricultural labor force.

Protective legislation, which began in the United States about 1900, reflected these changes. Institutionalizing "proper roles" for women who worked in factories and shops at one and the same time insulated them from their male coworkers and reduced the jobs available to them. It had little effect on the new office clerk, who normally did not work at night or in ill-ventilated factories or lift heavy weights. Working women found themselves subject to an increasing barrage of legislation limiting the hours of work, establishing minimum wages, and regulating the sanitary conditions under which they could work. These laws had the immense advantage of ameliorating the worst conditions of women's work, while offering to conserve the health and energy to rear present and future families. Their supporters quite specifically argued that legislation was in the best interests of the state. Oregon, for example, preceded its minimum-wage law with a preamble: "The welfare of the State of Oregon requires that women and minors should be protected from conditions of labor which have a pernicious effect on their health and morals, and inadequate wages . . . have such a pernicious effect."[56] Men did not benefit from minimum-wage laws in this period, and courts repeatedly struck down legislative restrictions on hours that applied to men.

At the same time, legislation had a significant impact on the workforce as a whole. In reducing the economic desirability of female employees, it limited competition with males. In the words of one authority, "The wage bargaining power of men is weakened by the competition of women and children, hence a law restricting the hours of women and children may also be looked upon as a law to protect men in their bargaining power."[57] Workingmen favored a minimum-wage legislation for women because it effectively reduced a downward pull on their wages.[58] The newly established Women's Bureau of the Department of Labor took great pains in the 1920s to prove that women were not displaced by factory laws.[59] While technically that seems to have been true, the bureau interviewed a number of employers who indicated that restrictive legislation rendered them unable to consider women for otherwise suitable jobs.[60] Despite job shifts that provided new opportunities, women's rate of labor-force participation remained stable until the late 1930s.[61]

With rare exceptions, employers did not suffer. Legislation was slowly and tentatively achieved, with due regard for the interests of manufacturers whose businesses were likely to be hurt. Sanitary and health regulations often went unenforced. By and large, regulation was opposed only by small manufacturers represented in the National Association of Manufacturers, whose interests often contradicted those of the corporations and labor unions that came to approve and lobby for protecting women.

Working women were confused about the legislation, and the trade unionists among them took contradictory positions in the early years of the twentieth century, finally opting for protection when organization seemed impossible. By the 1920s, when most industrial states had some legislation limiting hours and regulating night work, the conflict came to a head. Some feminists, largely business and professional women, protesting the assumption that women had special roles that required state protection, advocated an Equal Rights Amendment (ERA) to the Constitution, which would eliminate the body of legislation so painstakingly built up. Women trade unionists, the Women's Trade Union League, and the Women's Bureau led the fight against the ERA.[62] One woman supervisor in a Virginia silk mill expressed the conflict well: "I have always been afraid that if laws were made discriminating for women it would work a handicap upon them." By 1923, she had changed her mind: "[I]t would in time raise the entire standard, rather than make it hard for women."[63] Business and professional women, led by the National Woman's Party, supported the ERA. Many professional women's clubs forthrightly condemned labor laws for women.[64]

As the number of women in the workforce rose and the kinds of jobs open to them became more varied, segmentation among different groups of working women increased. Women considered certain kinds of jobs more appropriate than others. Rose Schneiderman, an immigrant who later became a trade-union organizer, recalls that when she left her department-store job to become a sewing-machine operator at the age of sixteen, her mother was "far from happy. She thought working in a store much more genteel than working in a factory."[65] Waitresses, considered by many in the early twentieth century as the most degraded of workers, had their own hierarchies. Those who worked where liquor was sold, and where tips were larger, were despised by the others.[66] As with men, employers used language and race to build barriers around employees. Garment-industry employers deliberately hired women who spoke different languages to inhibit communication in the workshop.[67] Tobacco processors most frequently hired black women to strip tobacco—a job white women would take only as a last resort.[68]

Schooling played a major role in segmenting women. New office jobs required not only facility in reading and writing English but a command of typing, stenography, simple bookkeeping, and business machines. In the early years of the century, manufacturers set up schools to train young women in the use of their products. Occasionally employers subsidized women who went to classes run by organizations like the Women's Educational and Industrial Union, which offered to teach department-store employees such subjects as English, arithmetic, hygiene, history of manufactured goods, art of politeness, and store diplomacy.[69] But most employers relied on an expanding network of manual or vocational training programs to discipline young women for the work world and to endow them with necessary skills. Beginning with the first vocational training school for women in 1899 and capped by the federal Vocational Education Act in 1917, these programs channeled suitable candidates into acceptable jobs. They preserved the dichotomy in women's roles by almost universally offering training in domestic science along with typewriting.

By the end of the 1920s the pattern had been confirmed. Most male and female workers were segregated from each other, largely by prevailing norms about proper roles, but increasingly by protective legislation and by an educational structure that reflected those norms and channeled women into jobs deemed appropriate. Within the female workforce, separate segmentation mechanisms were fairly widespread. Enticed by the image of the glamorous flapper, single women went to work in offices, department stores, and factories roughly according to their socioeconomic status. Schools and professional agencies opened their doors to those destined to become teachers, social workers, and nurses. Some women entered graduate school and became lawyers or doctors. But married women and poor women were encouraged to remain at home unless absolutely necessary, and industrial employers, discouraged by minimum wages and short hours, often looked elsewhere for labor. That compromise satisfied employers, who had an abundance of immigrant labor, and workingmen, who worried less about female competition.

But the compromise was never very effective. It began to flounder on the questions raised by women who confronted changes in their own roles at home and who, married or not, increasingly sought to work. It was finally scuttled by the insatiable demand for office workers.

The Compromise Collapses

The Depression of the 1930s obscured the long-term trend but could not challenge the essential compromise worked out in the preceding decades. If relative poverty inhibited consumerism and encouraged women once more to exercise economy and increase their productivity in the household, the continuing shift in job structures confirmed women's marginal but essential position in the workforce. Rising unemployment led to pressure to eliminate some married women from the state and federal civil service, yet many wives sought jobs to eke out family incomes. To some extent, men entered traditionally women's occupations like teaching. But, remarkably, women held onto the jobs that had been sex-role stereotyped. It is noteworthy not that women gained few jobs in the 1930s, but that they lost so little.[70]

Wartime prosperity succeeded the Depression, and women entered the labor force in large numbers. Though they breached sex lines in every imaginable job category, women faced at wars' end a major propaganda campaign to force them back into their homes.[71] Appeals to familial duty were only partially successful. Many women resigned their jobs, but a residue remained at work to be joined later by a steadily mounting number.

These women heralded a changing economy that, since World War II, has simultaneously opened new jobs and altered the nature of families and women's functions within them. Within the family, increased affluence and improved household technology as well as expanding consumer services have altered the kind of work women do at home, reducing their functions as producers but increasing their roles as consumers. Despite changes in household technology, rising standards of house care may have increased the actual time spent at household tasks. Longer life spans for men and women and declining birthrates have reduced the proportion of time spent in child rearing. For some sectors, relative affluence has reduced the need to instill values of thrift, hard work, and education, raising questions about how to socialize children.[72] Official policy still acknowledges the traditionally central role of the family as a stabilizing agency. But young people and women are beginning to explore alternatives that reflect doubt about old values.[73]

At the same time, job structures have shifted dramatically from primarily blue-collar and manual labor before World War II to white-collar and service work in the postwar period.[74] The expanding sectors—teaching, social work, the human services, health, publishing, and advertising—are all extensions of family functions and have long been acceptable areas for women. While the spread of mass education and the demand for office workers of various kinds have led women to enter the labor force, the concomitant need that these workers not seek advancement or high compensation has encouraged the belief that their work experience is and ought to be secondary to their home roles. Popular magazines, advertising, prevalent truths about child rearing, and the glorification of femininity have conspired to support this belief. But low-level clerical and secretarial jobs may be opening faster than they can be filled by the available pool of single or childless women.[75] Short of a dramatic rechanneling of men into office jobs, which would involve major adjustments in social values, large-scale bureaucracies will be forced to make allowances for women with children.

The problem is already evident in the changing composition of the workforce. Female workers are becoming older, better educated, less likely to take time off for childbirth, and more likely to be married and to have children. Fully 40 percent of all women over sixteen now earn wages, and two-thirds of the women in the labor force are married; 42 percent of the paid labor force is now female.[76] Because jobs have expanded in precisely those sectors in which women have been working, women have begun to reevaluate their commitments to the home and to seek occupational mobility. Women with seniority rights and prior experience become discontent when they are consistently overlooked for top jobs. For many women, the need for a job has given way to the demand for a career, and marriage is no longer an escape from the world of work.

Changing families and new job structures expose more clearly than before the fundamental tension between the demands of the labor market and the belief that social order is vested in the family. Women who are uncomfortable with confused family patterns and limited workforce options have begun to question their "proper roles." Ideas that assign them to secondary places in the workforce seem unacceptable. The feminine mystique seems no longer able to contain the contradiction. In contrast to the past, when only exceptional women agitated for more responsible jobs and release from their family roles, protest against the concept of roles is now becoming generalized. It is evident in attacks against images of women in advertising, on television, in popular magazines, and in movements to alter textbooks and clothing styles. While working women have frequently asked for higher wages and better working conditions, their failure to achieve them is explained by the continuing strength of ideas about women's roles. Some recognition that these ideas are losing credibility may be indicated by government-instituted affirmative action programs and successful campaigns to admit women to prestigious colleges and professional schools.

Some ways of containing these new challenges are already being tried. A few jobs are being opened up to women, and occasionally wages are being equalized. But the percentage of women holding prestige jobs has not increased, and on the whole, women's wages have not risen comparably to those of men.[77] Predictably, the issue of competition between men and women has undermined key questions about the nature of work and has produced something of a backlash, now known as "reverse discrimination." One can expect these reactions to worsen in the event of economic recession. But the most subtle and debilitating response has been its class-based nature. As in the early twentieth century, legislative responses are institutionalizing gains for the affluent and well-educated, while excluding most others from the workforce. Recent federal legislation encourages women who can afford the cost of child care or household help to work, while current executive action deprives those who are poor, but not on welfare, of federally financed day-care centers.[78] Affirmative action programs have benefited professional and business women far more than clerks and secretaries. Yet office workers have begun to organize, and trade-union women are beginning to talk about joint action.

The enormous number of women now working raises questions about whether their commitments to jobs will undermine the basis of the traditional family. High divorce rates, strong support for some form of abortion rights, and public affirmations of gay and lesbian lifestyles all testify to increasing conflict about the traditional role of the family and erosion of confidence about its social necessity. The decline of the family as an economic unit, valuable for the social insurance it provides, may herald women's freedom from it. Women who challenge the necessity for a sexually stratified workforce could expose the segmentation process that divides all workers. They could provoke other less well-defined groups to scrutinize their own particular sources of stratification. But if family roles have changed to the extent that society can afford to let women out of their homes, sexual stratification may give way only to be replaced for women by the traditional mechanisms of segmentation along class and race lines.

6

Independence and Virtue in the Lives of Wage-Earning Women in the United States, 1870–1930

Whatever the differences of race or class among women, a common ideological bond puts them in a relation to the labor force that has historically differed from that of men. For men, a sense of self has typically come from job-related skill, security, success, or achievement—or the lack thereof. But these are qualities not suited to home roles. Conversely, patterns of behavior and expectations ideally suited to family roles are not necessarily conducive to achievement in the male world of labor. The disparity between male and female expectations limits the validity of any analysis of women's labor that focuses only on such issues as occupational mobility, job consciousness, and even unionization, worker control, and resistance. Instead, it opens another kind of analysis that originates in the kinds of self-images that have formed the historical boundaries of women's labor-market behavior and experience.

Women's decisions to engage in wage work are deeply connected to "real-life" constraints that have historically emerged from women's roles in families. The number of babies, organization of the household and its income level, rural or urban settings, and ethnic or community approval all play a part in the varied patterns of women's workforce participation. These constraints have bred a series of ideological rationalizations that, in self-reinforcing fashion, maintain the original behavior patterns and roles and inhibit alternative modes of solving life situations. In the United States, ideas about what women should be have historically bred opposition to such notions as collective living, communal child care, and shared kitchens, and they have diverted us from questions

First published in Judith Friedlander, Blanche Wiesen Cook, Alice Kessler-Harris, and Caroll Smith-Rosenberg, eds., *Women in Culture and Politics: A Century of Change* (Bloomington: Indiana University Press, 1986).

about the naturally ordained nature of sex roles. The whole is, of course, sustained and reinforced by economic pressures that have changed over time.

If we explain women's ability to participate in the labor market in terms of the impact of real-life constraints on their historical choices, we are soon caught in the morass of differing experiences, each equally valid for the particular group to which it applies. Such a method teaches us little about what is common to gender, though it is useful for analyzing particular sociohistorical situations. But if we acknowledge that the same network of culture and socialization that affirms real-life choices operates as well *inside* the labor market and continues to influence women's behavior as wage earners in ways that sustain their social roles, we can perhaps reach a common ground from which to view the particular motivations and drives of female wage earners.

I would argue that, whether married or single, women's self-images begin in their relationships to home and motherhood, and I have labeled them *virtue*—shorthand, if you will, for conceptions of self that capture women's sense of being as it emerges from her "naturally" prescribed roles. *Virtue* manifests itself in a number of ways: attachment to the home, being a good mother, exhibiting genteel or "ladylike"—that is, "feminine"—behavior. In a society that rewards economic success, often achieved by means of aggression and self-assertion, women's instincts historically have been channeled elsewhere. But for those who engage in wage work, *independence*—my label for women's attempt to achieve without regard for family constraints—constitutes a more or less powerful pull. Notions of virtue have historically limited women's capacity to seek independence, so the relationship between the two notions can tell us much about women's work lives. The tension they create provides a framework for analyzing women's conceptions of their goals, their ambitions, and their own and societal expectations. The lack of such an analysis stymies our attempts to come to terms with some of the major problems we have faced in explaining women's consistently poor labor-market position.

We know that virtue or attachment to the home has sometimes been rejected by individual women; yet even when individual women flout the conventional notion of virtue, it remains central to their decision-making processes. And we know that, as ideologies do, the components of virtue have altered with changes in the family, in the labor process, and with labor-market needs. We now accept that ideas and their manifestations are relative to particular ethnic, racial, and class groups. But that is all part of what we need to explore. Only by understanding the ways in which definitions of female virtue change over time for different groups of women can we identify the historical experience of female wage earners. I would go a step further to suggest that so constant has been the importance of women's familial connection (in its varied forms) that it is precisely because the late twentieth–century women's movement challenges the ideas on which the connection rests that some find it so threatening.

In this essay, I make a case for looking at women's wage work outside the structural patterns imposed by male categories by illustrating briefly what happens when we do so in three areas. I look first at some expressed motivations for wage work among women who were cut off from male support in the 1860s and 1870s, reaching into the 1880s. Second, I examine self-imposed labor-market constraints in the period from the 1890s to about 1910. Finally, I explore the period from 1910 until 1930, when the notion of ambition emerged for women.

In the first period, women tended to justify their wage work in terms of the absence of male support. By the second, unmarried women had carved out a series of "proper" and appropriate jobs, and those who were married had developed elaborate rationales for job holding. Both of these periods reflect a notion of virtue that is emphatically rooted in women's roles at home. In the third period, after 1910, that notion of virtue changed to encompass economic support for the home, making room for women to declare their own job-related ambitions. In its full flower in the 1920s, and among some women, socially ordained roles at home gave way for the first time to an unapologetic notion of work for individual satisfaction. Virtue had produced its own contradiction.

These changes reflect abstract movements of ideas less than they suggest a tradeoff between the needs of the family and shifts in the labor process. While the work women did and the numbers of women working for wages changed dramatically over time, women's wage work, as these illustrations indicate, remained conceptually unaltered. Throughout the period, wage work affirmed virtue only in so far as it contributed to present and future family life. Independent women, in short, lacked virtue in society's eyes until the 1920s, when their roles as wage earners began to be seen as a more permanent part of the family economy.

The result of family-bound conceptions of virtue was such that even women who were in fact independent defended their positions as though they wished they were not. It was perhaps the conviction of their own virtue that enabled women to act politically. In the Civil War and immediate postwar period, for example, women played on the absence of male support, at first crudely, pleading for help because they were the widows, sisters, and daughters of men who had fallen on the battlefield. This argument underlay the militance of sewing women in 1863 who organized themselves into protective unions in response to visibly deteriorating conditions. And it was used by 1865 as a rationale for women to move into new fields of employment. "How inhuman," wrote a seamstress to a labor paper, "to refuse employment to women on the pretext that possibly they may marry. Many women now asking for employment gave up their husbands to die for the country."[1]

One suspects that the argument persisted because it worked, garnering public sympathy and inserting opening wedges in trade-union doors. It was the basis of successful petitions to President Lincoln in which women asked for direct access to arsenal work without the intervention of middlemen. It was picked up by the labor press—*Fincher's Trades Review,* for example, printed petition after petition urging higher wages for women whose husbands, fathers, and brothers had died in the war. And we can gauge its success to some extent because it was accompanied by a simultaneous excoriation of women "who are not in indigent circumstances, but who find time to earn the means of freer expenditures for dress or some other darling object of ambition."[2]

The reforming and middle classes who addressed problems of low pay and a glutted labor market offered solutions that ranged from the hope that women would marry to the suggestion of forced emigration to the West. A few feminists proposed to solve the problem by training women for decent jobs. But by and large it was thought that white women with husbands would not seek paid work and that men with sufficient incomes would keep their wives at home.

For many women, that solution held no promise. The *New York Times* estimated in 1869 that about a quarter of a million young women in the Eastern Seaboard states could never look forward to any matrimonial alliance because they outnumbered men by that much.[3] The surplus population of women contributed to a rising tide available for work, depressing wages to the lowest possible level and contributing to anxiety about wage competition.

If husbands were not to be obtained in the centers of population, there was always the possibility of westward migration. The editor of Boston's *Daily Evening Voice* proposed state intervention to this end in 1865. He knew "of no more useful object" to which the commonwealth could lend its aid than that of opening "the door of emigration to young women who are wanted for teachers, and for every other appropriate as well as domestic employment in the remote West, but who are leading anxious and useless lives in New England."[4]

Wage-earning women had different solutions. They agreed, at least on paper, that those who married should withdraw from the labor market to reduce wage competition. Some opted for organization, searching for allies among male trade unionists. But to do so, they had to struggle against a labor movement that accepted social notions of virtue.

The labor press, reflecting the opinions of a tiny though influential group of skilled craftsmen, bewailed the misfortune that permitted "sisters and daughters . . . to leave home, even for congenial employment in workshops and factories." "We shall spare no effort," proclaimed *Fincher's Trades Review,* "to check this most irrational invasion of our fireside by which the order of nature is reversed." The *Workingman's Advocate* concurred. "Man is and should be head in his own department, in the management of his business for the support of his family. Woman should be head in her department, in the management of household affairs, and in the care and government of the children." To sustain this division of roles, the editors suggested that a woman should be "sympathetic, tender, soft-voiced with faith, hope, and charity templed in her soul." Her strength lay "in the very weakness of her slighter nature and more delicate frame, and the charm, subtle and sure, of a feminine manner, is a more potent spell than enchanter wove."[5]

Women who wished to assert their independence—to organize—could expect little help there. And yet, despite these rigid conceptions of women's roles, the labor press recognized the need for women without husbands to seek jobs. "No one hesitates to give employment to a young man," Boston's *Daily Evening Voice* argued, "because of the probabilities of his entering the army. It is not so much a fear that business will suffer, as a determination to keep women in the track of domestic duties, that leads to this cruel ignoring of her necessities."[6]

Under these circumstances, women sometimes resorted to more devious means for protecting themselves. Denying their desire to flout convention, they played what was perhaps a tongue-in-cheek role. This is best captured by a group of Boston sewing women in April 1869. Meeting in convention, they petitioned the Massachusetts state legislature to give them homes. After years of suffering through the declining real wages of the Civil War, they asked for relief. While they protested their ignorance and weakness and appealed tearfully for care, these women had developed a comprehensive and well-thought-out scheme for public housing that would free them from economic dependence. They worked constantly, they argued. They were deprived of honorable society and religion and even reduced to "ruinous" avocations to make ends meet. They prayed the legislators to "think for us, care for us, and take counsel from your ever kind hearts to do for us better than we know how to ask." Then they presented their proposal.

> [W]e ask that an opportunity be given us to make homes. We pray your honorable body to cause to be purchased in the neighborhood of Boston, a tract of good cultivated land; and to lay out the same in suitable lots. . . . It is our desire that these lots should be let on lease to poor working women of Boston, to whom the state would be willing to furnish rations, tools, seeds and instructions in gardening, until such time as the women would be able to raise their own food or otherwise become self-supporting.[7]

It was not their fault, they argued in justification, that they had no husbands. Women far outnumbered men in Massachusetts. Nor was it strength that led them to ask for "a separate existence." That was evidence only of "a great distress." Women "collected together in a separate village" would, they claimed, be no danger to the community. Rather, they would "exercise a moral influence on each other." And to prove their good intentions, they declared their willingness to withdraw their petition entirely if the legislature would "give us good and kind husbands and suitable homes, make our conditions something distantly approximate to that of your own wives." With more references to their weakness and humility, the petition closed.

Predictably, the Massachusetts legislature did nothing. Yet these women brilliantly captured the core of tension: a restraining ideology rooted in revered familial relationships forbade effective solutions to the dilemma facing female wage workers. Having been placed outside bounds, through no fault of their own, they had been denied women's traditional protections and left to fend for themselves. Even before the Civil War, such women had become a visible "underclass." Had the Civil War not exacerbated the problem by reducing the numbers of potential husbands and creating poor widows of otherwise respectable wives, they might have remained so indefinitely. As it was, the march of economic events revealed their predicament in its starkest light. In exposing women's real economic conditions and removing the possibility of self-blame, it gave women license to protest and unionize. And it gave well-intentioned men, as well as those who feared competition, the opportunity to admit women into their organizations.

Among white women arguments for jobs for the husbandless left notions of women's roles unchallenged without hindering those in need from working for wages. At the same time, they conditioned women's decisions to engage in wage work, structuring the choice of jobs and the jobs available to them. As the labor market expanded, there followed, in the late nineteenth century, a discussion as to what jobs were appropriate for women to do—that is, which would be the least harmful to their home roles.

In the reforming and middle classes, this debate focused on whether the harsh conditions of work and the temptations to which women were exposed would forever inhibit them from becoming good wives and mothers. And it particularly emphasized sexual morality (which explains the boarding houses and working-girls' clubs of that period, as well as some early support for vocational education). But that form is not visible among wage-earning women themselves. Rather, wage-earning women eagerly took advantage of jobs in newly restructured areas to benefit from the rise in real wages current in the period and where the continuing subdivision of labor enabled them to take jobs formerly held by men. They were inhibited by their own notions of home needs—notions that differed among immigrant, black, and native-born women. Though gender was sometimes less important than class and race in decisions about whether to work, internal notions of virtue influenced choices about where to work. The visible manifestation of the decision-making process is in the expression of propriety. Important job shifts in potteries, in textiles, and, beginning in the 1880s, in offices reflected greater opportunity for women and fewer inhibitions among those seeking jobs. And a simultaneous and complementary rise in home work—apparently chosen by many women—confirms the sense that internal standards were operating among those able to choose among jobs.

In a broad sense, these notions of propriety served as the organizational principles for women's workforce participation. They created a reciprocally confirming system in which successful job experiences for women were defined in terms of values appropriate to future home life: neatness, morality, cleanliness, sex segregation, and clean language all defined appropriate women's jobs. Men's jobs, in contrast, reflected ambition, competition, aggression, and the search for increased income. Such definitions confirmed women's places at home, even while they engaged in wage labor, and legitimized their restricted roles despite visible evidence that the choices available to women often left them in indefensible poverty. Not incidentally, such restrictions also served to order the labor market in ways that benefited employers. They acted as devices to divide the wage-labor force, enabling employers to exercise greater control in a period of flux.

For women, internal standards emerged in terms of self-imposed hierarchies in jobs, self-exclusion from inappropriate jobs, and notions of "ladylike behavior." These self-imposed standards seem to be most visible between about 1890 and 1910, the years of the great expansion in the United States of the so-called new immigration. Women entered the labor force in jobs that reflected their class and ethnic positions. They worked for material necessities, choosing their jobs from the options offered by their particular racial, ethnic and class reference groups. Since the job market denied women self-directed ambitions towards upward mobility and cultural attitudes affirmed motivation to marriage and children, women were encouraged to adopt those forms of thought and behavior that would yield eventual marriage.[8]

Women talked about taking jobs because they attracted a "nice class of girls." Conversely, they remembered being warned away from other jobs. "Factory girls were immoral," was the advice given by an old neighbor to Mary Kenney when she went to Chicago to seek work.[9] Clean jobs within factories were more desirable than those that made hands dirty. And where they had choices, women refused jobs that required them to wear old or dirty clothes in the streets. Agnes Nestor, later a trade-union leader, described the women who worked on fine leather gloves in her factory as "looking down" on those who worked on coarser hides. Factory workers felt superior to menial domestic workers. A Cohoes, New York, newspaper reported in 1881 that operatives felt "they take a higher place in the social scale than is accorded them when they do housework."[10]

But factories took second place to what were then called mercantile houses—department stores. Department stores offered extremely long hours, low wages, and close supervision. Leonora O'Reilly remarked in 1899, "Department store women have a caste feeling about their work and think that persons working in a mercantile establishment are a little higher in society than the women who work in a factory."[11] Rose Schneiderman, later to become a Women's Trade Union League president, reported that when she quit her job as a department-store clerk to become a sewing machine operator at twice her former salary, her mother was "far from happy. She thought working in a store much more genteel than working in a factory."[12] The feeling of social superiority was reflected in different living styles. Despite low wages, shop workers tended to sacrifice food in order to dress well. Perhaps because their sexual morality was so often in question, they tended to live in better neighborhoods than factory workers with comparable wages. Factory workers, in contrast, ate better, at the sacrifice of the other amenities.[13]

What women gave up in ambition or independence on the job they compensated for in the home-related virtue that was thought to attach to particular kinds of work. High wages and promotion, though desirable, were not the measure of virtue for them. Just as department-store women willingly acquiesced to low wages because their jobs seemed to offer gentility, those who chose wages above "virtue" faced social censure. While waitresses often earned more than the ordinary factory operative, social disgrace attended the public character of their job. They were said to be "more free and easy in manner and speech" than other wage-earning women. Among waitresses, many disapproved of those who worked in restaurants that served liquor despite the significantly larger tips offered in these places.[14]

How any particular woman dealt with these issues in her own life reflected the tensions imposed by the constraints of her particular ethnic or racial group and the realities of the job market. For black women, faced with discrimination that confined them to the bottom of the labor-market pool and lacking social constraints against wage labor, gender disappeared as the primary operative category in work choice. Race was paramount. And virtue, having dictated the need to work, coerced most black women into accepting what was available. Other ethnic groups exercised their own constraints. Jewish women, whose culture validated economic contributions to family life, tended to take advantage of vocational training more rapidly than any other immigrant group. Like Italians, the unskilled among them worked together in their own ethnic group. Italians concentrated in New York City's garment industry (where 52 percent of all working Italian women were employed in 1910) and in candy making and artificial flowers, partly out of a desire to remain under the protection of kin rather than strictly as the result of free labor-market choice. Native-born white women most commonly emphasized nice surroundings. For them, one mark of genteel employment was the absence of immigrant co-workers. Observers noted that "native born girls of Anglo-Saxon stock prefer[red] when possible to choose an occupation socially superior to factory work,"[15] ranking jobs with the greatest percentage of "American-born" girls highest.

In its most virulent, self-imposed form, this notion of propriety probably lasted until the First World War. At that point one might argue that it had in some way become embedded into the behavior patterns adopted by immigrant women who wanted to be "Americanized." Among Jewish immigrant women in New York, efforts to emulate "ladylike" behavior ranged from attempts to dress like ladies to flat contradictions of an old-world culture that reinforced economic roles for women. It stirred trouble between mothers and daughters, emerging particularly in the generation that went to school in America. One immigrant offered the following description of what she learned about manners in night school: "We wore long skirts . . . and of course we were not allowed to lift it too high, only allow a little bit of the shoe to be seen. And [the teacher] used that as an example of our behavior in life. That we should be careful not to get any modernness."[16]

In the prewar years, less-privileged women ordinarily assumed not that marriage meant giving up work but that their continued wage work would depend on family needs. Those who put wage work first did so at the cost of family life. Rose Schneiderman, a frequently cited example, went to work at thirteen. The daughter of a widowed immigrant mother, she chose trade unionism as a career, knowing that it would lead to a life without marriage. Anzia Yezierska, a poverty-stricken child immigrant to America, learned English so that she could satisfy her burning passion to write. She abandoned a husband and gave up custody of her only daughter so that she could, in the words of her fiction, "make herself for a person."

Among the more affluent and those with some education, intimations of ambition existed in the period before the war. There had, of course, always been numbers of women who chose not to marry—whose restless energy had turned toward social settlements or the YWCA or found outlets in Greenwich Village rebellion. While the very talented, the very rich, and the hardy had long been able to mold the minds of Wellesley girls or pioneer their way into medical school, there was a sense around World War I and after that marriage and satisfying work need not be mutually exclusive alternatives. Charlotte Perkins Gilman's *Women and Economics* offers the most articulate theoretical statement of possibility in the United States. Crystal Eastman and her group of New Women before World War I offer the most dramatic examples. These women acted on the assumption that they were entitled to pursue careers and to marry.

But it was not until after the war that these attempts at independence became compatible with a measure of virtue. Changing definitions of virtue introduced into the labor market a kind of woman who had not earlier been seen there and for whom community and ethnic values carried less weight than they had for the poor women who early-on constituted the bulk of the female labor force. Labor-process shifts contributed to removing ideological constraints by creating the illusion of a technological imperative that necessitated training and the introduction of a tightly organized hierarchy to control the shop floor. To sustain that system required the introduction of incentive programs, in which women, as workers, had to be encouraged to participate. New organization forms in manufacturing and offices that emerged in the 1920s began to break down one of the major barriers to women's conception of themselves as full participants in the labor force, opening the door to work-related ambitions. Ironically, this happened first among middle-class women who had discouraged immigrant wives from making direct contributions to household income. Ambition crept into their vocabulary, producing what at first seemed like an irreconcilable conflict. To aspire, to achieve, not merely to do the least offensive job became at least a possibility for daughters as well as for sons.

Advice on how to "make it" flowed freely. "There is no such thing as limitation of opportunity in business," an audience of office workers heard in 1915. "The only limitation is the limitation we set ourselves."[17] Young girls still in high school were advised to sell life insurance as the "surest as well as most convenient means of providing for an independent old age." In 1916, the Boston Bureau of Vocational Information, set up by college-educated women for women, sponsored a series of lectures. "If you expect to get to the top, believe that you can get there, and then climb with all your might and main." Eliminate all thought of marriage: "If you have in mind that you . . . are going to do this for . . . years, perhaps all your life, you will be more likely to succeed."[18]

Paradoxically, ambition among the middle class may have legitimized the right for less-privileged women to work. Defensiveness disappeared as former household workers found jobs in candy factories, while candy dippers told their daughters not to "come with me to learn dipping" but to go to work in an office or department store, where the work was more certain and the pay steady.[19] Southern mill families urged their daughters to take "business courses."[20] Teaching jobs opened as possibilities for Colorado miners' daughters like Agnes Smedley and immigrant children like Anzia Yezierska. Secretaries interviewed in the early part of the 1920s reported that though they liked their jobs, they were discouraged about not being able to "get ahead" in them. So great appeared the desire for promotion among secretaries and stenographers that a barrage of literature attempted to persuade them that secretarial work was a satisfactory occupation in itself. But the influence of old notions of virtue had not disappeared. They continued to affirm personality patterns and social roles consistent with the home, reinforcing the occupational stereotypes that divided administrative and professional networks into those that threatened to negate home roles and those that did not. Women's mobility in the office and business world remained stringently limited. In contrast, careers in nursing, libraries, teaching, and social work drew on years of socialization and a consciousness bred to serve. They fitted the demand for personal satisfaction yet met the criteria for women's work. They were careers in the sense that they paid relatively steady salaries instead of poor and intermittent wages, but they offered only limited possibilities for advancement and therefore helped to curtail whatever ambition a young woman might have had.

The cycle was self-reinforcing, rewarding personality traits considered feminine and punishing others. One employment manager put it this way: "Select a woman who you think could be married at any time if she chose, but just for some reason does not."[21] Successful women often achieved their positions by utilizing their feminine characteristics. College women, for example, could do better in banks if they helped homemakers deal with savings, budget, and family problems that affected financial stability.[22]

Viewed from the perspective of a constraining ideology, the changing labor-force participation of married women seemed especially threatening. The new kinds of jobs women were entering tended to sustain or create gender-free illusions of mobility—illusions that had little to do with family lives and could best exist parallel to, but not in support of, their primary family roles. For it was in the jobs that hinted at upward mobility that the dangerous potential of an ambitious womanhood posed the greatest threat.

As a result, married women who had escaped or transcended the prevailing social constraints drew mixed admiration and doubt. The press emphasized their dual roles. "Woman President of Bank Does Housework in Her Home," trumpeted one headline.[23] Another paper captioned a photograph of the woman who invented tea bags: "Gertrude Ford proves that it is possible to maintain a house, be a devoted mother, *and* conduct a successful business."[24] Women could play two roles, but if the press were to be believed, success at work ought to be buttressed by a satisfying home life. A *New York Herald* reporter described the ascent of a young Scottish immigrant girl to an executive post at Western Union: "In spite of her sustained contact with the business world, she remains conspicuously feminine in dress and demeanor and believes in marriage and children for the average woman above all the rewards of the business world."[25]

Women did not "make it" in the 1920s. Married women of all classes faced persistent job discrimination. The labor market maintained, and in most areas rigidified, traditional patterns of job segmentation. Yet the attitudes with which women went to work in 1925 would have been unrecognizable in 1875. In the 1870s, wage-earning women demanded higher wages and better working conditions. By the 1920s, no longer content with doing better where they were, women asked for different jobs, upward mobility, and economically secure careers—demands that had historically been associated with men and that reflected the changing composition of the female labor force as well as the tempting new jobs available. Virtue still inhered in woman's ability to sustain family life. What had changed were conceptions of what families needed. One could speculate that the mobility aspirations that isolated working-class men into individualistic job consciousness had a different impact on working-class women. Among some groups—garment workers in the 1910s, for example, or southern textile workers in the 1920s—the freedom to boldly assert the right to work led women to identify as workers, an identification that made trade-union organization feasible, though it did not remove the real constraints against successful unionization.

My sense of what happened is that the changing labor process produced its own dilemma, creating for some women jobs that enabled them to see the possibilities for more satisfying wage work, and for less-educated women jobs that held the potential for combining wage and household work. For the better-off, possibilities were restrained in the 1930s by depression, manipulated in the 1940s by war, and rigidly channeled in the 1950s by a heavy dose of home and motherhood ideology, as well as by the incentives of household consumption. By the 1960s, they could no longer be contained, releasing in that decade a generation of repressed ambition.

Two opposing conceptions of wage labor inform women's current attempts to enter into work. One asserts women's new freedom from the family and claims the power to be as ambitious and success-oriented as men. The other insists that women must carry into wage labor some of the best of women's own "morality and virtue" and, by struggle, alter the conception of work for men and women. At the same time, we face the dilemma of how to organize reproduction and family life in a world that holds paid labor as virtuous for women as it is for men. That is our battle, but it would have drawn empathy from a young seamstress who asked in 1874, "Why is it can a woman *not* be virtuous if she does mingle with the toilers?"

7

A New Agenda for
American Labor History:
A Gendered Analysis and
the Question of Class

The question of how social history relates to and alters more traditional perspectives on American history has troubled historians since the field reached maturity in the mid-1970s. As a body of data, social history has successfully pointed up the rich diversity of American society and the enormous complexity of human motives that drive it. But it has not yet developed a way of understanding the past that might replace the easy and probably false coherence suggested by interpretations that posit a unified set of values. It poses the question of what understanding can emerge from a study of the lives of ordinary people.

No group of historians has taken this task more seriously than historians of labor. In the fall of 1984, about seventy U.S. labor historians met at DeKalb, Illinois, to discuss the question of "synthesis." In the light of new attention to the lives and experiences of working people, they asked, could the history of the working class become a vehicle for interpreting U.S. history? It turned out to be easier to identify the problem than to offer a way of thinking about the past that embodied a solution. The meeting stirred such rich controversy that the ideas it generated have framed an ongoing debate about the future of labor history. In this essay I use the conference to suggest what might be some of the difficulties of achieving a synthesis, or an interpretive framework, and then to propose a way of thinking about the past, through gender, that might cast some new light on American history as a whole.

On the face of it, a 1984 conference to debate new directions in labor history seemed not merely timely but ripe. It had been nearly twenty years since labor

I am especially indebted to Al Young for his perceptive comments on this piece. It was originally published in Carroll Moody and Alice Kessler-Harris, eds., *Perspectives on American Labor History: Towards a New Synthesis* (DeKalb: Northern Illinois University Press, 1987).

history had begun to edge its way into the canons of historical scholarship. Perhaps fifteen years had passed since historians had begun to talk about a "new" labor history rooted in the work of E. P. Thompson and exemplified by the pathbreaking essays of Herbert Gutman. And it had been more than a decade since labor historians had called a national meeting to define their enterprise. In the meantime, what had begun as a tentative exploration, peripheral to the dominant concerns of most American historians, had been catapulted, perhaps by force of circumstance, to the leading edge of social history. Labor history had benefited from the expanded vision of social history that emerged from the 1960s; and at the same time, the search for a history of the working class had stimulated new research of unprecedented depth and range.

The meeting began with every good omen. A small grant, a limited assembly (restricted at the cost of some hard feelings in order to enhance possibilities for discussion), papers in advance, and plenty of space for informal conversation—all these augured a fruitful outcome. Among the participants were the revered and those hoping to be so, a small but respectable representation of women and minority groups, and even a few social historians invited to provide distance and critical perspective. But after two days of discussion, no synthesis had emerged; no vision of a future agenda had materialized. Instead, many participants, as one of them noted, came away with negative feelings. Michael Frisch described them as "frustrated at best, disappointed on average, and cynical at worst."[1] The conference had not only been unable to achieve a synthesis, it seemed to have fostered dissension and confusion about what might be the agenda of labor history. In its aftermath, Eric Foner provided one version of the results. It remained unclear, he suggested, "how to reformulate labor history without simply incorporating race and gender into preexisting paradigms, abandoning class as a category of analysis, or creating an endless jigsaw puzzle of separate experiences lacking a coherent overview."[2] What accounts for the disappointment? How, in light of the tremendous richness of our empirical research, do we explain the failure to move towards a new paradigm? Part of the answer is rooted in the limits of our emerging research.

By the mid-1970s, most practitioners in the field had tacitly agreed that the history of organized labor was insufficient to explain the history of the working class. Following the lead of Herbert Gutman, they had redefined the history of workers to include every element of wage work and the family that supported it; and they had redefined the terrain to extend from unions to the factory floor, the neighborhood, and the tavern. Redefinition had opened the field to questions about the experience of a preindustrial labor force, which preceded formal organization, and to issues of working-class formation. To answer these questions, labor historians focused heavily on local history and adopted new quantitative and anthropological methods that attempted to reconstruct the lives and self-experiences of workers in their communities. In this "culturalist" approach, power was intrinsic in the capacity of workers to retain customs, values, language, and traditions in the face of a destructive capitalism. Workers' power resided in their capacity to use these indigenous attributes of their lives to confront, even to stave off, the initiatives of a dominant industrial elite and to shape the future of an industrial society.[3] The search for workers' resistance, wherever and however it appeared and whether in formal or informal institutions, replaced the history of structures.

But the process of exploring what David Montgomery called "the friction that comes out of everyday life" had fragmented the history of workers, producing, in practice, an eclectic pattern of behavior and belief that defied any attempt to locate a coherent vision or purpose among working people. In the absence of an identifiable working class, researchers focused on the unique rather than the shared qualities of workers. Implicitly as much as explicitly, they replaced the Marxian notion that consciousness comes from the social relations of production with a broader concept of culture, in which identity derives from an amalgam of factors such as race, skill, community, religion, and ethnicity. Increasingly, the particularism of the field undermined attempts to speak of common class interests.

Despite the efforts of Gutman and others to see power in the resistance embodied in working-class behavior, questions remained about the capacity of labor historians to explain larger political developments. The new techniques, after all, were rooted in data that affirmed the depth and strength of an empirically ascertained culture. For most of the assembled group, working-class experience mattered primarily because it offered alternative visions and challenges to a dominant bourgeois ethos. Rejecting interpretations of labor history that resided in such notions as American exceptionalism, the new historians saw in workers' culture a concern for values of community, equality, and justice that transcended particular and narrow interests and suggested the possibilities for alternative directions to capitalism.

Whether they resisted or adapted to industrial and postindustrial culture, workers projected values of cooperation, democracy, independence, virtue, and citizenship that were obscured by the dominant ideology as it appeared in government bureaucracy, court decisions, and the public press. Identifying these indigenous values was important—the more so because they had for so long been perceived as romantic ideology or written out of history altogether. Yet a troubling question remained: Why had the working class been so successfully incorporated? Within a framework of opposition, how do we account for the emergence and widespread acceptance of competitive individualism? How do we account for the undiminished, hostile role of the state in repressing the collective visions of workers? What could we say of the apparent support of most twentieth-century working people for a successful capitalism? The new labor history did not speak to the structures of power, nor did it lend itself to questions about the relationship of an ideology that sustained power to cultures of resistance. Labor historians thus faced the question of what their enterprise contributed to explaining the dynamic of American history.

As the culturalist approach floundered, an emerging body of literature emphasized the relationship between larger social and economic structures and political change. Challenges came from two directions: from economists and economic historians who sought explanations of macroeconomic trends, and from labor historians concerned with the expanding role of the state. Instead of placing workers and their struggles at the center of historical change, these scholars urged us to rely more heavily on analyses of economic trends and structural changes to explain the behavior and consciousness of working people. And yet, such approaches threatened to drown out visions of working-class resistance altogether. Culturalist approaches might beg questions of the relationship of workers to the exercise of power. But alternative structural approaches tended to subsume the culture of workers into larger patterns, making grassroots activities largely peripheral as explanations for social change.[4] Though we recognized the tension, we could not and would not abandon our work of the past decade.[5]

Resolution seemed to require an explanation of how resistance functioned in relation to capitalism; or to put it as it was so often put by us, an explanation of class relations in which the development of capitalism was rooted in the history of workers as they confronted the power of capital. Was such an explanation possible? Our answers diffused into discrete illustrations from which we could draw no general conclusion. Hindsight suggests that what divided conferees, disturbed a sense of equilibrium, and inhibited consensus among us was our failure to move the discussion of workers' culture to a different level. We did not want to abandon the notion. Far from it; most of us took its existence for granted. But, as eager as we were to acknowledge the various forms of worker resistance, we were reluctant to ask why resistance, in the long run, had failed to alter the structure of power. The tapes that recorded the conference suggest how and why we skirted that question. And they, therefore, provide clues as to how we might move the debate to a new agenda.

A piece of the answer lay in our own experience. The early excitement generated by the field of labor history had emanated from its overtly political purpose and vision. Reacting negatively to the liberal ideology of the 1950s, young scholars were drawn to the history of labor in part as an explicit rejection of the consensus history it spawned. Unlike the accepted version of the 1950s, which saw the United States moving harmoniously, if slowly, toward agreed-upon principles of equality and justice, the radicalism of the New Left sought explanations for conflict and diversity. It found them in the treatment of African Americans, Native Americans, and other ethnic minorities, and it looked to people's movements (among them the labor movement) as agents of change. As one participant put it, "Many of us ventured into labor history for political reasons . . . it was part of the whole project of changing something in the sixties." But labor historians who looked to the labor movement as a vehicle of change were frequently disappointed. Seeking there the innovative ideas and the political energy to redirect American society and redefine American democracy, they found only limited confirmation. To be sure, the crowd activity of preindustrial Americans and the workingmen's associations and cooperative societies of the early industrial period carried the seeds of change, as did the Knights of Labor in a later period. But the efforts of these groups were translated into ephemeral action and undermined by a self-definition that could not withstand capture by the prevailing ethic of power.[6] And the picture in the modern period is even bleaker.

Despite the general lack of social vision among most union leaders, a briefly revitalized labor movement, reminiscent of the 1930s, gave credence to the project. In the 1960s, a few unions joined with the civil rights movement. A few took active stands against the war in Vietnam. Others began to organize the unskilled and women.[7] Membership, in decline since the mid-1950s, stabilized only briefly. A decade and a half later, membership in trade unions had sunk to 18 percent of the labor force, and a conservative spirit ruled the land. Along with the decline of the labor movement went the sense of moral purpose associated with its revival. Increasingly, the instrumental orientations of the working people of America undermined whatever latent social vision remained in the movement, pointing up its bureaucratic flaws and its inability to represent the interests of all workers.

Though they hung, like stagnant air, over the conference, the questions raised by a pessimistic view of the contemporary working class and organized labor's possibilities remained unanswered. As the political arm of workers, the labor movement represented whatever was left of a millennial vision. And despite our disenchantment with unionism as a sufficient explanation of historical change, labor historians could not stop seeing trade unions as vehicles for conveying workers' aspirations and as the embodiments of their bravest achievements. Did labor's metamorphosis into an institution that represented particular rather than broader interests indicate that a history with workers at its center had romanticized working-class aspirations? An economy in which the labor movement played out its cyclical role relegated workers to the periphery rather than the center of social change. How, given these perceptions, would our enterprise change?

The marginalization of the labor movement implicit in culturalist approaches and the effort to seek change at the level of individual behavior, ideas, and values as well as in political activity have posed a set of powerful intellectual challenges. In part, these challenges had turned labor historians towards culturalism to begin with. For, as unions were seen as increasingly preoccupied with the material advancement of their members, they generated questions about their capacity to carry the banners of social justice and democracy for all. Where, then, did such ideas reside? We had found them in the heroism of ordinary lives as well as in everyday resistance to capital. But if we continued to look for them on the shop floor and in the working-class communities where we believed them to be nurtured, we would sooner or later confront the traditionalism of the working class. We would face a devastating uncertainty as to whether the evident conservatism of workers in the 1980s did not negate the hypotheses of the 1960s. Our sense of loss was so profound that Jesse Lemisch asked at one point if we were not merely saying Kaddish for the 1960s.

Although we sidestepped these issues at our meeting, the fundamental questions they raised created unease about the explanatory possibilities of a workers' culture. In some ways we wanted to rest on our laurels. A decade of scholarship in this arena had opened the door to an inclusive conception of what constituted the labor force. Culture served as an umbrella that incorporated race and gender, region and ethnicity, as well as skill. It had invigorated research into the preindustrial labor force and brought us closer to European forms of analysis. Stimulated by the work of E. P. Thompson and sustained by a romance with anthropology, the study of workers' culture had taken firm root among historians of the U.S. working class. Explorations of customs and ritual as they existed among different ethnic groups had produced rich troves of material detailing the lives of specific worker communities. Quantitative and anthropological techniques (including especially the capacity for "thick description" popularized by Clifford Geertz) satisfied a thirst to know what happened on the shop floor as well as at the family hearth, and they told us something of the connection between the two.

But, in the end, we never struggled with the meaning of culture.[8] We simply abandoned abstract Marxian conceptions of class and shifted to more comfortable Thompsonian versions without asking what, as a result, we had lost. In contrast to most interpretations of the 1960s (which defined *class* in terms of such abstractions as the relationship to the means of production and the consciousness that emerged therefrom), Thompson insisted on paying attention to social reality. Class, he asserted, is "a social and cultural formation, arising from processes which can only be studied as they work themselves out over a considerable historical period."[9] The definition extended a breathtaking invitation to explore class formation in historical context, but it carried the temptation of reifying the processes: of romanticizing the agency of working people and divorcing them from the power relations that created tension and change. Absent a way of understanding the class relations that inhered in culture, a cultural approach seemed merely to fragment our vision, without providing a mosaic on which to build. It failed to offer clues to the dynamic forces that sustained and resisted capitalism or to suggest possibilities of a new direction.

Reluctance either to shape and focus the conception of culture or to abandon it encouraged a hovering question about whether we were not succumbing to nostalgia. Like the "workerism" of the 1960s, which held that a political program was implicit in the self-identification of an individual as a worker, the labor history of the 1970s and 1980s seemed dangerously close to romanticizing workers past.[10] Every lost or broken tool could be interpreted as an act of sabotage; every stolen cigar or day off as an act of resistance. Sabotage and resistance were seen less as elements that shaped class relations than as attempts to preserve self, family, and community in the face of structural economic change. They did not so much actively resist capital as they provided an unstable (and readily destroyed) bulwark against it.

Culture seemed to have become a way of evading class rather than enhancing our understanding of the relationships among production, consumption, and politics. It had all the trappings of an exploration of consciousness. As historians developed the notion, it did not neglect social action; yet, because our study of culture remained resolutely empirical, it was not connected to larger questions of social order. As a result, although it avoided the dead-endedness of fights over abstractions, the notion of a workers' culture did not increase our understanding of how the whole functioned. It carried none of the political vision or the abrasiveness of Marxian class. In the hands of historians, preserving tradition seemed to be the central interest of most workers, ethnic roots their most powerful loyalty.

Yet, despite our evident discomfort with the use of Marxian notions of class as explanatory categories, we neither abandoned them nor replaced them with a more coherent conception of culture as an active phenomenon. Instead, we tried to use class in a way that incorporated culture but without fully integrating the concept. One speaker after another pointed out that their ethnic group or region had been forgotten or not appropriately accounted for. Sometimes we did this humorously. Worcester, Massachusetts, the setting of Roy Rosenzweig's perceptive exploration of working-class leisure, became a playful code that symbolized the new capacity to illuminate and the limits of the space illuminated. What emerged at the meeting was the question of whether, in engaging in extended explorations of process, we had not diffused the meaning of class, defanging it without simultaneously offering another model of social change.

The result was that the history of the working class had become curiously vapid and unthreatening; our enterprise contributed little to understanding how culture is connected to ideology or shapes the distribution of power. Rather, the method lent itself to exploring how workers used democratic forms instead of shaping them, or how they adapted republican ideas to their own purposes instead of departing from them. Ironically, in revealing the enormous inadequacy of traditional views of class, we seemed to have shaped a new consensus—to have written a history of how workers colluded in the development of liberal capitalism rather than one of how they constrained or structured it.

The core of discontent at the conference surfaced around these issues. At one extreme, we heard David Noble insisting angrily that we had been betrayed, offered a culture without content, left intellectually impoverished. At the other were those who still believed that uncovering the texture of American diversity lay at the heart of our enterprise and could not be abandoned lightly. But in the center, there was groping. For some, these extremes came together in a common understanding that we had outgrown the reification of culture. Being a worker was not, as Eric Hobsbawm put it, the equivalent of "having a culture." Insofar as we agreed that culture is not simply a passive phenomenon but an active agent in the formation of behavior and values, we knew we had to struggle to understand the connection of culture to theory. The problem lay in the perception of many that culturalist approaches had not simply led us astray but that, in emphasizing differences among workers, they had revealed the curiously empty meaning of class. Although enhancing our capacity to describe, research into working-class culture had undermined our capacity for understanding working-class transformation. Our work revealed a Marxian paradigm that was neither rich enough nor complex enough to incorporate the cultural diversity we had uncovered. Eric Foner put it this way: "[T]he 'culturalist' approach now appears inadequate as either a definition of class or a substitute for it. Producing a patchwork of local studies illuminating the diverse values and identities among working people, it has failed to provide a coherent overview of labor's historical development." And yet it did not solve the dilemma merely to articulate it. For, as Foner pointed out, "Nor does a return to a purely economic understanding of class, or to such time-honored paradigms as base and superstructure or 'false consciousness,' seem likely to explain either the history or behavior of today's working class."[11]

The tension between the richness of description and the need for analytic categories to explain change proved insurmountable at the conference. Unwilling to abandon our own contributions and unable to substitute alternative analytic frameworks, the group broke up dissatisfied.

We could have moved in a more fruitful direction had we listened more carefully to those who advocated race, ethnicity, and gender as analytic categories. These notions, suggested by the culturalist approach, have theoretical meaning that, accommodated to each other and to class, offer to illuminate class relations and to suggest ways of bridging the gap between culture and power. I can best illustrate the opportunity that was missed in failing to merge these conceptions to that of class by looking at gender.

Tensions in the group rose high whenever the issue of gender entered the conversation. Identified by Eric Hobsbawm (along with the decade of the 1960s, Edward Thompson, and Karl Marx) as one of the four ghosts haunting the conference, gender became a symbol of things forgotten, of items for which we could not account. Wrongly, I think, even sympathetic conferees used it as a symbol of the culturalist approach—an anachronism with which they knew they had to deal but that refused to speak to more pressing questions of power and authority. In so doing, the group failed to distinguish between gender as a theoretical construct and its empirical manifestations as reflected in the history of women. A discussion of the practical implications of the idea of gender turned into a conversation about particular women and their idiosyncratic forms of resistance.

Repeatedly raised by the female participants, gender was just as repeatedly passed over. In his summation, Eric Hobsbawm dismissed it, saying that he was not sure that "there was any very clear idea of what is meant by this." He then took pains to reject patriarchy as a useful historical category and turned to women as consumers, tertiary workers, and members of public-sector labor unions. Moving from questions of gender to the specifics of what women did changed the terms of the debate, repeating once again an emphasis on the fragmented nature of the working class at the cost of exploring the issue of how a system of ideas functioned to shape class relations in the workforce.[12]

Yet a discussion of gender (or race or ethnicity) could have enriched our understanding of the key issues into which we had become locked. Just as the history of African Americans is both separate from and a part of the history of racism, the history of women workers, which describes an aspect of cultural diversity, must be distinguished from that of gender. Gender functions as an analytic framework that is about women only insofar as they are its active subjects. Instead of focusing on women or men per se, a gendered exploration of the past explores how the social relations of men and women create and inhibit expectations and aspirations and ultimately help to structure institutions as well. Thus, a gendered exploration rests on an empirical base that can open the door to a system of ideas out of which reality is constructed.

I want to suggest that the concept of gender offers access to possibilities for understanding working-class culture, both as a material construct (in so far as we understand culture as consisting of behavior and traditions) and as a meaning system (the root of values and orientations that provide the basis on which people will act).[13] In this latter form, gender may provide a special service: first, in demonstrating how notions of culture might participate in conceiving, shaping, implementing, and resisting state policy; and second, in providing insight into the maintenance of internal divisions among workers and between workers and middle-class and elite groups that help to unpack some of the ways in which an accommodation occurs between workers and the industrial process. I suggest that fully integrating a cultural concept such as gender into labor history can illuminate class formation and class relations.

In offering an analytic category for looking at the culture of working people that transcends class divisions, gender provides a way of enriching notions of class. A gendered analysis functions in a way analogous to class, although not independent of it. Like class, gender is ideational and normative—a creator of consciousness that can be expected to tell us something about an individual's worldview and a part of any individual's perspective of what is right or wrong, acceptable or not. Though one might ask whether gender has shared meanings that transcend cultural and class lines, it is fairly easy to describe its manifestations under specific historical circumstances. And yet gender, like class, is a process. Paraphrasing Thompson's definition of *class,* one could argue that gender is a "historical phenomenon," not a "structure" or a "category" but something that happens in human relationships.[14]

Unlike class, which is said to be rooted in the material reality and social relations of the workplace, gender is rooted in the material reality and social relations of the household (which is sometimes also a workplace and, in any event, never unrelated to the workplace). But since neither household nor wage work is independent of the other, gender participates in class formation just as wage work participates in gender formation. Recent scholarship illustrates the point. We learn from Mary Blewett that gender influenced the "form and context of work" among preindustrial and industrial shoemakers, shaping the way men and women divided jobs and related to the workplace. At the same time, gender affected workplace struggle in various ways. Divisions between indoor and outdoor women shoe workers, for example, reflected differential family situations that conditioned the issues around which women would struggle and their perceptions of the importance of male alliances.[15] Together, class and gender help us understand how the particular forms of labor struggle between male and female workers and their employers are influenced by the different needs and expectations of the men and women who are workers.

In a gendered approach, women are not merely introduced into labor history. Rather, we begin to understand (more clearly at certain moments than at others) how ideology about male and female roles orders the behavior and expectations of work and family, influences the policies adopted by government and industry, and shapes perceptions of equity and justice. Because gender, like class, helps to construct consciousness, it operates at all levels—in the process of household production, on the shop floor, within the family, in the neighborhood, and in the community—to shape the ideas that form the core orientations on which working people will act. The historian's task must include an analysis of how gendered perceptions contributed to certain kinds of decisions and actions.[16] It is not enough to argue that men and women experience a social transformation in different ways. By demystifying seemingly natural roles, a gendered interpretation contributes to understanding how work (waged and unwaged) is organized, and it enables us to see how the larger political values and purposes of the society have been developed.

Many of the crucial concepts around which labor historians have organized their work have clear gendered content but are neither utilized nor understood that way. Compare, for example, the content of "republicanism" as it appears in the work of Sean Wilentz and the same word as it is used by Linda Kerber.[17] In the former, it describes direct participation in the polis and incorporates ideas of citizenship and virtue that, by dint of their public content, exclude women. The ideal of "possessive individualism" is legitimated as a way of achieving the respect required for participation in the polis, and the search for the common good becomes a by-product of enhanced self-esteem. In Kerber's analysis the public end or good of the commonwealth predominates. The content of republicanism is defined by women's attempts to find a voice in a revolutionary, preindustrial society, and the idea is defined with respect to gendered conceptions of order, hierarchy, household, work, and education. In the one case, the emerging content of republicanism is defined by pride in craft and the possibilities for independence and equality embedded in the rewards of skilled work. In the other case, its content reflects the constraints of the household as well as the pivotal place of community norms in the search for the common good. Tensions within republicanism reflected these dual meanings and shaped how men acted in the public arena.

Gendered ideas help to explain transformations in other key ideas as well. The idea of free labor rested on the notion that ownership of productive property yielded the independence necessary to participation in the public realm. Citizenship and skilled work were both incontestably male. In the post–Civil War battle that transformed this conception into the doctrine of liberty of contract, or the right to sell one's own labor, workers' capacity to defend their right to independence and dignity in the courts vanished. Not accidentally, however, these ideas find their way into arguments for the dignity of women, who, as wards of the state, are permitted and even encouraged to retain vestiges of the social conceptions of independence and equality that characterized free labor. The doctrine of equal rights is modified by notions of domesticity and in turn modifies them. Susan Levine effectively demonstrates the capacity of domestic ideals to transform a doctrine of equal rights into collective action.[18] And gendered ideas are apparent in descriptions of manliness at work—a key element in working-class resistance at the end of the nineteenth century.[19] But if notions of manliness helped to maintain the unity of the artisan class, they could also, as Patricia A. Cooper has shown, foster an exclusivity that helped to destroy the unifying organization.[20]

Gendered ideas tell us something about both sides of the power equation. They reveal how custom, expectations, and ideology with regard to sex roles affect the choices men and women make, as well as their willingness to undertake certain kinds of waged and unwaged work. And they tell us something about how the structures of power (religious and educational institutions, corporate bureaucracy, and government agencies) touch ordinary people in ways that create and affirm acceptable behavior and condition expectations. The social and economic policies adopted by the United States during World War II spring immediately to mind. Their explicit messages about the propriety of wage work for certain women and implicit support for the sexual division of labor reflected a general (though not universal) consensus about the roles of men and women.[21] Wartime needs notwithstanding, they protected the positions of men. Thus, gendered ideas can tell us something about the collusion of men across class lines in the interest of affirming a meaning system that transcends class itself.

At the same time, how gendered systems are preserved in different class contexts tells us something about how class divisions are maintained and how the process of class formation occurs out of the indivisible reality of home and workplace. We have begun to understand, for example, how the changing system of production in the antebellum United States produced a shared understanding of "women's proper place," or an ideology of "true womanhood," that played a powerful part in perpetuating traditional roles for women while they simultaneously pushed men into commerce and manufacturing, and thus toward a more rapid acceptance of the modern world. At the same time, the capacity of wage-earning women to resist that ideology was to some extent undermined by working men, who not only had a stake in keeping their wives at home but had an overriding interest in legitimating and protecting their workforce positions. As Christine Stansell's *City of Women* demonstrates, an oppositional ideology flourished among women outside the workplace and was sustained by community and neighborhood norms.[22] We know that the sexual and work behavior of women quickly became an important indication of class position and a factor in shaping class identification and control mechanisms.

Within the framework of gender analysis, the language of sexuality (in its literal sense and its symbolic usages) emerges as a code for family structure, class division, and notions of respectability that bind working-class women from certain ethnic and racial groups to particular kinds of home roles and that can serve as metaphors for such middle-class values as thrift and self-discipline. How far was the capacity of the elite to identify workers as "other" and to brutally suppress resistance derived from perceived differences between their own home lives and those of workers?[23] One could go on. We need to know more, empirically, about where and how ideas of the family wage are rooted in the development of a self-reinforcing ideological syndrome that had controversial effects on the structure of male-female wages and on the development of social policies that enshrined them. These illustrations suggest that class is not merely conditioned by gender but that gender (like ethnic allegiance or race in the United States) constitutes the bricks and mortar out of which class is constructed.

At another level, the values revealed by a theoretical construction of gender challenge the dominant ethos of liberal capitalism. One example should suffice. Central to capitalism's legitimacy in the United States in the late nineteenth and twentieth centuries has been the possibility of upward economic mobility. The constellation of qualities surrounded by the success ethic and an aggressive individualism is rooted in and reinforces notions of the free labor market on which it is built. The material and political equality for which Americans sacrifice so much and that they defend in war and peace is rationalized by a meritocratic ethic that holds that everyone has the chance to move up toward wealth, status, and fame. But women's historical experience (more clearly than that of people of color, because women share the class position of their male kin) calls into question the existence of a free market for labor and thus raises questions about the legitimacy of the egalitarian ethic. In so doing, it challenges some of the fundamental ideas by which we live. Describing the occupational structure of the labor force, then, requires paying attention to the effect of women's presence in the labor market on the idea that equality of opportunity is generally available. The practical effect of this understanding appears in the political campaigns for demands such as protective labor legislation for women but not men in the early twentieth century and contemporary demands such as government-subsidized child care, comparable worth, and affirmative action.

Issues of gender encourage us to think about the unity of home and work and to explore the values on which people act and at what level of consciousness. Interdisciplinary perspectives and an analysis of gender difference raise questions about the commonality of interests among men of all classes, transcending, at least at certain times, the class interests of working men and women. Heidi Hartmann suggested many years ago that the shared manliness of employer and employee contributed to occupational segregation and to the inability of trade unions to organize and represent women effectively.[24] But trade unions that fail to represent the interests of a large segment of workers undermine class cohesion and response. Theories of gender difference offer a mechanism that explains why, although it made little economic sense to exclude women from certain forms of production, employers and women workers have at times colluded in doing so in obedience to a shared understanding of culture. The resulting labor-market segregation affirmed women's dependence while contributing to arguments for men's power in the family and workplace.

The use of concepts like gender to translate culture from neighborhood to nation, to distinguish between discrete behavior and ideological overlay, moves culture from a passive, descriptive position to active agency. It illuminates how ideas about the social roles of men and women helped shape particular historical processes like proletarianization and class formation. It joins issues around a new series of questions. How does a gendered ideology (as opposed to women's behavior) alter the consciousness and expectations of male and female workers in ways that make it more or less likely that they will identify with other workers in sustaining and opposing dominant values and interests? How do gendered expectations around work and family lives create or inhibit structures of work for men and women? How do they participate in conceiving forms of resistance and accommodation? How do they manifest themselves in divisions and alliances among workers? On the other side of the equation, how do institutions accommodate and utilize gendered perspectives to create privilege, to act as models of exclusion, or to promote competition?

Let me speculate about a familiar example in this context. For years, we debated Werner Sombart's familiar question, "Why is there no socialism in America?" without reference to gender. Yet, when all the arguments are said and done and we have exhaustively explored the absence of labor parties, the existence of opportunity, and immigrant ambition, we will still have to ask whether the shifting gender relations that were characteristic of late nineteenth- and early twentieth-century America are not also part of the answer to that question. One notes such things as the incentive offered by an egalitarian spirit to cross class alliances of women that provided vents for despair; the immense desire for home ownership as a mechanism of family survival; and normative codes that restricted wage work for women whose families aspired to mobility—all of which played a special role in the United States. And we could argue that the roots of state action to defuse the worst features of industrialism and accommodate working-class protest originated in such female-based and sometimes wrongheaded voluntary organizations as those that fought for urban playgrounds, sanitation, and protective labor legislation in the workplace; for sexual morality, access to birth-control information, and child-rearing manuals in the home; and for assimilation in immigrant communities.

How does this help us to think about labor history, to integrate and understand the relationship of workers to the state? Just as we earlier agreed that labor history is not only about the labor movement, we seem to have come to the conclusion that labor history is not simply about workers, waged and unwaged. It is about class formation and the emergence of class relations, understood as a political and cultural as well as an economic process. But, as such, it must take account of the central organizing principle of human life, the sexual division of labor, and all that that implies for social relations. This principle is not simply subsumed into class once the process of industrialization begins but persists thereafter. We have begun to explore how it is manifested in the dynamics and feelings of workers. We know far less about how it is incorporated into the institutions, laws, and policies that frame the conditions within which workers struggle. Nor do we understand how the pressure of shared gendered assumptions can modify male behavior, inhibit class resistance, invoke sympathy, and so on. Analyses that utilize this central tension will be richer and more productive.

To omit this tension—to assume a shared set of interests between men and women—is to overlook a key source of dissension and division within the working class, as it evolves and as it attempts to resist the control of capital.[25] And it also ignores a key factor in the maintenance of class relations. Acknowledging gendered divisions, in contrast, opens the door to empirical research into how divisions work—who takes advantage of them and when, who benefits, and who suffers—as well as into such issues as the meaning of the provider role. These divisions teach us something of the dynamics of working-class life that are absent when shopfloor relations alone are the subject of empirical research.

The process by which gendered differences emerge and the political role they play is often blurred by virtue of their seemingly "natural" existence. Exposing these differences to examination opens questions of ideological influence within classes and among groups; and the process provides access to methods (like the analysis of symbolic language) that reveal something of the roots of behavior and tradition and thus touch directly on the relationship of culture to power.

In so far as a labor history embedded in the culture of workers has reached a theoretical stasis, it is in the interests of labor historians to shift the focus from explorations of culture as description to explorations that confront the issue of why power has been so elusive. Not culture itself but the process of transformation becomes the object of our enterprise. To do this in a manner that respects the self-experience of ordinary people requires an analysis of the major components of their cultural meaning systems. Among these, gender stands out. At the same time, since gender is such a crucial part of almost every meaning system, it behooves us to investigate the role it has played in shaping and regulating institutions of power. If we could do so, we might provide a way of thinking about U.S. history that transcends the working class and that could serve as a model for thinking about race and ethnicity as well.

It is arguable that, had we confronted gender, we would have been pulled into thinking about some of the larger issues of social process. Women historians at the conference were not alone in pressing the claims of their special group. Nor must the central importance of gender undermine the validity of thinking about the nation as a whole as a part of a culture-power nexus. Those who had studied ethnic groups, regions, and race insisted that each group provided access into problems that seemed discrete but were in fact common to all. They were right. An emerging synthesis must be not merely respectful of culture but cognizant of its active role in shaping work-related values, attitudes, and behavior. It must also be fully aware of competing values. The use of gender, race, ethnicity, and region are crucial as analytic categories for demystifying the workforce, putting cultural content into class and clarifying the relationship between class and social action. Gender may be only the clearest and perhaps the most persuasive example. It was therefore especially disappointing when conference participants converted gender into the readily dismissable examples of women and the controversial issue of patriarchy.

However we stood on the issues, tension and disappointment were the inevitable consequences of our failure to resolve the pressing questions of our field. In headier moments, labor historians believed the dynamism of American history could be explained by ordinary people acting in their unions, their communities, and their workplaces. The meeting did not dispel that notion so much as it forced us to construct a framework to support it. We failed in the challenge to translate the language, symbols, and celebrations that constitute the visible manifestations of what we call culture into viable interpretations of class formation and speculation about the structure and activity of the state.

The struggle to construct theoretical approaches that speak to the richness of our historical data is infused by ongoing conflicts within industrial society. Ethnicity, race, religion, and gender are the central features of that debate. They will continue to inform our discussions and to challenge our understanding of the relationship of class to working-class culture, and they will provide us with an opportunity to broaden our perspective. One conferee suggested that a history of American labor might, in the end, be nothing less than a history of American capitalism. Another noted that there can be no possible synthesis of American history without a synthesis of labor history. I suspect that both are right. And I suspect, too, that the frustration and the contribution of this effort at synthesis was its revelation that labor history, in grappling with the broader questions of social history (power, politics, and the state), has moved from the periphery to the center of the debate.

8

Treating the
Male as "Other":
Redefining the Parameters
of Labor History

Shortly after World War I, American women who wanted their hair cut stylishly short ("bobbed") began to desert their traditional female hairdressers and to patronize barber shops. To meet the demand, barber shops, especially in western and Midwestern states, hired first an occasional "lady barber" and then more and more women. For the exclusively male Journeymen Barbers' International Union, this posed a problem. Section 67 of their constitution prohibited female membership. Yet non-union women who worked as barbers were undermining union strength and bargaining power. The logical solution, to admit women to membership, seemed to present its own difficulties.

A memorable moment at the fall 1924 meeting of the Journeymen Barbers in Indianapolis captures the dimensions of the problem and sets the stage for what follows. Women, the barbers feared, lacked the skill, honor, financial incentive, and self-discipline to be good workers and union members. In a rising crescendo, union men articulated their visions of the future.

> In view of the fact of her physical make-up, is it not a fact that if she were comely to look upon, and possessed extreme charm, would it not have a tendency to create discord among the men, who up to the time of her admittance to membership, were real working brothers?

> Is it not a fact that the real reason for employing women in barber shops is the questionable worth or drawing power as a physical attraction, and not on account of their workmanship?

This essay was first delivered at the North American Labor History Conference in Detroit in November 1991. It was originally published In *Labor History* 34 (Spring 1993). My thanks to Elizabeth Faue for cogent criticism.

Allowing for her attractiveness, and also for her workmanship, would she be as capable at forty-five or fifty years of age, with her drawing power limited, and her attractiveness practically gone, as a man at the same age?

In view of the fact that we will probably pass on a pension fund . . . at this coming convention, does the female barber figure as an asset or a liability?

The questions continued until they culminated in the most serious question of all: "Finally, brothers, will it pay to have built up an organization to where it is to-day, running smoothly, gaining slowly but surely, and admit an unknown quality, who from the first of it will be nothing but a *blithering liability?*"[1]

The concerns of this group of skilled workers are as much about conceptions of masculinity as about anything else. Proud of their skill and derisive of the possibility that women could ever possess any equivalent, confident of their earning capacity and fearful lest women undermine it, these men rely for protection on their sense of themselves as "brothers." Women, they suspect, will create discord among them, destroying the solidarity that sustains their incomes and frames plans for future economic security. The work culture defended by these barbers transcended their participation in a job or a craft to reflect a sense of order delineated by male bonding. For, in the end, it was their brotherhood that enabled these barbers to create the secure environment that was now jeopardized by women. The barbers' questions derive from an understanding of manliness that shapes their sense of place and provides a structure for the world they live in.

Similar examples abound. Printers, cigar rollers, iron-core makers, and others spoke eloquently about the racial, ethnic, and gender boundaries that have historically ordered the worlds of American workers. The barbers alert us to the existence of a class-based, racially segregated, and gender-defined worldview that is instantly familiar. Their concerns illustrate the importance of the reciprocal tension between class and gender in accounting for the dynamism of our political and social culture. They reveal how gender—by which I mean the socially shaped cluster of attributes, expectations, and behaviors assigned to different sexes—participates in the construction of culture as an active agent. The barbers demonstrate that the culture we associate with class is firmly gender-defined and remind us that gender along with, and like, class provides the normative and ideational boundaries within which people will choose to identify themselves and to act. The barbers' comments suggest the degree to which a relational view of gender opens possibilities for seeing the dynamics of change. But if the barbers provide us with access to the contours of historical change, we have made little effort to follow their trail.

In the June 1991 issue of *Reviews in American History,* Richard Oestreicher offers some reasons for foot-dragging among labor historians. "Historians of women and historians of workers," he argues in a review of two books on women's labor history, "remain discrete and largely separated tribes with their own journals, their own conferences, and their own informal networks of communication."[2] This, he suggests, is because for labor historians the essential organizing concept is class. "Labor historians instinctively accept a materialist conception of history." Historians of women, in contrast, favor questions around the construction of gender ideology. Oestreicher exacerbates the differences. Labor history, he suggests, is "about class formation, about the development of class-based institutions and cultural practices, and about the collective efforts of the working class to alter the relations of production, the rules about who does what, and how the product gets allocated." Ultimately, labor history is about workers, "and what defines people as workers is their economic activity." But scholars dealing with gender, in his view, are concerned with "the ways that ideology limits the opportunities of women and the efforts of women to overcome the restrictions of gender roles."[3]

The sharp dichotomy between work and gender relies on formal definitions of production, wages, and labor that may not be viable in the light of recent scholarship.[4] Just as the history of male workers has come to incorporate notions of gender ideology, the history of women speaks of formal and informal relations of production: about people who sometimes work in the household and at other times outside of it; about efforts to alter the relations of production; and about economic activity. The tendency of labor history to separate historians of women from those of labor and to exclude women's activities from economic purpose—and therefore from a direct relationship to class and class formation—suggests the remarkably male terms in which class is still defined. Operating from a particular, and seemingly natural, standpoint, many labor historians have perceived the world through a lens that offers only partial vision: that of the male worker. In light of the rich veins of women's labor history uncovered in recent decades, it will not do simply to insist that women were present or to argue that we can incorporate women into existing conceptions of a male-centered history. It is not the legitimacy of women's history that is at stake here but the value of a concept of class that rides roughshod over the lived experiences of women and men. As the barbers' appeal suggests, class cannot be conceived, nor class formation analyzed, in the absence of gender as process and as ideology.

Failure to incorporate gender into the concept of class may be one reason for historians' growing discontent with the utility of materialist conceptions of history. As the participants in the 1984 DeKalb labor-history conference discovered when they attempted to create a new synthesis for labor history, defining class in terms of the daily lives of workers has its limits.[5] The cultural approach that emerged in the historiography of the late 1960s and 1970s

(spearheaded in the United States by Herbert Gutman) identified and valo-
rized the experiences of working people. It provided rich new information
and insights, but it had limited capacity to explain relations between classes
or between workers and the state. Thus it could not adequately address questions of power. It did have the enormous advantage of making room for
women largely by paying attention to their roles in the household and community and by asserting the relationship of domestic values to the workplace.
But the relationship of these domestic values to issues of class and power have
never received the attention they deserve. The role that gender plays in the
construction of the ideational and normative framework of working people
remains obscure.

It is time for a new strategy, a radical reconceptualization that takes on what
Oestreicher calls "the central organizing conception of labor history—class."
It is time to see what happens when we pull class apart—to ask if it is possible to construct a discussion of the relation of production and the allocation of its product in a way that more fully encompasses the consciousness
and identity of the people who participate in economic society. To do that, we
need to investigate the role of gender in shaping the ideas and actions of men
and women and therefore in structuring the economic universe.[6] We need to
acknowledge and account for a sense of order that derives from patterns of
male and female behavior and that enables us to locate the economic goals and
expectations of men and women. Just as the barbers located their concerns in
the possibility that women would threaten a traditional gendered economic
structure, so one suspects that, for most working people, consciousness and
action are systematically constructed around their sense of themselves as men
or women who operate within a profoundly gendered universe.

Seemingly fixed notions like "worker" and "working class" deserve our
attention if we are to understand how their various meanings change through
time. In the past, these terms have contained a set of meanings that are wedded to male categories of work. If we reconceive work, its locus, and its importance by adopting some version of what feminists have come to call standpoint theory, we may be able to reconceive class as well.

Using standpoint theory, feminists have come to understand the ways in
which all knowledge is socially situated and how in a gender-stratified society,
the claims to knowledge of the dominant group are conditioned by its desire
to preserve power.[7] In turn, these claims produce the institutional support
systems that validate them. Thus, human activity structures and sets limits on
what we can know. Standpoint theory enables us to assess the limits because it
exposes the stances of different groups of participants in human affairs. This
is not to imply that only women can do women's history—far from it. Rather,
it puts us in a position of problematizing all knowledge as the product of par-

ticular social situations. Analyzing claims to knowledge, in the view of the philosopher Sandra Harding, offers to maximize the goal of objectivity by overcoming "excessive reliance on distinctively masculine lives" as well as making use of women's lives in assessing the validity of claims to knowledge.[8]

I'm not arguing for a dual-systems theory that posits separately created and intersecting patriarchal and class structures. Nor am I advocating a struggle between the sexes to accommodate positions of power. Rather, I am suggesting that, in the formation of class, ideas about what constitutes work play a significant and even crucial role. Such ideas are explicitly gendered, and the identities out of which they emerge are constructed relationally: nurtured, shaped, and directed by the changing household and community. This framework suggests that male and female agency are equally constructed out of a historically circumscribed valorization and naming of masculine and feminine behavior. Thus, female agency can bespeak a variety of social experiences, ranging from motherhood to the workplace, and male agency can be expected to reflect a continuum that extends from workplace skills to family position. The actions of men and women can be said to reaffirm household identity and particular relations to production. Since it is the relation between the two that informs identity and consciousness, any discussion of class must construe masculine and feminine in relation to each other. To leave out either impoverishes both.

Joan W. Scott's critique of E. P. Thompson's *Making of the English Working Class* suggests a practical testing ground. She argues that those who have interpreted the behavior of working people through what we have called class have in fact adopted male categories as universal. Scott suggests that we explore the ways "the feminine is used to construct conceptions of class."[9] I want to adopt a corollary—to propose a stance—that problematizes the masculine in our understanding of class.

To do this, we have to lay siege to the central paradigm of labor history, namely, that the male-centered workplace is the locus from which the identity, behavior, social relations, and consciousness of working people ultimately emanates. We must challenge the notion that paid work, as a fundamentally male activity, inevitably reproduces itself in a closed system in which men derive their identity from the process of production (and then reproduce themselves by training other men), while women act in the household and in the workplace as the handmaids of the male reproductive system.[10] The social context that Thompson describes includes men who are shaped and formed by experiences that occur in institutions and structures that are themselves defined by relations of production. Its modification by Herbert Gutman to accommodate the lives and cultures of working people mingles ethnic and racial/ethnic traditions with the workplace. But the cultural context of class formation, which invokes the collective efforts of working people to alter the relations of production and the rules of economic activity, can readily accommodate a gendered stand-point as well.

The broader conception of economic activity encompasses the workplace and the household/community in a reciprocal and changing relationship where each participates in shaping the other. Part of the shaping process involves the subjective experiences, understandings, and expectations of men and women for whom gender may be the most salient part of their sense of social order. Earl Lewis's *In Their Own Interests* offers a useful formulation.[11] Lewis speaks of the importance to twentieth-century African Americans of the "home sphere," by which he means the nexus constituted by the household/neighborhood and community. He argues persuasively that in the context of racism this home sphere becomes the shaping force through which efforts to participate in and demand justice from the workplace emerged.

The implications of this formulation for gender are apparent. The experience of class and the politics that emerge from it are as much a product of gender as of social location and economic presence. For men, gendered politics might include organization around the family, workplace, or community, in trade unions or lodges, and meetings located in beer halls or around park benches. A particular political stance responds not to one experience or another but to an integrated conception of the home sphere and work relations. For women, politics might involve formal and informal neighborhood associations and women's clubs, petitions for shorter workdays for themselves, or parades and demonstrations with baseball bats in defense of their male kin. Traditional understandings of the inseparable relationship between paid and unpaid work of men and women underline women's protests against rent gouging or rising prices for bread, as do their efforts to secure higher wages and safer work. In this formulation, the structural separation of home and work achieves little resonance in the ideological construction of either class or gender.[12] While Lewis comes dangerously close to locating gender in the home, the broader application of his formulation enables us to conceive the work space as part of a reciprocal relation that includes domesticity and racial/ethnic sensibilities and occurs within a social context over which the actors can exercise only sporadic influence.

For most working people, men and women, the reciprocality of the gendered relation may be the critical component of subjective identity. But the naturalness of gender frequently renders it invisible. That doesn't make it less influential. As David Roediger astutely argues in *The Wages of Whiteness,* the continuing belief among white men in the absence of whiteness as a salient category had political and social consequences.[13] I would argue as much for gender. Though it has often been the case that men have failed to see themselves as men, rather than as normative beings, the historian quickly perceives the ways in which gender has defined how men look at themselves. This perspective promises to open up the ways in which relations of class are constructed out of a gendered sense of self. Situating ourselves at the standpoint of the home sphere may help us to see the effects of universalizing the male on definitions of work and reveal contemporary usages of class as particular and partial representations.[14] Not incidentally, it could help to rescue class from its currently vestigial position.

A long view of history supports the notion that fully incorporating community and household requires us to think about them as structures that preceded the development of capitalism and persist throughout it. We can agree that the commodification of labor and land that occurred during the industrialization process significantly altered social relations. But they did not eliminate civil society. In the process of industrialization, the struggle of men for power and influence was shaped by rapidly changing capitalist institutions.[15] Still, in our zeal to understand how pervasive these forces were, we have interpreted identity, social relations, customs, and culture as greater or lesser reflections of this process and of the narrowly defined class struggle. We have blurred aspects of a continuity located in households and communities. But fundamental forms of identity, derived from the household (created and shaped by women and men), survived even the depredations of capital. Is this a romantic view, another form of locating working-class resistance to capitalism? On the contrary, it is not resistance I seek: I search for the varied forms of participation, for aspects of continuity, that helped define and construct class relations. I seek the ways that gender and household participate in creating the relations of production and thus in shaping class.

Taking women's lives as our starting point, the particular relations of workplace and workers that we have called labor history appear to be ephemeral and to lack universality even for the period when they appear to be central. As the locus of human socialization and education, as the central provider of life-sustaining goods and services for most of historical time, an enlarged household provides a perspective from which wage work becomes merely another form of sustenance. Though wage work was surely a crucial aspect of many lives, the period when it constituted the central organizing principle of most individual existences can be more accurately conceived of as a phase—a historical moment—rather than as a universal truth. In our contemporary "postindustrial" period, older forms of identity are once again visible. The centrality of paid work, never entirely accepted even by male workers, has begun to diminish, not as a source of income but as a locus of identity. Workers increasingly define their sense of identity in terms of consumption and leisure activities; race, family, and ethnicity resurface as sources of political consciousness and of organizational strategy.[16]

How then do we understand the particular relations out of which some men rose to power? From the standpoint of women's lives and the household, it is not difficult to reimagine the transformations of character, belief, and values that encourage some people to participate in and shape relations in and around the workplace, and others to withdraw from them. At certain moments in time, different forms of masculinity become currency to be coined, hoarded, and traded in much the same way that female virtue was coined and traded among some social groups. And just as the value placed on certain kinds of masculinity (like brutality, intellect, and economic provision) shifted over time and space, so did the value placed on changing forms of femininity.

In some parts of the world, for most of the nineteenth and part of the twentieth century, wage work came to dominate and control the household by redefining power in gendered terms and in particular by constructing definitions of power that were exclusively male. Working-class men continually renegotiated forms of masculinity to create guilds, lodges, and craft and industrial unions that extrapolated the power of the household and utilized it in their struggle with employers. Their efforts were only marginally successful. Working men were both constrained and supported by the power retained by the household (and largely exercised by women) to create family and community networks, to identify the boundaries of community, and to organize local and neighborhood politics.[17]

In this context, one begins to see the century-long process that extends from household production to household consumption as an analytic framework and a determinant of how people think about themselves and their social experience. The activities of household providers (who may be male and/or female and who may or may not be wage workers) generate analysis. Workplace history is decentered. Formal labor institutions and informal associations of working people can be seen as outgrowths of male efforts to develop strategies for accessing economic power or to construct defenses against change. The meaning and significance of these institutions as agents of social change demand reassessment. Within the context of a persistent home sphere, relations of production no longer appear primarily as the products of a disembodied workplace; and class (defined as an outgrowth of a broader system of production that includes family, home, and community) becomes a subset of the effort to maintain culture, defined here as consciously created forms of value and beliefs. Political consciousness and activity are fruitfully interpreted as products of the household that, though deeply and differentially affected by the market, continues to shape working lives. The gendered struggle that emanates from households responds to the shifting demands of the market. It is translated into the workplace by formal and informal behavior patterns and by such state interventions as female regulation and exclusion. Gender is incorporated into public space by dint of formal and informal sanctions on male and female behavior. The household is no longer construed as a private domain; rather, in its enlarged form of home sphere it is the source of consciousness that generates public activity. External and self-imposed regulation of its inhabitants becomes a central subject of historical investigation.

Casting the broadly defined household as central encourages us to search for the construction of femininity and masculinity. It also, not accidentally, makes room for varieties of cultural experience (especially including that of black workers) that are often rendered invisible by the focus on particular sexually and racially segregated workplaces. Like race, gender is construed as a continually changing mode of identity and as an instrumental agent in shaping class relations. Both masculinity and femininity, but particularly aggressive masculinity, can be seen as instruments of economic organization—including the organization of conceptions about how wage work might be structured as well as the organization of the workplace in particular. We observe the household as the locus of work of all kinds. In tandem with the struggles of men and women in the workplace, those initiated in the household and neighborhood help us to explain the continuing tension between the powerful and the powerless as a product of household, neighborhood, and waged work.

The literature of labor history provides plenty of support for interpretations that move in this direction. In recent years, we have seen a surge of interest in issues of consciousness and motivation among working people that point towards multiple sources of ideology. Some of these emerge from Foucauldian notions that suggest that power is diffused among many arenas. Others pay special attention to changing modes and meanings of consumption as shaping agencies in the development of group identity. Together, they suggest that in the nineteenth-century United States, the home sphere did not disintegrate under the onslaught of republicanism in anything like the way we have previously imagined. Rather, they point to the changing ways in which households began to function with regard to political life. For example, Jeanne Boydston delineates the continuation of systems of household production and of a community life shaped by that system until well into the 1850s.[18] Women's work, in her view, provided a safety net for men eager to take entrepreneurial risks and a site in which traditional values were configured. Joan Jensen notes that, as a consequence of shifts in agricultural production that resulted from increased marketing of farm products, the influence of farm wives increased rather than decreased.[19] Before the Civil War and after, women who were denied public voice tried with varying success to use their work roles to claim access to the polity.[20] The urban street, according to Christine Stansell and Mary Ryan, was a space women could and did use to display themselves, to express their discontent, and to demand redress of grievances.[21] As an extension of the home sphere, streets provided locations of contest over values as well as arenas where otherwise silenced voices could be heard. Historians like Ryan and Stansell as well as Elliot Gorn and Joe William Trotter, among others, confirm that on the streets, ethnicity, race, and gender encountered and influenced each other.[22]

Students of late nineteenth- and twentieth-century women's history have provided equally strong support for the notion that the household did not exist merely as a creature of the workplace but participated in the structure of work as well. The importance of kin networks in finding and assigning jobs has been apparent for some time now.[23] But we are only beginning to understand how the household context shaped relationships to the workplace. Carole Turbin and Ardis Cameron have each tested the boundaries between home and work spaces and found them permeable. Boundaries fluctuated with the female life-cycle, and with opportunity and economic cycles as well. The result, these authors suggest, is an overlapping network of household and job-related concerns in which gendered constructs of community, culture, and work intermingle.[24] Further into the twentieth century, it seems clear that organizing strategies and possibilities rested heavily on the ties of men and women to their communities. Elizabeth Faue weaves together an intricate web of community lives and work needs to demonstrate how men and women constructed a successful campaign to organize in trade unions in Depression-era Minneapolis.[25] Lizabeth Cohen, though she does not pay attention to gender per se, ties successful protest in Depression-era Chicago to family needs, networks, and fortunes.[26] In a period of changing gender roles, ideas about appropriate and inappropriate work and about entitlement to wages and jobs rested heavily on the particular family and community commitments of men and women. Together, this work suggests that when historians ignore the role of households, they disguise the role of gender as a progenitor of class.

A second important component of the discovery of the home sphere has been the fruitfulness of exploring how the concept of masculinity has altered its definition in tension with changing structures of work. David Montgomery long ago pointed to the influence of notions of manliness in regulating workplace behavior, but only recently have historians and sociologists noted how exclusive and changing definitions of manly bearing have influenced work structure and expectations.[27] In consequence, we have a rich new trove of literature that looks at how working-class masculinity has assumed an active, even belligerent stance. Its continual and conscious redefinition appears to signal changing relationships to political and economic ends. For example, Ava Baron's work on nineteenth-century printers beautifully traces how male values and self-images are disrupted by challenges from young male apprentices as well as from women.[28] To meet this challenge, printers redefined their sense of themselves as men and attempted to use their new sensibility as an organizational rallying cry. Similarly, though Heidi Hartmann has suggested the importance of cross-class alliances of men in structuring the labor force, only recently has empirical data, such as that produced by Baron and Mary Ann Clawson, provided persuasive evidence of the importance of male solidarity in constructing particular kinds of political and work identities that separate them from the household.[29] Clawson's work on fraternal brotherhoods reveals the ways in which men sometimes bonded across class lines to stave off the threat of female encroachment. In this way, cross-class bonding could simultaneously signal the loyalty of working men to each other and divert their energies from working-class organizations that might have utilized gender differently.

We have begun to understand something of the way in which concepts of citizenship were released from class constraints by the uses of the language of masculinity. In the late nineteenth century, the capacity for citizenship inhered in the dignity and independence of the working person and therefore assumed that each person had equal rights or access to economic self-sufficiency. To define economic independence as the guarantor of effective self-representation and the perpetuation of a democratic republic, and to deny women such independence, not only created a different meaning for female citizenship but generated male solidarity and guaranteed male control of the household. The worker whose "manly bearing" enabled him to exercise authority in work-related decisions and who understood that manliness derived from solidarity with one's brothers surely understood that his identity and his wage were inseparable. Evidence of the close relation between a manly sense of self and the construction of citizenship appears in increasingly sophisticated versions of labor republicanism as well as in the ways in which female domesticity operates as its counterpart.[30] Nick Salvatore's biography of Eugene V. Debs employs Debs's changing perceptions of his own manhood to redefine the parameters of citizenship for working people. The work of Elizabeth Faue has also been useful in showing how definitions of masculinity fluctuate, becoming more and more violent, as the social demands for men to protect their households economically become ever more elusive.[31]

If definitions of masculinity are responsive to a range of influences located in the workplace and in larger economic changes, they are at least partly constructed out of ethnic, racial, and community structures that thus participate in forming economic policy. Mary Blewett discusses immigrant Lancashire mule spinners for whom deference and stability constituted part of their definition of masculinity. When they wanted higher wages, they adopted a deferential stance towards employers, considering it beneath their dignity to protest loudly. But they did not object when their wives, most of whom worked as weavers and who were not bound by such deferential norms, took to the streets on behalf of their menfolk. When the women failed, the mule spinners considered it unmanly to adopt the traditional American solution and simply leave.[32]

We have known for some time that definitions of masculinity form and shape expectations of the feminine and are in turn shaped by them.[33] While the relational nature of these two constructs has yet to be fully explored, we are already beginning to see how important ideological notions of women's rights in the family were for the middling sort. Working-class men and women seem to have developed their own measures of propriety based on gender-defined constructions of the household and changing perceptions of the relationships of women to the workplace.[34]

Thus the creation of a political strategy around protective labor legislation at the turn of the century was explicitly gendered and, within the working class, rose or fell on issues of masculinity and femininity. Among women, as Dorothy Sue Cobble has demonstrated, support for and opposition to particular kinds of protective labor legislation was closely related to women's economic positions within their families.[35]

The labor market is apparently not impermeable to gendered assumptions that help to create shared understandings of fairness and justice and regulate the expectations of both sexes. In my book on women's wages, I have suggested that these expectations could overwhelm otherwise rational market behavior by inhibiting employers from hiring women (or men) for certain kinds of jobs, and especially by conditioning the wage on what ordinary men and women had come to believe was appropriate for either sex, as well as for racial/ethnic groups within the sexes.[36] In this context, the construction of class relationships could be complicated by competition between men and women and by male, or white male, conceptions of privilege. Larry Glickman's work on the American standard of living confirms the notion that it was rooted in efforts of skilled male workers to define the family in ways that would enhance the services men could expect.[37]

Though constructions of the provider role differ historically, they are as important with respect to definitions of masculinity as with respect to those of womanliness—and both function as sources of economic and political initiative. What counts as resistance differs by sex (as well as by class and region and race) in accord with gendered norms. Efforts to preserve rural prerogative appear, for example, in the insistence of male mill hands in southern textile mills that they get days off to go hunting. Women, in contrast, negotiated time to do domestic chores, to nurse babies, or to supervise children.

Years ago, E. P. Thompson and Herbert Gutman urged us to look at class as a process in which the customs and cultures of working people play a significant part. Their work opened the door to an examination of institutions outside the workplace. But culture, in its anthropological definition, is a continuing and conscious creation whose central component may well be the relations of gender. With increasing knowledge of women's history, formulations of class and culture beg the question of how relations between men and women circumscribe those between worker and boss and shape the meaning systems around which power is constructed and legitimized. If we do not wish to abandon class as a concept, our efforts must be directed towards reconceiving it in a way that fully incorporates the multiple meanings that reside within it. Nothing less will do justice to the barbers with whom we began. Just as they could not separate the sexuality of encroaching lady barbers from their skill, wage-earning capacity, and commitment to work, so notions of masculinity conditioned their sense of order. The barbers were men, and this is as important a fact as that they were workers.

9

Reconfiguring the Private in the Context of the Public

J ohn M. imagined that his work would serve some very private purposes. In June 1930, he ruminated in the presence of a company supervisor about how he felt about the relationship between a job, a man's self esteem, and the responsibilities of employers:

> If a man is on a good job he should never be put down and given a worse job because you will find that when they do that the man never does the same work again. It tends to take his ambition away. It takes all the joy out of a man's life to have had a good grade of work and then be put down on something worse. I know that from my own experience. It is human nature to want to keep going on the up and up all the time . . . the company should . . . always see that a man is given a fair chance to keep rising going up all the time. His wages should keep increasing too.[1]

For John M., there was no clear line between public and private. He expected his employer—a huge corporation—to care about his private dreams and ambitions, if for no other reason than because he would be a better employee if they did so. His expectations reflect the persistently fuzzy boundary between the categories of public and private as they existed in the minds of generations of workers and came to a head in the period just before corporate capital abandoned the welfare of employees and the responsibilities of paternalism to the state. In this essay I explore the meaning of the public and private in the

The opportunity to formulate these ideas came at a conference on the Public and Private in American History. Family, Subjectivity, and Public Life in the Twentieth Century, sponsored by the Centro Bairati di Studi Euro-Americani, University of Turin, May 17–19, 2001. I am grateful to John Howell Harris for providing important comments. The essay first appeared in Rafaela Baritono et al., eds., *Public and Private in American History: State, Family, Subjectivity in the Twentieth Century* (Torino: Otto Editore, 2003). A different argument that makes use of some of the material in this article can be found in my book, *In Pursuit of Equity: Women, Men, and the Quest for Economic Citizenship in Twentieth-Century America* (New York: Oxford University Press, 2001). The names of those interviewed have been changed.

perceptions of workers and their employers. By examining the language of identity and family as it was used by male and female workers in a large industrial plant in the late 1920s and early 1930s, I hope to illuminate their implications for work-related policies and, indirectly, for claims to the prerogatives of citizenship.

I use the concepts of public and private in a somewhat idiosyncratic way. By "private," I refer to the emotional or affective sphere, to locations where individual satisfaction is sought and where narcissistic and subjective experiences are validated. By "public," I mean the sphere or location where more general interests are organized. Like the workplace, the family straddles the border in this definition. Historically, the household was a "public" sphere: until the late eighteenth century in most of Europe and the Americas, it functioned as a unit of social organization and a vehicle for controlling the individuals who resided within it. It incorporated work space; its head was responsible to the lord or king, and later to the polity. As work moved out of the household, the status of the householder changed, and the family increasingly became a location for the satisfaction of personal needs. Its members generally sold their labor in the marketplace, rendering work and the work space more and more a public concept.

As many historians have noted, gender constituted one of the main, ongoing organizational vehicles for regulating access to work and to the perquisites of citizenship it created. The separation of work from the household produced lengthy debates about the privatization of women, provoking the desire to protect their roles as mothers and wives who served the affective needs of men and children, and raising questions about whether their public work adequately served the needs of husbands and fathers. Through the late nineteenth and much of the twentieth century, women who functioned in public space (in wage work, for example, or in politics) occupied an ambiguous position, at once the private property of men and the bearers of individual rights to civil and political life. Women's involvement in the nonfamily workplace (itself public) therefore had something of a disruptive quality, simultaneously providing a potential vehicle for female political power and a focus of resistance among men who clung jealously to male turf.

Twentieth-century employers reflected and made use of this ambiguity by acquiescing to traditional expectations of men and women even as they paid women less to compensate for their understanding. In the first part of the century, as large corporate employers in the United States and in most industrial countries turned to paternalist mechanisms, attempting to incorporate some of the caring functions of the family into the workplace, confusion about what men and women could expect from the corporation that espoused affective goals even as it served public functions abounded.

In this essay I explore some of the complicated intersections between these public and private goals. Based on the admittedly limited but enormously powerful evidence drawn from one company, I suggest that the metaphors of justice and fairness used by workers and managers intersected with and sustained each other. When employers used the language of paternalism, they spoke to the most private sensibilities of women and men, engaging their imaginations as well as their labor in a common search for well-being. The success of the rhetoric of early twentieth-century industrial paternalism can best be measured not by the practices it engendered but by its capacity to weave a web of meaning that met the private, or familial, needs of workers as it fulfilled the demands of employers for more productive work. The workers whose words I have studied accommodated the goals of paternalist policies for loyalty, high production, and teamwork by invoking correlative rights to job security (or at least rational layoff policies), steady and increasing incomes, and predictable promotion patterns. They wove these expectations into the language of the family (measuring their own individual family needs against those of the company) in ways that articulated a coherent sense of justice and fairness for which they held the company accountable.

This reciprocal invocation of paternalism appears to have encouraged workers to capture its language and meaning and turn it to their own purposes. Company-sponsored paternalism resonated in the private as well as the public lives of workers and raised their expectations on both fronts, as workers imagined their own fortunes in the rhetoric of the company, linking their expectations to management's implied commitments and introjecting those promises into the value systems that dominated their lives, including providing for families, regulating job-related ambition, and articulating definitions of manliness. This interplay between public and private played a significant part in defining the mutual rights and obligations of corporation and worker and in the political process that re-created social policy as the economic depression of the 1930s took hold. I want therefore to look at the success of paternalist welfare policies at least partly as a function of their capacity to capture the intersection between public and private as they existed in the aspirations of male and female workers.

To do this, I use interviews and recordings of workers at Western Electric's Hawthorne plant in Chicago taken between 1927 and 1933. This cache of data emerges from one piece of a widespread movement to alter the human relations of industrial plants that took hold in the 1920s. In the years just before and around World War I, a few managers and some labor-relations experts came to believe that labor and capital could live in harmonious unity by adopting ideas of scientific management. Relying heavily on the ideas of Frederick Winslow Taylor, they became convinced that productivity could be increased and the rewards to labor and management multiplied by increasing efficiency and reducing labor turnover. At the heart of scientific management lay the idea that an individual worker would produce best if he or she were appropriately trained and monitored and allowed a generous share of productivity gains in the form of increased wages, rest, and other goodies. The new manager weeded out the inefficient worker, the one "naturally unfitted for his chosen work," and sought to "promote each worker to the highest notch he is capable of in his chosen life work."[2] In this context, male and female workers occupied different spaces in the imaginations of managers and workers alike.

Few employers adopted the full range of Taylor's ideas, but many subscribed to the notion of training and nurturing suitable workers. To find the best worker for the job, enlightened employers enlisted the new science of personnel management to streamline hiring practices. They undertook this with more or less extensive psychological inventories and informal interviews. The scientific-management movement paralleled and in some cases associated with a movement towards better human relations in the workplace that was motivated in part by poor conditions of unskilled labor, and particularly by increasing tension between women's work and family roles.

The leading experimenters in personnel policy, including such giants of production as Ford, General Electric, and Westinghouse, as well as smaller manufacturers such as H. J. Heinze, the Joseph Feiss Clothing Company of Cleveland, and retailers like Filenes of Boston, assumed that men and women wanted different things from work and adapted hiring, training, and promotion policies accordingly. They tried to determine whether potential employees possessed appropriate masculine and feminine characteristics for the jobs at hand as well as the appropriate virtues for each sex. By the 1920s, these practices had invaded the offices of the insurance and banking industries.[3]

Taylor had assumed that productivity gains would be shared with workers; in practice, however, most employers who adopted efficiency techniques returned little if any of the cost savings to employees and, if they paid attention to the resulting dissatisfaction at all, tried to ameliorate it by applying a range of "welfare" techniques derived from an amalgam of historical experience and refined by melding them with the supposedly more scientific findings of human-relations experts. We know from a variety of secondary sources that gender participated in the imagination of employers as they constructed these programs.[4] Employers supported gendered patterns in formal and informal ways, lodging them in a continuing rhetoric of economic independence that remained the prerogative of males. We can find them in the crude sex-segmentation practices of employers before the First World War, and we can see them in the new management techniques that reached their heyday in the 1920s. Scientific management, corporate welfare programs, and the new field of personnel management inspired by human-relations experts together reveal how readily, seemingly naturally, employers attempted to inscribe gender into the behavior of employees. Workers of both sexes held their paternalistic employers responsible for obeying gendered injunctions and felt betrayed when they did not. They also felt entitled to skimp on their work commitments when employers failed to adhere to their part of an implicit social bargain.

Employer strategies inscribed into the workforce gendered expectations that may not have differed dramatically from those of earlier generations but were certainly more formal. Many employers introduced showers, cafeterias, English-language classes, and medical services for all workers. Men got sports clubs and family picnics, designed to build loyalty. By the 1920s, some companies offered more valuable amenities, such as paid vacations, old-age pensions, and life insurance to skilled men. These typically incorporated longevity requirements that effectively barred women from benefits.[5] Many companies offered loans for home ownership to male heads of families. General Electric was among the employers that asked women to resign on marriage and restricted pensions to workers with twenty years or more of service—a constraint that excluded virtually all women. G.E. also made group life insurance policies available, but only to men.[6] By the late 1920s, an occasional company, like Western Electric, offered stock options to women as well as men. Generally, however, women received less in the way of financial rewards and more in the form of social amenities like lounge areas and sewing or cooking classes, along with occasional dances and summer camps. They also got rest periods and lunch-time recreation: sociability rather than job security.

If welfare programs were expected to create gendered solidarity among workers, they also served to reinforce traditional gendered divisions outside the workplace. At the Ford Motor Company, managers relied on a happy home life to increase steadiness, stability, and output. In 1914, the company offered its famous five-dollar-a-day "profit-sharing plan" (nearly doubling the wages of the least-skilled workers) to those who met its criteria for good citizenship. These included married men living with, and properly supporting, a nonworking wife and children. Single men over the age of twenty-two were eligible if they had thrifty habits and lived in good homes. To insure their continued worthiness, all workers were subject to stringent reviews of their domestic living arrangements and personal habits, including thrift, temperance, and appropriate respect for family life. The differences between these benefits and those offered to women contributed to developing a manly spirit among workers.[7] The company generally didn't hire married women with able husbands, but women could earn the advantageous five-dollar rate if they had "an immediate blood relation totally dependent" on them. All other women, like single men under twenty-two, found themselves ineligible for profit sharing. Since factory jobs were, at the time, among the best of blue-collar options for white women, we can imagine that despite pay and benefits significantly lower than those of men, most accepted the differences uncomplainingly. At Western Electric, women rarely compared their wages with those of men, though men and women discussed pay differentials with others of their own sex.

The most progressive employers deeply believed that ensuring male employees a modicum of economic security along with a rational and dignified work experience would not only fulfill their obligations to build good citizens but would generate increased profits and still the fires of radicalism as well. In this respect, they assumed that the invasion of the private sphere would serve a public interest in more efficient workplaces. This assumption echoed labor's conviction that manliness and democratic participation required dignified work and the capacity to support a family. Workers, in their own view, deserved not only adequate incomes and decent housing but assurances that their widows and surviving children would be cared for. A few companies tried to meet this goal by supporting orphanages or industrial homes, where women could be adequately employed and children educated to become the next generation of workers.[8] Others found work for widows. A sprinkling of companies acknowledged men's provider roles in other ways, by providing housekeepers to help out if wives became ill, for example, or setting up "little mother's clubs" where girls could learn the values that would make them good future homemakers and, not incidentally, train their parents as well.

At Hawthorne, as at other plants, paternalist interventions were the subjects of innovation and experimentation.[9] The Hawthorne works, located in Chicago, manufactured telephone, wiring, and switching equipment for its parent, employing thousands of workers to do a range of relatively routine jobs that required manual dexterity and speed. Dissatisfied with the output of workers and influenced by the human-relations movement in industry, personnel managers there began a series of experiments with workers to see what factors influenced productivity rates. Their first and most famous experiment involved raising and lowering the level of lighting for a small group of workers to see if production increased with changes in illumination. When they discovered that productivity increased regardless of the amount of light, they concluded that the heightened interest generated by the experiment itself increased productivity.

The company (already well known for its pioneering personnel policies) then brought in a group of industrial psychologists, including Donald Chapman, Clarence Stoll, Homer Harbirger, and later, William J. Dickson, in a series of efforts to measure the effects of increasing efficiency techniques against an array of workplace ameliorations and welfare benefits. They were soon joined by Elton Mayo, Felix Roethlisberger, and a team of researchers from the Harvard Business School. Over a six-year period, this group consulted on ways to extend the original exploration of the effect of lighting to research into the attitudes of workers. Their search began with first one and then another small test room and led finally to an extensive interview program conducted by plant supervisors. They set up test rooms in which they could listen to workers talk without their knowledge; they interviewed selected groups of workers at length; and over several years they arranged for all of the 10,500 workers in the plant to be interviewed, generally by supervisory personnel.

The effects of these experiments on workplace efficiency and productivity has been hotly debated. Official accounts published by Roethlisberger and Dickson suggested that the experiments were inconclusive as to the effects of illumination, rest periods, hours of work, methods of supervision, and wage incentives on increasing workers' rate of output. The "attitudes of employees," they concluded, were the key factors in tapping "the stores of latent energy and productive cooperation which clearly could be obtained from its working force under the right conditions."[10] But social scientists, skeptical of attributing changes in production to "attitudes," have repeatedly challenged the research methods used. The most balanced exploration of the literature, by the historian Richard Gillespie, offers a scathing indictment of the ways in which the interests of the critics as well as the researchers affected the published results.[11] In the end, the experiments affirmed earlier results, suggesting that the added attention given the workers was most likely responsible for any increases in productivity. Still, the researchers never wavered from the conviction that workers' mental conditions—their attitudes towards work—affected their productivity. This led them to produce a variety of records of worker attitudes by observing and recording the informal comments of workers in the test rooms and asking a select group of supervisory personnel to interview more than ten thousand women and men who worked in the plant.

The voices of the male and female workers recorded by interviewers provide a treasure trove of information about values, thoughts, feelings, and family lives, as well as about workplace issues, colleagues, supervision, and hundreds of other issues. They provide clues to some of the factors that motivate work for men and women and speak to how the ideology of work is gendered in particular ways. They suggest how that company and its workers accommodated each other, including how values shifted as a consequence of economic depression. And they reveal how paternalist policies participated in workers' sense of fairness and justice, conditioned their expectations, and shaped the imaginations of men and women—sometimes in similar and often in different ways. Most especially, they tell us that home and family lives invaded the thoughts of men and women, occupying their mental lives in ways that sustained some of the paternalist impulses of the company and perhaps operated as a constraint as well. I turn to the interviews now to see what they can tell us about how workers thought about their private lives.

The first and longest-lasting experiment, the Relay Assembly Test Room (RATR), set up by management in April 1927, consisted of five young women (aged eighteen to twenty-eight and consistently labeled "girls" by the researchers) whose repetitive but demanding jobs involved putting together telephone signal switches that would eventually relay calls from one cable to another.[12] A sixth woman determined the layout for the variety of switches on which the operators worked and acted in a semisupervisory position. Of the five women originally selected, two were replaced about nine months after the experiment started—presumably for talking too much. With the exception of a few months in the fall of 1932, when one worker briefly left, the new team of five "girls" remained together until February 1933. They more or less cooperated with management as their working conditions altered, their output steadily rose, and the depression around them deepened.[13] Other small groups of workers participated in shorter experiments. One of these, the Bank Wiring Test Room, established in November 1931, consisted of nine men and no women. It lasted barely six months, disbanded after the workers horrified management by regulating their own pace of work and thus restricting their output.

I draw heavily on their recorded conversations to illuminate issues of loyalty, fairness, and justice, many of which revolve around money, and to suggest some of the principles and constraints that guided their work. On one level, paternalistic treatment evoked quite similar responses from women and men. In apparently sharp contrast to the behavior of men, the women in the RATR, after a short period of adjustment, increased their production dramatically. Management praised the women for cooperating, and their room quickly became a model test. But the apparent gender difference dissolves on examination. As Richard Gillespie has pointed out, in both cases men and women were doing what seemed to be in their fundamental self-interest. The women, paid as a small group, knew that increasing their production would also increase their wages. And they had been promised no cuts in the rate of pay if the quantity of production increased. As a result, they quickly created a solidaristic group ethic.

But while the structure of the wage provided women with the incentive to use their power to regulate production, a different reward structure for men encouraged them to regulate their production in a different way. The men had been made no promise of level wages in the face of increased production; they continued to be paid as part of the larger section to which they belonged. Fearful that the rate for the job would be cut for all workers if they produced too much, and deriving little immediate benefit from putting out more work, they whiled away hours if it suited them. Asked by an interviewer if he was aware that others would be laid off if he produced too much, the worker replied, "[T]hat only stands to reason, doesn't it? . . . Suppose the fellows in the test room could increase their output to seven thousand. I think some of them can. That would mean less work for others."[14] To this man, the stint seemed a way of sharing work.

Men and women workers adopted the language of family unity, claiming their actions as essential to protect each other. Yet to the researchers, the men appeared "obstinately resistant to change," while the women were described as simply "immune to many of the experimental changes."[15] They attributed the continuously high production of the women to many factors, of which the high level of wages was only one. The informal organization of the men, who were described as having "a set of practices and beliefs . . . which at many points worked against the economic purposes of the company," clearly threatened management.[16]

Blinded by their own gender biases, the researchers never perceived the women's efforts to control the work pace. Roethlisberger and Dickson, whose book, *Management and the Worker,* provides the original and most comprehensive account of the experiments' results, describe the "girls" in the RATR and other test rooms without looking at or seeing women's control over their work. Instead, researchers tried to correlate women's menstrual periods, hours of sleep, and home responsibilities with their levels of production. They paid no particular attention to women's wages, though it is clear from the recorded comments of the test room "girls" that the dramatically higher wages they earned significantly increased their production, their eagerness to cooperate with the research process, and ultimately their loyalty to the plant.[17] In the end, Roethlisberger and Dickson credited the high levels of production to "a network of personal relations . . . which not only satisfied the wishes of its members but also worked in harmony with the aims of management."[18] In support of the women's cooperative stance, they cited such factors as company-sponsored social activities, afternoon tea breaks, and frequent rest periods. Though the women clearly enjoyed these perquisites, they registered most satisfaction in their capacity to work together to increase the income of each. One told an interviewer, "I'd rather work here any time, because in the other department we were working hard and others would be laying low on the job, and here when some girl is sick we speed, and when we are sick the other girls speed."[19] They used explicitly financial incentives to goad each other to work harder, to spell each other when tired, and to encourage attendance even when one or another was feeling under the weather. "You can't take a half day off tomorrow," one RATR woman declared. "You'll spoil the percentage. Get to work, girls. I'm getting thinner every day because I've got to make percentage for all. Shut up girls. I want to work."[20]

When researchers content-coded the 10,300 interviews for frequency and tone, they discovered far more similarities than differences among male and female workers. For both, income was the single most important compensation for work, a statement about personal worth as well as about the possibilities for consumption. Men and women measured the value of income in terms of its capacity to support families not merely at a level they considered acceptable but in a way that sustained their identities as family members and signified their capacity to maintain intimate relationships. Sam, a technical branch worker with eighteen years of experience on the job, felt aggrieved when he didn't get a raise. When his co-worker tried to make him feel better by pointing out that he really didn't need one because he had four boys of working age, Sam vociferously protested that he needed the raise precisely because "you can't expect [lads] like that to help you out. . . . I have always paid my own expenses and I never will expect them to."[21] Though Sam was relatively well paid, he believed that his expenses justified his demand for increased income. As he told an interviewer, "I have a great many things to which I have to pay money. I'm paying so much a week on AT&T stock. Then I am subscribing to shares of the Building and Loan. I put so much away in the Ready Money Plan and insurance. Then I am also still paying on my home." But he was also convinced that he was worth more than he was paid, considering "the class of work we're doing and the responsibility which goes along with a job like ours." Together this combination of his private needs and his service to the company provided a sense of entitlement to which he expected the company to respond.

Some of Sam's colleagues were able to put these expectations in a larger perspective, melding their private needs for sufficient income to sustain a home with the public interest in their stability as family men and as citizens. During an economic slump, another technical branch worker told an interviewer that he hoped the company would soon return to working regular hours because "a number of us have homes to pay on." He thought it important for a working man to have his own home. Remembering that before he had one, he used to gamble and play pool, he commented, "I think it makes better citizens out of the people because they won't waste so much time on the outside but will spend their time around home, working there and keeping it up."[22]

Like their male co-workers, women workers articulated an enormous interest in all things financial: they mentioned wages more often than men did, though they complained about them somewhat less. And women talked more about the "bogey," or target rate of production, even though men, and women were equally divided as to whether particular rates were set fairly and equally concerned as to whether they were earning enough. Participation in the company's stock-purchase plans and other benefit plans was at least as high among women as men, and perhaps higher. If women appeared to be less interested in working overtime to accumulate money, approximately equal proportions of men and women were willing to work night shifts to earn extra pay.[23]

Family needs tended to govern women's search for income as well as men's. Most women described their interest in work as a function of their capacity to earn as much as they could: when Sarah was asked why she worked at Hawthorne, she told her questioner that she had come from another job she liked better, but "[t]he Western was paying such good wages then I thought I would come out here and try for a job. There are very few places that pay the same money as the Western does to their shop girls."[24] Women believed they deserved jobs because they needed the income and that those who did not require money should give up jobs. While some welcomed the shorter hours mandated by the Depression ("Wish I could go home at 4:00 every day. Even if we only make 70 percent"), most weighed the loss in income on one day against the possibility of being less tired and so making more on another day. "When I go home at 4:00 I can make more on Saturday."[25]

In contrast to their shared perceptions of the importance of the wage, men and women articulated significant differences around the subject of advancement. The men at Hawthorne believed the company owed them a chance to "get ahead" and attached wages firmly to that entitlement. For them, the good company—the company that lived up to its paternalist rhetoric—was one that fulfilled promised opportunities for promotion. Men cited such promises at about three times the rate that women did and agonized about their "chances." They spoke about quitting jobs because "there wasn't much advancement" and complained about "how a fellow has to be here a long time in order to get ahead."[26] "Getting ahead" seemed to be part of the normal expectation of things. Asked if there was any other work that he would like to do, one young, married, male worker who had been with the company only a year responded, "[W]ell yes, I don't know what it is, but a fellow always likes to feel that he is getting ahead and working for something. . . . I always plan on getting ahead and promoting myself and some day I will see to it that I do."[27] Such self-expectations were integrally related to beliefs about how the company would treat them. As one worker put it, "When another job comes along you get rid of the guys that are not good, and the fellow that works hard does a good job, he stays here. That's the way it always is."[28] Another put it this way: "It is human nature to want to keep going on the up and up all the time. The company should . . . always see that a man is given a fair chance to keep rising, going up all the time. His wages should keep increasing too."[29]

The idea that good wages and advancement for men should go hand in hand was taken for granted, and bitterness emerged when for unknown reasons they did not. "What I consider an advancement," explained one male worker, "is when they take a person from one job and put him on another where he can learn more and at the same time make just as much money as he did before, but where a person is taken off of the job paying 45 dollars per week and to be placed on a job paying 25, I consider that a demotion instead of a promotion regardless of how much you are learning."[30] Absent a wage increase, a promotion had little meaning: as one worker put it when he refused a job as a gang boss at a pay cut of twenty cents an hour, he didn't "think it was fair" to ask him to take a cut "so that I could get a better job."[31] Static wages, for a man, could be interpreted as a negative signal about his "chances." One eight-year veteran with the company prefaced his despair about "only making a few dollars a week more than I made when I started to work for the company" with the comment, "I think my chances for advancement are zero minus."

The company's perceived commitment to advancing its own workers constituted what many workers understood to be the core of the paternalist contract. In September 1930, just before Western Electric began to respond to the Depression by cutting down hours and then laying off workers, one veteran assured his interviewer that the company wouldn't "kick the old timers out just because they can hire new men for less money." In the ensuing conversation, the interviewer responded with equal assurances: "You don't have to worry about the company doing anything that isn't fair. The men that are at the head of this company are too broadminded to play a mean little trick on a fellow."[32] Workers seemed to have faith in such assurances, again and again commenting, as one fourteen-year veteran did when he was faced with a wage cut: "I've still got a lot of faith in the company. I think they are going to come through with something that's going to help us out before long."[33]

Lacking the opportunity to move upward, men felt emasculated, and when the company did start to shorten hours and lay off workers, many used the imagery of childhood to express their disillusionment with a company that avowed paternalism and then treated men as children. Dignity required that they be treated as adults, whether that meant the capacity to take a sick day without being questioned or being heard when they complained of company policies.[34] The company that treats all its workers fairly, some believed, should distribute available work rationally, even at the cost of reducing everyone's pay. "I'd spread the work out," responded one Bank Wiring Test Room operator, when asked how he would handle layoffs. "Even if I could only give one hour a day to a man, I'd work it that way rather than lay him off completely."[35] Male workers believed that their employer had an unspoken contract to provide steady, reliable work, with regular increases in pay. When, during the Depression, the company failed to do so, they searched for explanations that relieved them of personal responsibility for failure. Some attributed success to those who had "drag." Others simply accused the company of failing to live up to its bargain with them. In response, men occasionally declared themselves free of the reciprocal manly obligation to marry: "I've seen . . . the troubles they're having and the worries that are continually on their minds because they got married. I got enough to worry about with just myself, so why should I get married?"[36]

For women a different set of standards prevailed. As Martha Banta has graphically put it, women would always be "boys" in the workplace, and even then, they would never be "real boys."[37] Such a stance was not unusual among paternalistic companies. Ford, according to the historian Stephen Meyer, "considered all women, regardless of their family status, as youths."[38] Mary Gilson, one of the early personnel-management counselors, recalls how stubbornly managers and the whole industrial relations field resisted women's promotion to supervisory positions, falling back on negative myths and stereotypes about women's behavior. In southern textile mills, which employed women in large majorities, she lamented that "no woman had a chance to rise to overseership."[39] Lacking a future in work, perceived to be without ambition, and absent the language of entitlement that permeated the attitudes of male workers, working women would remain boys who would never be granted the status of men. That was, in an economic sense, their advantage to managers. Small wonder that whatever hope most ordinary working women had was vested in the amount of the wage rather than in the job itself.

It doesn't take much detective work to ascertain how readily women might have been discouraged. The lack of incentives for women to get somewhere in the world prompted Ida Tarbell, perhaps the most successful female journalist of her time, to undertake a five-part series of articles exploring women's job possibilities in industry. "The number in executive positions has been so few and so scattered that there has been as general a belief that they were not adapted to industrial supervision as there has been that they were not capable of mastering mechanical tasks," Tarbell wrote in the last article of the series.[40] Mary Gilson concurred. Noting the limitations imposed by expectations of marriage and discouraging job possibilities, she commented how "little incentive was furnished to women by a world which spurred men to effort in opening all fields to them." The opposite was true for men, for whom marriage served as an incentive to make more income and to achieve promotions. As one noted, "[A] man gets married, he gets married to work."[41]

Small wonder, then, that when asked, working women at Hawthorne claimed the need for income, not the potential for advancement, as the primary justification for working. Unlike men, women who talked about working themselves up referred to a higher piece rate on an easier job—not to skills garnered. Julia was the fastest and most productive of the RATR test group workers—a young woman who financially supported and kept house for her unemployed father and three brothers and consistently goaded her teammates into ever harder work. She delightedly showed her high paychecks to her married sister, proclaiming, "I'm doing what I'm doing for money. . . . It's a bum making relays. Honest, I have no more ambition to make relays. . . . Oh, no marriage for me. I'm going to keep on making relays." She might have resolved the dilemma by seeking a different kind of job or by anticipating some marginal upward mobility. But Julia's high income (artificially higher than it might otherwise have been because of her involvement in the test room) served as a source of stability and pride, reducing any incentive to find another job that would pay more. Perhaps it was the only job she could imagine that would enable her to support her three unemployed brothers and widowed father.[42]

"Getting ahead" for factory women was more complicated, sometimes severing the positive correlation between income and status that men took as a matter of course. Julia gave up her dreams of secretarial work when she faced the need to earn relatively high wages. Her co-worker, a young woman in the technical branch, plotted her escape into a better job via a secretarial course—without mentioning wages at all. "I feel as though if I can say I'm a secretary and graduate with honors I won't have a hard time getting a job," she told the interviewer.[43] She had her future plotted out: she would work nights to get some experience, then transfer to a better job, perhaps even to one at Western Electric. But to conceive this plan, she believed she had to rule out marriage. She would not marry because she didn't think that she would "ever care to be domesticated." And if she did, she'd "feel humiliated to think I'd married somebody that couldn't take care of me."[44] For Julia and her teammates, savings suggested the possibility of loosening their commitment to work rather than enhancing it. If, like men, they talked repeatedly about how many "shares" they owned, they did so in the context of the incentive this would provide to their boyfriends to marry them. This sensibility contrasts with that of their male co-workers, for whom savings and pensions bred company loyalty.

These subtle differences around the attitudes of men and women towards work and wages served to maintain a broad array of traditions about manliness and womanliness, which workers expected the company to enforce. When Roethlisberger and Dickson argued that workers were motivated by a "logic of sentiments" to describe the "values residing in the interhuman relations of the different groups," they attributed to employees arguments for cherished beliefs around the right to work, seniority, and fairness. The data their researchers collected suggests not only that these concepts mattered but that workers used them to shape and order their daily lives. For the women at Hawthorne, the idea of working in a factory that cared for them evoked deeply embedded principles of justice, rooted in a moral economy of need that was reflected in workplace relationships. Inevitably this was linked to marital status. A young single woman described the tensions between the married and the unmarried:

> [B]elieve me, you have to be mighty careful you don't say anything about the married women. You know what they do? They holler at all of us young girls who are single. Now if you can't come in to work in the morning with a halfway

decent dress, they make fun of you, and if you do come in with a halfway decent dress on, they'll holler, "Where you going to sing tonight? Who's keeping you?" and all such remarks as that. But if you say a word about the married women, say, they'll holler their heads off. I hope to goodness I never get married until I'm able to stay home.[45]

When the Depression-generated scarcity of jobs magnified the idea that a fair distribution of work would sustain families, it sharpened an already tense debate over who possessed the right to work and the company's responsibility to family life. At the same time, it illuminated deeply rooted assumptions about women's secondary status in the workforce. As women's economic independence seemed to threaten the roles of husbands and fathers as providers, its value for insuring full citizenship seemed increasingly marginal in the popular mind. The common opinion at Hawthorne held that "[i]f the wife and mother were not working, the head of the house would of necessity have more steady work, and better pay."[46] Such attitudes delegitimized the rights to work of all women, allowing as exceptions only those who supported themselves or others. For women, occupations did not so much act as markers of citizenship as they served to meet personal and family needs. Every woman now had to prove that her job served that purpose. Among married women, the burden of proof loomed large, for insofar as marriage reduced women's needs to work, it also reduced her claims to it.

Like men, women expected the Hawthorne plant to police the boundaries of the moral economy. They used some of the same measures as men to assess the company's fairness, including length of service, quality of work, and commitment. But for women, need served as the essential marker. They believed the company's obligation to those with families to support should prevail over its demand for efficient work. "I can never forget how good the company was to me," one worker recalled of her early days at Western Electric, "one time when they go slack, all the minors were being laid off, and I explained that my mother was a widow and needed help, and they kept me on."[47] On the other side of the equation, when one of the RATR workers was removed from her job and replaced by a former participant, another operator responded by telling an interviewer: "I feel terrible, just terrible. That girl needs every cent she can make, and Anna [the replacement] has a husband to support her. She don't need the money." Defending her absent colleague, she complained about the company's failure to follow through on her proposal to juggle the workers in light of their relative need: "They didn't pay any attention. They don't care They're the bosses and they don't care. Antoinette needs every cent she gets. Her father is a paralytic and her mother is in the hospital a lot of the time and there are twelve mouths to feed at home."[48]

Marital status served as the easiest marker of financial obligation. Single women distinguished themselves sharply from the married, expressed curiosity about why married women would continue to work, required explanations from those who did, and applauded when the company laid off married women in moments of crisis. The married took pains to justify their positions as a product of family need: "If I could make more money on these jobs," declared one woman, "I'd feel better because then I would see some way of getting out of debt. My home needs to be paid for and my husband being out of work makes it very hard for me."[49] These attitudes suggest a cold calculus about the nature of jobs and claims to them. Nor did women workers believe their feelings unknown to supervisors.

Julia (our speedy RATR worker) repeatedly declared her ambivalence to marriage, insisting, "[I]f you get married you'll have to work anyway." Yet when she heard a rumor that married women were to be laid off, she said to her co-workers (a married woman among them), "Well, that's the best thing in the world I've heard them do. Now these poor single girls can have a chance to hold on to a job."[50] When layoffs began and the rumors proved unfounded, Julia's sense of fair play was outraged. "Why don't they lay off people that don't need the money? They always begin with the poor ones first." Julia had little question as to who the deserving workers were: "The office people—most of them—can afford it better than we can. And the way they go about it—say there are plenty of married women working whose husbands are working too. Do they lay them off? I should say not. We single girls first, and fellows too who are supporting families. Gee, they do things a hell of a way here." Her clear sense of justice led Julia to frustration at company policies that violated what she believed was a shared sense of caring.

Consistent to the last, Julia attacked Western Electric for laying off "a girl ... who had a family to support" and echoed the prevailing feeling that "the company ought to ... lay off all the married women first." She agreed in this respect with many of her co-workers, one of whom told an interviewer that "they should keep them when there is plenty of work but I don't think they should lay off a single girl and keep the married women."[51]

Whether the attitudes of workers like these influenced the company, or whether the continuing depression affirmed an already existing belief system, we might never know. But in October 1930, the Hawthorne works began giving six-month leaves of absence to married women. Thirty-nine-year-old Gertrude, the mother of a fifteen-year-old, was asked to take such a leave along with other women in her department whose husbands were working. She accepted it without much complaining: "It's a good thing as long as everyone gets it except those that really need a job," she told the interviewer.[52] Women who protested enforced leaves on the grounds that the company had made a mistake got a quick apology.[53] And those who were married and insisted on their jobs adopted defensive strategies to save face in front of their co-workers. A young woman who returned to work shortly after she married to help pay for her husband's unexpected and extensive medical bills reported, "I was criticized for coming back to work and I am always getting slams about being money hungry and work to support a man. . . . [I]f they knew my condition they would be more considerate of me."[54]

The attitudes of Hawthorne's workers sustain our sense that approval for women's wage earning increasingly resided in their provider roles, while the idea that work supported an autonomous female citizenship receded from the public mind. Marital status, if not a sure sign of eligibility for work, was certainly its most reliable signal. Married women increased their workforce participation during the Depression, but they did so in the context of an emotional discussion as to whether and how their work would affect the work opportunities of men and of single women as much as their family lives.

For the men and women who worked in the Hawthorne plant, the line between public and private was not nearly as clear as it seems to have been for their employer. For employers, the language of paternalism spoke to familial interests on which workers' concerns centered. By melding the public and private, managers created an arena of shared values and interests and a new threshold for measuring fairness and justice in which workers could believe and around which they could dream. Employers who invaded the private sphere in this way shored up particular visions of manhood and womanhood, each in a different way. By encouraging women but not men to indulge their dreams of leisure and frivolity and leading men but not women to imagine combining satisfying family lives with wage work, they sustained control of the workplace. For employees, the language of paternalism inevitably evoked familial concerns, leading them to hope that the company's attention to their private life could sometimes balance their interest in more efficient production. When that proved false, workers not only reimagined their relationship to the company but altered their life expectations as well. Seduced into believing that the public/private barrier had dissolved or diminished, employees repeatedly discovered their illusions in shards. But for a short time, at least, it mattered less whether managers lived up to their rhetoric than that they shared with the women and men who worked for them an apparently common language.

PART III

Labor and Social Policy

I became interested in the relationship between social policy and wage work for women because protective labor legislation ran like a thread through everything I touched. In the twentieth century, trade unionists offered up labor legislation as an alternative to the organization of women workers; reformers advanced it as a way to protect the family; employers supported it as an efficient mechanism for organizing the labor force; legislators and courts supported it as a way to maintain freedom of contract for men. Next to the welfare laws, protective labor legislation has had perhaps the most visible gendered effect of the many social policies adopted by the twentieth-century state. Its persistence for most of the twentieth century highlights the more obscure effects of other social policies and their uses in maintaining the sexual division of labor.

I turned to these uses first in two exploratory essays. In "The Just Price, the Free Market, and the Value of Women," I have tried to think about how wage policies have related to gender ideology over time. To disrupt the classical notion that wages are a product only of market forces, I explored some of the ways that the market has historically reflected gendered assumptions. "The Debate over Equality for Women in the Workplace" addresses this issue head on by confronting the question of whether gender differences play a role in current debates over what is fair for men and women. Finally, I discuss an important set of laws that regulated the capacity of women to work at night to assess if and how those laws embodied images of motherhood.

By now, however, I was interested in a whole palate of work-related social policies that, it seemed to me, had been influential in sustaining and perpetuating an ordered labor force. Some of these had already been analyzed from a racial perspective. I wanted to see how they might play out if one looked at their development as part of an effort to maintain an existing gender system. "Gendered Interventions" was my first foray into this sphere. From here it was easy to see the connections between social policies and citizenship—a subject that had entered academic discussion among social scientists but that historians had largely ignored. My research led me to look more closely at how particular social policies reflected gendered assumptions and produced gendered results. "Measures for Masculinity" provides an example of this thinking. It uses discussions of a proposed new federal unemployment insurance program in the 1930s to see how trade unionists and legislators imagined it in relationship to their notions of manhood.

10

The Just Price,
the Free Market,
and the Value of Women

For feminist historians, the 1980s might be described in the words with which Charles Dickens introduced his famous novel, *A Tale of Two Cities:* They are the best of times, they are the worst of times. On the one hand, the creative outpouring of historical scholarship on women is a source of energy and of continuing pressure for change. In the absence of a mass political movement, the enormous extension of historical knowledge (of which women's history is the center), if it does nothing else, should ensure that women's orientations are permanently imprinted in the vocabulary of the past. But there is another hand: our sense of purpose seems to have wavered, our direction to have become unclear. The feminist community no longer looks to history as the leading edge of scholarly research. Esoteric forms of literary criticism seem to have moved into that exalted rank. And even within the profession, women's history has lost some of its shine as accusations of partisanship and fears of politicization limit our courage and restrict our vision.

And yet, this is a moment when the voices of historians of women are needed more than ever. Some of the most significant social issues on the political agenda—family life, abortion, reproduction, and a range of issues having to do with economic equality—have a special meaning for women. As these become grist for legislative committees and judicial decisions, lawyers and policy makers increasingly invoke the past. In their hands, the history of women emerges as something other than the product of historians. Women appear historically

This essay is a slightly revised version of the keynote address to the Seventh Berkshire Conference on the History of Women, Wellesley College, June 19, 1987. It is reprinted from *Feminist Studies* 14 (Summer 1988), by permission of the publisher, Feminist Studies, Inc. Thanks to Susan Reverby, Dorothy Helly, and the program committee of the Berkshire Conference for inviting me to deliver the address and to Bert Silverman for sharing ideas and information.

as well as philosophically "other," as a single unified whole, instead of an amalgam of diverse experience.

A few examples will illuminate the issue. Feminist lawyers have disagreed sharply about whether to struggle for special treatment for women in the workforce or to opt for equal treatment with men. In 1986 and 1987, the argument focused on pregnancy disability leaves. In the case of *California Federal Savings and Loan Association v. Mark Guerra et al.,* (commonly known as the CalFed case), the U.S. Supreme Court upheld a state law that provided such leaves for women without providing comparable time off for disabled men. Feminists, who came down on both sides, agreed in repudiating protective labor legislation that "classified men and women based on stereotypical notions of their sex roles." But they differed vigorously on the message of the past. One side drew a parallel between pregnancy disability legislation and the discredited protective laws, arguing that special treatment for women had distorted the contours of the labor force, encouraging employers to discriminate against women and contributing to occupational segregation in the labor market. Opposing lawyers insisted that a law that provided pregnancy leaves differed from earlier legislation in that it focused on "how women's unique reproductive role affects them in the workplace." Pregnancy disability laws would not repeat the history of discrimination, this group suggested, but would instead enhance the possibility of achieving equality for women.[1]

In the 1987 decision, the Supreme Court sustained the affirmative action plan of Santa Clara County, California. The plan included gender among the qualifications an employer could consider in assessing candidates for promotion and hiring. The majority affirmation of this moderate plan evoked a blistering dissent from Justice Antonin Scalia, who called attention to the central issue underlying such cases: "It is a traditionally segregated job category," he noted of the road dispatcher's job in question, "*not* in the Weber sense, but in the sense that, because of long-standing social attitudes, it has not been regarded *by women themselves* as desirable work."[2] Scalia followed this up with his own historical commentary: "There are, of course, those who believe that the social attitudes which cause women themselves to avoid certain jobs and to favor others are as nefarious as conscious, exclusionary discrimination. Whether or not that is so . . . the two phenomena are certainly distinct." With all due respect to Justice Scalia, his description of these "two phenomena" reflects a historical consciousness to which many of us might object. Are conscious discrimination and social attitudes so easily separated? We once called this the difference between long-range and immediate causes.

A third example comes from an interview on comparable worth that appeared in *New Perspectives,* a magazine published by the U.S. Civil Rights Commission. In the last several years, the commission has been an outspoken opponent of most forms of affirmative action and of all forms of comparable worth. "We do not have massive evidence that there was wage discrimination against women over the past one hundred years," commented the interviewer, an editor of the magazine. "So why should we now pass legislation or have a court make a ruling that assumes that the difference between men and women is due to discrimination?"[3] Does anyone dispute the fact that invidious distinctions between women and men are deeply rooted in the history of women's work? What "massive evidence" would satisfy this interviewer?

These examples illustrate how public or popular conceptions of the past can construct the future. They remind us that we have a responsibility as scholars to speak to public issues—to shape the visible perception of a past whose contours we have so fundamentally altered. They suggest that history, as a way of thinking, speaks to contemporary issues—whether we, as individuals, will it or not—and therefore plays a crucial role in forming consciousness. A concern with contemporary issues enhances our capacity to think about the theoretical implications of the concrete empirical data in which we are immersed. Attention to historical reality encourages public policy makers to consider context, particularity, and diversity in the formulation of issues. A reciprocal relationship between history and public policy thus strengthens both areas, each on its own terms. And it offers us as historians of women a way of enhancing women's understanding of our traditions.

I want to illustrate how this dialogue might work by looking at one of the burning issues of the day, pay equity or comparable worth. A major tenet of the feminist demand for equality is equity or fairness or justice. The demand underlines affirmative action programs and equal pay slogans. But what is equity in the job market? Like surrogate motherhood, homework, and pregnancy disability leaves, the pay equity strategy evokes contrary responses among feminists as well as antifeminists. Antifeminists suggest that it could increase labor conflict, worsen America's international competitive posture, and encourage a destructive female independence that will finally destroy the patriarchal family. Feminists who dismiss these arguments worry that it might nevertheless produce a host of evils, including ghettoization in segregated occupations, economic inflation, expanded female unemployment, and increased female welfare dependency.

But comparable worth is clearly on the nation's political agenda. More than twenty states have some legislation that favors it, the 1984 Democratic party platform supported it, and the AFL-CIO and several of its constituent unions have made it a priority issue. Minnesota has already implemented it for state jobs. Washington is well on the way to doing so. Yet proponents and opponents of comparable worth differ sharply as to its justice or fairness.

Proponents suggest that the need for equity is self-evident. As one study observed, "[T]he work women do is paid less, and the more an occupation is dominated by women, the less it pays." That, they say, is manifestly unfair. But they disagree as to the basis for paying women more. Some argue that "jobs that are equal in value to the organization ought to be equally compensated whether or not the work content is similar."[4] Others suggest that the inequity resides in the market's failure to pay women a fair return on the human capital they have invested in the job.[5] Each calls on a different perception of history to solve two seemingly intractable historical problems facing women who earn wages—persistent occupational segregation and the stubborn wage gap between female and male workers. On the theory that low wages inhere in the job, which is itself sex-typed, advocates of comparable worth posit two central assumptions: first, that the free market has not worked for women, and second, that every job has an inherent value that can be compared with that of other jobs. Value, according to proponents of comparable worth, can be measured by such factors as the skill, effort, responsibility, training, and working conditions that are its requisites.

Critics ridicule the notion that value inheres in jobs. The market, they suggest—the demand for labor and the available supply—determines the wage paid. If women are not paid well, it is because they have made bad choices. And if these choices are historically conditioned, why should employers be held responsible? The language they use indicates something of the fear the idea evokes. Phrases like "the looniest idea since loony tunes" and "the feminist road to socialism" are the catchwords of the day.[6]

The historian hears these arguments impatiently, for whatever the abstract models preferred by economists, the historical record introduces the balm of experience. The market, as it functions in the daily lives of people, is not independent of the values and customs of those who participate in it. Justice, equity, and fairness have not been its natural outcomes. Rather, market outcomes have been tempered by customary notions of justice or fairness. The specific forms these take have been the object of struggle. And just as ideas of fairness influence our response to the market, so, too, do they influence how the market works.

Such notions go back to the earliest days of commerce. In the eleventh century, church authorities developed widely accepted notions of "just price" to resist an incipient market. Trying to avoid the inevitable disruption of traditional relationships that would occur if scarce labor were able (by means of restricting supply) to raise wages above those appropriate for its station, church authorities and educators who interpreted doctrine argued for an objective assessment of value. Measured by fair exchange or an equivalence of labor, value and therefore price inhered in every article of commerce and in the wage of every worker. Trade, in the minds of Thomas Aquinas and Albertus Magnus, might be a necessary evil, but it should be engaged in within the "customary estimate." Departure from that norm infringed on religious and moral codes.

From the beginning, the notion of just price embodied a subjective judgment. Because an important component of the wage and the price of the commodity to be sold was determined by the extent of the laborer's needs, just price rested on medieval conceptions of social hierarchy. "It corresponded," in the words of one economic historian, "to a reasonable charge that would enable the producer to support his family on a scale suitable to his station in life."[7] Economic historians still debate the extent to which that correspondence emerged from the "common estimate" or market value of an object. But everyone agrees that a complex array of exchange factors mingled with a sense of propriety to form the final price. Thus, in one sense, just price was a subterfuge that enabled public authority to regulate an emerging market.

Whatever the weaknesses of just-price theory and its rootedness in the moral concerns of the church, it passed down a continuing presumption that nonmarket notions have a place in the valuation of objects or wage rates. In a period of labor shortages, notions of just price restricted the wages of labor and prevented skilled workers from banding together in what were labeled "conspiracies." When labor shortages gave way to surpluses, and the consensual wage that had been used to keep wages down began to decline, artisans and laborers (sometimes organized in guilds) resorted to just-price theory to maintain a floor under wages. And as just price began to break down in the fifteenth century when the market expanded, notions that the wage ought to reflect some sense of need, rather than merely supply, persisted. Its components are visible in the market system that emerged in the fifteenth century and reached full flower by the nineteenth. The customary wage, the wage demanded by the craftsperson or laborer, reflected a social sense of how a worker should live, as well as of the amount of labor that entered into the product for sale. We have not yet abandoned these notions. Changing ideas of fairness are implicit in our evaluation of the market and influence the way we impose taxes and otherwise regulate its outcomes.

In the free market, theoretically, demand and supply determine price. But in practice, wage theorists recognize a variety of what the Harvard professor and former secretary of labor John Dunlop has called "exterior" factors in determining the wage.[8] These exterior factors are influences on the labor market that emerge from nonmarket factors like union contracts, seniority systems, and a sense of equity. Contemporary wage theorists have elaborate ways of describing how the market is restricted by these historical tendencies. Arthur M. Ross argues that wages move in "orbits of coercive comparison." This is simply another way of saying that traditional market forces do not have "compelling significance" in the determination of wages.[9] Rather, wages are influenced by the force of ideas about justice and equity and the power of organizations and individuals to sustain them. In this widely accepted model, workers compare their wages to those of other workers; pride and dignity prevent them from settling for less than what their peers are getting. Other economists talk about "job clusters": firefighters insist on parity with police; steelworkers strike to maintain equivalent wages nationwide, although, in fact, the market could easily pay less in some areas of the country. All these ideas and the social sensibilities that sustain them limit or modify market wages.

According to Ross, workers use comparisons to establish the dividing line between a "square deal and a raw deal." In a competitive market, where most workers do not leave jobs for wages but are promoted from within and rely on the job for security, a worker might not earn what he would like, but as Ross puts it, "[H]e wants what is coming to him . . . [it is] . . . an affront to his dignity and a threat to his prestige when he receives less than another worker with whom he can *legitimately* be compared."[10] I leave hanging for the moment the gendered content of "legitimately."

If wages reflect the relationship between some workers and others, they also tell us something about the relation between the craftsperson and the object produced, between the laborer and the employer, and among employers as well. Autoworkers, for example, agree that productivity and profits are appropriate factors to consider when determining the wage. They demand a share in the distribution of profits in good years and may reluctantly accept cutbacks in bad ones. Similarly, employers refuse wage increases that would raise the standard in an industry, even when their own profits make such raises possible. "Wage rates," as the economist Michael J. Piore suggests, "perform certain basic social and institutional functions. They define relationships between labor and management, between one group of workers and another," and they define "the place of individuals relative to one another in the work community, in the neighborhood, and in the family."[11]

Because wages function, like the labor market itself, to structure relationships, comparable worth provides a parallel rather than a substitute strategy for achieving equity. Some feminists criticize comparable worth on the grounds that it will ghettoize women. The wage, they suggest, is a function of jobs held, and the proper remedy for women who want equal wages is to seek access to traditionally male jobs where the pay is better. After all, the argument goes, affirmative action legislation, now in place, will open up the market to women's labor and eliminate the main cause of the wage gap: occupational segregation. The Equal Pay Act of 1963 will then insure that women are treated equally. Fighting for affirmative action increases women's admission to male bastions and, by encouraging them to act on male conceptions of the market, will secure for them permanent access to the best jobs.

But, like the wage, the labor market is itself a regulating device, the product of a long history of social relationships heavily influenced by traditional conceptions of gender roles. Although abstract market models indicate that people *choose* jobs, the historical record suggests that occupational segregation has been the product of deeply ingrained attitudes. What appears to be a "natural" consequence of women's social roles has to be measured against the specific shape of occupational segregation at a given historical moment. Ideas about women "following" jobs into the marketplace or choosing jobs that fill nurturing roles or preferring to satisfy some abstract social ethic rather than to make money are all ways of rationalizing nonmarket behavior by means of some other notion of equity. These and other specific social customs help legitimate the continuing and changing shape of the labor market. But they are and have been the frequent subject of negotiation and challenge by women. The historian who explores the workings of the labor market and reads complaints about its rigidities in particular times and places learns how segmentation functioned at certain moments and contributes to understanding the way in which gender roles have helped to construct the market as well.

Notions of craft and brotherhood, of masculinity and femininity, are embedded in and confirmed by the labor market, raising questions as to the definition of justice embodied in a "free labor market" in which inclusion and exclusion are a function of many things, including sex. Even a cursory glance at the rationalizations employers and managers have used to regulate women's participation leaves no doubt that the labor market has been socially, not abstractly, constructed. Thus, particular notions of equity are expressed by the London guilds that declared in the fourteenth century that "no man of the trade should set any woman to work other than his wife and daughter."[12] Medieval injunctions are echoed by those of many trade unions and male workplaces in our own time. As late as the 1960s and 1970s, employers explained why they had no women in certain jobs by calling upon customary ideas. "The nature of the work [did] not lend itself to employment in production of either women or the handicapped," said one wire manufacturer in 1973. And a pharmaceutical manufacturer told an interviewer in 1968 that the company would hire women in clerical occupations and elsewhere where the physical requirements of the task involved do not preclude it.[13] Such social attitudes continue to serve as guides to what is equitable in the labor market. A 1987 cover story in *Business Week* notes that women "are being promoted because they bring new management styles to the corporation." According to the article, experts report "that female personality traits such as an ability to build consensus and encourage participation are in demand today. . . . Women typically show more warmth and concern about human relationships and human sensitivities."[14] And when such qualities go out of fashion, will women be demoted?

We begin now to see why the idea of comparable worth is so threatening. Just-price theory imbued the market with a sense of equity that serves as a compelling (if sometimes unpredictable) influence on it. But whose sense of equity? An important element of equity, itself historically rooted, is a subjective evaluation of gender roles. A customary wage—one that reflects a social sense of how women and men should and do live—is partially an effort to preserve the status quo. Because the customary wage was built on a sense of the family as economic unit, it incorporated and passed down prevailing conceptions of gender. Because it was tied to continuing social hierarchy and women's restricted place, it affirmed women's secondary position. Thus, "a woman's wage" has long been a term of opprobrium among men. A male worker could not legitimately be compared with a female worker without violating his sense of dignity and justice. Nor did the sense of justice of most female workers historically require such comparisons.

But times have changed, and along with them, our conceptions of justice are altering. As Edward H. Carr put it, abstractions "are indispensable categories of thought but they are devoid of meaning or application till specific content is put into them." Like checks drawn on a bank, "the printed part consists of abstract words like liberty and equality, justice and democracy . . . valueless until we fill in the other part, which states how much liberty we propose to allocate to whom, whom we recognize as our equals and up to what amount. The way we fill in the cheque from time to time is a matter of history."[15] Many (but never all) women in the past accepted a model of equity in the labor market based on the ideology of the patriarchal family. Most arguments for female equality derived from male conceptions of justice and were debates about access, not about new rules. New material conditions have shifted the content of equity from a demand for equality with men to a challenge to male structures. The altered terms of the debate no longer ask how women can achieve equality in a predominantly male work world so much as how to revalue the world of work and workers in a way that incorporates female self-interest. Rooted not in the moral economy of the male but in the traditions, customs, and practices of women, the idea of comparable worth evokes a history that assesses the changing sense of right or dignity on which people will act.

That sense emerges from a historical context that alters definitions of what people are willng to accept. Disruptive conditions of early industrialization framed nineteenth-century arguments for a male wage sufficient to keep wives out of the workforce. Early twentieth-century battles for a wage adequate to sustain women who were not secondary earners reflected a mature industrial economy in which women had essential but apparently temporary roles as wage laborers. In the 1920s, the U.S. Women's Bureau fought bitterly to defend protective labor legislation—a battle rooted in historically conditioned understandings of women's primary task as childbearers and child rearers. By the mid-twentieth century, campaigns for equal pay for equal work reflected a shift in notions of equity rooted in the job to be performed rather than in an abstract conception of women's roles. Within the last ten years, the increasing pauperization of women and children in the United States has become a major incentive to redistribute income and thus an important argument for comparable worth. The campaign for pay equity reflects this new historical stage; because both women and men are recognized providers, the search for equity now includes a demand that jobs be evaluated on their own terms. Changing family structures have clearly played a political part in encouraging a revaluation of women's economic roles. The emergence of the argument is itself an indication that the conception of justice that underlined the legitimacy of a woman's wage is now called into question.

Like other redefinitions of equity, the consequences of this one are not self-evident. Thus, we argue over whether struggles for the family wage in the nineteenth century reflected women's interests in stable family life or men's desire to push women out of the labor market, over whether the capacity of women to earn wages yielded independence and autonomy or served to extend family obligations. Each stage reflects a social transformation that delegitimized certain customary roles and replaced them with others and from which some women benefited while others did not. And so it is with the struggle for pay equity for women. We can and must debate the way it will affect particular groups of women within a context that observes the social transformation of which the demand is a part.

Comparable worth now appears as part of a long political process within which women have tried to achieve some sense of equity and justice as it is defined in their historical period. It is so strongly resisted, in part, because a large and potentially powerful group of wage earners, in questioning the conception of the free market, challenges its ideological roots as well. And because it raises to consciousness the issue of equity on which the market rests, comparable worth challenges the legitimacy of gender lines. It purports to delegitimize one element of the market pattern—namely, sex. The end result would be to equate female and male workers; to threaten a male worker's sense of self, pride, and masculinity; and to challenge the authority of basic institutions that touch all aspects of social and political life. The federal district court that rejected the request of Denver nurses that they be paid as much as the city's tree trimmers caught the problem exactly. Such a change, the court commented, in a much-quoted decision, "'was pregnant with the possibility of disrupting the entire economic system of the United States.'"[16]

The point is that this might be true: In refusing to sanction gender distinctions, comparable worth raises a long line of earlier challenges to a new level.

The historical context reveals pay equity to be an issue of the gendered definition of justice and of the way justice manifests itself in the market. Seen from that perspective, comparable worth calls for nothing less than the revaluation of women. Its strength lies in its potential for acting upon female traditions, for it assumes that women have a right to pursue traditional roles and to achieve equity in that pursuit. Thus, it sustains those presumed qualities of womanhood—nurturance, community, and relational abilities—that are likely to have been products of women's cultural and social roles and that have, as a result, been traditionally devalued by the job market.

But comparable worth poses one other crucial challenge to historians. Because it rests on a redefinition of equity, which is historically specific, it confronts us with definitions of difference that are rooted in historical experience. The debate over comparable worth opens the question of what difference has meant to various groups of women and how it has manifested itself. The task is crucial to understanding changing forms of justice. If we allow abstract descriptions of "woman" and abstract notions of "woman's culture" to govern our interpretations of the past, we provide what Carr called a blank check. We offer empty categories that invite ideological uses of the past. We have seen (in the case of *EEOC vs. Sears Roebuck and Co.*) the consequences that this blank check can have in arguments that the nurturing and biological roles of all women preclude working women and needy women from seeking rewards in the workforce, discourage them from investing in human capital, and lead them to devote more time and attention to families.[17]

These arguments, which are partly sustained by appeals to recent philosophy and psychology of sex differences, and which rest on conceptions of the universal female, are negated by historical experience. It is not that most women have not performed traditional tasks but that the history of women's actual workforce roles demonstrates a far more complex set of struggles by which different women at different times and places have tried to find their own directions in their own ways. In the United States, immigrant women, educated women, black women, poor women, and married and unmarried women have each in their own ways come to locate their places within the shifting bounds of historical possibility.

Notions of universal womanhood blind us to the reciprocally confirming relationship of the workforce and gendered ideas of social role. Judith Long Laws talks about the labor market providing information that conditions aspiration and channels people's expectations along realistic paths.[18] The historical record reveals how readily information changes in wars and depressions, how selectively it is presented to poor women as opposed to those who are well off, how much more limited it is for women of color than for white women. It demonstrates that difference is not a universal category but a social specific. And it reveals that how women handle differences can vary dramatically with historical circumstance. Carole Turbin and Mary Blewett, among other scholars, offer evidence of "nondichotomous" differences.[19] They suggest that women can be different in terms of life patterns and family commitments and yet struggle in the workforce like men and with them.

We are led to two conclusions. First, although social and cultural differences between women and men surely exist, their abstract expression is less instructive than clear-eyed analysis of it in historical context. Second, such analysis should not be allowed to obscure differences among women and the historically specific ways in which they manifest themselves and serve as sources of tension and change. The poet Audre Lorde put it this way: difference, she argued, "must not be merely tolerated, but seen as a fund of necessary polarities between which our creativity can spark like a dialectic."[20]

In the labor market, difference provides the core of struggle. It is entrenched in the cultural symbolism of jobs. Outdoor, heavy, and skilled work is associated with pay/provider roles, and dexterity and compassion are tied to poor pay and secondary jobs. Difference is reflected in the struggle of women and men to maintain dependent as well as independent relationships. The working-class husband tells an interviewer that his wife "doesn't know how to be a real wife, you know, feminine and really womanly. . . . She doesn't know how to give respect because she's too independent. She feels that she's a working woman and she puts in almost as many hours as I do and brings home a pay check, so there's no one person above the other. She doesn't want there to be a king in this household."[21] And here he reveals something about his expectations of traditional roles that we need to hear. The women who opposed the Equal Rights Amendment because they feared giving up alimony are reluctant to abandon their conceptions of equity for new and unknown forms. But these are not universal statements. They are pieces of a historical struggle we need to understand. They tell us something about the distribution of rewards in a society and about the role that sexual constraints play in it, about the structure of power and about their gendered meanings. They therefore tell us something about the reciprocal relationship between sexuality and social power.

In negating individual and particular experience, abstract arguments from difference ride roughshod over the aspirations and motivations of most women. The undifferentiated "woman" becomes a reified object instead of a social category subject to analysis, an abstraction rather than an actor in the historical enterprise. This is not an argument against theory or against conceptualizing. Rather, it is a plea that our theories be conditioned by the experiences of real actors—an expression of concern that the "universal female" not become a device to negate the possibility of equity and inadvertently open the door to perpetual inequality.

We are brought full circle. History offers a picture of wage relations that are not systemic but constructed and processual—a picture from which most women were once excluded and into which they are now drawn. Like the labor market itself, the wage relation is constructed out of the subjective experience and rests ultimately on the legitimacy of historically specific notions of gender "difference." The historical record puts teeth into arguments for pay equity. As part of a changing battle for a changing definition of justice, its political parameters become comprehensible, and the meaning of the argument becomes more apparent.

Comparable worth illustrates how we construct consciousness out of historical experience. And it illustrates as well how the historian who explores the past in dialogue with the present can develop a richer understanding of the past. The struggle of women to redefine concepts like justice, liberty, and power, which reflect a vision of the future, pushes us to explore the past from which such ideas emerged. Because ideas don't come from thin air, our attempts to discover how they took shape—how diverse groups appropriated, shaped, and rejected them—enriches our understanding of the historical process and places content into what is otherwise a blank check or an empty box.

The reverse is also true. Without a history, public policy follows the paths of social myth. By entering the debate, we historians of women have in our hands the possibility of shaping the future. Without a history, our argument that women have a right to paid work can be turned into an excuse to push women with small children to take poorly paid, meaningless jobs. Without a history, our search for safe and accessible methods of birth control can be (and has been) translated into forced sterilization for the most vulnerable among us. Without a history, it is plausible for policy makers, legislatures, New Right groups, and ordinary women to interpret the problems women encounter in doing paid jobs as products of personal "choices" rather than as social issues. Without a history, employed women are asked to find solutions to what are called their own personal problems in their own ways.

An influential pair of sociologists demonstrated the consequences of an obligingly absent historical consciousness this way: when "family obligations come to be perceived as obstacles to self-realization in [women's] careers, individual women will have to decide on their priorities. Our own hope is that many will come to understand that life is more than a career and that this 'more' is above all to be found in the family. But, however individual women decide, they should not expect public policy to underwrite and subsidize their life plans."[22] To which the historian of women, politely eschewing the temptation to tackle the false historical assumptions contained in the statement, responds that as long as policy makers can invent a history that ignores the rich diversity of women's experiences, our task will not be completed.

11

The Debate over
Equality for Women
in the Workplace:
Recognizing Differences

This essay investigates women's continuing position in relatively disadvantaged places in the labor force. It argues that the failure of earlier strategies to alter this position derives in part from our failure to come to terms with whether in fact men and women are "different." It seeks to explore how dominant perceptions about women's nature have conditioned past and present strategies. Finally, it argues that for a variety of historical reasons, a strategy that accepts women as different might enhance the speed with which they can move toward equality.

What constitutes a "special" group in the workforce? Why is it that after all these years of striving for equality, we still refer to women workers as "special"? The familiar statistics belie any such categorization: 60 percent of all women work for a living, more than 70 percent of them full-time. Whereas the proportion of white women working for wages has expanded recently, black women have worked at these rates for most of the twentieth century. Currently almost half (47 percent) of the workforce is female. And women have demonstrated that they no longer fit the old stereotypes. Relatively fewer women than in the past quit when they have babies; their absenteeism and turnover rates are no higher than those of men holding the same kinds of jobs; and they are not more temperamental on the job.

What makes this large group of workers "special"? What separates them from male workers? What enables most of us without a second thought to cast them into an apologetic place in relation to work? This essay argues that wom-

An earlier version of this essay was delivered at the Eleanor Roosevelt Centennial Conference, Vassar College, October 15, 1984. My thanks to Louise Tilly and Marilyn Blatt Young for suggestions as to revisions. It was first published in *Women and Work: An Annual Review,* vol. 1, ed. Laurie Larwood, Ann H. Stromberg, and Barbara A. Gutek (Beverly Hills, Calif.: Sage Publications, 1975).

en's continuing "special" position derives in part from our historical failure to come to terms with whether in fact women are different from men. It seeks to explore how dominant perceptions about women's nature have conditioned past and present strategies for achieving equality in the labor force. Finally, it argues that for a variety of historical reasons, a strategy that accepts women as different might enhance the speed with which they can move towards equality.

At the core of the consensus that has shaped women's labor-market position is the family. To most historians it seemed self-evident that women's relationship to their families accounted for their unique labor-force position. Whatever our own predilections and lifestyles, historians of women understood that most women bore children, were responsible at some level for rearing them, and that they perpetuated the value systems of their communities in the home. Beyond this, the sheer physical demands of these tasks, as well as the special abilities developed to do them well, mitigated against successful labor-force roles. Given the realities of work in the home and the nurturing and self-sacrificing qualities most people believed were required to sustain a household, women could not be expected to perform effectively in the labor force. For when they entered it, they brought with them not the competitive and achievement-oriented attitudes required for success in that sphere but the more cooperative and relational spirit said to be cultivated in the home.[1] The attribution of family-related goals and norms to women thus constituted problematic, or even negative, features in the labor force.

To say that women have historically remained a "special" group, then, is to say that in the past, by and large, they did not act like male workers, choose the same responsibilities, make the same commitments, compete as effectively, or expect the same rewards. In the words of one recent historian of women and the family, "Women are still the primary child rearers, even when they work, and the purpose of their work in the main is to support and advance the family, not to realize themselves as individuals."[2] If this can be said of men also, an important distinction remains. The popular mind saw women as primarily responsible for the family's emotional and physical well-being—a function that conflicted with that of success in the workplace. For men, in contrast, responsibility for the family's financial needs fostered a search for more options in the labor force, and this, in turn, enhanced the possibility of individual fulfillment.

Economists have tended to rely on some notion of women's social place to explain their currently disadvantaged places in the labor force. Traditional or neoclassical economists argue that women's decisions as to when and how to enter wage work are based on their present or anticipated responsibilities for household care and child rearing. They argue further that investment in human capital determines how far and how quickly workers will be upwardly mobile and conclude that women occupy low-paying jobs because their family orientations and responsibilities discourage them from investing in their own skills or in human capital. And those who resort to the notion that employers simply have a "taste for discrimination" believe that, rightly or wrongly, people in charge of hiring attribute certain qualities to women that have emerged from their natural or culturally assigned roles.

The more radical perspective of labor-market segmentation theory seems to suggest at first that inequality is a function of the job and not the home. And yet segmentation theorists argue that income and rewards (especially in the lower primary sector) come largely from job training and socialization. According to Michael Piore, "[A] good deal of what is required to perform effectively on the job and is involved in the improvement of productivity during the 'training' period is the understanding of the norms of the group and of the requirements of the various roles which are played within it and conformity to the generalized norms and to the specialized requirements of the particular role or roles to which one is assigned."[3] But if learning on the job is a process in which custom and skill are handed down, it is also one that reinforces old roles: the more skilled teach the newcomers, and men tend to resist learning from women. Female workers cannot therefore be advanced beyond the point at which they are accepted by co-workers. The traditional values of the home are reinforced, in this schema, by the demands of production.

For feminists attempting to develop a theory of labor-force patterns that explains women's historically disadvantaged position and offers some hope for future equality, the notion that women derive their identity, self-esteem, and workplace personas primarily in families has constituted a central and precarious dilemma. Short of challenging the structure of work itself, and by implication the individualistic nature of work in the United States, it places women in the awkward position of either defending or rejecting the family in order to enter work on an equal footing with men. Some have insisted that the search for equality requires women to abandon traditional notions in regard to their family roles and to adopt the competitive and achievement-oriented hierarchy of the work sphere.[4] But, assuming that work lives remain demanding, that path also requires women to give up many of the comforting values associated with home and child care. Resistance to this direction is familiar, visible, for example, in the current concern for the family and its value. Troubling questions about the nature and scope of parenting remain even for those of us who accept these new workforce roles.

An alternative is to adopt what the philosopher Iris Young calls a "gynocentric" or woman-centered view of feminism—a view that accepts women's differences from men and argues that women bring to the workplace something of their traditional, socially and culturally inculcated behavior patterns.[5] This position, however, seems to return women to the beliefs of an earlier period when acknowledging family roles placed them in the position of perpetual outsiders in a labor force that bowed to their special needs only under legislative duress. It carries with it the danger that insisting on recognition of such qualities as cooperation or sharing above competition, and on such legitimate needs as child care, flexitime, extended parental leave, personal days, and so on, assigns to women the sometimes unspoken designation of "special," with all of its potentially discriminatory consequences. Either way, equality for women becomes a distant goal.

Can women move towards equality without either negating or reifying family roles? One way, of course, is to revalue these roles. If men nurtured others and sustained households, these roles would no longer be negative attributes in the workforce but simply part of the baggage all workers brought with them to the workplace. There would then be a greater likelihood that jobs would alter to accommodate family roles. Is this plausible? I want to suggest that it becomes more likely if we rethink social policy in regard to women wage earners anew, recognizing some of the lessons of history.

The apparent lesson of the past was that paying attention to the characteristics of one group of workers can overemphasize their special needs and result in discrimination. A second and now overlooked lesson is that ignoring difference tends to perpetuate existing inequalities. The bridge between these two lessons first conceptualizes difference as a broadly social phenomenon—one that touches all workers at some point—and, based on this understanding, proposes a pluralistic solution to broadly address difference. Second, it insists on sharing some of the social costs of family and child rearing that historically have been borne by women and have made them "special." We can more easily understand how such a strategy might work if we look back at the history, the assumptions, and the legacies of an earlier search for equality.

We must begin, if only briefly, with a sympathetic understanding of the plight of most working women in the late nineteenth and early twentieth centuries. Limited by widely accepted practice to relatively few occupations and paid little because it was assumed that they had homes in which husbands or fathers were the primary breadwinners, women's real or imagined attachment to home and family led to their widespread abuse as workers. While wage-earning women struggled to organize to combat the resulting problems of unemployment, overwork, malnutrition, and inadequate care for children, reformers and feminists developed two alternative and sometimes competing theories to inform social policy.

The first theory, which, following Iris Young, I have labeled "humanist," traces its roots back to the early campaigns for women's rights and beyond. It derives from the belief that by virtue of their common humanity with men, women are entitled to all the same rights and privileges. They share with men, the theory argues, a set of human rights that transcends biological/gender differences.[6] This tradition spawned Alice Paul's militant battle for suffrage in the early twentieth century and continued into the National Women's party in the 1920s. Governed by a belief that women are more like men than different from them, members of the National Women's party believed that dropping barriers to work for women would yield eventual workforce equality. They shared with other groups the slogan, "Give a woman a man's chance—industrially." And they sponsored the first Equal Rights Amendment (ERA), introduced into Congress in 1923. Its friends called it the Lucy Stone amendment after the nineteenth-century women's rights advocate, and its enemies labeled it simply the "blanket amendment" because, they said, it covered such an enormous variety of sins. The key phrase of that first ERA stated simply, "Men and women should have equal rights throughout the United States and every place subject to its jurisdiction."[7] The language has changed since then, but the assumption that human rights transcend any biological difference remains much the same. Current arguments from this humanist feminism assert women's capacity to participate in the workforce as equals, demanding only that barriers to fair competition be dropped.

In sharp contrast, the second or "women-centered" position emerged from the belief that women are inherently different from men. In the nineteenth century, such differences were commonly seen as spiritual or moral and, in the interpretation of today's historians, provided women with the strength and influence from which they could look after community welfare.[8] Doing good works, an extension of women's duty to guard national virtue, became a springboard for women's civic clubs and charitable and welfare acts, as well as for legislative lobbying and municipal reform. The same kind of argument— that women have special insights and special needs whose representation in the polity would uplift public debate—is widely credited for convincing a largely male electorate to give women the vote in 1919.

The goal of this group of women's rights advocates was not so much equality as a place in the public sphere for their own form of moral influence. Their position achieved public support partly because it did not explicitly violate commonly held views of men's and women's separate spheres and partly because it seemed to offer some moderate and sensible solutions to the social and economic problems produced by women's increasing wage-earning roles. But a position that contained the potential for obtaining equity for women in the political sphere proved to be more constraining when it came to economic issues. Those who believed in women's special attachment to the home and their more refined spiritual sensibilities deplored the idea of paid work for women as depriving the home of their guidance.

Applied to the workplace, difference arguments insisted that women required special protection. Their natural sensibilities, their greater delicacy, as well as the morality and spirituality they are destined to uphold were incompatible with the coarseness and competitiveness of the marketplace. And more concretely, excessive and poorly paid work might lead to fatigue, ill health, inadequate housekeeping, and neglected children. Faced with the need to work like men, so the argument went, women would be crushed, their capacity for uplift drained, their virtue tempted, and their bodies so weakened as to incapacitate them for healthy future motherhood. This argument, supported by social and scientific findings and researched by Josephine Goldmark of the National Consumers League, was incorporated in the 1908 Brandeis brief. It persuaded the U.S. Supreme Court to sanction special labor legislation for female workers on the grounds that the state has a legitimate interest in protecting the mothers of the race. The principle adopted mirrored the Supreme Court's rationale for denying protection to male workers. The Court would not sanction labor legislation that protected workers per se, but it could and did sustain laws that regulated working conditions for those whose safety or good health could be construed as in the public interest.[9] In the case of women, the public or state interest involved what the Court understood as a permanent or biological difference—women's childbearing capacity and concomitant child-rearing function.

Given the Court's repeated and consistent refusals to sustain labor legislation on other grounds, most female activists, working- and middle-class alike, accepted this difference argument and agreed that women ought to constitute a special group or "class" in the workforce. They took this position, as one proponent argued, not "because we want to get anything for women which we do not desire for men, but since protective legislation for men has been declared unconstitutional, the best means of aiding both men and women is to secure laws for women."[10]

The legislation that emerged from this widely shared understanding took a variety of forms. It limited the hours per day and days per week during which women could work, regulated night work, prohibited women from lifting heavy weights, and outlawed their employment in certain jobs altogether. Despite the attempts of fifteen states to establish minimum wages for women or to create a minimum-wage commission, protagonists of special legislation never succeeded in compensating for reduced hours through an adequate floor under women's wages. Efforts to do so were effectively stymied until the New Deal by a 1923 Supreme Court decision that invalidated a Washington, D.C., minimum-wage law for women, calling it a "wage-fixing law, pure and simple."

Most historians now agree that, whatever the short-term benefits, the consequences of protective labor legislation were in the long run negative for women, rigidifying separate niches in the labor market and depriving women of opportunities they might otherwise have had. Reading back into the past, they argue that the critical mistake of early social feminists was to accept, as the basis of legislation, the assumption that women's workforce roles rested on their biological differences from men.[11] But it is important to remember that in the 1910s and early 1920s, hard-fought battles for special legislation were treated as important victories by wage-earning women and reformers alike. So widely accepted was the notion that women occupied a separate sphere that the idea that they could win protection for their differences seemed like triumph indeed. And in the same years, other groups, from railroad workers to government employees, eagerly sought protected status. Advocates of protection urged the few working women who suffered from new laws to sacrifice their own interests to what the Women's Bureau concluded in 1926 was the well-being of the vast majority. Drawing a distinction between industrial equality and legal equality, Mary Anderson, head of the newly created Women's Bureau of the Department of Labor, defended her position in favor of special legislation by arguing, "I consider myself a good feminist, but I believe I am a practical one."[12]

The debate over strategy ushered in by this early twentieth-century conflict has continued in one form or another up until the present. Those who advocated social legislation to ameliorate women's family and work roles, usually called social feminists, have shared the notion of women's differences. Eleanor Roosevelt is a useful example. From the early 1920s, as her membership in such groups as the National Women's Trade Union League and the League of Women Voters indicates, she supported the notion that women are in fact different from men. Like other social feminists who belonged to these groups, she vigorously opposed the ERA, fearing that its passage would eliminate all special protection for female workers. In doing so, she rejected the arguments of what was then the more radical wing of the women's movement, the National Women's party, which believed in women's rights as a matter of justice and humanity. To Eleanor Roosevelt and the social feminists, career and job satisfaction were as important as they were to the National Women's party. But the notion that a married woman could value individual achievement and personal aspiration above the welfare of her family was inconceivable. "I never like to think of this subject of a woman's career and a woman's home as being a controversy," she wrote in 1933. "It seems to me perfectly obvious that if a woman falls in love and marries, of course her first interest and her first duty is to her home, but her duty to her home does not of necessity preclude her having another occupation."[13]

In the 1920s, short of women placing jobs first (that is, short of rejecting differences), possibilities for improving the working conditions and opportunities of even well-educated women seemed negligible. Even the trade unions conceded that among poor women improved conditions depended on legislation, a lesson learned from the unenviable position of most black women, whose work in domestic service and in agriculture excluded most from protection.

The Depression proved to be a watershed in which opinions began to change. It challenged an array of assumptions about women's difference, shaking the assurance that had surrounded three decades of mostly successful work for protective labor legislation and extending its benefits to many more workers.[14] As in the war that followed, New Deal policy makers introduced solutions to labor problems that undermined earlier certainties about the importance of difference. Together, depression and war, and the social policies they spawned, revealed that male and female workers shared more than they realized. Despite their differences, they could be equally protected.

To begin with, widespread economic privation destroyed the always tenuous illusion that families could be securely supported by a single male breadwinner. Among broader sectors of the population than had ever been true before, economic collapse meant that wives, as well as grown children, needed to earn wages and that more and more families were dividing the task of sustaining themselves among their members. As wives became more frequent and sometimes more permanent wage workers, they raised questions as to whether some of work's rewards could not also be theirs. Did personal aspiration conflict with family values? "Was work," as some asked, "an exclusive prerogative of the male portion of humanity," or was it "a fundamental right of every human being?" These questions were to reemerge in the 1950s. Despite desperate attempts to drive them out of the workforce, married women worked in ever-larger numbers, accounting for 35 percent of all women workers by 1940. Though they were abused in the public press and attacked by unmarried women, these new workers stood their ground. Some, like the San Antonio woman whose wages were deeply cut, did so because her job provided free meals, relieving her family of the need to feed her.[15] Others simply found work gratifying. Male and female workers experienced other commonalities. Unemployment and homelessness, for example, crossed gender lines.

The solutions of the New Deal summed up the similarities among workers. The same National Recovery Administration codes that discriminated against women acknowledged that male workers needed protection too and extended the arms of the state to them. Eleanor Roosevelt, Frances Perkins, and other social feminists fought consistently to defend the right of married women to work, to ensure equal pay for equal work, and to provide equal treatment for women on work relief. Partly as a result of this, public policy that at first treated women as if they always had somewhere to go was altered, and the New Deal made some crude attempts to find jobs and relief for women. Finally, the Supreme Court opened the possibility of general labor legislation. After decades of rejecting the idea that the state had any interest in the hours and wages of most male workers, the Supreme Court upheld the 1938 Fair Labor Standards Act, which for the first time legislated a minimum wage for many workers and successfully gave to men the kinds of legal protections against excessive hours from which women had benefited. Only twelve short years earlier, Mary Anderson had mocked what she called the "ultrafeminist" position for holding that such laws could be extended beyond women.[16]

Perhaps most importantly, notions of sturdy individualism suffered a severe blow as even the best competitive energies of male workers could not alter the bleak prospect of unemployment. A trade-union movement that had been at best ambivalent about recruiting women revitalized itself by relying at least in part on the energies of female workers as well as on the wives of male workers to sustain its expansion. Willingly or not, male unionists evoked the values of community, the virtues of cooperation, and family at its best as women turned their tradition and experience into mechanisms for survival. In significant ways, the Depression experience meant reduced differences. New laws or regulations extended the protections of women to many working men and in everyday life demonstrated the unforgettable lesson that family survival and wage work were inseparable.

By the end of the decade these changes had revitalized the movement for an equal rights amendment and reduced opposition to it among some women's groups. To many, equality now seemed a plausible as well as desirable goal.[17] The notion of difference, which in the 1920s had been largely reduced to biology as two groups of feminists adopted competing positions, was now broadened to include some notion of socially defined roles. Its champions responded to the challenge of women's new stature by drawing up what they called a Women's Charter. Conceived in 1936 by social feminists led by Mary Anderson of the Women's Bureau, the charter claimed to offer an alternative to a constitutional amendment by declaring the desirability of equality while acknowledging the need for protective labor legislation. Differences that earlier had been asserted as a means for women to achieve a place in public life were now claimed not to inhibit the goal of equality. But the difference argument itself was not abandoned. The argument put its proponents in the unwieldly position of asking for equal treatment and pay, on the one hand, and protected status, on the other hand. One protagonist commented that it asked for "'full responsibility and special privilege'" at one and the same time.[18] But though the issue tore the group apart, social feminists were not yet ready to assert equality if it meant abandoning their notion of womanhood. As one businesswoman put it, "'There are hundreds and thousands of the group I represent who are muddled by the whole thing.'"[19]

Like other social feminists, Eleanor Roosevelt found herself changing. Her concern and that of others increased during World War II, as challenges against notions of difference multiplied. During the war years, women demonstrated their capacity to work at the same jobs and as effectively as men. To support needed female workers, industry and government adopted new and imaginative policies for housing women and for feeding and caring for their children. What reasons now could be adduced for treating women as outsiders? For arguing that their positions as "mothers of the race" demanded special treatment? Toward the end of the war, Eleanor Roosevelt, although still opposed to the ERA, thought that the new circumstances warranted some compromise. "We must do a lot more than just be opposed to an amendment," she wrote to her friend Rose Schneiderman. "I believe we should initiate through the Labor Department a complete survey of the laws that discriminate against women and the laws that are protective; that we should then go to work in every state in the Union to get rid of the discriminatory ones and to strengthen the protective ones; and if the time has come when some of them are obsolete, we should get rid of them even though they were once needed as protective."[20]

Roosevelt had touched a historical nerve. She understood that the notion of difference, having emerged from a particular historical context, had taken on a shape appropriate to its time. As circumstances changed, the idea that men and women were different appeared to be undermining the equal opportunity that had been its goal. Further change was hidden below the placid surface of the 1950s. Public education expanded dramatically, offering new opportunities to men and women, and though women gave birth to more children, soon the need to educate them and to provide them with the benefits of a consumer society led mothers back into the workforce. Tempting possibilities of upward mobility in an expanding economy fostered a meritocratic ethic, posing a challenge to which women were not immune. Ideas of personal progress on the basis of individual merit nestled into an egalitarian framework. It was not only that some would make it; if ideology were to be believed, everyone who tried would do so. A decade of relative prosperity, shorter hours for everyone, and reasonable working conditions provided unusual optimism about the present and future possibilities of work. Although most activists still clung to the belief that women were not like men, pressures for equality mounted.

For women, new job-related opportunities still competed with notions that kept them tied to the family. Married women entered the workforce in unprecedented numbers. Although most would have argued that wage work was only a means to some other family end, the pressures of opportunity and mobility exercised their own influence. Old defenders of protection for women began to see it as no longer necessary. As Alice Hamilton wrote to one critic of her new position, "I have seen so great a change in the position of women workers in the last fifteen years or so that it seemed to me there was no longer any need to oppose the formal granting of equality."[21]

Arguments from difference were not merely rooted in an understanding of women's historical exploitation in the labor force. They had come as well out of a set of shared understandings about women's relationship to the home. And they persisted in the 1950s, despite new protections for all workers, because to abandon them was to leave questions about home and family unanswered. Short of arguing for an abstract equality or a humanist feminist position that most men and women in the 1950s did not support, solutions to women's disadvantaged labor-force position lay in addressing particular issues. In 1951, for example, the heirs of social feminism tried for three years to pass a Women's Status Bill that would have declared in national legislation that there be "NO DISTINCTION on the basis of sex, except such as are reasonably justified by differences in physical structure, or by maternal function."[22] The draft bill also recommended a presidential commission to review discrimination against women. Without confronting the fundamental problem of family-care responsibilities, the bill, like earlier demands for equal pay, simply insisted that women be treated equally in the labor force. But equal treatment for different people seemed hard to achieve, as a staff writer for the labor movement's *American Federationist* discovered in 1957. Vehemently opposed to the "misnamed Equal Rights Amendment," she argued that "an intelligent approach to women workers takes into account differences between men and women workers. On the other hand, these social differences in employment patterns should not be used to rationalize wage discrimination where women are doing the same job as men."[23] The author did not explain how if differences were taken into account, women could obtain the "same jobs as men."

Very much weakened, the old idea that women required special protection because they were different suffered its mortal wound at the hands of John F. Kennedy's Commission on the Status of Women. The commission, which Eleanor Roosevelt headed until her death in 1962, was recommended to Kennedy by, among others, Esther Peterson, the head of the Women's Bureau. It took an ambiguous stance, calling for more attention to preparing young women for motherhood at the same time as it explored job-related issues like training, selection, advancement, and equal pay. The commission also issued the first quasi-official public calls for "necessary supportive services by private or public agencies" to women in gainful employment. Here, at last, was a peacetime statement of social policy that acknowledged the double-sided nature of the dilemma of difference. Could women ask for equality at work without compromising their family roles? If they asserted a claim to motherhood, how could they justify demands for equal opportunity in the workplace?

In the context of the 1960s, the fight to acknowledge women's difference, still tarnished by biological notions and those of the centrality of motherhood, took on a defensive posture. The idea that women had family lives in need of protection had seemed a great and humane breakthrough in 1920 and 1930. By 1940 and 1950, women who wanted to advance in the sphere of work were willing to assign the issue of family lives to the private sphere. By 1960, to argue that women were different from men was tantamount to believing that little could be done to allow full work lives and quickly became a position largely held by those who preferred dependent roles. The old belief system was held responsible for limiting personal aspiration and for creating discrimination by fostering among employers the notion that women were not genuinely committed to wage work.

Simultaneously, the competing notion that women, not merely as equals to men, but like them, could and should be permitted to function as individuals at work—which had seemed to many in the 1920s at best an invitation to exploitation and at worst a threat to the separation of the sexes—had become by the 1950s more attractive to millions of women who now saw family lives as parallel to paid work. By the 1960s, the argument for equality seemed to those concerned with women's labor-force roles the only viable way to create job options for women and had certainly replaced notions of difference as the operative factor in the wage-labor force.

By the end of the 1960s, attempts to achieve special treatment for women in the workforce had come to an end. Most feminists, seeing what they took to be the consequences of "special protection," rejected the assumption that women were somehow different from men and argued instead that as far as the workforce was concerned, they were more like them than not. This humanist feminism insisted that it was because women had been treated as a special group that they continued to be disadvantaged. From their perspective, if women were to achieve equal status, they would have to give up the traditional attributes of their gender as well as the special treatments that were attached to them. Only by adopting the competitive and achievement-oriented values of the work sphere could women achieve equality. Informed by a new faith in more egalitarian household relationships that were thought to make possible job-related aspirations for women at work, new feminists believed that separating women's two roles would enable the married as well as the single to compete effectively for wages, promotions, and new opportunities. The result, as we know, was the spate of legislation that started with the Equal Pay Act of 1963, continued with Title VII of the Civil Rights Act of 1964, ran through Title IX of the Higher Education Act of 1972, and culminated the same year in the passage by Congress of an Equal Rights Amendment. Each of these bills attempted to remove some barriers to equality. And yet together they have had little discernible impact for women as a whole.[24]

The current movement has relied heavily on a strategy of dropping barriers to work and encouraging women, their opportunities purportedly equal, to fend for themselves. Even the addition of affirmative action has not brought anticipated gains.[25] Real advances have occurred for a few women in such professional and business areas as pharmacy, law, medicine, personnel management, banking, and accounting. And real alternatives have been created among women in intact two-income professional families—families that can afford to replace the services of the homemaker and child rearer—as well as among some who postponed childbearing or marriage until their thirties. In blue-collar jobs, women have made modest gains as bus drivers and repair persons, but in general equality has floundered. Fearful that demands for modified working conditions and benefits will be seen by male co-workers as coming out of their pockets and will leave women wondering whether such essentials as maternity leaves, day care, and flexitime will be used by employers as excuses to lay off women or reduce their chances for promotion, women have only reluctantly asked for them. Nor have trade unions actively pushed such issues. Instead, employers have taken advantage of women's assertion of equality to treat them more like men than as people with different needs. Since the early 1970s, we have seen a relative increase in the amount of female poverty, little reduction of unemployment in poorly paid workforce sectors, a small narrowing in the wage-gap (the ratio of female to male pay) to seventy-six cents for every male dollar, and only selective relief from occupational segregation.[26]

In short, for all its euphoric and insistent tone, the notion of dropping barriers to equality for women at work has not prevented women from becoming poorer and has only marginally increased opportunities for genuine mobility. Nor have affirmative action programs brought about any deep transformation of women's position in the workforce. Clerical jobs, always female-dominated in the modern period, have become even more so. And clerical jobs continue to be those held by the largest number of women. Women remain a disadvantaged group.

How then should we integrate this group into the workforce? At least one current strategy holds some promise. It revolves around two areas, each of which has, to some degree, abandoned the notion that women should adapt to male structures and returned to the idea that their differences require accommodation. Both represent what we have earlier called woman-centered or gynocentric feminism in that they recall the assumptions, if not the strategies, of the social feminists.

The first is best illustrated by the current strategy of the Women's Rights Project of the American Civil Liberties Union (ACLU). In a July 1984 amicus brief, the ACLU opposed the constitutionality of Montana's Maternity Leave Act—an act that entitled pregnant women to extended unpaid leave before and for several weeks after the birth of a child. Arguing that the effect of such a law would be to place women in a "special" category and citing the history of past discrimination that had "perpetuated destructive stereotypes about women's proper roles and operated to deny them benefits enjoyed by men," the ACLU proposed that the law be extended to permit health-connected unpaid leaves for all workers. The discriminatory effects of the act would be mitigated, the brief argued, and its "ultimate goals and purposes" supported if the court tied the act to Title VII of the Civil Rights Act of 1964, which forbade distinctions in employment on the basis of gender. The effect of such a link would be to extend leaves to all workers unable to work for reasons of health.

Here the ACLU argued that the law, while acknowledging gender-based differences, can encompass them instead of isolating or ignoring them. By extending rights granted to some workers to all, invidious discrimination is turned into a potential gain for everyone. The pluralism of the workforce is given its due, and each group of workers has access to the special treatment it needs.

A second example of current strategy emerges from the issue of comparable worth. The proponents of this effort to equalize pay acknowledge the existence of occupational segregation on the basis of prior discrimination and of structural barriers. They insist, however, that the social roles that account for women's segmentation not be penalized. Instead, they demand that some objective scale be devised to evaluate the education, training, responsibility, and initiative required for a range of jobs within firms and that pay be granted accordingly. Such a strategy promises to protect women's social needs even when they emerge as job preferences because it avoids the assumption that equality can be achieved only by dropping barriers, challenges the notion of the market as the fairest determinant of the value of work, and substitutes instead the idea that women's goals are as legitimate as those of men and deserve equal rewards. Such strategies emerge from an understanding of differences that acknowledges the social importance of familial roles and insists on the necessity of integrating them into a demand for equality. Insofar as these roles are traditionally preferred by women, sharing their immediate and opportunity costs by encouraging workplace compromises to accommodate them reduces the penalty women pay for engaging in them. At the same time, the workplace that accommodates family roles will exact fewer sacrifices from those who choose to emphasize the less individualistic elements of personality and thus it may encourage men to become less competitive as well.

As in the humanist feminist tradition, the basis of inequality in the work place in this approach is understood to lie in the privatization and separation of household and child-rearing functions. Such privatization, as many scholars have noted, perpetuates the inequality of women in the household, is characterized by dependence on male support, and is upheld by the value placed on femininity.[27] But these inequalities in the home are rooted in contributions and values that some women as well as men do not choose to give up. For all that they have been manipulated and abused, notions of nurturance, sharing, and the kinds of relational and affectional qualities of which Carol Gilligan writes are nevertheless valued by large numbers of people. Maintaining them has in the past required women to ignore inequality in the workplace and men to consciously foster it. A strategy that revalues these different qualities can create conditions that will enhance equality at home by making some of the real costs of family life and child rearing a social responsibility rather than a private one. This in turn will serve to increase the demand for equality.

I am not suggesting a new strategy so much as I am urging that we not retreat from an insight that has had mixed results in the past. Yet the attempt to deny differences has been equally mixed. A series of utopian communities in the nineteenth and early twentieth centuries attempted to confront and resolve the issues of child rearing and family care by fostering cooperation to share the burden. All were problematic. In her pathbreaking essay, *Women and Economics,* Charlotte Perkins Gilman proposed that these tasks be removed from the household. Several attempts to set up cooperative kitchens and community laundries provided no continuing model.[28] We must at least consider the notion that such proposals had little popular appeal because they ignored what many women have felt was most satisfying about their lives, namely, their relationships to family. More successful have been those few attempts to accommodate the workplace to family. Wartime experiments in housing women with families demonstrated the dramatic increase in productivity and family well-being that resulted from offering well-planned housing with easy supervision of children and on-site day care, laundry and banking facilities, as well as prepared hot meals.[29] This success offers a sharp contrast to the extension of female poverty that has resulted from the systematic decrease in the already minimal community and social services offered to poor women today. And it suggests that an earlier generation of feminists who asserted women's difference deserves a new look. For them, difference meant limiting or regulating the sphere of work for women—a strategy that, as we have seen, in the end undermined equality for women. But within the context of the service economy of the 1980s, difference could mean adapting workplace patterns for all workers to suit family lives.

In contrast to earlier notions of social or woman-centered feminism, the new understanding of difference proudly accepts the attributes associated with women's historically assigned roles, declaring itself antithetical to such male values as competition and achievement for their own sakes. It lacks the moralistic assumption that women's culturally or socially ascribed roles are in any sense more valuable while insisting that such qualities belong in the world and not in a separate sphere. Thus it argues that women bear responsibility for family lives but insists that they do not bear it alone. This perspective opens the possibility of placing what have previously been private issues onto the public stage. In doing so, it takes assumptions of difference that in Eleanor Roosevelt's time were rooted in biology and therefore isolated women as a group and turns them into a sociocultural form that holds the possibility of genuine equality.

These new arguments from difference suggest that a woman's sense of morality and responsibility and her behavioral codes (including those that derive from her sense of family and her childbearing capacity) are as much a public as a private resource, and they insist as a matter of social policy that the workforce recognize and make room for these alternative approaches to human relationships. Far from believing that women can act like men at work, this position asserts women's differences proudly, insisting that the workplace accommodate to women's biology as well as to society's need for those less individualistic qualities of personality and relationship that are her strength. At its most optimistic, this approach is nothing less than a belief that gender equality will be achieved only when the values of the home (which have previously been assumed to keep women out of the workplace or to assign them to inferior places within it) are brought to the workplace, where they can transform work itself. It opens the possibility that an ethic of compassion or tolerance, a sense of group responsibility to the world at large (instead of to self), might in fact penetrate the workplace.[30]

It differs sharply from the implications of a humanist feminism that argues that women can respond to the workplace like men and assumes at heart that women can and will play the game the way men play it. In this form of feminism, personal aspiration and individual achievement measure progress towards the goal of equality. The problem is that this theory makes room in the workforce primarily for those who wish to place nurturing roles in a secondary category and/or to acquiesce to the ethic of competition. It relegates to second place those who wish to function by their own more clearly female lights. In contrast, those who assert the validity of difference challenge the rules by which the game has been played, leaving room to extend protections won by women to men (as in the ACLU example) and opening up the opportunity to share the costs of childbearing and child rearing. Because this position accepts domestic life as a necessary part of the wage-work process, it encourages innovative thought in regard to housing programs, transportation systems, child care, and the allocation of community resources. It also insists on the need for compromises in the work situation that fully integrate women's orientations to work. At their most extreme, the two positions juxtapose the power of individualism against the force of some notion of collective good.

Lest it appear that one perspective is more radical than the other, let me add that both hold the possibility of major social transformation, and it is for this reason that I suggest what looks like a utopian possibility. Given the numbers of women entering the labor force for perfectly valid demographic, ideological, and economic reasons, and given their pressures to share in the American dream of success, some change in either the family or the workforce seems inevitable. If women are to function at work in competitive and achievement-oriented ways, they can and should fulfill all their drives for personal achievement. That goal offers a vision of a world without gender domination in the same breath as it implies the necessity for maintaining some form of hierarchy. It directly threatens the family in its patriarchal form and challenges traditional familial values. It begs the question of how the services normally offered in the home are to be provided in most families. In the end, it threatens the breakup of the family altogether.

The second direction, in insisting that women's orientation be publicly espoused, turns the attention of the state, the community, and extended friendship and kin networks to modifying the workplace and the home. As in the example of comparable worth, it places the market in second place behind an ethos of responsibility and fairness. Yet in insisting on shared values, this view challenges individualism, competition, and the profit system.

Both directions hold the possibility of conservative responses. The same group of people who argue that women can and should accept the rules as men have defined them implicitly accept the premises of individualism, namely, that people are by nature competitive, that some will not survive the struggle, and that although no one need starve, self-help is the key to eventual equality. Those who believe that difference should be honored, however, could respond positively to the New Right position that social order rests on reinforcing distinctions, not accommodating them. The logic of that argument is that women really belong at home.

If women's values become a force in creating and influencing work culture, if women can resist efforts to use their understandings to enforce old roles, then exciting possibilities could confront us in terms of cooperation and shared goals in the workplace and in family lives. As the material and other costs of rearing children and running households are shared or socialized, then no woman need fear an equal rights amendment. Once women's values are fully integrated into social relations, women will no longer constitute a "special group."

12

Gendered Interventions:
Exploring the Historical Roots
of U.S. Social Policy

Among the central paradoxes of American life is that of how the United States, among the wealthiest of industrial countries and practically alone among them, has failed to produce an adequate system of social welfare. This essay speculates about some of the historical roots of this paradox. I want to offer an interpretation that evokes not so much traditional explanations of American individualism and competitive drive but draws on shifting constructs of gender to help us understand contemporary attitudes towards social welfare. In the process, I want to illustrate some of the kinds of things we might learn by looking at gender (along with class and race) as an intimate participant in the construction of national identity.

This excursion will take us back into the nineteenth century; it will focus on how the lives and culture of ordinary working men and women were transformed by class-based appeals to shared gendered understandings. My intent is to demonstrate how at the end of the nineteenth century, working men and women were led to accept conceptions of their own identity that helped to translate notions of citizenship rooted in collective responsibility into gender-divided conceptions of citizenship based on legal rights and independence from state intervention that inhibited the growth of community. In this construction, gendered notions of citizenship provide the rationale and the motive force for particular forms of state action that measured the continuing relationships of the state to its citizens.

I delivered a version of this essay at the Japanese Association for American Studies, Kyoto, April 3, 1993. By then, I had been working on these ideas for some time and had floated other efforts at the Indiana Association of American Historians in October 1991 and the European Association for American Studies in Seville in March 1992. The essay appeared in this form in the *Japanese Journal of American Studies* 5 (1993–94) and in Maria Irene Ramalho de Sousa Santos and Mario Materassi, eds., *The American Columbiad* (Amsterdam: VU University Press, 1994). Thanks to Beatrix Hoffman and Stephen Robertson for research help and to Linda Kerber and David Thelen for cogent criticism.

We begin the story in the early history of the American republic, when contests over citizenship exacerbated the salience of gender. While the Revolution made it clear that women's citizenship was derivative of their spouses and that their political and economic rights were based on the assumption that they would marry and be "protected" by a male, it left unclear the degree to which, in the minds of ordinary people, ideas of republicanism were themselves gendered. Those ideas were still in flux. Some adhered to John Locke's conception of people as possessing universal rights. In their view, individuals had access to rights as a function of their being. On the grounds that each individual could protect his or her own rights, this conception provided a framework that allowed the polity to divest itself of responsibility for its members. Others were tempted by republican notions of rights as the legitimate by-products of status. This conception reserved access to at least some rights to those with particular and denned relationships to the polity. If it deprived some people of the full regalia of citizenship, it nonetheless offered them access to the state through a notion of collective interest.[1] Under this rubric, for example, republican principles justified the denial to some men of the right to vote by arguing that within a community of common interests, those with a "stake in society" would protect the interests of all of its members.

Constitutional historians have noted how the newly adopted document straddled the fence between these notions of collective and individual interest. The tension between individual rights (as it was expressed by the forces of economic change) and collective republican values (as they resided in the culture of families and working people) provided part of the dynamic of change in the nineteenth century. As the legal scholar Rogers M. Smith has suggested, "[T]he thrust of classical liberalism's oppositional language of personal rights is to cast the claims of all types of associations . . . as threats to personal liberty."[2] The pressures of an emerging industrial society led the nineteenth-century judiciary increasingly to construe rights as the property of individuals rather than of groups. Their efforts constrained the evolution of what David Thelen has described as a "sense of collective identity and goals."[3]

But judicial interpretation encountered two major repositories of collective or associational values: workingmen's societies and the family. In the face of efforts to reify claims to individual rights, both were defended with arguments and imagery rooted in notions of masculinity, manhood, and appropriate gender roles. The claims of women on both, and their interests in them, differed: a difference that, in the end, may account for the failure of these claims to prevail.

For working people whose rights often seemed most readily protected by associations with others, a legal framework of individual rights could be used to deprive them of collective protections. Organized workers therefore sought to lay claim to republican notions of collective interest through their attachment to work. But women in this period were subsumed by family law, which acted to reinforce traditional male prerogatives primarily denied by class interests. Women appear in legal discourse largely as the subjects of questions about whether and for what purposes they might be considered persons.[4] For them, a framework of individual rights offered the possibility of improved standing before the law. One practical effect of this distinction is that women could benefit from seeking access to individual rights, while many working men felt that such access might hamper their efforts to sustain a collective vision. The nineteenth-century effort to infuse family and work with individual rights thus created a continuing tension between gender and class.[5]

In the first half of the nineteenth century, tensions between the two were subdued. Skilled mechanics and artisans (distressed by changes in their trades) often succumbed to judicial pressure to participate in developing individual claims with relation to rights. A series of decisions in response to what we have come to know as the Cordwainers cases illustrates the coercive power of the courts.[6] When the skilled shoemakers who were members of New York's Journeymen's Cordwainers' Society tried to protect their prices by refusing to work with nonmembers in 1809, the master shoemakers who employed them leveled accusations of conspiracy. In a series of decisions that culminated in 1837, the courts compromised. They grudgingly agreed that cordwainers could meet to discuss wages, prices, and hours but asserted that workers had no right to enforce their collective decision. They could not persuade others to withhold their labor nor insist on an agreed price.[7] Though the resolution did not deny cordwainers the rights of association, it did reject their capacity to act together. The result was to leave them no alternative but the individual right to fight each other for any available work.

Such decisions coincided with the mobility aspirations of an emerging capitalist society and left skilled craft workers little alternative but to construe their collective assumptions in a political context. More and more, workers adopted notions of free labor that assumed that the collective voice and self-representation of labor as a whole ultimately relied on the dignity and independence of each worker. This perspective imagined that each person had equal rights or access to economic self-sufficiency, and that those rights were essential to the dignity and independence required to participate effectively in civic life.[8] Labor was free, in this view (which continued to be championed in the late nineteenth century by such working-class advocates as the Knights of Labor), when it had the capacity to represent itself. Thus, notions of an integrated or collective whole and of equal rights for workers that remained at the center of workers' consciousness ultimately embodied a notion of citizenship rooted in the possibilities of self-employment and independence from wage earning.[9]

As Jonathan A. Glickstein points out, however, the entire notion of free labor was patriarchally constructed.[10] It was built on a concept of independence in which skill at craft work was equated with manliness; it rested on a conception of male prerogatives built on an ordered and comfortable family life that relied on female labor at home; and it utilized these constructs to develop a conception of equal rights for workers that was to guarantee effective self-representation and provide the basis for the perpetuation of a democratic republic.

Women as individuals were virtually excluded from prevailing conceptions of free labor. They were not expected to be members of the polity in the same sense as men, nor was their wage work expected to offer access to independent judgment. Indeed, central to the male conception of republicanism was an ordered family life that incorporated male dominion over wives and children.[11] In men's eyes, women's wage labor, while sometimes necessary, could be dignified and offer access to self-support. But it was not expected to lead to independence and self-sufficiency. Rather, just as men's free labor was predicated on their capacity to support a family, so women's was assumed to sustain the family labor of men. Since it was expected that women would participate in the polity through their menfolk, it was assumed that any wage work women did would be in subsidiary positions. For if women's wage work competed with that of men, or threatened to undermine men's wages, it simultaneously challenged men's access to citizenship. The idea of free labor thus embodied the notion of separate spheres for men and women, explicitly discouraging women from participating in wage work except in ways that would help to maintain family lives.

Theory, of course, was never entirely sustained by practice. Women did manage to develop artisanal skills—those of milliners and printers, for example—and to set up businesses that parallelled the entrepreneurship of men.[12] Nor did the idea of free labor entirely quell the capacity of women to "steal" men's trades or the willingness of some men to teach their skills to daughters and wives. But for the most part, the idea of free labor neatly rationalized the sexual division of labor confining women to jobs that did not enhance their claims to citizenship.

For many women who did not earn their own wages, a different logic applied. Early nineteenth-century judicial interpretation treated women, collectively, as the dependents of men and of families. Though there were exceptions, women, as a group, remained largely legal creatures of the family.[13] While men acquired rights not only on their own behalf but on behalf of their families, women acquired rights through their families and might be denied access to property (and therefore practical liberty) by their fathers and spouses. What appeared to be "rights" for men were, from the earliest days of the republic, denied to women. It is true that some rights, like the freedoms of speech, assembly, or religion, were distributed without formal regard to sex, but they were often constrained by custom. Others, like property and liberty, frequently carried restrictions based on race and sex. Property, for example, typically passed through a woman to her male heirs; her right to establish her own domicile was limited. Women's capacity to resist (to keep some of their property, to claim their own wages, to engage in unorthodox behavior) required either the permission of their male kin or the intervention of the state on their behalf. At first, their efforts to be treated as individuals drew little response from the state legislatures that might have helped. But then the courts stepped in, increasingly allowing individual roles for women through interpretations of family law that protected individuals within the family.[14]

Thus the citizenship divide was born. For white men of all classes, the discourse of rights placed them in direct opposition to the state, which, by restricting the power of association, threatened to limit their liberty at every turn. But women (especially women of property) stood in a somewhat different relation to the state, which could, and sometimes did, act as a mediator between male prerogative and female dependence. For example, between 1839 and 1865, when state after state refused to concede the need for regulations of wages and hours for workers, twenty-nine states passed laws to protect the property of married women from improvident husbands. Norma Basch suggests the importance of these laws in extending "the individualistic egalitarian premises of the revolution to the women of the nation, not only in their capacity as women and mothers but also as independent citizens of the state."[15] By affirming the state's capacity to act on behalf of women, they ratified what the legal historian Lawrence Friedman has called "a silent revolution," a revolution that had already taken place.[16]

Poor women also seem to have perceived the state as a potential guardian of liberty. The generally abortive appeals of factory women to state legislatures for a shorter workday and the futile array of petitions to the U.S. Congress to abolish slavery affirm the willingness of women of all kinds to see the state as bearing a more benign aspect than the one it presented to most men, and especially to most ordinary working men. And indeed, there were early harbingers of success. By 1860, New York State included earnings protection in property laws. And in 1876, Massachusetts, which, like every other state, kept its distance from male working conditions, became the first state to limit the numbers of hours women could work.[17]

Still, these were limited gains. As long as women could be conceived as functioning largely in the private sphere (that is, as long as most women did not earn wages outside their homes), their legal standing derived primarily from their status. Efforts to access individual rights drew little public or legal attention. From the perspective of contemporaries, the state's denial of rights to women, when it was noticed at all, appeared "benign and paternalistic"; its offers of occasional protection were designed to preserve family well-being, not to undermine women.[18] To the historian, the invisibility of women in the Constitution affirmed what was thought to be their primary allegiance to a well-defined private sphere of family.[19] But the use by the judiciary of the family to mediate women's relationship to the Constitution foundered in the period after the Civil War, partly as the result of the women's rights movement, and partly in consequence of the salience of issues of class as a central category around which constitutional struggle emerged. Together these created urgent pressures on working-class families to reaffirm the republican tradition of collective rights in the face of a dramatic deterioration of practical liberty.

The passage of the Fourteenth Amendment to the Constitution and the subsequent debate around it exacerbated the conflict between working men and the state and the dissimilar relationship of men and women to it. The amendment, which affirmed a Lockean conception of human rights, explicitly assigned rights to all male persons, including especially freed slaves and people of color. Because it provided the basis for each individual to contract freely (liberty of contract), it provided justification for an all-out assault on notions of citizenship derived from the republican tradition of community. At the same time, it explicitly excluded women from the exercise of many of the political and civil rights to which men were entitled. The same courts that construed universal rights as adequate shelter for wage-earning individuals and defined individual rights in opposition to collective protection affirmed the state's capacities to refuse women the right to be persons under the law.

The twin assumptions about gender and class embedded in such interpretations are difficult to separate, but their consequences for the development of state policy are enormous. Briefly, this set of decisions turned women into a protected legal "class" on whose behalf the state could and did act, while it excluded male workers from comparable standing. If the workers happened to be women, they could seek protection on the grounds of their sex. If they were men, their diminished capacity to seek legislative and judicial remedies urged revitalized forms of association. The trade unions that developed, many of which explicitly excluded women, often coalesced around explicitly work-centered forms of masculinity. The ability of the courts in the late nineteenth century to distinguish family from labor law relied heavily on conceptions of women as part of a "separate sphere." When maintaining those conceptions became palpably impossible in the rapid industrialization of the 1870s and after, the resulting conflation of family and labor placed issues of gender at the center of a negotiating process over the meaning of democracy in the Progressive Era.

At first, it appeared as if the Fourteenth Amendment spoke most sharply to divisions between men and women. In a series of cases, the Supreme Court refused to acknowledge that women were persons protected under freedom of contract.[20] At the same time, however, it expanded women's rights in the home. Thus the meaning of its decisions and the cultural consensus they represented differed for different women. On the one hand, the courts allowed states to restrict women's access to political citizenship by such means as denying them the right to vote or to appear as attorneys before the bar. On the grounds that women's primary responsibility was to their families, the courts also allowed states to regulate women's access to economic citizenship by setting the terms under which they might earn a living, as Massachusetts did in 1876. Consistent with their concern for individual rights, however, the courts took a less indulgent view of state efforts to hamper women's rights within the family.

Perceiving opportunity, an active women's rights movement began eagerly to seek those rights, successfully pressing for enlarged access to child custody, divorce, and control over property. In practice, as women's rights in the home broadened, their liberty in the workplace narrowed, thus endowing women's citizenship with a double meaning: restricted in the public marketplace and enhanced in the household.[21] If working women gained what some activists called "practical liberty," the shift in stance nevertheless exacerbated the differences in the meaning of citizenship for men and women.

At the same time, the courts sharpened the differential relationship of men and women to the increasingly influential state by insisting that, whatever the disadvantages of liberty of contract for men, its exercise precluded any but an individual relation to the Constitution.[22] In the two decades before the turn of the century, the processes of rapid industrialization, urbanization, and immigration meant that the majority of the gainfully employed could no longer expect self-directed employment. Despite their efforts to encourage producer cooperatives and engage in political action, the defenders of free labor waged a futile battle against the challenges of a debilitating and all-encompassing wage system.[23] Eager for a rapid transformation of control into their own hands and anxious to maximize the possibilities of cheap labor, a new generation of industrialists and entrepreneurs treated workers as individuals, each capable of negotiating, and each protected by the Fourteenth Amendment's prohibitions on deprivation of property. Labor's freedom, they suggested, with the concurrence of the courts, inhered only in its right to freely contract to sell itself.

This view, commonly known as freedom of contract, appeared to extend democracy because it offered all workers (black and white, male and female) a putative equality from which to negotiate. Equal rights were embedded in the capacity of individuals (male and female) to compete freely against each other: to be free from restraint in selling labor. But the doctrine of freedom of contract also prevented workers from acting together to achieve ultimate economic independence, simultaneously negating the collective (or associational) possibilities inherent in republican conceptions of citizenship and preventing the state from acting on their behalf.

As a matter of formal and legal principle, the courts, beginning in the 1880s, ignored the vulnerable position of workers and turned the Fourteenth Amendment's prohibition on depriving citizens of life, liberty, and property on its head. Consistently, they interpreted freedom of contract to mean that men could not be prevented from entering into exploitative relationships with employers—as a ban on virtually all state efforts to regulate the relations between employers and employees.[24] In so doing, the courts effectively snuffed the associational dreams of working people, severing the connection between workplace dignity and manhood and negating the political visions of free labor. With a few specific exceptions, the doctrine of freedom of contract outlawed protective labor legislation for most workers, depriving them of state intervention, while employers were left free to impose their own conditions of work.[25] The crack in this system was gender.

Continuing to see women in terms of their status as family members rather than as individuals posed an incipient conflict, which emerged forcefully in the late nineteenth century. As women began to enter the "public" sphere of wage work in large numbers, increasing proportions of married women and of self-supporting women with children began to earn wages outside the home. Although this provided a large pool of "cheap labor," it also left women in vulnerable positions. Women who were treated as individuals for the purposes of the workplace and whose relative lack of skill subjected them to low wages and harsh working conditions could not fulfill socially necessary roles as family members. And jobs that undermined the working-class family by destroying women's health or fertility, or jobs that encouraged female aspirations to work at men's wages, could easily destroy the golden egg that produced the next generation of workers.

Male workers, the courts, and employers came together on the issue of women's family roles. Women could not be individuals in the same sense as men. Labor's conception of womanhood was rooted in the belief that effective civic participation demanded workplace dignity, which in turn rested on an ordered and comfortable family life. The value of male skills threatened with obsolescence, manly aspirations to independence undermined by wage work, claims to citizenship frustrated by shifting definitions of masculinity, manhood now located itself around the size of the wage packet. Women, seen either as individuals who competed with men for jobs or as family members on whose household labor men relied, belonged at home. If business's conception derived from the desire to preserve the family as an economic unit that could socialize future workers and provide incentives to stable and loyal workforce participation, still, for both, ideas of gender difference defined women as family members whose work roles were secondary. But for business, placing women in separate spheres meant that employers needed to treat women simultaneously as individuals from whose labor they wished to benefit and with whom they could freely negotiate pay and working conditions and as family members in whose nonwaged family work they had an indirect but important stake.

How this difficulty was negotiated reflects the dilemma of seeking equal rights for women at home in the context of a labor market within which male workers and employers resisted equal opportunities in the workplace. It signals the transformation of gendered meanings that moved women as a group from an invisible constitutional category to a protected class. As the idea of free labor (which located manliness in the independence derived from skill) gave way to that of freedom of contract (which located manliness in the more ambiguous independence derived from wage-earning capacity), the concept of citizenship as a community activity gave way to that of representation of the narrowly defined family. Though the virtue inhering in men's capacity to earn sufficient wages had always underlined male claims to citizenship, now the dignity of wage work became a new battle cry intended to unify the political interests of working people. But the cry was explicitly gendered.

It is difficult to read the labor history of the late nineteenth century without noting how explicitly reliance on gendered constructs shaped the meaning of work and helped to replace a sense of community with notions of independent self-sufficiency. By the late nineteenth century, wages, manhood, and citizenship were inextricably linked in a nexus that presented male workers as defenders of the home and justified tacit neglect of, if not opposition to, women's economic rights. Enhanced efforts to achieve a family wage or a living wage for men rested on continuing assertions of male rights to female labor inside the home and provided parallel illustrations of women's living wages that universally omitted any mention of support for the family.[26] At the same time, the struggle over the right of married women to keep their own wages pointed up the contradiction inherent in a manliness that relied on dominion over women and a woman's claim to individual rights.[27] Joy Parr captures the transition in the efforts of trade unions to persuade members to give up control over jobs in return for cash that would "smooth the way to domestic satisfaction, to all those things a couple shared when the wife was not nervous and the husband was doing what husbands should do."[28]

We can hear the muffled claims to manhood articulated in a range of late nineteenth-century working-class voices. The historian David Montgomery describes the manly bearing and mutual support that constituted the final defense of skilled machine workers for control of the workplace. For Montgomery, workers' dignity resided in the superior knowledge that made them self-directing at their tasks and in the supervision of one or more helpers.[29] The history of the declining Knights of Labor after 1886 reveals something of how as these claims weakened, skilled workers expanded their efforts to organize collectively around assertions of fraternity, defenses of their masculinity in comparison with slaves, and the exclusion of women from male crafts. More assertively, skilled workers, whose competence no longer guaranteed their power in the workplace, constructed new forms of masculinity at work to define their territory and restrain incursions on their influence.[30] The implications of declining claims to manhood for citizenship did not go unnoticed among male workers, who increasingly resorted to the language of republicanism to defend themselves. As the mechanics and laborers engaged in the 1892 Homestead Strike argued in response to a particularly egregious assault on their manhood, "'We believe that in this free land, all men should be free.'"[31]

The play of gendered ideas around the meaning of labor and access to individual rights heightened definitions of working-class masculinity that revolved around protecting homes. The resulting tensions in the family had substantive consequences for the meaning of republican citizenship among different women and men. Changing notions of manhood incorporated working-class males within a circle of individual rights that encompassed jobs as mechanisms for preserving homes, while locating the rights of women within an expanding definition of the home. Independence for working-class men all but required a conception of dependency in women, which served to sustain the new economic and psychological position of men. So, for example, by the early 1900s, skilled-craft trade unions routinely barred women from membership while simultaneously expressing moral support for the organization of women in female trades.[32] In the same period, Samuel Gompers, the president of the AFL, included among the inalienable rights of workers the right "'to protect their lives, their limbs, their homes, their firesides, their liberties as men, as workers, and as citizens.'"[33]

The shift left working-class women especially vulnerable. A working man's right to make a living (a family wage) could be and was interpreted as enjoining women from taking away, undercutting, or otherwise threatening the jobs and wages of men. The rights of men as husbands to the unpaid labor of their wives and daughters competed with the rights of women as individuals to train for good jobs, to work, and to keep their own wages. The right of employers to purchase labor at the market price could be—and, until 1908, generally was—interpreted as preventing state intervention in market dynamics that exploited the labor power of women.[34] And the right of working-class women to work could be and was interpreted by middle-class women as inimical to the interests of motherhood and child rearing. In contrast to men, a woman's right to a living was severely restricted by custom, her family's income and status, her marital status, and so on.

The same redefinitions of individual rights and gender sharpened distinctions of race. Squeezed into corners of the labor market by white male assertions of manly territoriality, white women assigned women of color into even narrower spaces. But this was only the beginning. While for poor white women, judicially conferred and legislated constructs split their class and gender identities, for African American women these constructs split racial identities as well. Since what Evelyn Brooks Higginbotham calls the "metalanguage of race" provided a different meaning for gender than the one that prevailed among white women, its practical effect was to exclude women of color from the category of "woman" in much the same way that white women continued to be excluded from the category of "person."[35] Translating this into policy produced very different legislative effects for women of color, as, for example, when the job categories in which they worked were systematically excluded from protective labor legislation, or when mothers were required to earn wages under circumstances where white women might have been exempted. It may also have created different patterns of solidarity, encouraging class alliances among African American women where divisions appeared among white women.[36]

The contested nature of equal opportunity in the workplace (with its consequent limits on job choice for women) restricted the kinds of political strategies that men or women might conceive to enhance the positions of both. At the narrowest level, strategies that embraced male job security limited female options. Unionized men increasingly defended their job rights with strategies that embraced higher wages, job security, and independent action, while becoming increasingly suspicious of state intervention in job-related arenas.[37] Working-class women, in response, located their job-related concerns in the protection of the home, allying with the movement of middle-class women who sought greater protection for individual rights at home and in the family. Together these provided an effective justification for poor and working-class women to seek state intervention and a rationale for lawmakers, reformers, and the judiciary to intervene in women's lives to protect the home. At the same time, it discouraged a politics of state regulation of industry on behalf of the efforts of working people to construct dignified working conditions. The ensuing renegotiation of gendered constructs may have finally eroded the republican/collective/community tradition on which workers had relied since the antebellum period and contributed to producing the compromises in which relationships of ordinary people to the state were rooted.

Some of these compromises are well known to historians. In summary, they include the resistance of the American trade-union movement to a political strategy that might have encouraged state intervention in the market and, most particularly, the stubborn refusal of most trade unions to countenance many forms of legislation that might have benefited workers. This stance minimally deprived Americans of any equivalent of the social democratic parties of Europe and might also be held responsible for the absence of the kinds of social insurance that came to be so valued by the workers of most industrial countries.

Second, they encouraged the intervention in the lives of poor women of a strong, largely middle-class, women's movement whose central goal was to protect the home. The welfare legislation that resulted is often labeled maternalist because it was designed to protect motherhood and the home. It defined all women, whatever else they did, as homemakers, reducing women's wage-earning roles to a secondary position. Middle-class intervention provided the single strongest voice in the passage of state legislation on behalf of women at home and in the workplace.[38] It had contradictory effects for different kinds of women, empowering middle-class women to speak on behalf of wage-earning women, discouraging working-class women from certain kinds of jobs, and excluding most jobs in which black women were heavily employed. It produced legislation that was simultaneously maternalist and regulatory but not universally applicable in that its rationale for including women rotated around the family and mothering. Occasional gestures and government workers excepted, federal workplace regulation did not attempt to cover most men until the 1930s.

Third, the language utilized to legitimize passage of legislation on behalf of women inhibited the capacity of social-justice legislation to assume a more universal aspect because it framed issues that might have been in the domain of the workplace in ways that turned them into women's problems or placed them in the nexus of the family, where they became appropriate subjects for middle-class influence and state action. While in many European countries maternalist legislation occurred in the context of a broader acceptance of state intervention in the market, in the United States gendered language negated the possibilities for achieving universal job protections, encouraging men to see them as inimical to their familial or personal interests. In consequence, efforts to acquire legislation regulating the hours and wages of workers were, with few exceptions, restricted to women.[39]

That huge confluence of legislation we call protective labor legislation provides a case in point. Rooted as it was in arguments for the protection of motherhood and in efforts to reify the home at the expense of female independence, there was little chance for the legislation to serve as a model for men. The debate around restricting night work, for example, was articulated in language that explicitly denigrated the employability of the women who were said to need it.[40] One might argue that it turned motherhood and maternalism into an instrument for undermining the universal rights that workers in other industrial countries were beginning to acquire. That it did so in the name of the workers' self-interest in the home is the more remarkable. Legislation passed for women, made possible because of their differential relationship to the state, thus served to deter redistributive efforts.[41]

Fourth, redistributive policies did not seriously appear on the agenda of U.S. social legislation until the crisis of the 1930s, at least a generation later than in most of Europe. Before that, sporadic efforts to develop a rationale for achieving such entitlements as health care and unemployment insurance fall foul of a gendered language that roots manliness in self-protection or, like workmen's compensation, confines it to programs in which employers agree to participate. One explanation for the tentative nature of such redistributive strategies as the 1920s mothers' pensions initiatives (which were punitive in nature, discriminatory in their application, and incorporated requirements that revolved around women's successful performance of their home roles) lies in their violation of male claims to providerhood.

Fifth and finally, because the construction of women's rights in relation to the home restricts the parameters within which social legislation is discussed, some issues remain out of bounds. Maternity legislation, the cornerstone of European protections for women workers, is the most vivid example. While in many European countries, some combination of legislation offering medical care and time off with job protection to women workers at childbirth was standard by World War I, in the United States such legislation was seriously considered by only one state (New York) and passed in none. Florence Kelley, the director of the National Consumers' League and a champion of protective legislation for women workers, explained that she opposed "'any law which provides for recognition by the state, of the practice of sending childbearing wives out of the home into industry.'"[42] At the same time, attaching women's rights to the home fosters disputes among women around such issues as whether married women have a right to a job, the nature of "respectable" versus "disreputable" jobs, and whether the state should support unwed mothers.

From our perspective, what is significant about this period is the cross-class construction of individual rights and equal opportunity as gender-linked prerogatives—available to men in some ways and to women in others. Their differential application to the home and workplace resulted in legitimizing appeals to the state for protection for the family and the women within it at the cost of conceiving any broader state role in the workplace. No longer invisible in the light of the Constitution, gendered constructions of the rights of citizenship emerged at the turn of the century as articulated rationales for the way democracy was to evolve and for restricting or enhancing the role of the state. The close relationship of equal rights under the law for men and the denial of economic opportunity to women justified and enhanced the dependence of working-class women, constructing access to citizenship as a condition of gender and fostering a variety of strategies that implicitly linked the well-being of men and their families with demands for access to economic democracy that tended to exclude women. The result was to exacerbate class and gender conflict in ways that limited conceptions of a welfare state.

The process affirmed the unwillingness of the state to mediate between the market and workers while providing a mechanism for state intervention between the market and women/mothers who sometimes happened also to be workers. Men of all classes participated in this strategy because it helped to bond them together regardless of their economic position.[43] The gendered association on which the strategy builds—between independence, manliness, and freedom from state intervention, on one side, and dependence, community, regulation and femininity, on the other side—creates conflicts among workers. At the same time, male workers, denied access to universal benefits, develop a compensatory ideology of the home that purports to limit competition in the labor market. Female workers, in contrast, struggle among themselves to define the boundaries between regulations designed to benefit the home (which now fall within the state's jurisdiction) and their access to jobs that are threatened by efforts to preserve their motherhood.

The gendered lens illuminates the particular circumstances that encouraged the disintegration of a community of interest, and it helps us to see how notions of individual rights altered the relation of women to the state. At the same time, it discloses how working men constructed themselves with relation to the state in ways that made them not only "not women" (not dependent) but magnified their claims to equality of opportunity at the cost of the potential benefits of collective interests. To ignore this piece of the gendered equation by focusing, for example, on the influence of women alone obscures the complex array of negotiations that illustrates how, in a difficult economic moment, efforts to reconcile and reshape prevailing conceptions of liberty, contract, and labor within the context of familiar gendered understanding culminated in the restrictive system of social justice we sometimes call the semi-welfare state.

13

The Paradox of Motherhood:
Night-Work Restrictions
in the United States

A
mong western industrial countries, the United States was a late-
comer to maternal protection. It did not pass national legislation to
protect women's jobs in the weeks before and after childbirth until
1993. With the exception of New York, where a provision for paid job
leaves and medical insurance for pregnant working women was discussed and
then defeated in 1919, the states have also largely ignored the issue of maternity
leaves for most private-sector workers.

Considering that concern for the welfare of mothers has dominated the discussion of protection for women workers in the United States, the absence
of maternity leaves, which constitute the backbone of protective labor legislation in most other countries, is puzzling. In the early twentieth century,
when the search for protection became a legislative priority, advocates of maximum hours, night-work regulation, and safety and health measures rooted
their arguments in the need to protect the family roles of women. At the same
time, independent of the workplace, reformers struggled to address high levels
of infant mortality through clinics for pregnant women and young children,
and they argued successfully for mothers' pensions that would permit some
mothers of small children to stay out of the workforce.[1] Yet neither in this early
period nor until recently has maternal protection for women in the workplace
seriously entered the U.S. legislative agenda.[2]

The silence about maternity legislation can hardly be explained as a function of the peculiarities of American labor legislation, which until the 1930s
was rooted in gender differences. Gender-neutral legislation, offering minimal

From Ulla Wikander, Alice Kessler-Harris, and Jane Lewis, eds., *Protecting Women: Labor Legislation in
Europe, the United States, and Australia, 1880–1920*, copyright 1995 by the Board of Trustees of the University of Illinois. Used with permission of the University of Illinois Press. I am grateful to Ulla Wikander
for Inspiration on this subject.

protections to industrial workers without regard to their sex, did not emerge in the United States until the late 1930s. Before that, with few exceptions, protective labor legislation was designed for women only. The exceptions involved the working conditions of federal and some state and municipal employees as well as workers whose health and safety affected public well-being. The hours of railway workers, for example, were reduced by federal law, and those of miners were reduced by many states because of the danger that exhausted workers might hurt passengers or other workers. However, in a precedent-setting 1905 case, the U.S. Supreme Court refused to allow New York State to regulate the hours of bakers because there was nothing intrinsically unhealthful in allowing bakers to work as long as they wished.[3]

While this case and others effectively stymied gender-neutral laws, legislation specific to women progressed rapidly. Between 1908 and 1920, an astonishingly wide array of laws emerged from state after state. Thirty-nine of the forty-eight states regulated hours for women; thirteen states and the District of Columbia passed minimum-wage laws; sixteen states passed laws that expressly forbade night work for women. Because the progress of this legislation varied from state to state and because its impact has been well documented, I will not summarize it here.[4] Rather, I want to focus on the larger meaning of this body of legislation by looking at the case of night-work laws.

License for the several states to regulate women's right to work under conditions of their own choosing derived from the Supreme Court's decision in the 1908 case of *Muller v. Oregon.* The Court sharply distinguished between what was appropriate for men and what was desirable for women. Arguing that the state had an interest in women's present and future roles as actual mothers and as "mothers of the race," the Court upheld Oregon's effort to reduce the hours of women workers.[5] It thereby inscribed into precedent the notion that women, all of whom could be viewed as potential mothers, constituted a separate class and a proper subject for legislative action. For the next three decades, the basis of American protective legislation resided in women's capacity to become mothers. But no effort was made to address one of the central issues of motherhood: the difficulty of giving birth and of holding down a job at the same time. In sharp contrast to the frequent discussions of maternal and infant health, concern for maternity leaves for wage-earning women rarely entered the agendas of state legislators or female reformers.

Part of the explanation for this curious gap may lie in how the debate over protective legislation was constructed in the United States. First, in contrast to most other countries, the debate was not primarily the province either of political parties or of the labor movement. No socialist or social democratic party was powerful enough to dominate the debate; neither of the leading parties (Republican or Democratic) took on the issues as a national cause;

and the struggling trade-union movement was too weak to provide leadership. For most of the first two decades of the twentieth century, the dominant American Federation of Labor resisted efforts to legislate on behalf of men and acquiesced reluctantly and ambivalently to efforts to legislate for women. Trade-union leaders believed that the only real protection for workers derived from effective organization, and they convinced themselves that if male workers were unionized and earned a family wage, women would not have to work at all. In the meantime, union leaders offered lukewarm support for the efforts of groups like the Women's Trade Union League and the National Consumers' League to pass legislation for women only.

The failure of political and working-class leadership left the legislative initiative in the hands of a loose coalition of mostly female reformers. For the most part, the campaign for protective legislation was led on a state-by-state basis by middle-class women who possessed a vision of family as traditional as that of trade-union men. Recent discussions of Florence Kelley and the National Consumers' League suggest that the political coalitions they formed to campaign for reduced hours, night-work laws, and minimum wages for women led the drive to regulate women's paid labor.[6] Their efforts derived from concern for family life, and their strategies were shaped by the constraints of the legislative and judicial systems rather than by the agendas of poor working women.[7]

A second critical factor in the U.S. experience was the role of the courts. The legal debate over protective labor legislation intersected two discussions in U.S. law. The first, from the perspective of labor, was the conflict between the doctrine of freedom of contract and that of the police power of the state. By the late nineteenth century it had become pretty much settled law that the courts would not interfere with a worker's "individual right" to negotiate with an employer. This doctrine, known as "freedom of contract," held that every citizen had the right to decide when and under what circumstances he or she would work. Since, in the judgment of the courts, a practical equality existed between employer and employee, legislation that would impinge on the contractual relation was held unconstitutional. The state could intervene by regulating hours, wages, and working conditions only when it perceived the public interest or the general welfare to be at stake. In practice, court interpretations deprived even well-intentioned lawmakers of the opportunity to legislate for workers, except when the health of the worker was threatened in such a way as to damage public well-being. The police power of the state could thus be used to limit freedom of contract only in special circumstances.

Because she belonged to a class of people who could become mothers, a female worker turned out to be a special circumstance. From the perspective of family law, the state perceived and the courts upheld a primary interest in the family. By the end of the nineteenth century, they had constructed an image of married women as individuals entitled to limited citizenship rights. Yet this class of citizens had particular claims on the courts by virtue of its role in preserving family life.[8] The entry of large numbers of women into the industrial labor force compelled legislatures and the courts to consider how women could simultaneously exercise the freedom of contract implicit in citizenship and demand the protection of the police power of the state to preserve their own health and that of their present and future families. At the heart of this debate lay the meaning of womanhood itself.

As in most other countries, debates over social legislation took place in the ferment surrounding a rapid industrialization process. Many commentators have noted the absence of feudal and other obligatory constraints and the particularly predatory nature of U.S. capitalism at the end of the nineteenth century. This period has been labeled the "age of the robber baron" due to the rapid consolidation of capital, the speed of industrial mergers, and the concentration of major production industries. Historians have commented on the Darwinian rationalizations adopted by leaders of industry and on such notions as the "gospel of wealth" to justify unapologetic and increasingly sharp divisions between rich and poor. A massive influx of immigrants (some twenty million from foreign countries, and some eleven million from rural to urban areas in the United States between 1870 and 1920) made industrial workers particularly vulnerable. The process and its ideological justifications led to deteriorating working and living conditions for all workers and created special concerns about whether or not family life among the least skilled and most vulnerable might deteriorate to the point where the poor would no longer be trained to participate in the labor force. These concerns were exacerbated by the increasing numbers of women drawn into wage labor. By 1900, women constituted 25 percent of industrial workers. Though relatively few married women were employed (perhaps 6 percent) in 1900, they represented about 15 percent of all women workers.

Political, judicial, and economic parameters together heavily influenced the nature of the discourse on protective labor legislation. This discourse, which ultimately shaped visions of what was possible in the legislative sphere, created the paradoxical situation in which the idea of motherhood became the object of protection in the workplace, while women who became mothers acquired no job protection at all.

The debate around prohibiting night work, which began in the United States in the late nineteenth century, provides a useful illustration of how this paradox came about. As part of the movement for shorter hours, the debate over night work added complexity to an already difficult issue. Historically, the debate emerged from discussion regarding maximum hours. Restricting night work was a heuristic device designed to encourage employers to obey the shorter-hours legislation just beginning to emerge and to facilitate its enforcement.[9] Contemporary reformers understood that their efforts to reduce the daily hours of women wage earners would be stymied if women worked split shifts or if they took a second job. To solve the problem, reformers called for prohibiting night work altogether. Their efforts quickly found justification in a range of arguments about the importance of family and the humane effects of shorter hours. Like arguments against the long working day, those formulated to prohibit women's work at night frequently confronted the equally salient issue of male night work. Though reformers were often sympathetic to laws that might have prohibited night work for men as well as women, legal precedent and a hostile judiciary vitiated this possibility. Thus, the moral effort to ensure that no one would work at night confronted the legal conviction that the work of adults could not be regulated. To resolve this standoff required exaggerating gender differences and placing the qualities of women, not social justice for workers, in the forefront of the debate.

At the time of the Bern conference in 1906 (to which the United States did not send delegates because the individual states were empowered to legislate working conditions), only four of the forty-eight states had laws restricting the employment of women at night.[10] In one of these (New York), the state's highest court would declare night-work laws unconstitutional in 1907. The Bern conference's resolution restricting women's night work seems to have had little effect on U.S. legislation.[11] No other states even attempted to restrict night work until after the Supreme Court declared in 1908 that women were in effect wards of the state whose prior interest in their health and mothering capacity permitted intervention.[12] In the aftermath of this decision, several states included the regulation of night work among their laws restricting women's work. But even by 1918, only twelve states had such laws, as compared with forty-two that had adopted maximum-hour laws for women workers.[13]

The debate over night work for women heated up in the years following World War I, and in the early 1920s four new states (New Jersey, North Dakota, Washington, and California) passed restrictive night-work laws.[14] Two other states moved in the opposite direction: Maryland and New Hampshire explicitly acknowledged women's right to hold night jobs by limiting to eight hours the length of time a woman could work at night. In 1924, the Supreme Court decisively upheld the constitutionality of legislation that restricted night work for women but not for men, but state legislatures did not respond. The total number of states regulating women's night work remained at sixteen—only one-third of all the states.

Even that number exaggerates the kinds of protection women could expect. The laws varied dramatically from state to state as to the hours during which restrictions applied and the industries covered and exempted. For example,

Indiana, Massachusetts, and Pennsylvania covered only manufacturing plants; South Carolina covered only retail stores; Ohio regulated night work for female ticket sellers; and Washington singled out elevator operators.[15] Even states with stringent regulations permitted exceptions: nurses, hotel workers, and those employed at seasonal agricultural and cannery labor were most frequently allowed to work at night. But other states, in no discernible pattern, thought it unnecessary to restrict the hours of women employed, for example, as domestics, actors and performers, or cloakroom attendants. Some exempted store workers for the two weeks before Christmas; others refused to restrict women who worked in small towns no matter what their occupation.[16] Most regulations prohibited work from 10:00 PM until 6:00 AM. Massachusetts denied textile mills the right to employ women from 6:00 PM until 6:00 AM but allowed other businesses to utilize women during the evening hours. Some rural states with almost no industrial workers, such as North Dakota and Nebraska, passed restrictive night-work laws, while heavily industrialized states like Illinois refused to do so. The Women's Bureau of the Department of Labor, surveying with some dismay this chaotic array of legislation in 1924, concluded that night-work legislation was "found not only in a much smaller number of States than is legislation limiting the daily and weekly hours of work, but in many States which have both types of legislation, the night-work laws cover a much smaller group of industries or occupations."[17]

The wide array of laws, and the refusal of many states to adopt them, may reflect the fact that relatively few women earned their livings at night. A 1928 Women's Bureau study of twelve states found that on the average slightly more than 2 percent of all female wage earners worked during the night hours.[18] Mississippi, the state with the highest percentage, counted 6.4 percent of its working women in night jobs; Alabama, South Carolina, and Virginia each had between 4 and 5 percent. The heavy concentration of night work in these southern states can be traced to the textile mills, which employed 40 percent of all night workers (87 percent of whom were employed in Alabama, Georgia, Mississippi, South Carolina, and Tennessee).

If night work was confined to a relatively small group of women, these women were crucially placed. Among the night workers, as the Women's Bureau noted, "all but a negligible proportion were in the years of development or of highest childbearing capacity, the years precisely when all the characteristic injuries of night work are most disastrous."[19] Of the women who worked at night, some 75 percent were between the ages of twenty and forty, and an equal percentage were mothers of young children. Other studies confirmed these figures. In Passaic, New Jersey, ninety-six of a sample group of one hundred night-working women surveyed in 1919 were married; ninety-two of them had children; only five were widowed or did not live with or have husbands.[20]

These figures stand in sharp contrast to the female workforce as a whole in 1920, less than 15 percent of which was married,[21] and probably no more than one-third of whom were mothers of small children. The problem was that night work confronted a reluctant legislative and court system with what to do about working mothers. This phenomenon shaped the debate, structuring perceptions of the workforce as a whole and leading to a formulation of gender distinctions that encouraged the continuing exclusion of males from legislative protection and legislative silences about women who became mothers during their working years.

An examination of the rhetoric of the debate around night work that occurred in the late nineteenth and early twentieth centuries appears to explain how this happened. The debate locates itself in three areas: in the effort to modify harsh working conditions for all workers, regardless of sex; in the creation and precise definition of an idealized version of women (a universal woman); and in the problem of how to regulate competition in the labor force. These are neither uncontested nor mutually exclusive; arguments for all three are sometimes made by the same person in the same sentence. Commentators also frequently acknowledged disagreement when offering their own strongly felt opinions. But distinguishing them allows us to see how ideas play themselves out in ways that produce regulation and reflect a particular construction of gender.

Since the discussion of night work arose from an effort to restrict the role of capital and to humanize its uses in the treatment of all workers, night-work legislation, like other protective legislation, initially was meant to incorporate an apparently gender-neutral concept of workers. Eliminating night work was necessary to increase the possibility of leisure, to allow full family lives, to provide access to education, and to encourage effective participation in political citizenship. These arguments continued through the first decades of the twentieth century.

Night work, it was argued, was not good for any worker. Thus, the secretary of the male Bakery and Confectionery Workers International Union used the following language to condemn it. Night work, he suggested, was "one of the greatest evils against humanity." Its deleterious effect on bakers "makes them dissatisfied and warps and spoils their dispositions because they are prevented from enjoying proper rest which they cannot get during the day. Furthermore they are prevented from sharing in the joys of family life or the opportunities of educating themselves for a better station in life."[22] Note that the deleterious consequences are said to detract from the lives of all individuals, not specifically men alone. Contrast this with the language used in Josephine Goldmark's influential 1912 study, *Fatigue and Efficiency,* which identified the negative features of night work in gender-neutral terms. The "characteristic and invariable effects" of night work, she argued, were "the loss of sleep and sunlight," with its "inevitable physiological deficits." But, she continued, the evil effects of night work on everyone's health produced in women the additional problems of "loss of appetite, headache, anaemia, and weakness of the female functions."[23] With few exceptions, advocates of night-work legislation turned arguments for its abolition into special pleadings for women. A typical article in the *American Journal of Public Health* would begin by asserting, "I am not in favor of night work for anybody," and then turn to the particular ill effects of night work on women.[24]

Failing to establish effective legal grounds for regulating capital's ability to buy labor, reformers turned to women as examples of what the state might appropriately do and sometimes offered them up as the vanguard of state activity. This discussion was inevitably influenced by the sharpening conflict over definitions of womanhood. Calling attention to the problem of night work for women in particular presented the issue as a social problem that could and did require state intervention, for the state, as many reformers pointed out, did not hesitate to exercise its police power when public health was at stake. This strategy at first stumbled on the roadblock of freedom of contract—defined as a right of citizenship.

While even the most ardent reformers hesitated to infringe on the citizenship rights of men, those of women proved to be much more vulnerable. When the issue first emerged in the landmark case of *Ritchie v. the People,* the court held that "if one man is denied the right to contract under the law as he has hitherto done under the law, and as others are still allowed to do by the law, he is deprived of both liberty and property." It struck down an effort to regulate women's hours as a "purely arbitrary restriction upon the fundamental right of the citizen to control his or her own time and faculties."[25] But within five years, women's citizenship rights came under pressure. In 1905, Pennsylvania's highest court allowed the state to regulate women's hours, asserting that "the fact that both parties are of full age and competent to contract does not necessarily deprive the state of the power to interfere when the parties do not stand upon an equality, or when the public health demands that one party to the contract shall be protected against himself." The state, the court added presciently, "retains an interest in his welfare, however reckless he may be."[26] The male adjective aside, we should not let this warning to womankind go unheeded. Later events were to sustain the court's notion that women's citizenship rights were vulnerable to legislative and judicial determinations about the public health, with or without the consent of the women involved. What was at issue, then, was not whether women needed the protection but whether to sustain state intervention required a modification of women's rights.

The slow pace of legislative activity, especially around night-work legislation, tells us something about the skepticism with which this interpretation was initially viewed. In reviewing New York State's early attempts to put night-work clauses into legislation, the economic historian Elizabeth Faulkner Baker notes that "there was quiet question in the minds of New York labor officials from the start as to the right of the legislature to prohibit *adult women* from working at night." As late as 1906, the state's labor commissioner argued,

> [T]here is no present necessity in this state for the prohibition of night work by adult women. On the other hand, if enforced, it would deprive some mature working women, employed at night only, at skilled trades, for short hours and for high wages, of all means of support. And the prohibition in its application to factories only seems rather one-sided when we consider that probably the hardest occupations of women, those of hotel laundresses and cleaners, are not limited as to hours in any way.[27]

Because protective labor legislation relied on a special effort to restrict the citizenship rights of one class of people, the hope that it would serve as a vanguard—an example that would be followed by regulations for all workers—seemed doomed before it began. The discourse over night work quickly transformed what might have been a general struggle into a woman's issue, constructing contrasting pictures of gendered citizenship rights, organizational capacity, and natural and social circumstances.

How this happened can best be explained by looking at the rhetoric that formed the core of the debate over a period of more than two decades. Taken as a whole, the rhetoric creates a concept of an ideal, or universal, woman. To make the case for special legislation for women required riding roughshod over class, race, and ethnic distinctions and ignoring questions of life-cycles and personal choice. The debate situated all women within a single framework defined as "natural" and located within childbearing and child-rearing functions. It sought to portray a world in which these attributes dominated—and therefore justified the sacrifice of all others. The words of the New York State court that in 1914 articulated the standard for all other night-work decisions drew on and extended the decision in *Muller v. Oregon*. Night work in factories, as contrasted with day labor, wrote the court, "substantially affects and impairs the physical condition of women and prevents them from discharging in a healthful and satisfactory manner the peculiar functions which have been imposed upon them by nature." The court offered little sympathy to the many women who did not exercise these functions, suggesting that such differences among women did not tempt it to modify the decision. Moreover, the court acknowledged that "this statute in its universal application to all factories will inflict unnecessary hardships on a great many women who neither ask nor require its provisions by depriving them of an opportunity to earn a livelihood by perfectly healthful labor although performed during some of the hours of the night."[28] But, the court insisted, such women should turn to the legislature, not the courts, for relief, for the prerogative of defining public welfare lay in legislative hands.

If this decision did not repeat the language of the public debate, it and the 1908 U.S. Supreme Court decision that sealed approval of all such restrictions certainly reaffirmed what would by the mid-1920s become a prevailing theme. That debate, firmly rooted in the traditional family and in women's place within it, identified women in terms of their family roles and articulated the expectation that they would reproduce. The debate was conducted as if all women were mothers or potential mothers. The evil effects of night work on both men and women receded in the face of its consequences for those who would bear or care for children. Rather, legislatures attempted to persuade the courts that women's health in particular required state intervention. Drawing heavily on the research utilized by successful European advocates of night-work prohibitions, American supporters painted a distressing picture. Their language invoked the female's "delicate organism" and cited at length the injuries to women's reproductive systems, menstrual cycles, and general vitality that the state had a special interest in guarding. Inevitably, women's physical capacities were described as being far less than those of men. "No-one doubts," wrote the judge who issued the opinion in *The People v. Schweinler* (1914), "that as regards bodily strength and endurance [a woman] is inferior. . . . As healthy mothers are essential to vigorous offspring, the physical well-being of women becomes an object of public interest and care in order to preserve the strength and vigor of the race."[29]

Advocates did not fail to add, nor courts to take notice of, the social burdens imposed on women by household tasks. Women's double day, suggested Frances Perkins, the industrial commissioner of New York State, provided the rationale for protection. "Night work," she argued, "bears with special severity on women who under these conditions tend to work all night and discharge family and home duties most of the day."[30] Louis Brandeis and Josephine Goldmark, in their brief to the court hearing the New York State case on night-work legislation, wrote, "Women who work in factories are not thereby relieved from household duties—from cooking, washing, cleaning, and looking after their families,"[31] and the court concurred. Housework, it noted in its favorable ruling, filled "most of the day" for those who worked at night.[32]

These arguments were not uncontested. Medical opinion differed as to the effect of night work on the menstrual cycle,[33] and many experts testified to the disadvantages of long hours, long periods of standing, and the stress of responding to machines. Attempts to place the discussion in the framework of poor working conditions in general proved successful in only two states that limited night work to eight hours, rather than banning it altogether.

In general, however, the effects of poverty and malnutrition and the debility caused by overwork were identified as the peculiarly gendered consequences of night work. Infant mortality and higher morbidity rates for working women were widely laid at its door. "It goes without saying," Brandeis and Goldmark dismissively wrote in their New York State brief, "that many other factors besides the mother's employment contribute to a high infant mortality, such as poverty, inadequate attendance at birth, wrong feeding, bad sanitation, and the like."[34] Though studies conducted by the U.S. Children's Bureau confirmed European research that demonstrated an overwhelming relationship between infant mortality and fathers' wages, arguments that an increase in male wages might solve some of the problems of malnutrition and long hours fell on deaf ears.

The possibilities inherent in higher wages for men (which would have required a different kind of regulation) were rarely pursued by investigators who preferred instead to depict the horror inherent in night work for women. In the textile mills of Passaic, New Jersey, night-working women were described as "weary, tousled . . . half dressed, trying to snatch an hour of sleep after [a] long night of work in the mill." Their children were "aimless" and "neglected," the tragedy of their lot reflected in their "woebegone and wistful faces."[35] A government investigation described the children of night workers as "pitiable drifts and strays deprived of anchorage."[36] The homes of these women night workers were "as dismal and neglected as similar homes were found by investigators abroad."[37] Implicitly these descriptions blamed poor health, household disorder, and neglected children on the problems of night work, exonerating the role of desperate poverty. These descriptions also encouraged an image of women who deprived their families of domestic comforts, negating a healthy moral as well as physical environment. "Young women who work at night," wrote Goldmark in 1912, "are deprived of all the restraining influences of home life." And when the mother of a family "spends the night or evening in work, disorder is almost unavoidable, and the comfort of the men as well as of the children dependent upon her ministrations is lost."[38]

The subtext that appealed to the legislative instinct was the helplessness of women engaged in night work. What kinds of women would abandon their homes and children to such depravity? The literature described them as foreigners: "Poles, Hungarians, and Russians," women who "speak little English" and were "always willing to work overtime." They were also "poor negro women" employed as substitutes for boys; or they were the "lintheads" of the southern textile industry.[39]

The language used to describe women's nighttime experiences affirmed their helplessness. Louise Kindig, the twenty-three-year-old woman who tested the constitutionality of New York State's night-work law in 1913, was described as "a frail girl" who "represented hundreds of working women who, night after night, are employed in the factories and workshops of New York." Like other such women, Kindig was "forced to go outside for meals at midnight"[40] and was "'turned into the streets at a late hour of night or at early dawn.'"[41] Women night workers were "ignorant women" who could "scarcely be expected to realize the dangers not only to their own health, but to that of the next generation from such inhuman usage."[42]

This message was eagerly, even anxiously perpetuated by male and female reformers for whom protective labor legislation, and particularly restrictions on night work, seemed to respond to a need to regulate a chaotic labor market. Here the emphasis shifted to the need to protect the male provider role, both in its economic aspects and in its social assumptions of patriarchal entitlements. Employers, union men, and reformers, as well as some wage-earning women, debated efforts to restrict night work and sometimes unilaterally limited women's ability to work at night as a function of implicit understandings about who should support the family and what constituted an appropriate job. The discussions reflect and affirm a sense of entitlement on the part of males that turns women's refusal to submit to regulation into a selfish act that threatens to undermine the family.

Assumptions about male roles may explain why so few women worked at night to begin with—partly out of their own expectations, and partly out of what the Women's Bureau described in 1928 as "an astonishingly strong feeling among employers in industry against the employment of women at night, irrespective of legal regulation."[43] These feelings, affirmed by union men, were not independent of generally shared assumptions about female roles. Lurid sketches of opportunities for immoral behavior inherent in female work at night, accusations that unscrupulous employers fed their female workers "liquor and narcotics to overcome exhaustion," and the conviction that the bad character of some night workers would infect even decent women—all these conspired to construct an image of night work that negated the possibilities of respectable family life.[44]

Opponents of night-work restrictions adopted the same language but gave it a different twist. Conceding that family life was the most important issue at stake in whether or not legislation should be passed, they constructed images of sturdy, self-supporting women who used the extra income they could earn at night to support families in modest comfort. They repeated such stories as that of the female elevator operator whose family situation deteriorated when she lost her relatively comfortable job only to end up as a poorly paid charwoman. They circulated hardship stories of skilled women printers who could no longer keep their families after they lost their night jobs. Waitresses who could not work at night when the tips were highest complained that the hat-check girls and cabaret singers, who were exempted from the law, were less likely to have children and families in need.[45]

The language of male prerogative and of family values translated directly into the workforce. Elizabeth Faulkner Baker, in a thoughtful discussion of the problem, noted that both sides of the argument understood that if legislation passed, then "men will always be preferred . . . leaving women to earn a scanty living out of the left-over jobs—a part of the luckless mass of underpaid, unskilled, and unorganized workers who toil long and hope little."[46] Such job segregation would inevitably follow night-work restrictions because whole categories of jobs would be removed from female competition.

Perhaps more significant in the long run, the explicit rejection by unionized men of the need for protective legislation was sustained and supported by a false perception of the role of trade unions that played off images of women's weaknesses. One popular magazine, for example, advocated night-work restrictions for women because "working women and girls, less able to organize for self protection need, if they are to fulfill the functions of motherhood, to be protected against the exploitation of their physical and mental life by a greedy and inhuman industrialism."[47] In 1907, perhaps 12 percent of America's urban male workers belonged to unions—a figure that rose to nearly 20 percent during World War I and then declined again in the 1920s. Not until the mass-organizing drives of the mid-1930s did the proportion of organized men in industry reach even 25 percent. Still, advocates of night work insisted that women needed the protection of laws to offset a protection already negotiated by men. Frances Perkins, for example, noted that women who were poorly organized could not be expected to reproduce the experience of men, who had "in many instances created excellent industrial conditions for themselves without legislation and through the medium of the trade union and the strike."[48]

Distinguishing men from women in this way preserved benefits for the relatively few, mostly skilled men who were union members—a boon to which working men were not insensitive. For example, when New York's unionized female printers, deprived of their night jobs under state law in 1914, petitioned the legislature for relief, they were opposed by a significant proportion of the membership of their own union. When in 1921 an exception was made in women's favor, union men and foremen placed obstacles in the paths of their return to their old jobs.[49] Despite a Women's Bureau finding that streetcar conducting was healthful outdoor work, the New York State legislature refused to grant an exemption when male workers fought against it. As a result, 83 percent of New York City's female streetcar conductors lost their jobs.

A rhetoric that obscured male needs and took its stance from questionable depictions of the character and lives of women concealed some of the larger issues of the debate. Though reformers frequently raised questions about the efficiency of running factories late at night, such questions did not enter the agenda until the discussion broadened in the 1930s. Rather, manufacturers thought about the problem in terms of control of the workforce, constructing images of women that accorded with their own and with community perceptions of present and future labor-force needs. Generally, it was easier to play the sexes against each other than to exclude one sex or the other. "Night work for women," concluded Agnes de Lima, "is fostered by the low wage scale for men, coupled with a comparatively high wage level for women which tempts them to enter the industry."[50]

This very cursory, tentative examination of the rhetoric surrounding night-work legislation in the United States reveals a public culture in which men and women differ dramatically in their possession of citizenship rights. Night work, equally evil for men and women, was regulated only for women (albeit ambivalently) because their claims to citizenship rights were subject to public perceptions of appropriate behavior for females in family life. Such perceptions inhered in women's role in social reproduction and in the characteristics of person and physique assumed to be necessary to fulfill that role. Assumptions about women's roles and attributions to them of qualities that inhibited their capacity to function effectively in the workforce turned the debate over night work into a discussion of women's functions. In the face of this onslaught against women's physical stamina and character, other alternatives such as nurseries for children, minimum wages for men, and police patrols for dangerous streets became invisible. The shape of the debate, framed in terms of settled assumptions about motherhood and domesticity, contributed to the passage of laws that exacerbated differences between men and women. Rooting legislation in this manner did more than characterize and disadvantage women; it discredited protective legislation for men. The unspoken message that legislation was necessary for the weak and inferior implied that only the weak and inferior would seek it. Mature adult males could be left to the mercy of an unencumbered capitalism.

Equally important, the particular construction of citizenship that facilitated legislation for women was rooted in the states' right to protect motherhood and family roles, not in a woman's right to protect her job. The discourse that made such a division possible created a vision of motherhood that precluded an amalgam of wage work and mothering in the public mind and therefore mitigated against maternity leaves to protect jobs and instead supported maternal protections that saved babies. A rhetoric that reduced women who worked to inadequate mothers left little room for policies that might allow mothers more rights at work. Instead, it encouraged ways of removing mothers from the workforce through such devices as mothers' pensions.

What emerged in the late nineteenth and early twentieth centuries was at best a limited and hard-fought consensus on social reproduction and women's place in it. But it was costly. To assert women's primary roles as childbearers and child rearers meant subsuming their role as providers. The result was that women's individual rights as citizens were regulated on behalf of motherhood. The powerful images invoked in the debate enabled the public to accept the loss of economic rights for women in favor of the states' desire to protect the rights of all women to be mothers. Consistent with the judicial antagonism against economic rights for all workers, as well as with the preferences of American industry, the courts did not protect the rights of women as workers. Instead, they offered women, conceived in terms of motherhood, the right not to work at all, setting up a contradiction between motherhood and work that made asking for maternity legislation all but inconceivable.

14

Measures for Masculinity: The American Labor Movement and Welfare-State Policy during the Great Depression

istorians who have investigated how gender shapes the welfare state have paid a good deal of attention to the consequences of maternal claims and the social movements organized around them. We now understand how such claims influenced the development of health insurance, protective labor legislation, mothers' pensions, and aid to dependent children.[1] But we know less about claims made on behalf of manly ideals. In this essay, I suggest that ideas of gender may have a more subtle impact in shaping legislation than we have yet imagined. I argue that by constructing the imagination out of which the legislative agenda emerges, gender infuses the language with which individuals articulate demands for change. Notions of masculinity, I suggest, specifically influenced the nature of the U.S. welfare state that emerged in the 1930s. Conceived in and through the American labor movement, images of masculinity governed the political possibilities and ultimately constrained the capacity of legislators to provide European-style benefits.

For most of the nineteenth century and the early part of the twentieth, American courts prohibited state intervention in the lives of individual workers. With the major exception of women and a few male workers on whom the public relied for its own safety and well-being (like railroad engineers), the federal government and most states had resolutely stayed out of the business of regulating the hours, working conditions, and wages of labor. Nor did the separate states provide much in the way of minimum standards for the health

First published in Stefan Dudink, Karen Hagemann, and John Tosh, eds., *Masculinities in Politics and War: Gendering Modern History* (Manchester: University of Manchester Press, 2004).

Material for this essay is drawn from Alice Kessler-Harris, *In Pursuit of Equity: Women, Men, and the Quest for Economic Citizenship in Twentieth Century America* (New York: Oxford University Press, 2001), chap. 2. It is used here with the permission of the press.

and well-being of any but white women workers. Despite a good deal of pressure from socialist groups and reformers of various kinds, not until the 1930s did general labor legislation enable the United States to join the ranks of the already emerging welfare states of Europe. In what follows, I focus on how one set of ideas influenced the fate of two important pieces of social legislation.

An emphasis on individual attachment to wage labor best distinguishes the welfare policies of the United States in the 1930s from those of most industrial countries. The pattern honored the fears of organized labor, which, weak as it was, sought to speak for all workers. In the late 1920s, organized labor represented only about 5 percent of American workers, most of them skilled, white males. African Americans belonged to a few mainstream unions like the United Mine Workers of America and the Sleeping Car Porters' Union. If women organized at all, they joined unions in the garment, textile, and incipient electronics industries, where the largest proportions of women workers concentrated. Still, the American Federation of Labor (AFL) was certainly the most powerful voice of workers, and when the Depression of the 1930s inspired large numbers to organize, the AFL acquired a strong voice in labor legislation.

As represented by the AFL, organized workers definitively did not want government intervention, even when it seemed to be in their self-interest. Until the early 1930s, the AFL clung obdurately to the idea of voluntarism as it had been developed by its revered longtime leader, Samuel Gompers. Voluntary organization—the right of citizens to define and pursue their goals in free association—was a call for action and a mantra for masculinity.

In the first guise, voluntarism embodied the economic self-interest of the trade union by assuring members that an investment in collective efforts would bring greater benefits and leave them less vulnerable than government intervention. Union strategy assumed that jobs were scarce resources to be distributed and protected by workers in defiance of employers' claims to control them. It invoked American ideals of individualism in defense of organization and constructed solidaristic appeals to labor to preserve its collective self-interest in jobs without fear from, or benefit of, government intervention. Voluntarism presumed that wage earners had the courage, independence, and economic power to protect their own interests. In the best of worlds, that included controlling the supply of labor to guarantee its price. Its advocates assumed that dignity—a man's dignity—resided in the capacity to do so.[2] Because it relied on the unified strength of skilled workers, partisans of voluntarism freely excluded those who might undermine labor's power, including the unskilled, most people of color, and women.

In the second guise, voluntarism closely wove the liberty of members to pursue collective ends into a pattern that reflected manly identities. The labor movement marshalled words like "courage," "dignity," "self-respect," and "independence" in defense of workers' liberty and freedom, associating them with manly conceptions of virility and economic power. It recognized that threats to liberty did not come only from clubs and rifles but from more subtle assaults on workers' conceptions of their own strength. And it found the idea of government regulations for male workers particularly threatening. Such regulation would inevitably privilege employers and undermine the manly character on which collective action rested, turning the worker into a cowardly and subservient creature forced to go hat-in-hand to the state for benefits. Fearful of the consequences, the AFL, under Gompers's leadership, consistently opposed even the most apparently beneficial interventions out of the fear that they "would build up a bureaucracy that would have some degree of authority or control over all the workers of the state."[3] It acquiesced reluctantly to workmen's-compensation programs in the 1910s. But fear of government bureaucracy and administration led it to oppose reformers' efforts to introduce even such seemingly benign benefits as health insurance in the late 1910s.[4]

At the heart of voluntarism lay a uniquely American version of manhood. Closely tied to American ideals of self-sufficiency and upward mobility, it was rooted in the notion that those who gave up control over their own fate gave up a precious source of liberty and would become lesser citizens. In this respect, the stance of American workers differed from forms of social democracy supported by European labor, which encouraged alliances between labor and social insurance advocates. American trade unionists believed "socialistic" programs that created universal entitlements available to all would undermine manhood by creating dependent and cringing males. Unlike some Europeans, who believed they could turn government to the purposes of male providers and their families, American labor leaders profoundly suspected government as the instrument of business and capital. As Samuel Gompers wrote: "[F]or the government to intervene would be wrong and harmful; wrong because such interference is destructive of personal (and inalienable) rights, harmful because it destroys initiative, independence, and self-reliance."[5]

No equivalent inhibition guided the AFL's position on women's relationship to government. Many craft unionists supported special protective laws for women on the grounds that women could not organize effectively and that these laws protected male bargaining power and jobs. They shared with social feminists a commitment to maintaining male wages and believed, with them, that employers who took advantage of women's cheap labor would undermine the family wage. AFL leaders acquiesced, as early as 1911, in plans to regulate the hours and wages of women and children in several states. By 1916, the Federation ardently supported them. Powerful voices saw labor legislation for women and children as a way of shoring up the family by discouraging employers from hiring women in the first place, while ensuring reasonable conditions for those who did enter the labor force. Regulating women's work also promised men less competition over jobs, sustaining the solidarity and collective-bargaining possibilities of men's unions. But unlike social feminists, who often proclaimed labor legislation for women "an entering wedge" that would ultimately lead to protection for all workers, the AFL's leaders continued to believe that labor laws would never do for men whose faith in collective bargaining embodied the manly force of workingmen's liberty. Yet both groups could agree on the central importance of family life and on male jobs to sustain it. Consensus on this issue may have enhanced the voice of a relatively weak AFL in national legislative councils.

Ideals of manly liberty, never far from the labor movement's self-image, asserted themselves in campaigns for a shorter work week, sought in the 1920s by many as a strategy for reducing unemployment. Acquired through collective bargaining, shorter working hours represented the power of American labor. Achieved by legislation, however, they seemed to many to be a source of weakness. Legislative processes, they argued, never had achieved and never would achieve progress for the labor movement. Instead, they invoked "the great mass of workers" who had "progressed successively from twelve to ten hours, then to eight hours, and now, in many instances, to forty-four or forty hours weekly through the power of their economic organizations."[6] Some of their number disagreed. "We have come to a point in the history of labor," argued one delegate to a 1932 convention of the Federation, "when we must of necessity change our previous attitude and opinion of regulation of hours of labor by legislation. ... I am not afraid of the United States government; it is bad enough, but it is not as bad as having eleven million men walking the streets looking for work."[7] Still, the convention roundly rejected a resolution to support a Twentieth Amendment to the U.S. Constitution mandating a thirty-hour work week.

In the AFL's discussions, fear of the legislative quick fix prevailed. "Do you know what it would mean to give this power to the Government to rule the hours of labor?" asked Andrew Furuseth of the Seamen's Union. "How do you know that you will not get twelve hours instead of four hours?"[8] Thomas Donnelly of the Ohio State Federation of Labor pitched in: "You attempt to fix the hours of labor for the working people of America, and just as soon as you do you take away from the adult worker his fundamental inherent right to work one hour, two hours, six hours, or eight hours."[9] The AFL's president, William Green, agreed. While he remained convinced that only shorter hours could permanently end unemployment, he wanted the labor movement to negotiate them. Anything less threatened labor's manly honor. "It will ultimately rest upon labor to utilize its economic strength in a constructive and practical way in order to secure this great change," he roared to a standing ovation.[10]

But the pressure on labor to change its stance escalated in the winter of 1932–33 when two members of Congress, Senator Hugo Black of Alabama and Representative William Connery of Massachusetts, introduced twin bills to forbid the shipment in interstate commerce of goods produced in a facility where "any worker was permitted to work more than five days in any week or more than six hours in any day."[11] With its ranks disrupted, its position as spokesperson for working people in question, and its own economic self-interest at stake, the AFL reluctantly shifted gears and supported the bill. Even as it did so, its leaders feared for the future of manly liberty. "Personally," John Frey told the Senate hearing called to consider the bills, "I have always been opposed . . . to regulating the terms of employment for adult males through legislation. I have believed that free men should work out their problems instead of having the legislature endeavor to do for men what they were capable of doing for themselves; but I have reached the conclusion now we are in a position where men are not capable of doing these things unless Congress says."[12] Philip Murray, then a vice president of the United Mine Workers, picked up the theme. He was driven to support the bill, he said, by the need to "sustain character" among those who would otherwise be idle. Men, he told the committee, "want to keep their economic independence. They do not want to become objects of charity. . . . [T]hey seek to maintain their relations as normal citizens toward society."[13] Could they do that if they relied on government intervention? For many labor leaders, confusion over a shorter-hours bill reflected the distress of a complicated effort to solve the practical problem of unemployment while defending its vision of manhood as the last bastion of freedom and liberty.[14]

Energized by the optimism around Franklin Delano Roosevelt's inauguration as president, hopeful that the wages issue could be resolved, its sponsors reintroduced it in March 1933. By early April, it had already passed the Senate.[15] With labor's reluctant backing and the issue of unemployment staring the administration in the face, shorter hours seemed like a popular and ready-made solution. Speaking for Roosevelt, the secretary of labor Frances Perkins publicly accepted the principle of reducing unemployment by reducing hours but insisted on making the bill "more flexible and workable."[16] In an act calculated to raise the worst fears of labor leaders, she proposed a three-member board empowered to "license" a six-hour day in industries that met minimal requirements; minimum wages established by boards to determine appropriate wages in each industrial sector; enough flexibility to extend the thirty-hour limit to forty in some industries; and a relaxation of antitrust laws where a thirty-hour week was imposed. This was everything that labor detested: a bureaucracy that could exercise discretionary powers over men's freedoms, loss of control over wages, and untrammeled influence for industry. Fearing entrapment, the AFL withdrew its support, and the bill went down to defeat.

Would the bill have met such a precipitous end if labor had compromised over the imposition of bureaucracy, had its manhood not been offended by the very idea of a regulated wage? What if labor had swallowed its concern for voluntarism and exercised the power of a countervailing force? Would Congress have overcome business's objections to a rigid thirty-hour provision? We have no way of knowing. The AFL continued to make a reduced work week the keystone of its collective-bargaining demands until the passage of the Fair Labor Standards Act in 1938. Yet its continuing commitment to the manly qualities encoded in voluntarism restrained its enthusiasm for legislative regulation of hours. Though passage of a thirty-hours bill was never a foregone conclusion, once the proposal no longer fit the gendered imagination of a skittish labor movement, it became less likely.

As it turned out, the struggle over a legislated thirty-hour work week was a skirmish in the ensuing campaign for unemployment insurance. By the 1930s, unemployment insurance should have been an idea whose time had come, and there were many advocates for a comprehensive and rational system. At one end of the political spectrum, socialists, communists, and radicals of every variety folded unemployment compensation into wide-ranging proposals to eliminate economic inequality and provide generous government support for the young, the aged, and the ill as well as the unemployed. At the other end, conservative voices of small business insisted that the federal government keep its hands off. Between these extremes lay more moderate groups whose members searched for stability and social justice within a business-oriented framework. Two proved particularly important in setting the tone of public conversations and in the policy debates within the subcommittees of the Committee on Economic Security, both of them active for a couple of decades. The first consisted of reform-minded advocates of social insurance, many of them deeply influenced by European-style programs; the second included proponents of employment stabilization through the cooperative action of government, business, and labor.[17]

The social-insurance model had a good deal of support from ordinary workers as well as from social reformers of all kinds. Championed in the United States by two somewhat controversial figures, Abraham Epstein and Isaac Rubinow, it took several different legislative forms. But at bottom, all of them offered to create a pooled fund from employer contributions and general tax revenues that would provide a minimum income to everyone who could not earn wages for reasons of sickness, disability, unemployment, or old age. The plans differed as to the level of income they offered, and at least one offered maternity insurance; but they agreed on coverage for all workers, including the self-employed, farmers, professional workers, and wage earners.

AFL leaders quickly rejected the social-insurance model, noting that it subjected all individuals equally to potential government supervision and control, and therefore suggested the helplessness of union members. It wanted a program to which workers would be entitled by "right" rather than one that smacked of government charity or relief. So leaders threw their lot on the side of those aimed towards employment stabilization.

In the United States, John Commons had early conceived and campaigned for such programs. Commons was, in 1934, recently retired from teaching at the University of Wisconsin. His *Institutional Economics* had just been published, and the third volume of his *History of Labor in the United States* was about to go to press. In these books, he elaborated his notions of the economic institutions that sustained a democratic capitalism. Most forcefully, he advocated the notion that workers, like capitalists, were "citizens of industry," each with a stake in prosperity.[18] Industry's part of this compact was to provide employment—to stabilize work and ensure its availability. Commons believed that large employers should shoulder the responsibility for seasonal and technological employment fluctuations, arguing with most of his fellow economists that they, after all, caused most unemployment. Given adequate incentives, employers could prevent it.[19] Commons conceived the right to work as essential to the exercise of citizenship, for, as he wrote early in his career, "the right to work is the right of access to the land, the machinery, the capital, whose products support life and liberty"; "[T]he rights of liberty and property are the conditions on which personal character and responsibility are based."[20] To this end he supported the collective individualism of the AFL, with its deep commitment to liberty earned through the manly freedom to work.

In practice, Commons's ideas translated into a narrow unemployment-insurance program based entirely on contributions from employers and either directly or indirectly from workers' wages. It restricted itself to large employers (those who could stabilize industry) and to regular workers, whose maintenance in the labor force would benefit industry as economic cycles changed. Benefits would be no longer than several weeks—for the expected duration of a brief economic downturn. Advocates of Commons's point of view disagreed as to whether the funds contributed by employers should be controlled by industry or by state agencies and about the level of the unemployment stipend and the length of time it should be offered. But they tended to agree on the kinds of industries to be covered and the need to exclude part-time workers and those, like women, who were only "marginally" attached to the labor force.

For the AFL, what appeared to be a choice of technical solutions to a serious economic problem represented far larger conceptions of who was and was not a man and how the dignity and freedom of workers were to be preserved. As might have been expected, they applauded the lesser reliance on the good-will of employers in which the Commons-based models were rooted while objecting vehemently to the demand that workers be required to contribute that constituted a feature of one such model.[21] Leaders protested the inclusion of business in economic planning, the self-policing of employers, and the role of government intervention. These raised the threat posed by bureaucracy to manhood. Aiming at the idea of joint contributions, they asked why employers, who had created the unemployment problem, should be able to get off scot-free (they would, after all, pass costs on to consumers) while workers suffered from reduced wages. They objected to the helplessness of workers placed in this situation. And even as they applauded the idea of pooled funds, they protested the likelihood that government would collude with a coercive employer to exercise "'leverage over the employment term.'"[22]

In distinguishing what kinds of wage work would promote eligibility for unemployment insurance and tying rights to particular patterns of labor-force participation, the Commons-based programs conceptualized participation in ways that discounted the lives of the vast majority of African Americans, members of other minority groups, and most women. If this was obscured with regard to African Americans by a rhetoric that paid obeisance to the responsibility of industry and the rights of states, it was crystalline with regard to women. Only relatively large, producing industries (where most women of any color and most African Americans did not work) could conceivably regularize work or develop the individual insurance fund necessary to provide even minimal compensation. Only workers who remained in the labor force for lengthy periods could reap benefits. The idea of regularizing work reflected a notion of rights to work that explicitly excluded women who were not providers and tacitly dismissed all women as actually or potentially married. The employment stability plans thus promised to extend new citizenship rights to men in particular (largely white) labor-force sectors, while denying them to other men and to virtually all women in the labor force.

Still, even as the representatives of African American organizations leveled sharp criticisms at the exclusions embedded in these proposals, most women did not challenge their exclusionary biases. Even when the Commons plan became the basis for conversations within the Committee on Economic Security and ultimately the root of the unemployment compensation system adopted by Congress, women remained silent. Informed by popular beliefs about the significance of marriage in the lives of ordinary wage-earning women, most maternalists pursued social policies designed to reinforce women's continuing family roles. Instead of fighting for women's rights to work, they successfully placed motherhood at the center of the legislative agenda for women workers and encouraged and sustained prevailing conceptions of women's working lives as adjuncts to the family. Perhaps we should not fault them, for they acted on definitions of family developed through fights for protective labor legislation and won, in consequence, means-tested plans that would enable poor women to care for children without wage work. Their relative failure to address work-related issues not only left the sphere of wage work to men but arguably allowed greater scope for the AFL's concern for manly liberty.

To be sure, the leaders of these two groups shared with other social activists a commitment to male providerhood, but they deeply disagreed over whether a government that sustained it would not simultaneously undermine the self-respect and independence that defined manliness. While maternalists placed great faith in government's capacity to shore up the family, the AFL remained committed to the idea of manly independence. In support of this idea, successive AFL conventions had voted against government unemployment insurance, while supporting private union-employer plans and a negotiated thirty-hour week. What seemed like simple justice to many felt to labor like an attack. "You can't have unemployment insurance," declared William Green, "without agreeing to a set-up that will, to a large degree, govern and control our activities. . . . [T]hen you must be willing to give up some of the things you now possess. You can't have an unemployment insurance plan without registration. You must report, you must subject yourself in every way to the control of the law."[23]

The AFL was no monolith, and pressure from several state federations and local and international unions led it to reconsider its position beginning in 1929. Several years of long and heated disputes within AFL councils and on the convention floor followed. Opponents decried handouts from government and protested cowardly submission to state authority. Did American workers, asked the 1930 Executive Council, echoing the language of the courts that justified protective labor legislation for women, want to follow the pattern of European schemes "under which the worker becomes a ward of the state and subject to discipline by employers under state authority?"[24] "It involves the question of whether the American Federation of Labor shall continue to hew to the line in demanding a greater freedom for the working people of America, or whether liberty shall be sacrificed in a degree sufficient to enable the workers to obtain a small measure of unemployment relief under government supervision and control."[25]

At issue were some of the same things that had emerged in the labor movement's attack on shorter hours: First, the creation of state bureaucracies that, as Gompers had put it, would undermine the principle of voluntarism by making "the means for life and thus liberty dependent on government supervision of the conditions of leaving employment."[26] Second, the construction of a fearful administrative apparatus. "Every system," argued the Executive Council in a report that rejected the idea, "contemplates supervision and control by both federal and state governments and will require registration, not only of the aliens among the workers, but of all workers." And finally, the power it provided employers even over the jobless. Any compulsory unemployment insurance program, insisted the AFL vice president Mathew Woll, would remind a worker constantly "that his employer holds what in effect amounts to at least a temporary veto power over his right to benefits when unemployed." This would, he argued, inevitably increase the power of the employer and lead to "a virtual surrender on the part of the workers . . . of their right to organize. . . . Shall we be content to carry industrial passports because they have a government label?"[27]

Enmeshed in the fear of structures they could not influence or control, AFL leaders offered up a conception of liberty demanding defense by courageous men. Throwing down the gauntlet to the cowards among them who would place their faith in the false promises of government authority, Woll demanded to know if members had "lost courage to the point where we regard freedom no longer as the greatest essential of life and the most necessary element in human progress."[28] Nor did he shrink from religious symbolism: "In return for a slice of bread—a mess of pottage, as it were—the workers are being asked . . . to yield up their birthright, to practically surrender in their struggle for liberty."[29] In this struggle over liberty, family support and personal well-being alike would take second place: "Have we come to that position in our labor movement," asked Olander incredulously, "that we are about to say that one of the most precious liberties we have . . . must be surrendered forsooth, because our people are hungry and they must eat?"[30]

To combat this strong language, supporters of unemployment insurance constructed an alternative conception of manhood. James Duncan of Seattle's Central Labor Council tried his hand at creating one. Invoking William Green's presidential address, which had demanded a new right ("the right of men to work"), he insisted that if the government denied "us the right to work" it "must at least provide some means of feeding our families while we are waiting for the opportunity to work."[31] Unemployment insurance, he suggested, far from degrading a man, would give him "a chance to stand up and say, 'No, I will not go in and work for less than my fellows get. I at least will not starve to death.'"[32] Against the Executive Council's defense of freedom, liberty, and independence, Duncan, making common cause with social reformers, invoked a different form of manliness: solidarity with fellow workers and family provision. "I want men to get the sustenance from somewhere so that they can stand up like real men and say, 'No I am getting enough to get by on. I don't have to undermine my fellows, I will stick to my unemployment insurance until I can go to work with my fellows and maintain my self-respect.'"[33] And Philip Ickler of the Pensacola, Florida, Central Labor Council offered yet another justification for the manliness of unemployment insurance. "I don't believe," he argued, that "we are making beggars out of all who need it . . . it furnishes at least a little help to keep our fellow workers in the militant fighting spirit."[34]

Would unemployment insurance contribute to beggary or fend it off? Some of the same labor leaders who had enthusiastically promoted legislation on behalf of women could not contemplate its negative consequences for manly independence. Andrew Furuseth of the Seamen's Union is a good example. A friend of Louis Brandeis and an enthusiastic supporter of special laws for women, Furuseth mounted a last-ditch resistance to unemployment insurance. After the 1932 convention finally accepted the idea, he rose to articulate what he called his unalterable opposition. No such law, he declared, had been enacted "as will retain the working man his independence and courage. . . . I think you are making a mistake, men. . . . I can't stop you, but the road you are traveling is the road that leads to the destruction of humanity and the destruction of this nation and of all other nations that can find no other way than to make out of a man a pleading beggar and a man who must go for his goods to others."[35]

By the time Furuseth spoke, the Executive Council had acted. Overwhelmed by pressure to combat existing unemployment, it reversed its position in November 1932 and persuaded William Green to reverse his. While it decried the continuing economic crisis and once again repeated its conviction that a thirty-hour week would provide the surest solution to unemployment, it offered the convention an industry-funded plan that it thought it could live with.[36] In withdrawal, Green tacitly aligned himself with the Commons proposals. "If compulsory unemployment insurance is forced upon our industrial, political, and economic life, it will be because industrial ownership and management has failed to provide and preserve these opportunities for working men and women," he told convention delegates.[37] Workers, the Executive Council affirmed, "are as much entitled to work security, to enjoy the opportunity to work, as the owner of capital are to returns from their investments." Industry's failure should be charged to it by the imposition of compulsory unemployment insurance, paid for by employers alone. It should be "clearly recognized as a legal right earned by previous employment within the state."[38]

But no one was completely happy with this solution, and the Executive Council continued to be wary that the "right" contained in unemployment insurance be absolute, insisting, for example, that drawing on unemployment insurance not infringe on rights of suffrage or on other civil rights.[39] This would be a new, an added, an "earned" right. "We are going to propose and insist," Green told the AFL's leaders in the fall of 1934, "that Congress and the State legislatures enact unemployment insurance legislation, old-age pension legislation, the abolition of child labor, and the development here of a social order that will make for the highest degree of citizenship."[40] The gesture meant little. By then, the president had already convened the Committee on Economic Security to draft a social-security program, and its staff and technical committees were hard at work. William Green, who had a seat on the Advisory Council, remained a largely silent member, leading the executive director Edwin Witte to dismiss labor's role in the formulation of the final act. It was not, he wrote later, "a major player."[41] But Witte was wrong. As much as anyone, the labor movement had set the terms within which the debate would be conducted.

On the table before the Committee on Economic Security in the fall of 1934 was a proposal for a federal tax on payrolls, 90 percent of which would be forgiven (or offset) for employers who contributed to either their own state-supervised reserve accounts or to statewide pooled accounts. The offset, which removed the federal government from a direct relationship to the recipients of unemployment compensation, was meant to avoid questions of constitutionality; it also provided states with maximum discretion to develop whatever unemployment-insurance program they wished. Employers' contributions were to vary with the employment records of the employer: those with stable workforces would pay less. Everything else, including the level of benefits, possible employee contributions, and eligibility for coverage, would be determined by the states. It was not a bill that labor could like very much, for it left the states (and their most powerful employers) huge discretion. Yet Green reluctantly testified in favor of it when it was presented to Congress in the spring of 1934. "We believe," he told the assembled legislators, "a man will retain his independence and his manhood better if he is permitted to earn a living." In the absence of jobs, "we are inevitably forced to this position."[42] The AFL continued to support it halfheartedly when a modified version entered the Social Security bill.

Organized labor, which disliked the flexible provisions that emerged, had little choice but to ally itself with the Committee on Economic Security plan. The AFL had backed itself into a corner. Equally suspicious of state bureaucracies and legislatures and of employer influence, uncertain whether unemployment insurance would cool workers' loyalties to their trade unions, Green had failed to take a strong stand either in the council of the Committee on Economic Security or before Congress.[43] Green would have preferred, he told the Senate Finance Committee, a plan that filtered contributions through the federal government so that one entity could more readily impose standards for eligibility and benefits; he deplored the possibility of individual reserve accounts, which failed to provide workers with security; he hoped no state would exact contributions of workers; he thought the payroll tax could easily be raised from 3 to 5 percent so that a more generous benefit might be paid. Most especially, he wanted to insure benefits sufficiently high to guarantee that labor could maintain its purchasing power.[44]

Though the AFL would have preferred to give vastly less discretion to the states (and might have allied itself with African Americans to this end), its commitment to voluntarism bound it to a contributory program. It did not believe employers could or would, given incentives, prevent unemployment. But it liked the idea that benefits were offered to workers in light of the contributions of their employers and therefore available as a "right." It was more willing to hazard the risks of individual reserves than to fund a program with general revenues that might threaten to dilute the relationship of benefits to contributions and undermine male independence. If unemployment benefits were inevitable, they must be tied to employers' contributions. Everything else was secondary, including what the leadership quickly recognized as the unfortunate consequence of legislative discretion in excluding awkward categories of workers.

Labor had given up a lot to get benefits that sustained male dignity, available as a matter of right, without administrative or bureaucratic discretion. Bounded by a conception of unemployment insurance largely designed to provide incentives for employers to "regularize" employment, the issue of who was appropriately defined as a "worker" assumed paramount importance. Gender was a major constituent in that definition. At every turn it emerged as a dynamic agent. It participated in the initial conception of which jobs should be "regularized" and which not. Its hand was strengthened by the issues of voluntarism prominent in the labor movement, where notions of masculinity fostered suspicion of government intervention of every kind. It was sustained and enhanced by the attitudes of women reformers, whose shared sense of the nature of breadwinning for the family blinded them to possibilities for supporting women's wage work. And gendered understandings fueled issues of "coverage" and "availability" that continued to wreak havoc with the desire for uniformity. But the labor movement had preserved its image of masculinity. And who is to say that it was alone in undermining a broader social-insurance program that might well have laid the foundation of a more generous welfare state?

PART IV

New Directions

Early on, my work on wage-earning women led me into networks of women and men outside American borders who were also interested in these issues. Early contacts with British, French, Scandinavian, and Italian women proved particularly important in identifying areas of similarity and uniqueness. Shared conversations with Leonore Davidoff, Sally Alexander, and others opened up a realm of family and work issues that Europeans thought of in very different contexts from those normally used by American labor historians. Their approach to "the state," for example, has been particularly instructive, since it posits government as an active agent in the lives of workers rather than an obstacle to be overcome. I drew on these ideas when I wrote "In Pursuit of Economic Citizenship."

The essay itself came out of a continuing dialogue with the Swedish economic historian Ulla Wikander, who first introduced me to European approaches to the sexual division of labor. With her, I began to make cross-national comparisons that have proved useful in isolating specifically gendered behavior. We explored the impact of religious, ethnic, and political differences on the regulation of gender in the workplace. Ultimately this work led me to conceptions of economic citizenship—a notion that has helped me to synthesize women's relationship to family and wage labor in more complete ways.

These conversations also gave me the courage to accept a challenge issued by the American Historical Association to write an essay on global women's work. Was there a way, they asked, to think about women's work across time and place? What could be said that could help us to categorize it and to understand its historical development?

"Reframing the History of Women's Wage Labor" is a first stab at answering that question and an effort to take the arena of women's labor history into the world where it belongs.

I close this collection with a reflection on how my intellectual life has been shaped by action as well as dialogue. Returning to my Welsh roots and to my work within the trade-union movement, I offer a personal reflection on the intersection between activism and thought, and between autobiography and ideas.

15

In Pursuit of
Economic Citizenship

I n the autumn of 1967, the U.S. Congress passed legislation designed to encourage states to require wage work among mothers who received welfare payments on behalf of their small children. The provision was hotly contested, and the Senate hearings and subsequent debate drew delegations of supporters and protesters to the nation's capital to plead their case. Among them were a group of mothers from New York City who came to petition the Senate committee charged with drafting the bill to preserve their capacity to remain at home with their young children. Failing to get on the Senate's agenda, the mothers made something of a fuss inside and outside the hearing rooms. Senator Russell B. Long, who chaired the subcommittee in charge of drafting the legislation, responded angrily. Labeling welfare mothers "female broodmares" and "riffraff," he declared his distress at being beseiged by "mothers who sat around this committee room all day and refused to go home." Along with their claims, Long rudely dismissed the rights of these mothers to petition Congress: "Why can't those people be told that if they can find time to impede the work of the Congress they can find time to pick up some beer cans in front of their house?"[1]

Long's abrupt refusal to hear the voices of welfare mothers illustrates a persistent tension between the political and civil rights of individuals and their access to social citizenship. It suggests that in the modern world, where the market has intruded into the lives of families everywhere and social rights are increasingly vulnerable, the exercise of political voice may be at odds with claims to social citizenship. When welfare deprives its recipients of the privacy

Special thanks to Ulla Wikander, Gro Hagemann, Jane Lewis, and Ann Orloff for help in working through these ideas. Originally published in *Social Politics* 10.2 (Summer 2003). Reprinted by permission of Oxford University Press.

of their homes, when children who take drugs or who play truant from school expose parents to eviction from their homes or a reduction of their family allowances, the prerogatives of social citizenship are conditional on political whim. Far from expanding their participatory potential, claiming the benefits of social citizenship may limit the capacity of women and men to participate fully in the polity.

This poses something of a conundrum. From the perspective of a historian of women, it appears that we have described categories of citizenship—civil, political, and social—that limit our ability to act strategically, and disempower large groups of individuals from exercising the social rights meant to ensure full participation. The history of past struggles for economic independence and for social justice for women of every class and race suggest that we have been unable to work our way out of the conundrum because we have adopted a normatively gendered, conceptual framework for citizenship that has inhibited more imaginative strategies for achieving equitable treatment of gender issues. They encourage us to begin to imagine an additional category of citizenship whose achievement will mark an equitable (fair) society that can effectively meld caregiving interests (for children as well as elderly and ill relatives and partners) with market-driven self-interest. If our goal is to preserve the social rights of men and women to caring and healthy family lives without undermining the political and material desires whose satisfaction is contingent on well-paying jobs, then we need to imagine a gender-encompassing right to care and a gender-encompassing set of economic privileges. I'm especially concerned with how we do this in a world where the spread of the market makes the rewards of paid work necessary for almost all women and increasingly tempting to many (including mothers). At the same time, the combination of market pulls and state pushes undermines the capacity of all but the wealthiest families to undertake the caring work that lies at the heart of satisfactory human relations. In every class and in every industrial state, the three-way tug among caregiving, family life, and wage labor poses severe challenges to achieving gender equity and full citizenship.

I suggest that we have not been able to imagine a workable solution to this problem because we are imprisoned within ideas of citizenship whose gender dimensions turn them into oppositional categories. I argue here for a new category of citizenship—economic citizenship—to supplement, not supersede, T. H. Marshall's three traditional categories. I would include in economic citizenship some of the rights that Marshall would have put elsewhere: the right to work at the occupation of one's choice (where work includes child rearing and household maintenance); to earn wages adequate to the support of self and family; to a nondiscriminatory job market; to the education and training that facilitate access to it; to the social benefits necessary to sustain and support labor-force participation; and to the social environment required for effective choice, including adequate housing, safe streets, accessible public transportation, and universal health care. The achievement of economic citizenship can be measured by the possession and exercise of the privileges and opportunities necessary for men and women to achieve economic and social autonomy and independence.[2] The fulfillment of economic citizenship resides in the standing or status that enables women and men to participate fully in a democratic polity. In the rest of this brief essay, I argue that just as the distortion of "caring" rights has emerged from a false dichotomy between women's and men's interests in social citizenship, so the achievement of full citizenship for all is contingent on a political strategy that imagines a gender-encompassing economic citizenship. My examples come primarily from the U.S. experience, partly because I know it best, but also because it provides the most egregious example of the market-driven cleavage between social and other forms of citizenship in the industrial world.

Social theorists, beginning with Britain's T. H. Marshall, have generally argued that along with the achievement of civil citizenship, the rights and concurrent political participation of men and women were extended in the nineteenth and twentieth centuries by two familiar forms of citizenship: political and social. Marshall rooted the growth of economic rights and obligations in the civil and social arenas.[3] In his view, the civil protected the opportunity to work; the social protected the right to economic security (not to starve). While these two sets of economic rights should have been complementary, their gendered application has often left them at odds. As many commentators have pointed out, who gets what kinds of economic rights (whether civil or social) has rested on sometimes hidden, normative, assumptions about who "cares" and who "works"; who deserves what sorts of rights; and who requires protection from the market.[4]

Marshall called the right to work "the basic civil right," identifying it as the "right to follow the occupation of one's choice in the place of one's choice."[5] Like religion or speech, such a right seems self-evident, and yet it has not historically been available to women and remains circumscribed by custom and culture. As a practical matter, "the right to follow the occupation of one's choice"—the right Marshall identified as the most basic civil right—has never been secure. In some sense it is no right at all. As the political philosopher Jon Elster points out, it has no equivalent in the construction of citizenship. Classical political rights like freedom of speech and religion are, as Elster notes, "largely negative, in the sense that they protect the individual from interference by others or by the state."[6] The right to work, in contrast, is a positive right, enforceable not by legal mandate but implicit in the expectations inspired by an emergent nineteenth-century democratic decision-making process. Walter

Korpi calls such rights "proto-rights." They are "norm based" and influence "the distribution of resources that form the basis for material inequality." They also affect a person's "capability and freedom in many different areas of life," including most especially interaction patterns in the family.[7]

The historical record powerfully supports the notion that the norms sustaining the right to follow the occupation of one's choice were gendered. It suggests that since the Enlightenment, the liberty of men to freely contract their labor remained, and nowhere more than under America's version of liberal theory, a deeply rooted gendered prerogative. For men, economic independence, full economic citizenship, has traditionally constituted a de facto goal, a measure of male status, and a necessary foundation for political voice.[8] In contrast, not only has women's economic freedom never been accepted as axiomatic, but the rights meant to accompany it were further restricted by marriage and motherhood and by treating unmarried females in the workforce as if they were potentially married and would eventually be mothers.[9] In part, the denial of this civil right has produced a reciprocally confirming reaction. Denied access to good jobs, their economic independence constantly at risk, women have sometimes retreated to dependent roles, and at other times found themselves fighting for access to an economic independence that many men understood as their due.[10] Gendered assumptions about rights to work legally ended in our lifetimes, but they have continued to reside in custom if not in law. Far from being axiomatic, as Marshall had insisted, "the principle of individual economic freedom" has rendered the labor market a site of gendered struggle in which the ideologies of female domesticity and male breadwinning justified men's generally rapacious treatment of women.[11]

If democratic citizenship was closely tied to earning, then the right to work constituted a rather precarious guarantee even for skilled free white men, and none at all for the women of every race whose status Marshall found "in some important respects peculiar." Lacking property in their own labor, which was vested in their husbands or fathers and at the disposal of their families, women have rarely had the same kinds of occupational choice, an absence that virtually eviscerated some of their other civil rights (including the right to own property, to contract, and freedom of domicile). The peculiarity lay in the normative assumption that women would spend most of their lives in household production and maintenance and in biological and social reproduction. That assumption not only restricted economic opportunity but imposed a range of ancillary duties on women as well. As Carole Pateman argues, given the paramount duty of the citizen to work, restrictions on women's opportunities in that sphere assigned women to a secondary citizenship based on their roles as family members and subject to male domination.[12]

Echoes of this sense of gendered entitlement persist. Western industrial countries have typically reserved certain kinds of skills and jobs to males, refusing membership in guilds and later trade unions to most women. When employers' devices like differential wages and occupational segmentation by sex have proved insufficient, workers have resorted to their own, sometimes informal strategies to enforce customary understandings of sex boundaries. As late as the 1950s, these included sex-segregated seniority lists and separate "help wanted" advertisements. Despite the success of 1970s affirmative action programs, which attempted to redress customary bias, male entitlement remains a persistent workforce phenomenon. It reveals itself in the persistent occupational sex segregation that characterizes every industrial country and among men who refuse to mentor female trainees, provide negative job assessments for women who aspire to men's jobs, enforce glass ceilings, and engage in the still-unresolved and contentious behavior we call sexual harassment on the job.[13]

These are the perhaps inevitable results of what I have called elsewhere the "gendered imagination."[14] Historically thought of as appropriate, they have only recently come to be seen as unfair. For instance, American courts persistently applied the notion of economic rights as if women's liberties fell into a different category from those of men. Under the equal protection clause of the Fourteenth Amendment, the U.S. Supreme Court repeatedly and fervently upheld rights to work for what it called "all" citizens when it meant the rights to be held by males. The right to work in legitimate occupations, it declared in a pathbreaking 1915 decision, "is of the very essence of the personal freedom and opportunity that it was the purpose of the Fourteenth Amendment to secure."[15] And yet for two generations after, it restricted women's access to that right. Senator Robert Wagner thundered popular faith in the notion when he declared: "[T]he right to work is synonymous with the inalienable right to live. . . . It has never been surrendered and cannot be forfeited."[16] Yet with respect to women, the idea that such restrictions were "an offence against the liberty of the subject" dueled with the widespread belief that the liberty of women could and should be curtailed if it menaced the health of the family.

In contrast to the individual rights that undergirded civil citizenship, and which most women did not claim until well into the twentieth century, many of the social rights that have enhanced self-respect and political participation were won in what Björn Wittrock and Peter Wagner describe as the cradle of national consolidation. They appeared as extensions of the idea of community—as a way to enhance state power rather than to restrict that of the market.[17] Marshall understood social rights as the "universal right to real income which is not proportionate to the market claims of the claimant."[18] An expansion of social citizenship was not necessarily designed to reduce social inequality, although it included "a modicum of economic welfare and security" and dangled "the right to live the life of a civilized being according to the standards prevailing in the society" as well as "a general enrichment of the concrete substance of civilized life."[19] Rather, expanding social citizenship involved something closer to equal membership in the community of citizens, an enhancement of voice through self-respect.

For men, the struggle for social citizenship involved a demand for social access that could sustain and support rights to work, above all for the family wage, which included within its dimensions the privileges of "keeping" a wife who would manage his household, rear his children, and service his sexual needs. This conflation of economic and social elements (which includes workmen's compensation for accidents, unemployment insurance, old-age pensions, and vacations with pay) was considered natural for males and, though the object of struggle, understood finally as the perquisite of an informed and involved citizenry.[20]

For women, however, the achievement and the content of social citizenship have differed in ways that have produced tensions among women and between men and women. Differently developed by different nations, the distribution of social rights was invariably tied to normative gendered assumptions—to notions of fairness or equity for men as well as women. In the early part of the century, fairness could comfortably accommodate privileging male wage earners by granting them citizenship rights quite different from those granted to women. It could also privilege dependent female careers.[21] Fairness for women, however, meant something else. The British, the Dutch, and the Americans all developed something variously called an "endowment for motherhood" or "mothers' pensions," which, with limited success, enabled certain widows deprived of male support to hold families together without benefit of wage work. For those who earned, social citizenship rights differed too. France provided crèches for infants of working mothers; Austria offered shorter working days to the mothers of young children; and every western industrial society produced some form of protective labor legislation designed to preserve women's maternal and family roles in the face of insistent labor-market pressures.[22]

Where social rights were granted as prerogatives of citizenship—sometimes of birth, sometimes of residency—gendered tensions diminished. Access to the National Health system in Britain or to unemployment insurance in Ireland constitute examples. In the United States, however, the best social benefits were attached to work. Within the American constitutional and judicial framework, where notions of freedom of contract largely prohibited government intervention to regulate the labor-market work of men or women, policy makers and advocates of women chose to protect the social rights of women through families rather than insisting on civil rights to work. Protecting women's standing as caregivers proved a more effective conceptual and practical strategy for enhancing their citizenship and that of men than seeking constitutional change. It soon became the goal of women as well as men. Marriage thus constituted an alternative source of social provision for women but not for men, against whom the state enforced the injunction to provide and protected their capacity to do so. Women who did market work (whether sheltered by marriage or not) found themselves in a different relationship to the state than those who did caregiving work.

The result placed women in a different relationship to the Constitution than men, constructing paid work for them as secondary to caregiving work. The continuing division of civil and social rights sometimes pitted men and women against each other, as members of each group struggled to situate themselves to advantage in the labor market. By assigning some social benefits through wage work and others through state indulgence, a divided labor force limited possibilities for either sex to create balanced lives, inhibiting political participation for women and family participation for men. And yet, in the course of the twentieth century, social policy repeatedly reaffirmed the division even as women's labor-market participation slowly increased.

The United States perhaps provides the archetypical illustration. There, social policies establishing and regulating labor standards, unemployment insurance, old-age pensions, and income-tax codes invariably reflected a gendered order, and when they did not try to alter its boundaries, they reproduced its inequities. The legitimacy of early twentieth-century protective labor legislation, for example, was rooted in conceptions of women as "mothers of the race" in need of state protection because they were weak and defenseless.[23]

Such conceptions provided a range of beneficial special legislation for women workers, including safety and sanitation, hours and wages, and exclusion from certain kinds of jobs. At the same time, they constrained women's civil rights to work in ways that did not apply to adult males.

The 1935 Social Security Act provides another case in point. It dramatically extended the social citizenship of women and men by granting old-age insurance as a by-product of contributions made from the wages of a limited number of largely male jobs. Its initially unpopular provisions were legitimized by the inclusion of a thoroughly gendered set of family benefits in 1939. Until the 1970s, only husbands and fathers had the capacity to extend their benefits to widows, aged wives, and surviving children. Wives and mothers had no such rights; but if a deceased father left minor children, their mother might claim benefits for taking care of them until she remarried or the children reached adulthood—whichever came first. The distribution of unemployment-insurance benefits offers another example. Confined to particular kinds of workers and assigned on the basis of availability for work, most states specifically excluded pregnant women, mothers of young children, and those forced to move to keep their families together. Thus, men and women found themselves with different kinds of social rights, each of them considered quite fair.[24]

Extending the benefits of social citizenship seemed to be the route to improving women's lives, while efforts to extend civil rights (to jobs, for example) left the social existence of men and women untouched. Good pensions, health care, paid vacations, and so on are unavailable to those without good jobs. The result is a deeply class- and racially-divided system that leaves those without work (often women, African Americans, recent immigrants, and the poorly educated) with a problematic form of social citizenship and a questionable "right to work" that smacks more of obligation than of benefit. Thus, professional and middle-class women find that their educations and family circumstances enable them to take advantage of the newly wrought privileges of access, while poor women are forced by the new welfare rules into wage labor even at the cost of tremendous disruption to the lives of their children. Many people objected to the Temporary Assistance to Needy Families rules adopted in 1996 not because they required people to work for benefits but because they required mothers of small children to work without adequate support systems.[25]

While an expanding social citizenship has been designed to reduce the impact of unequal earned incomes on social status and security—there is little question that it has done so in the instances of old-age pensions and unemployment—in practice its gendered application has left many women vulnerable to bureaucratic requirements and reduced rather than expanded their capacity to participate in the polity. Witness, for example, the image of Senator Russell Long excoriating welfare mothers for taking time to lobby Congress for more generous benefits when they should—in his view—have been at home cleaning up beer cans. Relying on gendered norms and gendered expectations, social and civil citizenship continue to constrain the legislative imagination within the borders of a sometimes problematic traditional family. They have disserviced women and the poor of both sexes.[26]

As women began to enter the labor market in larger numbers, and particularly as the two-income family became necessary for the support of a middle-class lifestyle, norms changed. In the United States, the differential civil rights and their attached social benefits applauded by citizens of the 1930s seemed by the 1970s to be patently unfair, and some of them were labeled discriminatory. The normative systems that emerged in the 1970s in the United States (unlike the Swedish system but much like that of Britain) took the shape of extending civil rights, retaining the connection of social rights to employment, and promising equality to women by dropping barriers to their access to the labor market.[27] While social rights tied to male work habits and defined as social insurance continued to enhance the self-respect that theorists like

T. H. Marshall and Judith Shklar have thought essential to democratic participation, those not so tied undermined self-esteem and voice.[28] And yet our political strategies for extending equity continued to rely on extending social rights that did not generally protect the participatory rights of many poor and working-class women as well as of men. This created two kinds of problems. It revealed the rights offered to those who did not engage in wage work as of a lesser participatory value than those tied to wage work; and it created divisions among women who now found themselves eligible for different kinds of social rights depending on how effectively they could take advantage of the economic rights attached to civil citizenship.

In the modern world, lodging economic security and the right to earn within separate categories of civil and social citizenship exacerbates the conflicts between caring and earning roles, especially for women. The two-income family now encompasses the vast majority of all families with children in the United States; and in 20 percent of these families, women earn more than their male partners. The proportions of women earning wages has now leveled off at about 48 percent of the total population of wage earners; both men and women increasingly desire choices about whether to care or to earn wages. These patterns influence and participate in those of a global economy that everywhere drives women away from their homes and into the job market— sometimes across borders and oceans—to seek ways to support their own families while enabling more affluent women to support theirs. At the same time, it places pressure on unemployed and underemployed males who cannot yet imagine caring roles for themselves. Worldwide, just as a gendered social citizenship marks many social rights as inferior, so a gendered civil citizenship limits opportunities and renders women's wage work vulnerable.

Because social rights have so often been predicated on differential male and female relationships to economic civil rights, they left gendered distinctions intact, far more effectively challenging class inequality than affecting issues of gender or racial exclusion.[29] The tensions that resulted from imagining that the right to work was an individual freedom possessed primarily by the male sex and offered only to women who for idiosyncratic reasons needed or earned it resulted in a double bind: on the one hand, an uneven and demeaning expansion of social rights, and on the other hand, a punitive insistence on the obligation to work.[30] In practice, their gendered limits rendered the participatory potential of social citizenship problematic, especially as they affected women of different classes.

A wide variety of political theorists has affirmed the idea that without economic independence, vested for most people in claims to jobs and acknowledged as the social right to work if not as a claim to a particular job, political participation remains a chimera.[31] This has been especially true in the United

States, where many rights that are elsewhere the universal entitlements of citizens, including old-age pensions, unemployment insurance, and medical care, have been vested in each citizen's record of work. "We are," in the words of the political scientist Judith Shklar, "citizens only if we 'earn.'"[32]

Under these circumstances, requiring wage work as a condition of survival undermined rather than reinforced democratic participation for women—the opposite of Marshall's expectation that expanding social citizenship would provide greater participatory options for citizens. The effort to increase access to public education and release workers from "soul-destroying" hours of labor arguably provided greater self-esteem and voice for men. But extending social citizenship to women as mothers or wives has served as often to encumber their political access and their civil rights as to expand it—as, for example, when mothers receive parenting leaves that are not taken by men and thus jeopardize their job standing, or when wives and widows receive old-age pensions on the basis of their spouse's records and are thus denied the privilege of independent remarriage; or when the welfare state demands that, in return for benefits, mothers work outside the home as well as inside it. Granted on these normative, gendered terms, (rather than on the more encompassing terms that prevail in some social-democratic countries like Sweden) state intervention in, and support for, women's caring roles has tended to diminish the self-respect of recipients, to reduce rather than enhance their capacity to exercise voice.

Nor have social benefits provided on the basis of class generally paved the path to economic independence in the United States. To encourage poor women to enter the job market, welfare programs provided subsidized health care, child care, and limited access to public housing, job training, and education. But once in the market, most of these benefits phased out or dropped away. Persistent poverty rendered the participatory potential of social citizenship problematic, especially as it affected poor women who could not take advantage of even the same "rights to work" as their middle-class sisters who could buy education and household support. The social rights attached to employment dissolved into entitlements for eligible (largely male) workers, while those available to most women remained identified with poverty.

In the absence of an integrated concept of economic citizenship, differential social rights divided women against each other. As more privileged women (including skilled female workers, union members, and professional women) sought access to the labor market in the 1960s and equal treatment in it, on the basis of their individual abilities, they inadvertently offered up a model that disadvantaged less-fortunate women. If women of the middling sort could earn wages, why shouldn't women of the poorer sort be asked to earn rather than to remain dependent on state subsidies? Senator Russell Long refused to heed the requests of welfare mothers specifically on this ground. "Other mothers are supporting their families," he argued. "[I]t seems to me those welfare mothers could strive to do the same thing."[33] Demanding the right to work opened up an apparent duty to work from which many women, and especially mothers, had been exempt.

But poorer women, held to the duty to care, lacked sufficient perquisites of social citizenship to compete effectively in the labor market, including the capacity to choose not to work or to choose part-time or temporary work. For example, 1960s job-training programs admitted twice as many black men as women on the theory that men more fully deserved access to better employment. Absent job training and education, women were poor competitors. While these were often promised, little effort was made to place women in "good" jobs. Once in the labor market, they found themselves without either the social benefits of welfare (including subsidized child care, medical and dental care, or rent) or the economic advantages of good jobs (which include reasonable wages, appropriate skills, paid vacations, and union representation).

For middling-income women, the United States provided little in the way of social rights for the families of workers, continuing to pit caregiving against the demands of the market. And the market offered few compensations: until 1992, many corporations offered no maternity or parental leave at all, and few, even now, offer paid leaves. Most attach no benefits to part-time work, and only a small percentage will arrange flexible working hours.[34] Better-off women faced another sort of dilemma: pushed to compete in the job market, they sacrificed their affective lives to the chance to make it, suffering from what Arlie Hochschild has dubbed "the time bind."[35]

The idea of economic citizenship plucks economic freedom (the right to a job) from the category of civil citizenship and economic security from that of social citizenship, turning them from subsets of something else into basic measures of human dignity. In breaking down the categories of social and civil citizenship, it offers a more encompassing notion of citizenship that captures those rights and obligations attendant to the daily struggle to reconcile economic well-being and household maintenance with the capacity to participate more fully in democratic societies. It distinguishes between women's efforts to participate in public life and to achieve respect as women (sometimes as mothers and family members) and the efforts of men and women to occupy equitable relationships to corporate and government services.

Attaching economic citizenship to wage labor for all acknowledges the power of the market while attempting to temper its influence. In most countries, for most of historical time, the basic rights of social citizenship have rarely been granted without payment in terms of work. One thinks here of the eighteenth-century parish doling out the widow's mite in return for sewing or child care; of the nineteenth-century "Poor House" from which residents could hardly emerge because they earned too little in wages to sustain body and soul; and of the twentieth-century U.S. two-track state, which allocated social benefits to men "as of right" while conditioning the eligibility of poor women on their adherence to rigid moral standards.

By attaching economic rights to care, economic citizenship provides language with which to inscribe caring rights into the larger economic structures, enhancing their normative weight. At their utopian edge, these rights promise to inhibit rather than increase market influences—countering the argument that "economic citizenship" runs the risk of commodifying all labor. One can imagine, for example, government policies that treat women as individuals, not family members. Such policies might (as they already do in Sweden) include individually based income taxes, social benefits based not on marital status but on individual records, and mortgage credit for single parents. They might also include sharing the costs of childbirth and child rearing; equalizing parental responsibility for children's medical, financial, and social well-being; and the elimination of discriminatory gendered protections in the realm of employment, education, and political participation. Rights offered as benefits of citizenship rather than as corollaries of market work, rights offered without means-testing and without regard to the family status of the recipient, may enhance participatory potential. Family allowances in much of Europe fall into this category, as does free public education for children, access to public housing and child care in Sweden, National Health insurance in Britain, and so on. In some countries there is a seamless border between the rights offered as corollaries to wage work and those meant to care for families, as is the case with unemployment insurance in Ireland, which melts into the dole after a finite period. But elsewhere individuals who have engaged in wage work find themselves entitled to a greater share of social rights than those who have spent more time in caring work. The Swedish case is a good example—offering basic old-age pensions to every older person to fend off poverty, but greater sums to those whose wages enabled greater savings. The distinction disadvantages women who have remained outside the labor market to care for children or elderly parents.

The United States offers the most dramatic example of the effect of wage-related and hierarchically structured social rights. Unemployment benefits, to cite only one example, go to those with strong work records and are denied those engaged in part-time, temporary, and contingent work. They are also denied to anyone deemed not to be "available" for work—a category that, at the discretion of the administrator, might include anyone "loosely attached" to the workforce. Married women, women not willing to move to new cities for jobs, mothers of small children, and for many years pregnant women fell into this category. So did people who quit their jobs for any personal reason.

And despite years of trying, women's groups have still failed to convince state legislators to make unemployment funds available to pregnant women and new mothers on maternity leaves or to men on parental leaves.

The distinction between civil and social citizenship is arguably sharpest in the United States, where social benefits for mothers and children have not only been deeply means-tested but accompanied, historically, by severe penalties for violating traditional standards of sexual and personal relationships. At various times and in various states, women have been denied benefits when they have male companions. Their benefits have been reduced if their children missed too much school or were found with drugs. Some states have refused to provide benefits for the third child in a family where the first two children received them. These penalties were justified on the grounds that women had not "earned" their benefits. They ensured that expanding social citizenship to privilege working mothers eliminated neither economic insecurity nor social inequality for the women and children most deeply affected. And punitive regulations also ensured that social benefits did not significantly expand women's capacity to participate in the polity. Rather, welfare was said to destroy character because it provided something for nothing; its recipients were demeaned as "lazy" and even their political participation impugned as detracting from their duties as mothers.

In contrast, when expanded civil rights accompanied an extension of social rights (as in the Scandinavian countries) a rapid expansion of political participation ensued.[36] This was less the case in the United States, where women successfully challenged many labor-market barriers (they won job-training programs, or vocational education) without significantly enhancing their political power.

Our excursion into the past suggests the central importance of a unified concept of economic citizenship for the global citizens of a new world. Melding the two categories more readily vests rights in domestic labor. If women's right to work (as a civil right) succumbs to normative assumptions about the family, then social rights will fail to adequately accommodate families without male breadwinners. A continuing tension between social citizenship and the "economic element" of civil citizenship—a tension rooted in gendered normative assumptions—appears when women make demands for rights to work and/or when the state fails to provide appropriate social benefits. These tensions are reduced when there is a consensus that civil rights belong as well to women—a concession that fosters a redefinition of particular social rights relating to family life. States with a commitment to universal social rights, including child care and paid maternal and paternal leaves, have tended more generously to legislate workplace arrangements to accommodate family life, including shorter hours, flexitime, and paid vacations. Those committed to individual economic freedom, like the United States, have acted less gener-ously to meet caring needs.[37]

Conceived as a civil right, economic opportunity illuminates a history of gendered conflict in the labor force. Some have argued that it reflects male values and that incorporating women into its competitive value system would negate female nurturing values. Conceived as a social right, economic security is the last bastion of the defenders of the affective components of life, includ-ing the family and the humane workplace. Some have argued that it is the loca-tion where women's values might prevail—where a caring society might find financial and structural support. But in fact, as our brief excursion suggests, the two are not separable. Only when they are melded into economic citizen-ship can we begin to imagine a world where men and women have genuine choices—to work at home, in caring jobs, or in the marketplace.

Perceived as the prerogatives of economic citizenship, policies that are oth-erwise punitive invoke a range of rights that apply to both men and women. Imagine, for example, the tactics that swim into view with regard to wel-fare when we think of economic citizenship as our goal. Imposing a "duty to work"—now the target in the United States even for mothers of small chil-dren—would require policies that guarantee a fully integrated labor market that permits, but does not assume, domesticity for either sex. It would also require "family-friendly" labor-market policies like well-paid part-time jobs with benefits, community child care, shorter hours at full pay, paid maternity and parental leaves, and so on. Such compromises were suggested by Dutch women when they were asked to imagine the most desirable model for their own lives.[38] At the same time, the concept of economic citizenship alerts us that a gender-encompassing "right to care" would require an equivalent set of economic access routes, including income tax and pension credits for non-wage-earning mothers and paid parental leaves and generous child allowances as well as universal health care, at least for children.

In Marshall's world, it was enough simply to be free to work—the market would sort out the rest, and where it failed, the state could be counted on to extend the kinds of social rights that would enable full participation. In the early and mid-twentieth century, it appeared to many that state supple-ments would ameliorate the worst excesses of the market, foster labor-market participation, and enable women to join in as full citizens. In the new world, where global financial markets curtail the civil and social rights of men and women, and where national boundaries no longer provide effective protec-tions for either, the time has come to make common cause. Citizens of this new world have already begun to recognize that they cannot fight effectively on "two fronts," divided by gender, but must unite along a single border that everyone can cross together. Unlike citizens of the 1960s, those of the twenty-first century hold in their hands the possibilities for both men and women to enjoy caring and wage work. To illuminate their choices, to give voice to those who seek to understand how the market has constrained individual lives, we might well turn to a new category of citizenship—to ask how states have conferred and restricted economic citizenship and for which groups of citizens. That strategy would reveal an interdependent group of rights and obligations and render participation plausible to growing numbers of male and female citizens of the world.

In 2003, the Supreme Court of the United States issued a pathbreaking decision affirming the validity of a federal law that required the separate fifty states to adhere to the provisions of an act giving twelve weeks of unpaid leave to family members who needed time to care for others, including newborn babies. Little as this leave is, its passage constitutes a major breakthrough in the United States, which has never, as a nation, protected the right to either maternity or parental leave. In a stunning recognition of the potential of "economic citizenship," the Court recognized the linkage between women's caring rights and wage work, holding that requiring states to provide family leaves acknowledges and redresses long-standing "stereotypes that only women are responsible for family caregiving and that men lack domestic responsibilities."[39]

16

Reframing the History of Women's Wage Labor: Challenges of a Global Perspective

W hen the United States embarked on a war against the Afghanistan Taliban in the fall of 2001, its apparent motive was to eliminate a regime that had harbored those it believed to be responsible for the devastating destruction of September 11. To justify its actions, the American administration provided a long list of grievances against the Taliban, none of them more persuasive than its pernicious treatment of women. One of the reasons the U.S. was going to war, the administration argued, was to free Afghanistan's women, who had been closely sequestered within households, denied even rudimentary education, and dismissed from jobs. Without the possibility of earning a living, women's health had declined, maternal deaths had soared, and women were reduced to absolute dependence and penury. Americans responded to this story with alacrity. Ignoring several centuries of their own past tradition, they expressed outraged sympathy over rules that restricted girls and women to the home. They waxed particularly indignant at regulations that prohibited education for girls and refused even highly trained women access to paid employment.

It isn't surprising that the Bush administration should have made effective use of the confinement of women to evoke a sympathetic response. The history of colonialism reveals that western nations have frequently invoked women's plight to disrupt traditional power structures and to open recalcitrant regimes to capitalism.[1] What is surprising is the empathetic response of an American

This essay draws on my pamphlet, "Gender and Work: Reaching for an Overview," prepared for the American Historical Association. I want to thank Bonnie Smith and Liz Lunbeck for their help in thinking through these issues and Eileen Boris for a crucial last-minute critique. This essay appeared as "Gender and Work: Possibilities for a Global Historical Overview," in Bonnie Smith, ed., *Women's History in Global Perspective* (Urbana: University of Illinois Press, 2004). This version was first published in the *Journal of Women's History* 15.4 (Winter 2004): 186–206.

public that has long been ambivalent about the tension between individual rights and family responsibilities among women. Astonishingly, "freeing the women" became one of America's major justifications for war, and jobs for women rapidly became the measure of female liberty. As the National Public Radio correspondent Ann Garrols put it in December 2001, after the bombing had all but ceased, Afghani women believed "jobs . . . are the first step towards restoring their freedom."[2]

The story and the comment suggest something of the importance of rethinking women's labor history—a process now well under way. When historians of women (myself among them) began to write about women's wage work in the early 1970s, our vision, like that of most historians, was bounded by the intertwined borders of family and nation. Whether we were writing about Europe, the United States, Africa, or Asia, our questions tended to emerge from theoretical frameworks rooted in the western Enlightenment and the practical lessons of the western industrial experience. We wanted to know how women were incorporated into wage labor and (after Engels) whether women's wage work had any emancipatory potential for women. We explored the consequences of industrialization for the relationship between family work and paid labor for women, and we focused on the extent of economic autonomy, political and civil liberties, and agency available to women caught in economic developments not of their own making.[3]

Whatever our own positions on these issues, we could hardly imagine women's wage work without raising questions about family life and assessing the relationship of the different roles of women and men to individual mobility and achievement.[4] If the notion that women lived in "separate spheres" lacked verisimilitude among historians of western women's work, the powerful vision of an enduring tension between wage work and unpaid home work for women nevertheless infused the patterns we imposed on the structure of the labor force, demanding explanations when men and women functioned in seemingly unorthodox ways. Inescapably, our own gendered expectations infused historical interpretations, infiltrating our description of how each sex contributed differently to capital accumulation and the demands of industrialism.[5]

These interpretations melded into those of nation building. Nineteenth- and early twentieth-century nationalists thought of families as the building blocks of capital accumulation, from which more advanced civilization derived. In their view, the spread of "civilization" justified national accumulation of colonial possessions, which would help to sustain the place of the "mother country" in the modern world. At the base of the pyramid was the patriarchal family, with its strict control of reproductive and productive female labor inside the home as well as outside, if necessary. Imperial forces everywhere counted on family structures to reproduce an endless supply of labor by imprinting appropriate values on the next generation and regulating the daily behavior of their female members. Given the predisposition of regional cultures to utilize male and female labor in accord with particular traditions and family formations, the historian who sought to understand how women's work participated in the nexus of capital growth, accumulation, and expansion learned to pay attention to the tensions within and among racialized and gendered patterns of nation building.[6] By the 1990s, historians could document how colonizers transmitted and utilized gendered understandings to organize the labor of the colonized.[7] Yet from the perspective of western industrialism, colonists could still appear to have effectively generated civilizing tendencies through family organization and western notions of morality: they had, after all, reined in tendencies to seclude women or veil them, to demand dowries and purchase concubines in the interests of a more efficient organization of labor.

The literature on colonialism and postcolonialism reveals how western efforts to extend Enlightenment notions of natural rights and individual freedom filtered into the work choices offered to and made by colonized women and men.[8] Even when, as was often the case, historians noted the resistant responses to colonial efforts to frame family work in relation to male breadwinning and female homemaking, they often did so from a perspective that placed family work and wage work in tension with each other. Indeed, the measure of women's contribution to nation building (in the mother country as in the colony) remained their dual capacity to sustain family life while participating first in the agricultural and then in the industrial labor force. Depending on time and place, colonizers manipulated incentives to mobility for men or women, often tempting men but not women to migrate to distant work sites. But they could also encourage unmarried and childless women to enter factories, while insisting that married women and those with children remain at home, where their labor could be exploited by paid home-work industries and justified by the need to maintain moral and healthy families.[9] Unsurprisingly, incentives to female wage labor produced palpable tensions between and among women of different generations, marital status, racial and religious backgrounds, and social classes.

In this light, women seemed to mediate between the nurturing traditions of the family, whatever its form, and the competitive values of a relentlessly invasive market. Women appeared to many labor historians as the vanguard of tradition—simultaneously the protectors of patriarchy and its subversive agents. For example, we assessed the impact of change in the preindustrial period in terms of women's increasing or declining status within families and communities.[10] We measured the horrors of slave labor for women, but not for men, by the extent to which women lost control over their own reproductive lives, could not effectively maintain families, and were forced to engage in field work. We gauged the human damage of industrialization in terms of its negative effects on the emergence of a "normal family" headed by a male breadwinner who earned a family wage.[11] We investigated whether unmarried female wage earners worked for the sake of their families of origin, in unpaid or paid labor.[12]

Nor were notions of state formation exempt from the consequences of our visions of the reciprocal relationship between women's dual roles and patriarchal social order. In response to the sometimes unacceptable costs to family life exacted by nineteenth-century industrial demands for female wage labor, many early twentieth-century states attempted to constrain capitalism, sometimes with appeals to manufacturers to adopt "civilized" standards; at other times with policies that enhanced national images of humane and compassionate state power.[13] To shore up patriarchy and insure effective reproduction of the labor force, mature industrial states developed elaborate social-policy regimes that incorporated subsidized housing, family tax systems, and unemployment, health, and pension benefits into tightly knit webs that tacitly affirmed or discouraged particular gendered formations for the purposes of effective economic development. Such policies undoubtedly benefited women workers and their families at the same time as they strengthened capitalism and helped to rationalize its attendant inequalities. They continue to be administered in "core" countries, where their gendered content plays important roles in sustaining the vestiges of patriarchal power in families.[14]

As impressive as the search for women's labor history has been over the past several decades, the field now seems to be taking a new turn, inspired in part by the growing visibility of women workers worldwide and by efforts to understand how gender participates in shaping and constraining the economies in which they function. Perhaps more than any other historiographical trend in recent years, the new global perspective has exposed the particularity of western cultural standpoints, encouraging us to ask questions about how racialized-gendered power relations infuse the distribution of work and shape the meaning of family. I do not want to dichotomize these elements, or to juxtapose the "core" against the "periphery," as if one could parse the elements of culture, analyze the effects of one segment, or group countries into unified categories. Rather, I want to suggest that the global and comparative stance of recent scholarship exposes the multiple ways that gender participates in structuring changing systems of work organization. By revealing the sometimes subtle ways that gender functions to legitimize and order power relationships, a global and comparative stance suggests the continuing importance of a labor history rooted in the relationships of men and women in and outside the family, the community, and the nation.

The global economic transformations now occurring, including the rapid spread of the transnational corporation with its disregard for national borders, provide the framework from which scholars have begun to think anew. As the twenty-first century opened, women everywhere were being drawn into the labor force. In East and Southeast Asia, their rates of participation equalled those in the developed world.[15] Yet despite increasing levels of education, the large majority of women continued to find themselves either employed within their families or in low-paying routine jobs. The promise of freedom dangled by new jobs and access to new forms of income remains elusive. The vocabulary of Western European and American scholarship sheds little light on the relationship between the dramatic economic transformation now occurring and cultural and ideological incentives to stasis and change. But recent research in the history of women's work around the world suggests how quite different notions of gender have constrained as well as encouraged the development of particular kinds of labor forces. In what follows, I try to identify some of the directions in which this work leads. These are, of course, highly idiosyncratic, meant to be suggestive rather than exhaustive and to articulate only a few of the challenges that emerge from scholarship that pushes beyond the traditional boundaries of labor history. I've grouped the challenges into four large areas: ideology and culture; the sexual division of labor; labor migration or the flow of labor; and issues of power and status.

Ideology and Culture

From a global perspective, the household and family (as structure and tradition) no longer seem broad enough rubrics to explain the position of either male or female workers: new scholarship reveals them as far more than the evolutionary economic structures that the Marxian tradition described. Instead, it demonstrates how closely tied the organization of labor is to local customs and to national and religious interests.

To be sure, the family functions everywhere as a mediating device—providing the restrictive or permissive environment that fosters or excludes education, job training, and the care of the ill and weak. But deeply rooted traditional gendered norms and values appear to play a far larger role in influencing labor patterns than material interest alone. A global standpoint calls attention to the different ways cultural values and ideological commitments participate in influencing family norms and shaping the labor force. A labor history that takes global experience into account illuminates the significance of ideas of loyalty, dignity, faith, and hierarchy in valuing different forms of work and in constructing the gendered relationships that manifest themselves in exclusion and inclusion in particular workplaces. A Moroccan village provides one revealing example. There, according to Susan Schaefer Davis, one of the most prestigious and well-paying women's jobs (that of bath-mistress) was reserved for widows and divorced women whose natal family status, rather than any particular skill of her own, entitled her to respect.[16]

The same example encourages us to think beyond traditional descriptions of the nuclear family as an "independent" or explanatory variable in accounting for particular labor-force patterns. It leads us to ask about how definitions of "family" differ, revealing complicated and varied conceptions of kin and honor that can influence women's labor-market choices and result in apparently idiosyncratic distributions of women's labor. For example, in parts of Africa, where each of several wives was entitled to a share of land, the number of wives and the effectiveness of their labor historically determined the ability of a family patriarch to accumulate land and wealth. But in Brazil, where a father might beat his daughters if they hinted at wanting to work in factories, additional female hands did not increase family wealth.[17]

Enormous variations in family and child-rearing patterns also open up new ways to view women's labor. We sometimes see women's labor as part of an integrated continuum that extends from paid and unpaid employment in the home to work in the family fields. At others, we see its products as market-oriented even as the rewards for labor serve the needs of the family. Yet again, a global view of women's labor reveals an expansion of autonomous choice among women, sometimes strengthening ties with family, and in other cases leading to a loss of contact with family members. The interplay of cultural circumstance and economic incentive emerges everywhere. My favorite example comes from the work of Ursula Sharma, who points out that among Muslim Bengalis, disgrace attaches to even the most poverty-stricken Bengali farmer who allows his wife to work the fields of non-kin for a wage. But the same farmer comfortably accommodates the wife who works the fields of near and distant family members. Her work then is not considered public, and so, profitable though it might be, his family honor is retained.[18]

Though we now know something about how females served as the means through which families accumulated capital, a global view suggests that the inverse might also be the case. Because families seem, at least occasionally, to have served as vehicles for female acquisition of economic capital, the interrelationship between family and waged and unwaged work appears newly complex. In western parlance, the language of separate spheres captures the dual roles of women in and outside the household, explaining what appears to be a near-universal sexual division of labor: varied as to jobs, but consistent within cultures. In other contexts, however, where domesticity participates in the extension of family wealth or provides essential capital for trading children as marriage partners, the idea of separate spheres for men and women is far less persuasive as an explanatory frame. Take, for example, the degree to which traditional Confucianism reinforced a wife's work for and in the home, increasing her production of silk, textiles, and other commodities for sale. These in turn served as the tangible wealth that enabled families to marry their sons and daughters into greater material comfort. Unlike the proto-industrialization process in Western Europe, which is often interpreted as a function of the impact of enclosures and an expanding market, a parallel process in some parts of China appears to have been more directly influenced by religious and ideological incentives that mandated that work for public well-being occur within the privacy of the family.[19]

Similarly, western tendencies to correlate increasing industrialization with lower fertility rates assume a simple calculus based on the value of labor power to the family. In neoclassical economic theory, the opportunity costs of keeping women out of the labor market rose with industrial expansion, encouraging more and more women to postpone marriage. Simultaneously, when rearing children for an industrial rather than an agrarian labor force became more expensive, incentives to produce large families declined, and women were increasingly tempted to enter the wage-labor force. But a more complex rendering of the household, including varieties of child-rearing patterns and extended family support systems, suggests that different cultural practices and ideological convictions constrained the range of choices open to women. As Sharon Stichter tells us, in much of Latin America and the Carribbean, the tendency of women to rely on extended families for help with child care leaves women much freer to engage in the labor market. And yet men and women developed a variety of heady rationales to keep women out of the nonfamilial work space.[20] Governments sometimes intervened to disrupt ideology and practice, as when they adopted the tactics of forced sterilization and population control widely acknowledged to have occurred in 1950s Puerto Rico.[21] Nor, given the employment opportunities available to women in developing economies, can an economic calculus explain tendencies to value male over female children and the continuing destruction and abandonment of female infants in countries like China and India. These phenomena seem to be rooted as much in such factors as religious injunction, spiritual belief systems, and the growing individuation of women as in the economic needs of family life.

Cultural conditions that enforce women's seclusion, as David Landes and Kumari Jayawardena among others have pointed out, are detrimental to capitalism. As Landes puts it, "[T]he best clue to a nation's economic growth and development potential is the status and role of women."[22] But others have noted that conditions of seclusion are not necessarily detrimental to the personal growth of women; they can provide opportunities to develop in gender-specific service industries and professional jobs and enable female ownership and control of midlevel enterprises. Despite the fact that North Africa and the Middle East display the lowest levels of female labor-force participation worldwide—a factor largely attributed to the role of Islam in confining women to the household—the economist Richard Anker argues that professional women constitute a startlingly "high concentration of their largest non-agricultural occupations."[23]

Such unusual configurations speak to the complex relationship between feminisms of different sorts and women's wage labor. Wage work sometimes seems to be a precondition for feminism—as in the United States, where the late twentieth-century entry of married women into the labor force fueled a campaign for equal employment opportunity. But elsewhere, the search for economic and social freedom is often the source, rather than the result, of feminist impulses. The power of women within families, rather than their labor-force experiences, seems to account for women's political influence. Here the central examples come from two areas: the use of feminist demands by women in colonized areas to fuel resistance to imperial control, and evidence of the capacity of women to take advantage of family status to accrue professional and political power to themselves.[24] The latter may account for the otherwise surprising rise of women to high-status business and political leadership positions in countries like India, Burma, and Pakistan, where many women still lack economic autonomy.

A global perspective also reveals the essential ways that women's waged and unwaged labor has served the cause of nationalism. Key here is the close relationship between the use of women as cheap labor in industrial capitalism and the reliance on industrialism to build national wealth, status, and military power. In the classic industrialization scenarios of China, Japan, Western Europe, and North America, women constituted at least a quarter of the first factory labor force, and sometimes an absolute majority. Employed first in cottage industries and home-based workshops, women found themselves working increasingly to the specifications of the middlemen who marketed their products. They entered semiskilled factory jobs when the introduction of machinery rendered their handmade products no longer competitive in increasingly complicated markets. As the division of labor became more complex, increasing numbers of new tasks required relatively little training and demanded a large and flexible workforce amenable to close supervision. Jobs opened to women in many sectors, including raw-material extraction and construction, but almost everywhere women found their metier in the textile factories that constituted the dynamic heart of modern industrialization.[25] In Shanghai, women were fully two-thirds of the total industrial workforce, and more than half—a third of the Shanghai proletariat in the first half of the twentieth century—worked in cotton mills.[26]

At first concentrated primarily in the production of textiles and clothing, women moved quickly into manufacturing shoes, paper, and prepared foods, and then into assembly-line manufacturing of all kinds. Their participation was often rationalized by subtle forms of argument that linked expanding industrial production to national ideals of strength and service. In China, at the moment of transition to a commercial economy, women's household output of cloth generally paid the taxes that allowed families to participate in the polity and fostered national progress towards a full-fledged market economy.[27] The cheap labor that women provided fueled the industrial revolution, and nations everywhere tried to pull them into the labor force. Britain manipulated its poor laws so as to force women to earn their livings in workshops and factories. Administrators in Meiji Japan sent their own daughters to work in the new textile mills to demonstrate the economic and spiritual value of women's labor outside the home.[28]

Over the global terrain, notions of domesticity have fused in complicated ways with national self-interest to stimulate a coherent viewpoint on the relationship of wage work to national interest. Like the industrial entrepreneurs of Meiji Japan, nineteenth-century employers who hoped to attract women to work in Lowell, Massachusetts, provided ideological rationales that drew on women's eagerness to support their families from a distance. At the same time, colonial regimes everywhere fostered programs that pulled men into mining, the construction of infrastructure, and urban domestic service, while encouraging women to stay at home. For most former colonies, as Kumari Jayawardena tells us, the rhetoric of modernization and development, of national prosperity and strength, incorporated an "emancipatory" rhetoric designed to free women to enter industry even as it sustained women's ties to their rural and village homes. Such a rhetoric was sometimes complicated by the need for women to labor for pay in their own homes—a phenomenon that ironically sustained the idea of the home as a private place.[29] The contradiction between the need for women's labor, on the one hand, and a rhetoric of women's roles derived from the desire to retain traditional patriarchal family forms, on the other hand, may account for one of the continuing puzzles of women's labor-market participation, explaining why, despite women's skills and experience, their labor remains relatively cheap.

The Uses of Sexual Divisions of Labor

The commodification of female labor that has everywhere accelerated in recent years encourages us to pay more attention not only to the persistence of a sexual division of labor and its economic functions but to the mechanisms through which it is established and perpetuated. It highlights women's central roles in household maintenance and child care, even as it uses these roles to justify segregation in the labor market. Richard Anker concludes a recent study of labor markets throughout the world by remarking that occupational sex-segregation is "extensive in every region, at all economic development levels, in all political systems, and in diverse religious, social, and cultural environments." Not surprisingly, he finds the phenomenon not only detrimental to women, but "*a major source of labor market rigidity and economic inefficiency.*"[30] Historians of women's work have frequently noted this phenomenon, of course, but its near universality and its persistence over time and space despite its apparent economic dysfunction remains a historical puzzle whose unraveling will require comparative as well as transnational analysis.

From a global perspective, we learn something of the way occupational segregation has helped to preserve and has participated in continually redefining masculinity. Like the wages of whiteness, the wages of a normative masculinity include a sense of entitlement to particular kinds of jobs, skills, and economic security. And as the concept of white privilege is imbued with gendered prerogatives, so the concept of male privilege is imbued with racial license. This is transparent in colonial regimes, from which we have learned much about the mechanisms of gendered control; but it is also evident in the efforts of many countries, past and present, to metaphorically as well as literally emasculate racialized men who attempt to garner gender privileges that the dominant group wants to reserve for itself.[31] Such emasculations are not limited to colonial relationships. Leela Fernandes's perceptive study of Calcutta jute mills describes the restrictions placed by different castes on certain jobs among men and the further limits in distributing jobs to widows of families who belong to the right castes.[32]

While western industrial nation-states have typically utilized their own understandings of masculinity to organize the labor force and inscribed appropriate family roles for men and women into legislation and social policy that protected patriarchal patterns of family life, global differences shed light on enforcement mechanisms. I think here of early twentieth-century Australian wage boards and of the history of "protective labor legislation" for women in industrialized states, which was designed not to protect women but to regulate their labor in the interest of the patriarchal family. Each tried to ensure women's continuing commitment to social reproduction by restricting their capacity to compete with men in the labor market and restraining the temptation of employers to exploit their cheap labor.[33] And each drew on cultural tropes that depicted women's bodies as delicate, weak, and incapable of simultaneous nurture and labor. Such gendered images disciplined men as well as women: imposing "provider" roles on men and limiting women's labor-market participation in the service of national rather than narrowly familial interest.

The measure of resistance to these patterns is visible in the degree to which colonial rulers tried to impose it on their colonies. Each prescribed a familiar and often racially imbricated sexual division of labor to categorize and organize its labor force, differentiating among the kinds of jobs that black and white men and women could and could not do. Heedless of quite different bodily imagery and the labor patterns it spawned, colonial powers attempted to develop loyalty, economic dependence, and morality at one divisive stroke. This could involve, as it did in colonial Northern Rhodesia, a preference for male rather than female domestic servants. The preference, argues Karen Tranberg Hansen, reflects "a complex interweaving of cultural factors and social practices with economic forces and questions of power."[34]

The shift of economic power to the transnational corporation has subsumed national interest (including vested patterns of family and household labor) into the effort to attract jobs and industry by providing cheap labor. It threatens the power of nations to sustain local gendered cultural patterns and illuminates the degree to which labor standards have historically reflected national and familial interests. Wedded to economic efficiency and the search for cheap labor, mobile in terms of plants and capital, the relatively autonomous transnational corporation operates without concern for local cultural norms or family maintenance. It reveals the good and the bad sides of a gendered organization of the labor force—at once threatening traditional family patterns by providing women with far greater opportunity than they could previously have conceived, and at the same time subjecting them to economic and sexual exploitation that defies local and national efforts at resistance.

The extreme case of exploitation lies in the traffic in women, to use Emma Goldman's felicitous phrase. Early in the industrialization process, western concerns for the health of the traditional male-headed family led to moral condemnation and sometimes regulation of female sex workers who relied on their bodies to make a living. A global perspective quickly reveals the particularity of the moral rationale while leaving open questions about how women make labor-market choices. "White slavery" came to the attention of western reformers at about the same time in the late nineteenth century as protective labor legislation began to take root. A global perspective suggests something of how women's bodies served a broader economic purpose and calls for an analysis of the subjective experience of sex work. Luise White has demonstrated that women migrated to Nairobi to provide an essential service to displaced male workers. Sex work was supported by family, involved little or no stigma, and produced not only a degree of economic autonomy but respect for women who used its proceeds to help sustain their families of origin as well.[35] In contrast, while some of the female sex-workers who occupied Donna Guy's Buenos Aires voluntarily chose to migrate to cities, others were forcibly imported as white slaves. Because their presence was central to economic as well as moral and political order, the authorities condoned it, enabling many women to live lives of relative independence. Though often geographically restricted and sometimes medically examined, women encountered minimal intervention.[36]

In the current world, the financial rewards of sex work so far outweigh other alternatives that many highly educated women willingly hazard its risks, including those of HIV/AIDS.[37] Further examination of the complicated negotiations between women's efforts to maximize their economic potential and state and local efforts to narrow women's sphere could well illuminate the conditions that foster the cruel sex trade that is now a global phenomenon. This is not to ignore the powerful symbolic functions of sex work, particularly as it has emerged in the literature of colonialism, where the claims of white males to the services of nonwhite females have helped to establish racial hierarchy as well as to affirm the sexual division of labor.

Interdependence and Labor Migration

A global perspective draws attention to labor migration as a subject of analysis and as a historical constant in the formation of effective labor supplies. At the same time, it encourages historians to explore the gendered aspects of migration and especially to consider the relationship between domestic pushes and labor-market pulls. As many women as men have left their homes to move (voluntarily and involuntarily) to sometimes distant workplaces, often for similar reasons: involuntarily because they have been captured and/or deported; voluntarily because they seek income for themselves and their families. Racial, ethnic, and national migration patterns point up the overlaps and the differences among male and female migrants. Thus, the forced migration of enslaved populations, which included white Europeans in the early modern period and prevailed in much of Asia until the early twentieth century, was largely a movement of women in many areas. The rapid spread of African slavery to the Americas in the seventeenth century, in contrast, appears as predominately male, as does the transport of indentured servants and imprisoned convicts. The gendered differences tell us something about labor-force needs, and they speak to the assumptions of slavers about appropriate gender activities in particular markets.

Migration flourished under ideologies of free labor, which permitted men but generally not women to sell property in their own labor. Students of Western Europe and North America have often critiqued the paradigm of "free labor"—the capacity of men and women to negotiate the price of their labor and to control their own earnings—for exposing male and female workers without effective bargaining power to indefensible exploitation. But they have also noted that women have everywhere struggled for this right, and still not everywhere achieved it. In western industrial countries it took more than a century for women to win the right to decide when and if to work, to keep their own earnings, and to choose to work for their own satisfaction rather than out of economic duress. The absence of such choices sometimes inhibited women's capacity to migrate and at others encouraged migration for the sake of family well-being.

A global perspective calls for a different paradigm, one that renders the idea of free labor incomprehensible. It suggests that labor-market choices rely as much on the power of traditional expectations of family loyalty and hierarchal position as on individual desire or motive. Paradoxically, perhaps women may achieve far greater mobility, and sometimes autonomy, in the service of their families than in their own self-interest. Studies of the sub-Saharan African continent, for example, reveal multiple patterns of labor-force mobility. Rural to urban migrations of women could and did occur without family supervision and without control of female income. Luise White's study of women's decision to move to Nairobi, where they sold their services as companions and housekeepers to men whose families had remained in rural areas, provides only one example. Their considerable profits sometimes accrued to the benefit of their families and as often resulted in comfortable lives for themselves. For generations, Chinese women could be and were sold as wives, concubines, and for sexual services, moving to their new locations in response to traditions of service. When the daughters of Japanese farmers left their homes to work in nineteenth-century textile factories, they did so for the sake of families who negotiated multi-year contracts for their labor and received the designated wage.[38]

In the modern world, where capital seeks out the cheapest source of labor, a global perspective reveals the difficulty of separating individual goals from family and community needs. This seems to be the case in countries that have experienced economic growth as a result of the rise of export-based production industries. The women who typically work in the garment factories, food processing, and electronics assembly lines of Puerto Rico, Mexico, Taiwan, Thailand, and many other countries may well experience their capacity to earn wages as liberating. Young women tend to migrate to urban and industrial centers, free from family supervision if not from the financial dependence of family members.[39] Relative economic independence doesn't necessarily provide them with more respect in their own families, but it does yield greater self-reliance and a tendency to cast off dependence on males.

Similarly, women's capacity to earn changes their relationship to social reproduction. Among the largest flows of labor has been that of female "carers"—a group that includes nurses, nannies, and domestic servants. It is fueled, on the one hand, by the expansion of opportunity for women in the affluent world who require child care to sustain professional jobs and careers, and on the other hand by the financial incentives it provides for women who live in places with few job options to support their families. Initially undertaken for money, however, these jobs often turn into attachments based on love and caring.[40] At their best, they can satisfy the desire for independence from family constraints. But they are not without irony and even pain, trading daily association with biological children for the bonds of another child's affection and complicated by the interdependence of women who earn on each other, across regional and national lines. In this respect, a global perspective draws attention to the central importance of social reproduction and to the varieties of ways that women have fulfilled that task. It draws into focus the relation between care work (paid and unpaid) and other forms of wage labor.

If the economic independence of some women builds on the ability of others to assign the tasks of social reproduction to extended family members, extending economic opportunity to women across the globe tends to pit workers from opposite ends of the earth against each other. Thus, what appears to be a "runaway" shop to female textile workers in North Carolina translates into job-providing industry to rural women in the Philippines or Malaysia. The migration of capital turns women who might be said to share class interests into rivals for the same jobs, pitting poor workers in rich and poor countries against each other.[41] Advances in technology have extended this process into such white-collar areas as processing financial data, answering telephone inquiries, and responding to Internet help lines. They challenge the capacity of some countries to maintain trade-union-negotiated labor standards and of others to create jobs for their unemployed workers.

Issues of Power and Status

A global perspective complicates the notion that female gender generally signifies powerlessness with respect to workforce position. While early modern historians of the West have often argued about the degree to which women's economic roles declined with increasing urbanization, and modern historians endlessly debate the impact of industrialization on women's status within and outside the family, a global view of women's work reveals something of how gender participates in establishing power relationships in a larger social context. In particular, it illustrates the active role of women in sustaining and maintaining power relationships through their economic intervention and in thereby enabling the family unit to provide a voice for all its members.

Involved in local and simple labor markets, where family-produced products are exchanged and sold, women tend to report positive accretions of power and status in their own families. But their incursion into more complex markets and migration to distant places to find jobs prompt questions about how their earnings affect gendered power relationships within the family, the community, and the state. On the island of Java, for example, families encouraged their young daughters to find work in local factories to reduce the cost of their upkeep. But the net contributions of these young women were so small as to mitigate any additional influence they might have gained from more significant additions to the family pot.[42] When they remained at home and participated in the family's daily routine, including working in the fields, the same young women found themselves with increased authority.

The historical and contemporary evidence suggests that young women who migrated to distant factories or to domestic service jobs, far more than men, sent money home to families. But if sending a daughter or a wife out to work promised to bind her more tightly to families whose economic survival depended on multiple earners, neither wives nor daughters found themselves, as a result, with greater voice or influence at home. The migration of a wife seemed especially to increase struggles over the distribution of power within the family, intensifying conflict over decision making. Even the possibility of such power struggles sometimes renders women's labor-force access more remote. Among Moroccan Berbers, for example, wives are systematically excluded from access to the wage-labor market, working instead for barter or in family agricultural enterprises. Fears that women with earned income will upset the patriarchal power structure and increase an already high level of divorce render women's efforts to access broader labor markets useless.[43]

While women's capacity to make decisions about distributing family income and to participate in the management of their earnings, if not to control them, challenges patriarchal and hierarchal relationships and models in some cultures, in other instances power over spending decisions seems less related to who earns the income. Female control over household purchases and expenditures varies culturally. While in the West, women's voices tend to diminish as the expense rises, in other places different patterns prevail. Japanese women, who generally lack workplace mobility, nevertheless have control over domestic expenditures—often including the purchase of houses, cars, and other "large" goods. Many African women decide on their family domiciles, building their own homes, sometimes with their own hands.[44]

These questions impinge on the relationship of class to gender, particularly as they rotate around the power or powerlessness of ordinary people. In so far as the increasing economic visibility of women in the past two centuries has been translated into feminist struggles for political power, women's political access may rise even as the economic power of the nation-state declines. Increasing education and professionalization of women yields greater voice. And wage work enhances women's capacity to claim nonpolitical leadership positions, for example in trade unions, where they have been largely responsible for incrementally raising labor standards. Especially where political parties dominated by labor exist, modest social benefits and reasonable working conditions and pay enable moderate livelihoods for men and women.

As the labor market has come to incorporate women more fully, it has engaged issues of human rights, particularly with regard to reproduction and economic opportunities. Perceptions of rights—to a reasonable standard of living and to a job that provides for oneself and one's children—suggest that women's self-esteem and status improve, if not their power to change their lives. The silver lining in the increased visibility of sexual harassment worldwide is its reflection of women reaching for good jobs. But the dark clouds of opportunity denied still hover, bringing malnutrition or even starvation (as in Afghanistan) to women and their children.

Conclusion

We are left with more questions than answers. Like the Industrial Revolution of the nineteenth century, the unstoppable wave of globalization carries the promise of a higher standard of living and the threat (for better or worse) of disrupting long-standing gender norms. Tracing how these two have existed in tension with each other throughout the past, and imagining how they will continue to coexist, is a task that will surely occupy historians for years to come. How have the continuing changes in women's work patterns affected the lives and lifestyles of ordinary people? How have they altered the attitudes and mores of ordinary people? What has been the impact of the transnational corporation on labor standards and the sexual division of labor? How has the transnational corporation influenced political and social power structures in ways that will impact on women and their families. Historians (compared to some sociologists) have yet to turn their skills to microstudies of how change happened and its consequences. We have yet to examine the gendered responses of male and female trade-union leaders, of rich and poor women's organizations, and of men and women who aspire to political leadership.

Whether, as individual historians, we do our own work within or beyond national borders, our questions will in the future be informed by recognition of the complexity of the issues. The paradigms of our field have shifted to encompass gendered analysis as part and parcel of every issue, from the largely economic questions embedded in family decision making to the spiritual and emotional issues captured by organizing a labor force to sustain resurgent nationalism and nourish ethnic and racial identities. A nonwestern perspective opens labor history to questions of ideology, sexuality, interdependence, and power, revealing to every labor historian new paths for understanding the working lives of women and men.

17

"History Is Public or Nothing": Learning How to Keep Illusions in our Future

I trace my lineage in American studies back to no traditional training. I did not sit at the feet of one of the inspiring practitioners in one of the great programs at Yale or Minnesota. And though I am, somewhat inadvertently, the grandchild of one of the masters, my intellectual roots and passion for our discipline came initially from outside the mainstream of American studies—from exploring the history of labor and of women and gender. Both have been contested arenas within American history partly because of their propensity towards interdisciplinarity and partly because each is bound to a political trajectory or movement. And both have found comfortable homes in American studies, participating in the successful efforts of a generation of scholars to alter the meaning of "American culture" or "cultural studies" to reflect subjective and vernacular experience as well as artistic and literary commentary on it. The lineage I trace draws on the politics and the insights of three decades of flux in American studies. But it also reflects the intersection of politics with the life of the mind that has simultaneously tormented and inspired a generation of Americanists who work within the United States.

My story is perhaps as useful for what it reveals about a changing and contested field as for what it says about one idiosyncratic journey. Still, I focus here on that journey. It starts when I was a graduate student in the 1960s. I sought out Rutgers as a place to do graduate work for reasons not unfamiliar to women of my generation. Already married, I needed an institution within

This essay was first published as "Moving Towards a Future with Illusions," in Rob Kroes, ed., *Pre decessors: Intellectual Lineages in American Studies* (Amsterdam: VU University Press, 1999); it was republished in *Rethinking History* 5 (2001). Earlier versions were presented at the North American Labor History Conference, Wayne State University, Detroit, fall 1997; the Warren Susman Graduate History Conference, Rutgers University, New Brunswick, N.J., April 1998; and the Amsterdam University Amerika Instituut conference on "Predecessors: Intellectual Lineages in American Studies," April 1999.

commuting radius of New York. In the early 1960s, Rutgers had a reputation for exciting social history, and it was not tainted by the just-emerging hints of involvement in the cold war that colored the images of other institutions.

Within a semester I had encountered one of the transformative minds of his generation, Warren Susman. Himself a student of Merle Curti and a participant in Curti's efforts to use numbers to assess the reciprocal impact of social change on the lives of ordinary people, Warren persuaded his students that particular kinds of historical consciousness could and did participate in constructing culture. In a field still resolutely antitheoretical, he used to torment and bully his students into efforts to comprehend what we would now call our subjective positions as narrators. "Every history," he insisted, "is an autobiography." He put it more fulsomely in the 1984 preface to his excruciatingly compiled volume of essays, *Culture and History:* "The writing of history is as personal an act as the writing of fiction. As the historian attempts to understand the past, he is at the same time, knowingly or not, seeking to understand his own cultural situation and himself."[1]

Susman believed that such an understanding transcended the search for individual identity. "Attitudes towards the past," he argued, "frequently become facts of profound consequence for the culture itself."[2] In a pathbreaking 1964 *American Quarterly* essay, he laid out his theory about the relationship of myth to history. For him, myth proposes "fundamental goals" of society, while history "defines and illuminates basic processes involved in achieving those goals." The tension between using history to affirm myth and evoking it in a more traditional ideological way produces culture. Historical interpretation thus underpins any generation's understanding of its own culture. It is, thought Susman, most readily identified by intellectuals and artists who, in turn, help to perpetuate particular interpretive stances. Eighteenth-century ministers, early nineteenth-century writers, and late nineteenth-century artists were among those who believed they could offer "a vision of . . . history that would be more meaningful for culture." And Warren had great hopes that by the early 1960s, intellectuals who had emerged from the cold war would be among those whose rewriting of history would produce a fuller and more profound understanding of cultural development and thus help to change the world around them.

This was 1962: Kennedy's election and the optimistic rhetoric that surrounded it had opened promises around civil liberties and expanding democracy that no one was prepared to fulfill. An increasingly militant civil rights movement began to provoke confrontation around voting rights and public accomodations. Within a few short years, branches of the labor movement rallied in active support of Martin Luther King's antipoverty crusade. Other branches carefully shepherded medical care for the aged through Congress.

Vietnam was in the air, challenging cold-war platitudes about dominoes and begging questions about the authority of governments. A generation bred in comfort discovered huge pockets of poverty that defied illusions of affluence.

It was beyond imagination that my generation of graduate students would continue to read the past through the rosy lenses of a shared consensus, or that we could stand by while change happened around us. Events seemed to challenge us to develop an "engaged" history, one that would alter the shape of American culture to come. The standard explanatory frameworks lacked resonance for the challenges of the moment. Discontented with the brilliant expositions of sociologists like William H. Whyte and David Riesman, whose descriptive analysis offered little hope for change, we turned to the new sociology of knowledge.[3] We sought the roots of what Peter Berger later called "the social construction of reality" in investigations of psyche and personality, looking to the likes of Norman O. Brown to find the connecting links between identity and social action and joining a stream of young scholars like John Higham, Daniel Bell, Leo Marx, and Richard Hofstadter, who already believed with Susman that culture is rooted in visions of the past. We discovered Karl Mannheim's argument that no human is immune to the ideological influence of social context. As "ideology" (which Mannheim euphemistically transformed into "wish dreams") crept back into the historical vocabulary, it reaffirmed the possibility that ideas could be engines of change.[4]

We dipped into a deeply tainted Marxism, cherishing our rediscoveries of a dialectical historical process and the explanatory power of theories of labor value. Yet we resisted the idea that materialism was all, or, as the British historian E. P. Thompson (of whom no one in America had yet heard) put it later, that human relationships could be entirely defined by the economic.[5] Instead, we found in the early Marx the electrifying notion of false consciousness. The historical Marx put teeth into our new history, enabling us to believe that our work could unearth the roots of consciousness in order, to paraphrase only a little, to enable people to shake off the chains of illusion and "cull the living flowers."[6] We learned that if the historian's task was "to establish the truth of this world," the student of American culture had a wider obligation: to discover the meaning of that truth and to disseminate it. The "New Left" for us was not simply a utopian dream; it had roots in the history we were creating.

For help in that quest we looked beyond American borders. The British theorist Richard Hoggart had already published *The Uses of Literacy,* which linked the worlds of economic and media culture to the construction of expectation and aspirations and jolted us out of the benign assumption that individuals could control their own wishes.[7]

Then came Herbert Marcuse, bringing even the laggards back to Marx; Antonio Gramsci swam into view, affirming the political force of ideology.[8] By

the mid-1960s, we had the beginning of a new vocabulary and a way of understanding the world. It was a world where questions emerged from political and
social circumstance and where "culture" had become the source of interpreta-
tive authority as well as the object of study. It was a world where culture and
politics were reciprocally empowered, and where history was the engine of
change in both arenas.

Warren Susman's brand of cultural history provided a crucial set of hooks,
resisting without rejecting fundamental notions of the dialectical process
of history and offering culture as an access route to comprehending whole
social systems. His notion of "ideologies as systems that account for everything" demanded that we place ourselves within, not outside, the process of
collecting and evaluating data and take responsibility for our use of words. In
retrospect, his effort to rethink notions of culture resonate with those of other
historians. Natalie Zemon Davis, for example, had already discovered that she
could use anthropology to look for "whole relationships."[9] Herbert Gutman
was busily developing a labor history within which culture constituted a "lived
experience." His conception begged for explorations of leisure that inspired
some new directions.[10]

For his students, what was special was Warren's excitement about defining
culture with us in it. Our sources expanded to incorporate the "naive." We
read fiction, convinced that it promised access to the worldviews or historical frames of the authors who had touched American lives. E. P. Thompson
was later to claim that much of his work had come from teaching literature.
We added up numbers for the same reason: they seemed such unproblem-
atic signals to behaviors that reflected belief systems. We hunted for ethnogra-
phy everywhere, inventing the term "oral history" to legitimize our complete
absence of method. Though Warren himself focused on the visible and the
iconic, his willingness to think about "culture" as a synonym for experience
nurtured alternative possibilities. As he used the term, it embraced a politics
of human behavior that interrogated the dualisms of self and object within
every artifact of analysis: strikes and mentalities, consumption and production, photography and the photographer. It freed us to think about how ordinary actors—African Americans, workers, immigrants—created culture as
they engaged with their worlds both high and low. No, there was as yet no
thought of women, but in retrospect, I believe the groundwork had been laid.

In this context, the dissertation topic I chose—on Jewish immigrant workers in New York City in the 1890s—seems to have been overdetermined. Labor
history at the time existed largely as a subset of economic history. Generally
located in economics departments, it was infused by little conception of culture. It drew its theoretical parameters from an institutional economics that
respected institutional boundaries of enterprises, trade unions, and govern-

ment policy without exploring anything of the lives, experiences, or voices of workers, male or female, black or white. Notions of individual agency tended to disappear into conflated categories like class or business or regions. Immigrants occupied a marginal place in the consciousness of students of American culture. Lumped together in groups like "Southern European" or "Nordic," their history was characterized by words like "assimilation" and "adaptation." This world smacked little of culture, a word for which Matthew Arnold provided the boundaries, and whose narrow and explicit meaning encompassed nothing of ordinary life.

And yet exploring the relationship of poor people, and especially of working-class Jews on New York's Lower East Side, to the reformers who tried to ease the path to Americanization would allow a continuing rebellion against established notions of culture and the freedom to locate the conflicts that fueled illusions about the future. I intended to explore the American dream enacted in the life of the mind of immigrant workers. This seemed pretty brave to me. At a moment when the distinguished colonialist Carl Bridenbaugh publicly bewailed the admission to the profession of children of immigrants who threatened its destruction, I, a child of refugees, not once but twice an immigrant, firmly believed that I had crept into graduate school by the back door. I neither intended nor wanted to battle the establishment. But I did want to write a history that reflected something of my own lost culture. Who was writing about workers, or Jews, or poor people and their connection to politics? John Hope Franklin was hardly a name to be reckoned with. Herbert Gutman had just begun to publish. Joe Huthmacher had just produced a piece that connected labor and politics. But the Rutgers department offered the kind of atmosphere available perhaps nowhere else on the East Coast. My dissertation would test the radical potential of the field—a double redemption and a double subversion. Every history, Warren had said, is an autobiography. In the end, I lacked the courage to reify experience, and the dissertation, completed in 1968, fell far short of its unspoken goals. Not only did I skirt the "real" experience of immigrants, but I left women completely out.

Perhaps this was inevitable, for while I had opened up one piece of a culture, I had neglected the relationship of history to politics and experience that was a key piece of Susman's maxim. In the late 1960s, my work began to draw new inspiration from an active engagement with the labor movement and with feminism. As I began to understand that my own notion of culture participated in how I conceived working-class history, and that I would need to engage with trade unionism to fully interpret its history, I sought to infuse my work with a more active commitment. Once again my timing was off, for by the late 1960s, the American labor movement had largely rejected the idea of intellectuals as partners; Left intellectuals, in turn, had become disillusioned with the possibilities of labor's transformative influence. They shared a view of labor history that reified myths of its institutional isolation.

To be sure, intellectuals, many of them factory workers, and other university-trained idealists had involved themselves in every phase of the late nineteenth- and early twentieth-century American labor movement. But by the 1960s, the purges of the McCarthy period had turned whatever relationships continued into largely passive alliances. Conflicts over the war in Vietnam produced active hostility. For many years the trade union had embodied intellectuals' hopes for a transformed society. Generations of socialist and communist thinkers had dreamed of using the trade-union movement as the vehicle of economic and social change. Radicals of all kinds had chronicled their successes along with the lessons of their failures. Brookwood, a pioneer school for union leaders and workers, and other labor education centers had employed intellectuals to construct socially conscious agendas. Yet the record revealed an enormous disparity between what most American union members and leaders believed and the agendas of their putative instructors. For the most part, American unionists mistrusted left-wing ideas that did not advance the immediate economic self-interest of union members. They rejected actions that threatened their ability to negotiate with the capitalists who wielded power.

Labor historians had for decades affirmed the vision of contest that permeated the history of unions. Their history functioned as a description of the labor movement's continuing resistance to broadening its agendas and a warning notice to aspiring academics like me, beginning with Selig Perlman's conviction that "scarcity of opportunity" must guide trade-union actions: his urgent calls for a limited trade-union program responsive to the psyche of workers, and his fear that a utopian intellectual agenda would undermine dynamic job consciousness and therefore had no place in the world of unions.[11] Perlman's eloquent appeals offer a prescription that could justify the Congress of Industrial Organizations' (CIO) leadership's exclusion of communists who had contributed to its strength, their willingness to turn the idea of the intellectual into a code for communist.

A different kind of labor history threatened to undermine the union movement. At a moment when the trade-union movement was still sore from its battles with intellectuals, the American labor historian Philip Taft penned an impassioned plea against the idea that labor had gained anything at all from the intellectuals in its midst. Union members, he argued, had not objected to communists, as long as they had salted their ideas with hard-edged gains. In Taft's view, visionary unions of the past, including miners, machinists, brewers, garment workers, and many more, "were not superior in most respects, to others." Pointing to the labor movement's "practical idealism," he extolled its leaders' ability to "protect their members' interests."[12] By that standard would the labor movement judge itself. I recall Douglas Fraser, the UAW president in the late 1970s and 1980s, commenting in 1990 that trade-union leaders could never move too far beyond rank-and-file members. And by that standard, the labor movement was, in Taft's mind, an unmitigated success.

At the time Taft wrote, many intellectuals would have preferred labor to take a different route—not the socialist extreme, but one that more closely resembled the social unionism of some European trade unions. C. Wright Mills, who entered the postwar period optimistically predicting the movement's turn to social unionism, thought that no longer possible by the mid-1950s.[13] And in that "golden age of capitalism," social democrats like Daniel Bell questioned union willingness to trade off increased productivity for higher wages, arguing that unions, eager to provide economic security, were already beginning to lose their force for social change. Such economistic goals, he thought, would limit the latent potential of the unions to lead a social movement. Bell at one point hoped leaders like Walter Reuther (to whose visions of social justice Taft gave such short shrift) might constitute a repository of that movement—for his championship of issues like better housing, more schools, adequate medical care, and the creation of a more humanistic work atmosphere in the factory.[14] But—rightly, as it turned out—Bell predicted that the labor movement as a whole would never fully trust that direction.

Still, I had to try. In the early 1970s, I abandoned traditional academic teaching to help create a school for workers that started classes within trade-union headquarters in 1976. District 65 was a small, maverick kind of catch-all union formed by Left intellectuals during the Depression. For a while it floated in and out of the CIO, finally ending its years as a UAW local. District 65 was a very good union by almost every imaginable standard, and one that tried to translate transformative notions into day-to-day practice. This was a union whose slogan was "organize the unorganizable" before that was popular; that sponsored hootenannies before anyone knew what the word meant; that refused the check-off on the grounds that members ought to reaffirm their support frequently. It was a union that in the 1950s traded off seniority rights for racial equality. Its president, the late David Livingston, who marched at Martin Luther King Jr.'s right hand in 1963, was an outspoken opponent of the war in Vietnam. But District 65 was something of an outcast in the labor movement, bouncing from the CIO to independence and back again. And Livingston so feared the loss of his power and influence that he had never allowed a second generation of leadership to develop. When our program began to develop those leaders, we ran into trouble.

What I did not then understand was that in the memory of even the most progressive and open-minded labor-movement leaders, the history of practical accomplishment overwhelms and underlines any campaign for larger goals. The culture they sought, and perhaps still seek, to resurrect is a culture of accomplishment. John Sweeney captured pride in that history when he reminded a 1997 audience of labor and academics of the continuing validity of Samuel Gompers's request for "more." For him, the 1950s was a golden age precisely because labor leaders avoided larger agendas. Working people in that decade knew that "if we got up every morning and did our jobs, then we could earn a better life for ourselves and a better chance for our children."[15]

With some significant exceptions, most elements of the American labor movement have neither wished nor intended to transform society, even as they have participated in doing so. On the whole, American trade unions have built themselves on an interpretation of the past that agrees that workers have struggled to achieve such things as an "American standard of living," justice in the workplace, and dignity in poor jobs. They have sought to develop and use the power generated by numbers to bargain with employers, to speak for their members and their needs, and sometimes to curtail corporate greed and irresponsibility. To the extent that these noble goals have been achieved, they helped many workers to reach Gompers's goal of "more": more comfortable family lives, more education for kids, and more leisure time for everyone.

The women's movement in those years, though less suspicious of larger goals, was equally locked into a past that continued to shape women's expectations. It aimed to open economic opportunity, political access, and reproductive freedom to more and wider groups of women. But to do this required a new way of seeing how gender functioned as an ideological system in all its class and racially rooted complexity. For historians like me, questions of ideology and consciousness were inevitably rooted in issues of evidence and interpretation. If ideologies were "systems that accounted for everything," then gender was a piece of the whole. If every history was an autobiography, the multiple sources of one's own identity surely deserved exploration. What piece of my collective self (our collective selves) was I omitting when I ignored gender? What understandings of class and race were restricted by omissions of women and of the relationships of men to women within racialized class contexts? Trained by Warren Susman and schooled by the 1960s to reconcile experience with illusion, was I to be an accomplice in perpetuating the idea that gender did not matter? Yet when I turned towards the histories of wage-earning women that became my life's work, Warren shook his head in despair. "When are you going to do something serious?" he would ask, in a voice that implied that I had yet to learn what it meant to be a historian.

But I had been well trained. Once immersed in the women's movement, I could see that Warren was wrong. Herbert Gutman helped to confirm my intellectual direction. I met him shortly after I defended the dissertation in the spring of 1968. In a long afternoon of conversation, he offered me his own take on how to historicize issues of class and race, leading me finally to position myself as a new-style labor historian. In American history, it was Gutman who released a generation of young people to write histories of workers in and outside trade unions and led them to examine the meaning of community and of nonwork lives. For many of us, the approach illuminated ways of melding women—working women—and the families of working men into analyses of social change. It opened to question the difference between a culturally based labor history and a celebratory history of women and begged a notion of class that could successfully accommodate women. This would be my contribution to lifting the veil of illusion: surely a project serious enough even for Warren. I set to work.

Like many of my generation, I turned first to Marxist-feminism. My study group saw this as a theoretical tool for understanding how women participated in processes of production and reproduction and a practical instrument for furthering the socialism that we remained convinced was just over the horizon. But the tensions between them remained palpable. We used to joke about them: "What does it mean to be a Marxist-feminist?" we asked. The answer: "Twice as many meetings." A curious intersection of cultures helped to resolve the problem.

I encountered Raymond Williams in the effort to find a definition of culture and ideology that could encompass the lived experience of working people at about the same time that I discovered Allen Ginsberg. This might appear a rather improbable combination. Williams was by then already a distinguished socialist theorist and Cambridge don. His deep respect for the power of historical interpretation contrasted sharply with the irreverent and ahistorical stance of Ginsberg, the Beat poet. Yet the two shared something that I, too, cherished: a tiny piece of Wales called the Wye Valley where Raymond Williams grew up, Allen Ginsberg drew inspiration, and I found some of my most precious escapes as a child. This valley, as I remember it and as Ginsberg describes it, is one of the most beautiful places on earth. In his eyes, its gentle, grassy hills are without menace. They contain neither craggy peaks nor dangerous precipices. All year round, they remain a comforting cheerful green, dotted only with clumps of ash and birch and spotted with wandering sheep. When Ginsberg discovered it, he fell to his knees, seeing before him "a solid mass of Heaven, mist-infused." There was, he thought, "no imperfection in the budded mountain." There, "valleys breathe, heaven and earth move together." Only erotic metaphors adequately describe Ginsberg's ecstasy. He lay down, he tells us, "mixing my beard with the wet hair of the mountainside."[16] I could go on to quote more of the sheep, the flowers, the dancing horses that persuaded him that in these hills he was seeing "the myriad-formed soul" of Buddha. But I stop here to remark only that the poem is twice-dated. One dateline reads August 3, 1967, London. The second: July 27, 1967, LSD.

Raymond Williams (born and raised in those valleys) and I (who grew up just south of them) knew, as Allen Ginsberg could not have (in or outside of his acid-laden trance) that the country he perceived was an illusion, hiding under its gentle hills and green valleys the seams of the coal mines, sources of the contradictions that have long made the Welsh a desperately poor and fiercely proud people. By the mid-nineteenth century, at a time when the majority of the English still lived off the land, more than half the Welsh earned their livings in and around the mines. Fully a third of the men and boys worked underground. But the real contradiction (which Ginsberg could easily have seen had he peered just over the next mountain) was what the mines had done to the shape of the land. A century and a half's worth of coal leavings had thrown up thousands of ugly slag heaps whose grey shapes competed with the green of the hills and often dwarfed them.

Let me try to bring home the starkness of the contrast. In the fall of 1966, only a few months before Ginsberg put his gossamer illusions into words, and less than ten miles from where he prostrated himself on the grass, one of those slag heaps began to move. Sliding at first slowly down, then bursting into a frenzied pace, it produced an avalanche of gritty, grey, dusty waste, coming to rest on top of the tiny schoolhouse in the village of Aberfan where it buried 116 children and their twenty-eight teachers alive.

I wish I could say that the slag heap was the end of my illusions. That after this, I saw them beside every rolling hill. I cannot. Like Ginsberg, I repeatedly returned to those valleys for solace. But the contrast between the thundering power of refuse and the gentle valleys of Ginsberg's imagination and my youth created an urgent need for reconciliation that paralleled and informed a growing sense of myself as a labor historian. Not much later, I discovered Raymond Williams.

From where I had lived in Gabalfa, Aberfan was "up the valley," one among dozens of mining villages, each of them a row of terraced miners' houses, headed by a church and a schoolhouse. The villages lay just south and west of the site of Raymond Williams's childhood. To be honest, I have to say that I discovered Williams before I knew he was Welsh. It was 1973. The New Left had already disintegrated into its ignominious end. What remained focused on ending the Vietnam War finally and at last. I was still in a Marxist-feminist study group. We had read all three volumes of *Capital* with increasing skepticism and a diffuse anger towards a Marxian theory that could not accommodate our growing conviction of the power of social and biological reproduction. Then I came upon "Base and Superstructure in Marxist Cultural Theory."[17]

"Base and Superstructure" refused the old dichotomy between the material and the ideological, suggesting the ultimate futility of conversations around economic determinism and invoking the power of culture and the necessity of exploring it as an analytic entity. It awakened me to the central importance and complicated mechanisms of deeply rooted cultural identity in human consciousness and behavior, opening new ways to see gender (and ethnicity and race) within the framework of a dialectical process. The piece led me in search of Williams's other work, but it was only later that I came to believe that without his experience—our shared experience of Welsh history and culture—he could not have written as he did.

That insight came when, in my efforts to follow Williams's attempt to locate culture as the central trope of human experience, I encountered his essay on the Welsh industrial novel. For the Welsh miner, wrote Williams, the pastoral remained a visible presence, not as an ideal contrast, but as the slope, the skyline, seen immediately from the streets and from the pit-tops, tangible in the "sheep on the hills" that often "strayed down into the streets of the settlements." The shape of the mines and the hills, wrote Williams, trying to explain the tenor of the Welsh imagination, accounted "not only for a consciousness of history, but for a consciousness of alternatives" that shaped the miner's persona and framed his aspirations and possibilities. That consciousness came, as he put it, from the contrast between "darkness and light, of being trapped and of getting clear . . . here on the ground in the most specific ways."[18]

Turning from efforts to describe how past and present (pastoral and industrial) continuously confront each other, Williams proposed instead that we engage the contrasts—live with them and feel them. Exploring the meaning of contrast became for me a new way to view the historical process. Williams's autobiographical novel, *Border Country,* articulates the play between elusive dissimilarities and underlines their central importance to those who lived with them. In his fictional persona as a historian returned from his university post to the Welsh village of his childhood, Williams stumbles over his failure to complete a book on Welsh population movements during the Industrial Revolution. "'I've lost heart, I suppose,'" the protagonist tells his father's friend. "'For I saw suddenly that it wasn't a piece of research, but an emotional pattern. Emotional patterns are all very well, but they're our own business. History is public or nothing.'"[19]

In our lifetimes as historians and students of American culture, we have come to understand, as Williams eventually did, that "emotional patterns" are not our own business at all but the stuff of which history is made—the living texture out of which people make decisions. Williams's theoretical work contributed as much to that as anyone's, providing for me a conception of culture deeply embedded in class *and* place, in work *and* community. Yet much as those emotional patterns (cultures, if you will) have been integrated into our research, we resist them in our politics—they remain unspoken sources of the tensions we face as we grapple with the real world, always there and always mocking our efforts to rethink the past with us in it.

Not long after my encounter with the Welsh industrial novel, I went to visit my friend Nora, who still lives where the coal mines once existed. Nora's father-in-law is a retired collier (pit man) who arranged for a friend to take us down into one of the now-closed pits. Our guide had followed his father into the colliery as a fourteen-year-old in 1936. Now he was old, ill, and somewhat bitter. As we shared the dank, cold, and dark, miners' lamps strapped to our heads, he walked us, bent-headed, through to the low seams where he tried to evoke the feeling of being eternally trapped. He described how the new seams were extended by miners who lay flat on their backs in eighteen-inch-high openings, chipping the coal above them. Often rats ran over a man's body. Tiny rivulets of water dripped down, soaking the miner to his skin. I listened to our guide's voice, feeling the gnawing sharp teeth and shivering with the wet in my bones. Commiseration overwhelmed analysis as I burbled sympathy about this surely being one of the hardest jobs of work. "You'll never understand it," he said, a bit of contempt creeping in. "You'll never understand it till you understand about the smell. That was the worst." Then he elaborated. Until electrification began in the early 1950s, the coal was pulled out by pit ponies. Because they balked at going from sun to dark, the ponies were kept underground, usually for a year at a time. They were fed there, and there they eliminated their waste. The residue not only accounted for the rats but for what was by his account a stench so unbearable that many miners could literally not stomach it. I leave the rest to your imaginations.

Is it only an illusion to imagine that as historians we can capture a culture that will reflect the heartbeat of working people as they earned their livings and lived out their dreams, not ours? Is it hubris to believe that as intellectuals our work can produce patterns and pictures that honor labor for what it did rather than for what we wish it had done? Raymond Williams and Allen Ginsberg give me comfort.

When I think of the seams of coal running under the poet's heavenly mountains; of the miners' lives shaped by light as well as dark; of the sheep that ran in the streets where the pit heads spewed their grit; of the miner in his prideful masculinity daily meeting the humiliating stench—I think as well of how the historical process moves forward because these experiences cannot be reconciled but must be lived in all their oppositional intensity. The contrasts persist everywhere we look: the skilled trade unionist lives in a world in which the job is his only turf and seniority protects it. Yet "fairness" demands that he give up his claims and share his rights to work with others. The working mother's days contain the desire to be with her children and to leave them in order to earn the money that will give them a better future. The idea of social justice (translated into issues like set-aside programs, job-related affirmative action, and welfare stipends without work) appears as blatant injustice to working people on the margins. Preferential admission of alumnae children to the best universities draws no comparable protest.

My explorations of culture, like those of many of my generation who have come to understand the relationship of history to culture, continuously confronts the complicated tensions exposed by simultaneously existing yet potentially conflicting goals. The generation of scholars that grew up rejecting the idea that the histories of workers and unions were coterminous sees workers in multiple ways and remains cognizant of the contradictions embedded in their lives. Workers are producers, consumers, and citizens; they are family members and wage earners; they are white and "raced"; they make products and produce offspring. We begin to understand that skill at work can be the source of self-esteem—the glue that cements families—and the foundation of discrimination as well. We watch how games like baseball that were once "play" become big business, generating unions for players and leisure for observers. We understand that people who identify as "men" or "women" find their activism enhanced and inhibited under different circumstances; that an immigrant mentality affirms and negates racism; that radicals can be sexist even while espousing the woman question.

On one level, American cultural historians have accepted the effort to more fully understand the multiple consciousnesses of most people. At another, we want to write histories in which social movements embody only our best and most precious aspirations. The U.S. labor movement, with all its flaws, serves as a metaphor even as it has provided a touchstone for me for so many years. Many intellectuals (and perhaps most of those who, like me, came of age in the 1960s) wanted from the labor movement more than it could provide. Persuaded of the need for a trade-union movement that would serve as a vehicle for social justice, if not for some future transformation, we have wanted to write histories in which it carried the banners of equality, justice, and freedom. We have wanted it to stand for racial and, more recently, gendered fairness; to speak for and on behalf of a community of interests of all workers. As the distinguished economist Albert Hirschman might put it, we have wanted an institution that could function as a voice for them; that could pave the way for a nonracialized, gender-encompassing workplace. In short, there are those among us who have wanted it to represent a spiritual and moral vision, even at the cost of the gritty realities that surround most people's lives and lead them to seek narrower social and economic goals. Like Ginsberg's view of the Welsh mountains, our own fog of metaphorical LSD obscures some critical illusions. And yet, it has served me well as a lesson in comprehending the meaning of cultures.

Warren Susman's sense that social order is justified and sustained by theories of history mediated by cultural interpretation has remained a permanent legacy, exemplified by our own experience. The broader goals of social justice and equality and the more specific ones of economic security have receded in our time. Myths of the free market abide. The rising tide of the 1950s, along with its skilled craftsmen, mass-production workers, and seemingly endless productivity gains, is a thing of the past. As the tide turns, it carries with it not only any immediate possibility of social democratic consensus or socialist dreams but it tosses aside more limited goals like good jobs, public housing, health care, and education as well. The social unionism of the American past that once appeared a modest goal to intellectuals has become, in AFL-CIO president John Sweeney's energetic hands, the agent for new coalition. Yet it seems inadequate even to defend past gains, much less to achieve new ones. The global market stifles the most generous visions of the old social unionism, preventing even the best-intentioned governments with strong union movements from sustaining the most benign welfare system. It also releases corporations from responsibility for polluting and destroying the environment, for job training, and for the quality of community life. The upshot is a world of contrast: great wealth and great opportunity for some, along with stark and growing poverty and enhanced racial/ethnic division.

The global market exacerbates contrasts. On the one hand, it produces a work/family dynamic that calls for greater attention to the world outside of work, including the consumption patterns and leisure lives of workers. On the other hand, the family and work become oppositional categories, forcing a reevaluation of the meaning of women in the workforce and in the labor movement and provoking skepticism about the meaning of families. Class reemerges as a pivotal force in understanding the ideology of workers' lives, and women become a key dimension in its definitions. Suddenly my own efforts to understand the complicated culture of work move to center stage, and I want to thank Warren Susman for introducing me to the notion of an engaged history. At the same time, I can't resist the temptation to declare victory: women's history is more "serious" than you or I ever imagined.

These lessons were brought home to me sharply a few years ago. I had agreed to introduce my husband (who had never been to my part of Wales) to some of the memories of my childhood. We drove from the Cotswolds, through Hereford and the Wye Valley, stopping at some of the scenes of Ginsberg's raptures, to smell the grass and to watch the sheep. He was as taken with my captivating valleys as Ginsberg had been. I urged him, impatiently, forward. Come on, I said, it's not like this, wait till you see the slag heaps. It's all grey where I come from. Five more miles, then ten, and still green, a country I did not recognize. Through Abergavenny and down from Merthyr into Pontypridd. I was in my valley, and still it was green. Then the dawning recognition came: the slag heaps were covered with grass. The last of what had once been upwards of three thousand coal mines had been closed, and the European Economic Community had paid to turn what had been grey into green. The new hills marked the end of one set of contrasts forever obscuring the world that had fostered in Williams such clear vision. But they reminded this student of American culture that the search for historically specific cultural explanations is not always easy; that truth can be hidden by beauty as well as slag.

Notes

Introduction

1. It would be impossible to list all the titles that come from the resurgence of interest in women's work in the 1970s, but a few of the key volumes would include Nancy Cott, *Bonds of Womanhood: Women's Sphere in New England, 1780–1835* (New Haven, Conn.: Yale University Press, 1977); Margery W. Davies, *Women's Place Is at the Typewriter: Office Work and Office Workers, 1870–1930* (Philadelphia: Temple University Press, 1982); Thomas Dublin, *Women at Work: The Transformation of Work and Community in Lowell, Massachusetts, 1826–1860* (New York: Columbia University Press, 1979); Joan Jensen, *Loosening the Bonds: Mid-Atlantic Farm Women, 1750–1850* (New Haven, Conn.: Yale University Press, 1986); S. J. Kleinberg, *Shadow of the Mills: Working-Class Families in Industrial Pittsburgh, 1870–1907* (Pittsburgh: University of Pittsburgh Press, 1989); Meredith Tax, *The Rising of the Women: Feminist Solidarity and Class Conflict, 1880–1917* (New York: Monthly Review Press, 1980); and Mary Roth Walsh, *Doctors Wanted; No Women Need Apply: Sexual Barriers in the Medical Profession, 1835–1975* (New Haven, Conn.: Yale University Press, 1977).

2. See Mary H. Blewett, *Men, Women, and Work: Class, Gender, and Protest in the New England Shoe Industry, 1780–1910* (Urbana: University of Illinois Press, 1988); Eileen Boris and Cynthia Daniels, eds., *Homework: Historical and Contemporary Perspectives on Paid Labor at Home* (Urbana: University of Illinois Press, 1989); Ardis Cameron, *Radicals of the Worst Sort: Laboring Women in Lawrence, Massachusetts, 1880–1912* (Urbana: University of Illinois Press, 1993); Jacquelyn Hall et al., eds., *Like a Family: The Making of a Southern Cotton Mill World* (Chapel Hill: University of North Carolina Press, 1987); Joy Parr, *The Gender of Breadwinners: Women, Men, and Change in*

Two Industrial Towns, 1880–1950 (Toronto: University of Toronto Press, 1990); Carole Turbin, *Working Women of Collar City: Gender, Class, and Community in Troy, 1864–86* (Urbana: University of Illinois Press, 1996); and Winifred Wandersee, *Women's Work and Family Values, 1920–1940* (Cambridge, Mass.: Harvard University Press, 1981).

3. See, for example, Dorothy Sue Cobble, *Dishing It Out: Waitresses and Their Unions in the Twentieth Century* (Urbana: University of Illinois Press, 1991); Patricia Cooper, *Once a Cigar Maker: Men, Women, and Work Culture in American Cigar Factories, 1900–1919* (Urbana: University of Illinois Press, 1987); Nancy Gabin, *Feminism in the Labor Movement: Women and the United Auto Workers, 1935–1975* (Ithaca, N.Y.: Cornell University Press, 1990); Elizabeth Faue, *Community of Suffering and Struggle: Women, Men, and the Labor Movement in Minneapolis, 1915–1945* (Chapel Hill: University of North Carolina Press, 1991); Dolores Janiewski, *Sisterhood Denied: Race, Gender, and Class in a New South Community* (Philadelphia: Temple University Press, 1985); Ruth Milkman, *Gender at Work: The Dynamics of Job Segregation by Sex during World War II* (Urbana: University of Illinois Press, 1987); and Victoria Ruiz, *Cannery Workers, Cannery Lives: Mexican Women, Unionization, and the California Food Processing Industry, 1930–1950* (Albuquerque: University of New Mexico Press, 1987).

4. My favorite examples include Annelise Orleck, *Common Sense and a Little Fire: Women and Working-Class Politics in the United States, 1900–1965* (Chapel Hill: University of North Carolina Press, 1995); Alice H. Cook, *Lifetime of Labor: The Autobiography of Alice H. Cook* (New York: The Feminist Press, 1998); Elizabeth Faue, *Writing the Wrongs: Eva Valesh and the Rise of Labor Journalism* (Ithaca, N.Y.: Cornell University Press, 2002); Elliott J. Gorn, *Mother Jones: The Most Dangerous Woman in America* (New York: Hill and Wang, 2001); and Yevette Richards, *Maida Springer: Pan Africanist and International Leader* (Pittsburgh: Pittsburgh University Press, 2000). See also Dorothy Sue Cobble, *The Other Women's Movement* (Princeton, N.J.: Princeton University Press, 2004), on the generation of labor feminists.

5. Ava Baron, "Gender and Labor History: Learning from the Past, Looking to the Future," in *Work Engendered: Toward a New History of American Labor,* ed. Ava Baron (Ithaca, N.Y.: Cornell University Press, 1991), 1–46.

6. Edward Hallett Carr, *What Is History?* (New York: Knopf, 1962), 26.

7. Ibid., 44.

8. Ibid., 164.

9. I did this, for example, with Emma Goldman's June 1894 speech to a crowd of Jewish immigrants in which, in Yiddish, she urged them to take bread if their demands for it were refused.

10. See, for example, Herbert G. Gutman, "The Missing Synthesis: Whatever Happened to History?" *The Nation,* November 21, 1981, 521, 553–54.

11. Gayle Rubin, "The Traffic in Women," in *Towards an Anthropology of Women,* ed. Rayna Reiter (New York: Monthly Review Press, 1975), 157–210.

12. Joan Kelly-Gadol, "The Social Relation of the Sexes: Methodological Implications of Women's History," *Signs* 1 (Summer 1976): 809–23; Joan Scott, "Gender: A Useful Category of Historical Analysis," *American Historical Review* 91 (December 1986): 1053–75.

13. This work drew on Mary Ann Clawson, *Constructing Brotherhood: Class, Gender, and Fraternalism* (Princeton, N.J.: Princeton University Press, 1989); Ava Baron, "An 'Other' Side of Gender Antagonism at Work: Men, Boys, and the Remasculinization of Printers' Work, 1830–1920," in *Work Engendered: Toward a New History of American Labor,* ed. Ava Baron (Ithaca, N.Y.: Cornell University Press, 1991), 47–69. More recent work on this subject includes Steven Meyer, "Workplace Predators: Sexuality and Harassment on the U.S. Automotive Shop Floor, 1930–1960," *Labor: Studies in Working-Class History of the Americas* 1 (Spring 2004): 77–94; and Roger Horowitz, ed., *Boys and Their Toys: Masculinity, Technology, and Class in America* (New York: Routledge, 2001).

14. Ulla Wikander, Alice Kessler-Harris, and Jane Lewis, eds., *Protecting Women: Labor Legislation in Europe, the United States, and Australia, 1880–1920* (Urbana: University of Illinois Press, 1995).

15. For an early example of such questions, see particularly Sarah Eisenstein, *Give Us Bread but Give Us Roses: Working Women's Consciousness in the United States, 1890 to the First World War* (New York: Routledge and Kegan Paul, 1983). I also found useful Charles Sabel, *Work and Politics: The Division of Labor in Industry* (New York: Cambridge University Press, 1982); Frank Parkin, *Class Inequality and Political Order: Social Stratification in Capitalist and Communist Societies* (New York: Praeger, 1971); and Kathleen Canning, *Languages of Labor and Gender: Female Factory Work in Germany, 1850–1914* (Ithaca, N.Y.: Cornell University Press, 1996). My thoughts on these matters appear in *In Pursuit of Equity: Women, Men, and the Quest for Economic Citizenship in Twentieth-Century America* (New York: Oxford University Press, 2001).

16. Andrew Heinze, *Adapting to Abundance: Jewish Immigrants, Mass Consumption, and the Search for American Identity* (New York: Columbia University Press, 1990); Lizabeth Cohen, *A Consumers' Republic: The Politics of Mass Consumption in Postwar America* (New York: Knopf, 2003); Dana Frank, *Purchasing Power: Consumer Organizing, Gender, and the Seattle Labor Movement, 1919–1929* (New York: Cambridge University Press, 1994); Meg Jacobs, *Pocketbook Politics: Economic Citizenship in Twentieth-Century America* (Princeton, N.J.: Princeton University Press, 2005).

17. That the organization of the workforce is related to gender-determined household needs has been one of the truisms of popular opinion. The most deeply felt requirement of a nineteenth-century male worker, for example, was for a wife and children who lived in a home he could govern; the patriarchal family relied on women to accumulate capital; and neither miners nor farmers could function without a "wife." See particularly Leonore Davidoff, *Worlds Between: Historical Perspectives on Gender and Class* (London: Polity Press, 1995); and Leonore Davidoff and Catherine Hall, *Family Fortunes: Men and Women of the English Middle Class* (New York: Routledge, 2001). See also the voluminous recent literature on "caring" work and how it is to be managed in the face of the twenty-first-century transformation of women's roles: for example, Nancy Folbre, *The Invisible Heart: Economics and Family Values* (New York: New Press, 1989).

18. Hobsbawm's declaration was made at the conference on "The Future of American Labor History: Towards a Synthesis," Northern Illinois University, DeKalb, October 1984.

19. Richard Oestreicher, "Separate Tribes? Working-Class and Women's History," *Reviews in American History* 19 (1991): 228.

20. Jefferson R. Cowie, *Capital Moves: RCA's Seventy-Year Quest for Cheap Labor* (Ithaca, N.Y.: Cornell University Press, 1999); Barbara Ehrenreich and Arlie Russell Hochschild, eds., *Global Woman: Nannies, Maids, and Sex Workers in the New Economy* (New York: Metropolitan Books, 2003).

21. David Roediger, *The Wages of Whiteness: Race and the Making of the American Working Class* (London: Verso, 1991); "Scholarly Controversy: Whiteness and the Historical Imagination," *International Labor and Working Class History* 60 (Fall 2001): 1–81.

22. R. W. Connell, *The Men and the Boys,* (Berkeley: University of California Press, 2000), 46.

23. Alice Kessler-Harris, "Gender and Work: Possibilities for a Global Historical Overview," in *Women's History in Global Perspective,* ed. Bonnie Smith, (Urbana: University of Illinois Press, 2004), 145–94. Literature in anthropology is helpful here. See especially June Nash and Patricia Fernandez-Kelly, *Women, Men, and the International Division of Labor* (Albany: State University of New York Press, 1983); and Eleanor Leacock and Helen Safa, eds., *Women's Work: Development and the Division of Labor by Gender* (South Hadley, Mass.: Bergin and Garvey, 1986).

24. For an entry point to these issues, see Geoffrey Eley and Keith Nield, "Farewell to the Working Class?" *International Labor and Working-Class History* 57 (Spring 2000): 1–30.

25. Luise White, *The Comforts of Home: Prostitution in Colonial Nairobi* (Chicago: University of Chicago Press, 1990). See also Ann Laura Stoler, *Carnal Knowledge and Imperial Power: Race and the Intimate in Colonial Rule* (Berkeley: University of California Press, 2002).

26. Mrinalini Sinha, *Colonial Masculinity: The "Manly Englishman" and the "Effeminate Bengali" in the Late Nineteenth Century* (Manchester: University of Manchester Press, 1995); Sueann Caulfield, *In Defense of Honor: Sexual Morality, Modernity, and Nation in Early Twentieth-Century Brazil* (Durham, N.C.: Duke University Press, 2000).

27. Maria Patricia Fernandez-Kelly, *For We Are Sold: I and My People* (Albany: State University of New York Press, 1983). The relationship of family values to the worldwide organization of the labor force is the subject of many fascinating studies. See especially Lourdes Beneria and Shelly Feldman, eds., *The Crossroads of Class and Gender: Industrial Homework, Subcontracting, and Household Dynamics in Mexico City* (Chicago: University of Chicago Press, 1987); Leela Fernandes, *Producing Workers: The Politics of Gender, Class, and Culture in the Calcutta Jute Mills* (Philadelphia: University of Pennsylvania Press, 1997); and Diane Lauren Wolf, *Factory Daughters: Gender, Household Dynamics, and Rural Industrialization in Java* (Berkeley: University of California Press, 1992).

28. As the economic historian David Landes noted in *The Wealth and Poverty of Nations: Why Some Are So Rich and Some Are So Poor* (New York: W. W. Norton, 1999), "[T]he best clue to a nation's economic growth and development potential is the status and role of women" (413). More generally, see the still relevant Ester Boserup, *Women's Role in Economic Development* (New York: St. Martin's Press, 1970); and Kate Young,

Carol Wolkowitz, and Roslyn McCullough, eds., *Of Marriage and the Market: Women's Subordination Internationally and Its Lessons* (London: Routledge, 1981).

Chapter 1: "Where Are the Organized Women Workers?"

1. Fannia Cohn to William Green, March 6, 1925, Fannia Cohn Collection, box 4, New York Public Library.

2. Figures are derived from John Andrews and W. D. P. Bliss, *History of Women in Trade Unions*, vol. 10 of the Report on the Condition of Women and Child Wage Earners in the United States, Senate Doc. 645, 61st Cong., 2d Sess. (Washington, D.C.: Government Printing Office, 1911), 136–39; Leo Wolman, *Ebb and Flow in Trade Unionism* (New York: National Bureau of Economic Research, 1936), 74, 116; Leo Wolman, *The Growth of American Trade Unions, 1880–1923* (New York: National Bureau of Economic Research, 1923), chap. 5. *The Growth of American Trade Unions* estimates that about 40 percent of organized women were in the three garment-industry unions: the ILGWU, Amalgamated Clothing Workers, and United Garment Workers, unions that were either literally or virtually nonexistent before 1910. See also Alice Henry, *Women and the Labor Movement* (New York: George Doran, 1923), chap. 4, for discussions of the difficulty of collecting trade-union figures. Henry illustrates the numbers of women in specific unions.

3. The proportion of foreign-born and native-born daughters of foreign-born women declined slightly in this period, and women continued to shift from manual sectors to low-level clerical sectors of the workforce. See U.S. Census, *14th Census of Populations*, vol. 3 (Washington, D.C.: Government Printing Office, 1920), 15. Such occupations as taking in boarders, homework, and working on a husband's farm or in a family business are not counted by census takers. Including these legitimate forms of labor would create drastic upward revisions in the proportion of working women, but we have no way of knowing by how much. The figures include black women, more than 40 percent of whom worked for wages, compared to about 20 percent of white women. However, about 32 percent of married black women worked, compared to less than 6 percent of married white women. Black wage-earning women are far more heavily concentrated in agricultural and domestic-service jobs than their white counterparts. Figures are from Joseph Hill, "Women in Gainful Occupations: 1870–1920," *Census Monographs*, no. 9 (Washington, D.C.: Government Printing Office, 1929), chaps. 5 and 9; Janet Hooks, "Women's Occupations through Seven Decades," *Women's Bureau Bulletin*, no. 218 (Washington, D.C.: Government Printing Office, 1947), 37, 39.

4. Andrews and Bliss, *History of Women in Trade Unions*, 138–39. Even before the great uprising of 1909–10, women, who made up 63 percent of the workers in the garment trades, represented 70 percent of the trade-union members. This is all the more remarkable because their skill levels did not, by and large, match those of men. Women comprised 32.5 percent of hat- and capmakers and 54 percent of the trade-union membership. Women made up 50 percent of bookbinders and 40 percent of the trade-union members in that industry.

5. Ann Blankenhorn, miscellaneous notes, p. 12, box 1, file 23, Ann Craton Blankenhorn Collection, Wayne State Archives in Labor History and Urban Affairs, Detroit.

For another example, see interview with Netti Chandler, Virginia Home Visits, Bulletin no. 10, Accession no. 51A101, Women's Bureau Collection, Record Group no. 86, National Archives, Washington, D.C. (hereafter WB/NA).

6. Faigele Shapiro, interview in Amerikaner Yiddishe Geshichte Bel-pe, August 6, 1964, pp. 2, 7, YIVO Archives, New York.

7. *American Federationist* 6 (November 1899): 228.

8. Quoted in Andrews and Bliss, *History of Women in Trade Unions*, 173.

9. New York Women's Trade Union League (WTUL), "Report of the Proceedings," *4th Annual Conference of Trade Union Women*, October 9–10, 1926, 18.

10. Vera Shlakman, "Economic History of a Factory Town: A Study of Chicopee, Massachusetts," *Smith College Studies in History* 20.1–4 (October 1934–July 1935), 216; Andrews and Bliss, *History of Women in Trade Unions*, 166.

11. Andrews and Bliss, *History of Women in Trade Unions*, 168; Massachusetts Women's Trade Union League, *History of Trade Unionism among Women in Boston* (Boston: WTUL, n.d. [ca. 1907]), 22–23.

12. Theresa Wolfson, "Where Are the Organized Women Workers?" *American Federationist* 32 (June 1925): 455–57.

13. Andrews and Bliss, *History of Women in Trade Unions*, 151.

14. *American Federationist* 17 (November 1911): 896; James Kenneally, "Women and Trade Unions," *Labor History* 14 (Winter 1973): 42–55. Kenneally describes but does not explain the AFL's mixed feelings.

15. Eva McDonald Valesh, "Women and Labor," *American Federationist* 3 (February 1896): 222.

16. Selig Perlman, *A History of Trade Unionism in the United States* (New York: Macmillan, 1923), 166. For illustrations of AFL policies, see James Weinstein, *The Corporate Ideal in the Liberal State, 1900–1911* (Boston: Beacon Press, 1968), esp. chaps. 1 and 2; Ronald Radosh, *American Labor and United States Foreign Policy* (New York: Vintage, 1970); and Stanley Aronowitz, *False Promises: The Shaping of American Working-Class Consciousness* (New York: McGraw-Hill, 1973).

17. Samuel Gompers, "Should the Wife Help Support the Family?" *American Federationist* 13 (January 1906): 36. See also Stuart Reid, "The Joy of Labor? Plutocracy's Hypocritical Sermonizing Exposed—A Satire," *American Federationist* 11 (November 1904): 977–78.

18. "Mainly Progressive," *American Federationist* 3 (March 1896): 16; "What Our Organizers are Doing," *American Federationist* 10 (April 1903): 370.

19. Editorial, *American Federationist* 11 (July 1904): 584.

20. "Trade Union History," *American Federationist* 9 (November 1902): 871.

21. John Safford, "The Good That Trade Unions Do," pt. 1, *American Federationist* 9 (July 1902): 353, 358; "Talks on Labor," *American Federationist* 12 (November 1905): 846

22. William Gilthorpe, "Advancement," *American Federationist* 17 (October 1910): 847.

23. Safford, "Good That Trade Unions Do," 423.

24. Edward O'Donnell, "Women as Breadwinners; The Error of the Age," *American*

Federationist 5 (October 1897): 186. The article continued: "The wholesale employment of women in the various handicrafts must gradually unsex them as it most assuredly is demoralizing them, or stripping them of that modest demeanor that lends a charm to their kind, while it numerically strengthens the multitudinous army of loafers, paupers, tramps, and policemen."

25. Safford, "Good That Trade Unions Do," 357–58.

26. Gompers, "Should the Wife Help Support the Family?" 36.

27. Ibid. See also Louis Vigoreux, "Social Results of the Labor Movement in America," *American Federationist* 6 (April 1899): 25.

28. "Women's Labor Resolution," *American Federationist* 5 (January 1899): 220; "Talks on Labor," *American Federationist* 10 (June 1903): 477.

29. Massachusetts WTUL, *History of Trade Unionism among Women in Boston,* 13; Elizabeth Baker, *Technology and Women's Work* (New York: Columbia University Press, 1964), 33.

30. Mildred Rankin to Mrs. Raymond Robins, March 30, 1919, Margaret Dreier Robins Collection, University of Florida, Gainesville. In 1918, two women members of the federation offered a resolution to the national convention urging the addition of two women to the all-male Executive Board. It was quietly suppressed.

31. Gompers, "Should the Wife Help Support the Family?" 36.

32. Alice Woodbridge, "Women's Labor," *American Federationist* 1 (April 1894): 66–67; Valesh, "Women and Labor," 222; and Massachusetts WTUL, *History of Trade Unionism among Women in Boston,* 32.

33. WTUL Action of Policies, Proceedings of the 1923 AFL Convention, pp. 3, 8, box 4, Accession no. 55A556, WB/NA; See also Massachusetts WTUL, *History of Trade Unionism among Women in Boston,* 32.

34. Ann Blankenhorn, manuscript notes, chap. 4, p. 17, box 1, file 24, Ann Craton Blankenhorn Collection, Wayne State University Archives in Labor History and Urban Affairs, Detroit. Such examples of family unity are not unusual in the mine and mill towns of western Pennsylvania and the Appalachian Mountains. Women helped to picket during strikes, provided essential support services, and sometimes spearheaded attacks against mine management.

35. Pauline Newman, interview in Amerikaner Yiddisher Geshichte Bel-pe, n.d., p. 21, YIVO Archives, New York. Gladys Boone, *The Women's Trade Union League in Great Britain and the USA* (New York: Columbia University Press, 1942), recounts a similar incident as having taken place in 1918 (166). I suspect that it might be the same one and that her date is incorrect. Andrews and Bliss, *History of Women in Trade Unions,* notes that women practically disappeared from this union between 1905 and 1910—a period in which master bakers were rapidly being eliminated by machinery (149).

36. Mildred Rankin to Mrs. Raymond Robins, March 30, 1919, Margaret Dreier Robins Collection, University of Florida, Gainesville.

37. Boone, *Women's Trade Union League,* 167; Henry, *Women and the Labor Movement,* 102.

38. Interview with Vail Ballou Press, "Effects of Legislation: Night Work Schedule," New York, WB/NA.

39. See, for example, Mildred Rankin to Mrs. Raymond Robins, March 30, 1919, Margaret Dreier Robins Collection, University of Florida, Gainesville; and M. E. Jackson, "The Colored Woman in Industry," *Crisis* 17 (November 1918): 14.

40. New York WTUL, "Report of the Proceedings," 14.

41. Undated interviews, unions, for Bulletin no. 65, WB/NA.

42. Hilda Svenson testimony, CIR, p. 2307; the testimony was taken in June 1914.

43. Florence Sanville to Rose Schneiderman, November 28, 1917, box A 94, Rose Schneiderman Collection, Tamiment Institute Library, New York University. For examples of union discrimination, see Massachusetts WTUL, *History of Trade Unionism among Women in Boston,* 13; Andrews and Bliss, *History of Women in Trade Unions,* 156–57; and Alice Henry, *The Trade Union Woman* (New York: Burl Franklin, 1973), 150.

44. Testimonies, box 15, Accession no. 51A101, WB/NA. The women had been hired when the war broke out.

45. Emma Steghagen to Mary Anderson, January 15, 1919, WTUL Action on Policies, Accession no. 55A556, WB/NA.

46. United States Education and Labor Committee, *Report upon the Relations Between Capital and Labor,* vol. 1 (Washington, D.C.: Government Printing Office, 1882), 453. See Andrews and Bliss, *History of Women in Trade Unions,* for Strasser's often-quoted, "We cannot drive the females out of the trade but we can restrict their daily quota of labor through factory laws" (94) and for Samuel Gompers's fears of female competition as expressed in 1887 (155).

47. Interview with Mr. Salerno, Amalgamated Clothing Workers, Accession no. 51A101, WB/NA.

48. Interview with Mr. Hurley, July 1919, Women Street Car Conductors, Accession no. 51A101, WB/NA.

49. Sir Lyon Playfair, "Children and Female Labor," *AF* 7 (April 1900): 103. See also Martha Moore Avery, "Boston Kitchen Help Organize," *AF* 10 (April 1903): 259–60.

50. Ira Howerth, "The Kingdom of God in Modern Industry," *AF* 14 (August 1907): 544.

51. Mary Anderson, "The Federal Government Recognizes Problems of Women in Industry," *AF* 32 (June 1925): 453.

52. Individual interviews, Massachusetts, April 12, 1920, Accession no. SA101, WB/NA. Her preference rested on the union's ability to ask for wage raises to compensate for the reduction in hours.

53. Individual interviews, Massachusetts and New Jersey, Accession no. 51A101, WB/NA. See especially interviews with A. J. Muste, Mr. Sims, secretary of the weavers union, and Amalgamated meeting of workers at Princeton Worsted Mills. These are undated but must have occurred in early 1921.

54. Fannia Cohn to Dr. Marion Phillips, September 13, 1927, box 4, Fannia Cohn Collection, New York Public Library.

55. Interviews with Tony Salerno, Amalgamated Clothing Workers Union and Hat and Cap Makers Local 7, Boston, Accession no. 51A101, WB/NA; Massachusetts WTUL, *History of Trade Unionism among Women in Boston,* 11.

56. Lizzie Swank Holmes, "Women Workers of Chicago," *AF* 12 (August 1905):

507–10; Eva McDonald Valesh, "Women in Welfare Work," *AF* 15 (April 1908): 282–84; "Mainly Progressive," *AF* 3 (March 1896): 16.

57. Faigele Shapiro, interview in Amerikaner Yiddishe Geshichte Bel-pe, August 6, 1964, p. 25, YIVO Archives, New York.

58. *Justice* (April 1919): 2.

59. Ann Blankenhorn, manuscript notes, chap. 13, p. 4, box 1, file 25, Ann Craton Blankenhorn Collection, Wayne State University Archives in Labor History and Urban Affairs, Detroit.

60. For example, see Mary Dreier's address to the New York WTUL in New York WTUL, "Report of the Proceedings," 14. Dreier referred in this speech to the WTUL's initial difficulty getting female workers to serve on the executive board. See Nancy Schrom Dye, "Creating a Feminist Alliance: Sisterhood and Class Conflict in the New York WTUL, 1903–1914," *Feminist Studies* 2 (1975): 24–38. Kenneally, "Women and Trade Unions," treats the WTUL's relations with the AFL at length.

61. Individual interviews, California, effects of legislation, Accession no. 51A101, WB/NA.

62. Quoted in a letter from Mary Van Kleek to Mary Anderson, February 2, 1923, Mary Van Kleek Collection, unsorted, Smith College, Northampton, Mass.

63. Breman and O'Brien, individual interviews, Massachusetts, accession no. 51A101, WB/NA. Such sentiments must, however, be treated cautiously. We know, for example, that the National Consumers' League in Philadelphia orchestrated an anti-ERA letter-writing campaign by wage-earning women in 1922. The league urged women to write letters arguing that the ERA would limit or eliminate protective labor legislation. See Barbara Klazcynska, "Working Women in Philadelphia, 1900–1930" (Ph.D. diss., Temple University, 1975). Janice Hedges and Stephen Bemis point out that most "protective" legislation has now been invalidated by EEOC decisions ("Sex Stereotyping: Its Decline in Skilled Trades," *Monthly Labor Review* 97 [May 1974]: 18).

64. Rose Schneiderman with Lucy Goldthwaite, *All for One* (New York: Paul Erickson, 1967), 59; Faigele Shapiro, interview in Amerikaner Yiddishe Geshichte Bel-pe, August 6, 1964, p. 9, YIVO Archives, New York.

65. Elizabeth Maloney testimony, Final Report and Testimony of the Commission on Industrial Relations, Senate Documents, vol. 21, 64th Cong., 1st Sess., vol. 3, 1914 (hereafter CIR), pp. 3246–47. See also M. E. Jackson, "Colored Woman in Industry," 12–17.

66. Agnes Nestor testimony, CIR, p. 3389; Elizabeth Dutcher testimony, CIR, p. 2405.

67. Elizabeth Maloney testimony, CIR, p. 3245.

68. Leon Stein, *The Triangle Fire* (Philadelphia: J. B. Lippincott, 1952); Agnes Nestor testimony, CIR, p. 3382.

69. Ann Blankenhorn, manuscript notes, chap. 4, p. 17, box 1, file 24, Ann Craton Blankenhorn Collection, Wayne State University Archives in Labor History and Urban Affairs, Detroit.

70. Agnes Nestor testimony, CIR, p. 3382; Hilda Svenson's testimony (CIR pp. 3382 and 2308) reveals the degree to which this was an attempt to undercut union strength. See also an unsigned typescript, "Personnel and Management in a Retail Store: A Study

of the Personnel Policies and Practices of William Filene's Sons Co., Boston, Mass.," p. 14, in the Mary Van Kleeck Collection, unsorted, Smith College, Northampton, Mass.; and Marie Obenauer and Charles Verrill, *Wage-Earning Women in Stores and Factories*, vol. 5 of the Report on the Condition of Women and Child Wage Earners, Senate Doc. 645, 61st Cong., 2d Sess. (Washington, D.C.: Government Printing Office, 1911), 48; Hilda Svenson testimony, CIR, p. 2309.

71. See Cambridge Paper Box Company, Long Hour Day Schedule, accession no. 51A101, WB/NA.

72. U.S. Department of Labor, Bureau of Labor Statistics, Bulletin no. 145, 1914, 37.

73. *The Cotton Textile Industry*, vol. 1 of the Report on the Condition of Women and Child Wage Earners, Senate Doc. 645, 61st Cong., 2d Sess. (Washington, D.C.: Government Printing Office, 1910), 608.

74. Mary Anderson, "Industrial Standards for Women," *American Federationist* 32 (July 1925): 21.

75. See Massachusetts WTUL, *History of Trade Unionism among Women in Boston*, 7, 32; New York WTUL, "Report of the Proceedings," 21.

76. Henry, *Women and the Labor Movement*, 108.

77. Typescript of "Complete Equality between Men and Women," published in the December 1917 issue of the *Ladies Garment Worker*, Fannia Cohn Collection, box 7, New York Public Library.

Chapter 2: Organizing the Unorganizable

1. In 1913, 56 percent of the workers in the industry were Jews, and 34 percent were Italian; 70 percent or more were women. See Hyman Berman, "Era of the Protocol: A Chapter in the History of the International Ladies Garment Workers Union, 1910–1916" (Ph.D. diss., Columbia University, 1956), 22, 24. Jewish women were much more likely to be working inside a garment shop than were Italian women, who often preferred to take work home. 53.6 percent of all employed Jewish women were in the garment industry in 1900. Nathan Goldberg, *Occupational Patterns of American Jewry* (New York: Jewish Theological Seminary University Press, 1947), 21. The relative proportion of women in the garment industry declined between 1900 and 1930. In addition to dresses and waists, women were heavily employed on kimonos, housedresses, underwear, children's clothing, and neckwear. For a good description of conditions in the garment industry, see Melvyn Dubofsky, *When Workers Organize: New York City in the Progressive Era* (Amherst: University of Massachusetts Press, 1968), 72–75.

2. The industry was characterized by the rapid turnover of its employees. In 1910, about 50 percent of the dress and waist makers were under twenty years old. The best estimate is that less than 10 percent of the women working on dresses and waists were married. See U.S. Senate, *Abstracts of the Report of the Immigration Commission*, 61st Cong., 2d Sess., 1911, S. Doc. 747, vol. 2, 336. See also, Berman, "Era of the Protocol," 23.

3. The proportion of women in the Jewish immigration between 1899 and 1910 was higher than in any other immigrant group except the Irish. See Samuel Joseph, *Jewish Immigration to the United States, 1881–1910* (New York: Columbia University Press, 1914), 179. This can be accounted for in part by the high proportion of family emigra-

tion and in part by the numbers of young women who came to America without their parents to work. Rose Pesotta, Rose Cohn, and Emma Goldman fall into this category.

4. Unpublished autobiography no. 92, YIVO Institute, New York (see also no. 160, p. 8); Etta Byer, *Transplanted People* (Chicago: M. J. Aron and the Lider Organization of Chicago, 1955), 28.

5. Flora Weiss, interview in Amerikaner Yiddishe Geshichte Bel-Pe, June 15, 1964, p. 4, YIVO Archives, New York. See also Anzia Yezierska, *Bread Givers* (Garden City, N.Y.: Doubleday, 1932), 28.

6. Rose Pesotta, *Bread upon the Waters* (New York: Dodd, Mead, and Co., 1944), 4. The novels of Anzia Yezierska, who arrived in America from Russian Poland in 1901, beautifully express these aspirations. See *Bread Givers; Arrogant Beggar* (New York: Grosset and Dunlap, 1927); and her semifictional autobiography, *Red Ribbon on a White Horse* (New York: Charles Scribner's Sons, 1950).

7. Ruth Rubin, *A Treasury of Jewish Folksong* (New York: Schocken, 1950), 43, 97.

8. See, for example, Rose Schneiderman quoted in Zoe Beckley, "Finds Hard Job Unionizing Girls Whose Aim Is to Wed," *New York Telegram,* June 18, 1924; Julia Stuart Poyntz, "Marriage and Motherhood," *Justice,* March 18, 1919, 5; Matilda Robbins, "My Story," unpublished manuscript, p. 38, Matilda Robbins Collection, Wayne State University Archives in Labor History and Urban Affairs, Detroit. Mechanics of organizing women are illustrated in chap. 1 of this volume.

9. Although the same tensions existed for women of other cultural backgrounds, one does not always get the impression that non-Jewish women were quite so torn. Mary Kenney, for example, continued to be active after she married John O'Sullivan. The most prominent Jewish women who remained active after marriage married outside their ethnic group. Anna Strunsky Walling and Rose Pastor Stokes are two examples. In some ways, Emma Goldman's life acted out the protest many women must have felt but expressed in more limited ways. See Blanche Wiesen Cook, "Emma Goldman and Crystal Eastman," Paper presented at the annual meeting of the Organization of American Historians, New Orleans, April 1973.

10. Rose Schneiderman with Lucy Goldthwaite, *All for One* (New York: Paul Erikson, 1967), 50.

11. Interview with Pearl Halpern, n.d., p. 8, in Irving Howe Collection, YIVO Archives, New York.

12. U.S. Senate, *Abstracts of the Report of the Immigration Commission,* vol. 11, 517. In 1910, 23.9 percent of Jewish men belonged to trade unions, as opposed to 14 percent of Italian men.

13. See, for example, unpublished autobiography no. 160, pp. 8 and 12, YIVO Archives, New York.

14. Rubin, *Treasury of Jewish Folksong,* 23.

15. Ibid., 97. These songs, with their hope of escape, should be compared with the hopeless and agonized verse of Morris Rosenfeld. See Rosenfeld, *The Teardrop Millionaire and Other Poems* (New York: Manhattan Emma Lazarus Clubs of the Emma Lazarus Federation of Jewish Women's Clubs, 1955), 14, 19.

16. "Manhattan's Young Factory Girls," *New York World,* March 2, 1913.

17. Lillian Mallach to David Dubinsky, December 18, 1964, Glicksberg Papers, YIVO Archives, New York.

18. Flora Weiss, interview in Amerikaner Yiddishe Geshichte Bel-Pe, June 15, 1964, p. 11, YIVO Archives, New York. The same woman recorded the influence the legend of Mother Jones had had on her (20).

19. Schneiderman, *All for One*, 49. Officially, ILGWU policy was to organize whoever was in the shop, regardless of sex. It was easier in practice to discriminate against women, since they were often employed in sex-segregated jobs.

20. Pauline Newman, interview in Amerikaner Yiddishe Geshichte Bel-Pe, June 26, 1965, p. 19, YIVO Archives, New York.

21. Schneiderman, *All for One*, 61.

22. Isaac Hourwich, *Immigration and Labor: The Economic Aspects of European Immigration to the United States* (New York: G. P. Putnam, 1922), 373. These figures are for the period from 1880–1905.

23. *Life and Labor* 1 (February 1911): 52.

24. "Manhattan's Young Factory Girls," *New York World,* March 2, 1913.

25. Flora Weiss, interview in Amerikaner Yiddishe Geshichte Bel-Pe, June 15, 1964, p. 28, YIVO Archives, New York.

26. Faigele Shapiro, interview in Amerikaner Yiddishe Geshichte Bel-Pe, August 6, 1964, p. 9, YIVO Archives, New York.

27. Constant D. Leupp, "Shirtwaist Makers Strike," in *Selected Articles on the Employment of Women,* ed. Edna Bullock (Minneapolis: H. W. Wilson, 1919), 126.

28. Louis Lorwin, *The Women's Garment Workers: A History of the International Ladies Garment Workers Union* (New York: B. W. Heubsch, 1924), 156.

29. Julia Stuart Poyntz, "What Do You Do with Leisure," *Justice,* February 22, 1919, 13.

30. Unpublished Autobiography no. 160, p. 13, YIVO Archives, New York.

31. Pauline Newman (hereafter P. N.) to Rose Schneiderman (hereafter R. S.), September 20, 1910, box A94, Rose Schneiderman Collection, Tamiment Institute Library, New York University (hereafter RSC).

32. Rose Pesotta (hereafter R. P.) to David Dubinsky, February 6, 1935, Rose Pesotta Collection, General Correspondence, New York Public Library (hereafter RPC).

33. Jennie Matyas to R. P., February 25, 1935, RPC.

34. For one encomium, see Flora Weiss, interview in Amerikaner Yiddishe Geshichte Bel-Pe, June 15, 1964, p. 32, YIVO Archives, New York. For the WTUL side of the story, see Nancy Schrom Dye, "Creating a Feminist Alliance: Sisterhood and Class Conflict in the New York Women's Trade Union League, 1903–1914," Paper presented at the Conference on Class and Ethnicity in Women's History, State University of New York at Binghamton, September 22, 1974; and Robin Miller Jacoby, "The Women's Trade Union League and American Feminism," *Feminist Studies* 3 (Fall 1975): 126–40.

35. "Joe" to R. S., November 8, 1911, box A94, RSC.

36. P. N. to R. S., April 17, 1911, box A94, RSC.

37. P. N. to R. S., February 9, 1912, box A94, RSC.

38. P. N. to R. S., April 17, 1911, and P. N. to R. S., August 9, 1911, box A94, RSC.

39. P. N. to R. S., November 14, 1911, box A94, RSC. Three months later the ILG fired

the new organizers, and Pauline crowed, "I tell you, Rose, it feels fine when you can say to a secretary of an International to 'go to hell with your job together' and after have the same man beg you to work for them again!" P. N. to R. S., February 22, 1912, box A94, RSC.

40. P. N. to R. S., January 17, 1912, box A94, RSC.

41. P. N. to R. S., February 9, 1912, box A94, RSC.

42. P. N., interview in Amerikaner Yiddishe Geshichte Bel-Pe, June 26, 1965, pp. 21–22, YIVO Archives, New York. See also P. N. to R. S., May 17, 1911, box A94, RSC, where Newman expresses sadness at not being able to attend a conference to discuss the "woman problem." "You must tell me about it in your next letter."

43. P. N. to R. S., April 11, 1910, box A94, RSC.

44. P. N., interview in Amerikaner Yiddishe Geshichte Bel-Pe, June 26, 1965, p. 2, YIVO Archives, New York.

45. P. N. to R. S., March 5, 1912, box A94, RSC.

46. P. N. to R. S., November 7, 1911, box A94, RSC. Newman had already had a similar experience with the Ladies Garment Worker (Justice's predecessor), which mutilated an article on the WTUL she had written for them.

47. P. N. to R. S., October 29, 1911, and November 7, 1911, box A94, RSC.

48. P. N. to R. S., July 11, 1912, box A94, RSC.

49. P. N. to R. S., October 19, 1910, and April 11, 1910, box A94, RSC.

50. P. N. to R. S., October 29, 1911, and November 7, 1911, box A94, RSC.

51. Faigele Shapiro, interview in Amerikaner Yiddishe Geshichte Bel-Pe, August 6, 1964, p. 17, YIVO Archive, New York.

52. "On Lightheaded Women," Justice, March 8, 1919, 4.

53. Juliet Poyntz, "The Unity Corner," Justice, March 29, 1919, 3.

54. "The Problem of Life for the Working Girl," Justice, February 1, 1919, 3.

55. "Women Who Work," Justice, March 15, 1919, 5.

56. B. Maiman, "Conference on Women in Industry," Justice, January 19, 1923, 4.

57. Fannia Cohn, "With the Strikers," Justice, February 22, 1919, 3.

58. Fannia Cohn (hereafter F. C.) to R. S., January 24, 1929, box 4, Fannia Cohn Papers, New York Public Library (hereafter FCP); see also E. Christman to F. C., October 2, 1915, box 1, FCP.

59. James Shotwell to F. C., December 31, 1926, box 1, FCP; F. C. to James Maurer, March 6, 1931, box 5, FCP.

60. F. C. to Helen Norton, February 9, 1932, box 5, FCP. The rest of the letter reads in part: "It hurts me also to know that while 'men' frequently come to each others' assistance in an emergency, 'women' frequently remain indifferent when one of their own sex is confronted with a similar emergency. Of course, a woman is expected to assist a man in his accomplishments, but she (the woman) is forced in her aspirations—in social and economic field—to struggle along. She is compelled to depend upon her own resources, whether this be material, moral, or intellectual."

61. F. C. to Dorothea Heinrich, February 3, 1937, box 5, FCP; F. C. to Mary Beard, January 23, 1940, box 5, FCP.

62. Theresa Wolfson to F. C., November 19, 1923, box 1, FCP.

63. F. C. to Helen Norton, February 9, 1932, box 5, FCP.

64. F. C. to Evelyn Preston, September 21, 1923, box 4, FCP.

65. F. C. to Wm. Green, March 6, 1925, box 4, FCP.

66. F. C. to R. S., October 5, 1926, box 4, FCP.

67. F. C. to Dr. Marion Phillips, September 13, 1927, box 4, FCP.

68. F. C. to Theresa Wolfson, May 15, 1922, box 4, FCP.

69. F. C. to Evelyn Preston, September 9, 1922, box 4, FCP; see also F. C. to Evelyn Preston, February 19, 1924, box 4, FCP.

70. F. C. to Theresa Wolfson, May 15, 1922, box 4, FCP.

71. Fannia Cohn, "A New Era Opens for Labor Education," *Justice*, October 1, 1933, 9. The article may be more hopeful than realistic. Cohn said, in part, "the women strikers, many of whom were married and their younger sisters, too, increasingly realized that no longer do they want a strong union as a temporary protection for themselves but as a permanent safeguard for their present and future families." There is no question, however, that the industry's workers were increasingly drawn from married women and older women.

72. R. P., diary, June 9, 1934, RPC. In her autobiography, *Bread upon the Waters*, Pesotta wrote that "the voice of a solitary woman on the General Executive Board would be a voice lost in the wilderness" (101).

73. R. P. to Rae Brandstein, April 9, 1934, RPC.

74. R. P. to David Dubinsky, April 26, 1934, RPC.

75. R. P. to David Dubinsky, March 3, 1934, RPC. Pesotta on this occasion stayed in a YMCA because it was "respectable."

76. R. P. to Jennie Matyas, April 16, 1935, RPC.

77. R. P. to Paul Berg, February 15, 1934, RPC.

78. R. P. to David Dubinsky, September 30, 1933, RPC. Pesotta's snippy attitude comes through in the rest of that letter: "Now, my dear President, you will have to come across with the help we need, namely: financial, moral, and the representative for a week or two. After we'll pull this through you will come to visit these whores and I am confident that you will see with your own eyes that enthusiasm is not such a bad thing after all."

79. Rose Schneiderman called the codes "the Magna Charta of the working woman" and characterized them as "the most thrilling thing that has happened in my lifetime." *New York Evening Journal*, October 24, 1933, 15 (clipping in box A97, RSC); R. P. to David Dubinsky, February 1, 1935, RPC.

80. R. P., diary, November 3, 1931, RPC.

81. R. P., diary, February 24, 1934, March 12, 1934, August 9, 1934, RPC.

82. R. P. to Powers Hapgood, February 21, 1937, RPC.

83. F. C. to Jess Ogden, June 25, 1935, FCP. A second play described how two working sisters nevertheless waited on their brother at home because they had to atone for earning less than he did.

84. Quoted in a clipping, "Says Chivalry Stops at Door of Workshop," unidentified newspaper, 1912, box A97, RSC.

Chapter 3: Problems of Coalition Building

1. Ruth Milkman, "Organizing the Sexual Division of Labor: Historical Perspectives on 'Women's Work' and the American Labor Movement," *Socialist Review* 10 (January–February 1980): 95–150.

2. I am moving away from the question of organizability, partly because I am convinced that how and why trade unions recruit women is a function of some of the other phenomena I will discuss, and partly because recent scholarship has provided a fairly clear sense of the social and industrial factors that inhibit and encourage women's organizing efforts. These include factors such as occupational segregation, the kinds of industries organized, the historically high turnover rates of women, and especially sex-role socialization, which often instills in women a sense of deference to men, involves them in time-consuming household commitments, and suggests an alternative set of roles to those offered by waged work. For access to this literature, see chapter 1 in this volume; Heidi Hartmann, "Capitalism, Patriarchy, and Job Segregation by Sex," in *Women and the Workplace: The Implications of Occupational Segregation,* ed. Martha Blaxall and Barbara Regan (Chicago: University of Chicago Press, 1976), 137–69; and Milkman, "Organizing the Sexual Division of Labor."

3. Helen Sumner, *History of Women in Industry in the United States* (1910; reprint, New York: Arno Press, 1974), is probably still the best summary of the nineteenth-century experience. See also Barbara Wertheimer, *We Were There: The Story of Working Women in America* (New York: Pantheon, 1977); and Philip Foner, *Women and the American Labor Movement: From Colonial Times to the Eve of World War I* (New York: Free Press, 1979).

4. It was not the total number of women who worked for wages that was at issue. The proportion of such women expanded only modestly during the decade. But the kinds of women who worked (native-born, married) caused concern, as did the seemingly more permanent nature of their jobs.

5. Leo Wolman, *Growth of American Trade Unions, 1880–1923* (New York: National Bureau of Economic Research, 1924), 97–98. By 1914, the number of organized women had dropped to 250,000, and the figure increased only slightly over the rest of the decade. Theresa Wolfson estimated that the number of organized women was only one-thirty-fourth of all women then earning wages. See Theresa Wolfson, "Trade Union Activities of Women," *Annals of the American Academy of Political and Social Science* 143 (May 1929): 120.

6. Incentives mentioned in the 1920s, but only rarely employed, included women organizers, discussion groups and social occasions, women's bureaus within unions, and vacation houses.

7. Wolman, *Growth of American Trade Unions,* 98–99, 107, estimates that one-quarter of all organized women in 1910 were in New York State.

8. See the account of the 1919 New England telephone operators' strike in Maurine Greenwald, *Women, War, and Work: The Impact of World War I on Women Workers in the United States* (Westport, Conn.: Greenwood Press, 1980), 218–22.

9. Anderson was thirty-eight years old and single when she wrote this. Mary Ander-

son with Mary N. Winslow, *Women at Work* (1951; reprint, Westport, Conn.: Greenwood Press, 1973), 46.

10. Victor Turner, *Dramas, Fields, and Metaphors: Symbolic Action in Human Society* (Ithaca, N.Y.: Cornell University Press, 1974), 45–47. For a sense of how this worked in practice, see Nancy Schrom Dye, *As Equals and as Sisters: Feminism, Unionism, and the Women's Trade Union League of New York* (Columbia: University of Missouri Press, 1980), chaps. 2 and 4.

11. Rose Schneiderman, for example, commented on high turnover rates among women: "'I wish they would realize that joining the union would bring untold benefits during the five years they are in trade, not to mention how it would help the girls who come after them.'" Quoted in Zoe Beckley, "Finds Hard Job Unionizing Girls Whose Aim Is to Wed," *New York Telegram,* June 18, 1924, 4.

12. Agnes Nestor, "The Experiences of a Pioneer Woman Trade Unionist," *American Federationist* 36 (August 1929): 926.

13. General Executive Board Minutes, May 1, 1913, p. 39, International Ladies' Garment Workers' Union Archives, Industrial Relations Archives, Cornell University, Ithaca, N.Y. (hereafter ILGWU Archives). See chap. 1 of this volume for additional examples.

14. Theresa Wolfson, *The Woman Worker and the Trade Unions* (New York: International Publishers, 1926), 81, 86–87.

15. "Yes, Women Are Discontented, but What of It?" *Advance,* May 6, 1927, 6.

16. Charles F. Sabel, *Work and Politics: The Division of Labor in Industry* (New York: Cambridge University Press, 1982), 80.

17. Herbert Gutman, *Work, Culture, and Society in Industrializing America: Essays in American Working-Class and Social History* (New York: Alfred A. Knopf, 1976), chap. 1.

18. See especially Nancy Chodorow, *The Reproduction of Mothering: Psychoanalysts and the Sociology of Gender* (Berkeley: University of California Press, 1979), chaps. 2 and 11. I explicitly disagree with formulations of women's work that measure self-experience in terms of ties to family or community of origin. The prime example is Louise Tilly and Joan Scott, *Women, Work, and Family* (New York: Holt, Rinehart, and Winston, 1978).

19. "A Union Leader: Fannia H. Cohn," in *Women in the American Economy: A Documentary History, 1675–1929,* ed. W. Elliot Brownlee and Mary M. Brownlee (New Haven, Conn.: Yale University Press, 1976), 223.

20. Anderson with Winslow, *Women at Work,* 66. The technique could be used by both sides. The organizer Sarah Shapiro reported to the general strike committee of Local 25 that she had almost won a lengthy strike of Italian girls, when "the bosses finally succeeded in getting them back by giving them an increase in wages, and in some cases shorting the hours, and giving them parties and dances in the shops." February 21, 1919, Benjamin Schlesinger Collection, box 3, file 16, ILGWU Archives.

21. Frank Parkin, *Marxism and Class Theory: A Bourgeois Critique* (New York: Columbia University Press, 1979), 44–46, 74.

22. *American Federationist* 36 (August 1929): 914.

23. Parkin, *Marxism and Class Theory,* 98.

24. Wolfson, *Woman Worker and the Trade Unions,* 73.

25. Ibid., 77–78. For more on the barbers, see chap. 8 of this volume.

26. This process was successfully used by professional organizations like the American Medical Association and the American Bar Association as well.

27. Baroff report in General Executive Board Minutes, September 26, 1921, p. 1523, ILGWU Archives.

28. Sigman in General Executive Board Minutes, October 17, 1923, p. 1825, ILGWU Archives. See also Halprin in General Executive Board Minutes, March 26, 1923, p. 1736, ILGWU Archives.

29. General Executive Board Minutes, April 24, 1917, p. 641, ILGWU Archives (see also comments of John Pierce on p. 655).

30. ILGWU, *Report of the General Executive Board to the 15th Biennial Convention of the International Ladies' Garment Workers' Union* (New York: ILGWU, 1920), 90; see also General Executive Board Minutes, September 26, 1921, p. 1552, ILGWU Archives.

31. General Executive Board Minutes, June 11, 1923, p. 1800, and September 26, 1921, p. 1552, ILGWU Archives.

32. Report of Vice President Seidman, in General Executive Board Minutes, April 24, 1917, p. 675, ILGWU Archives.

33. Transcript of interview with Israel Breslow by Henoch Mendelsund, March 2, 1982, ILGWU Archives, pp. 5 and 14.

34. Ann Washington Craton, "Working the Women Workers," *The Nation* 124 (March 23, 1927): 312.

35. *Justice,* February 16, 1923, 4.

36. ILGWU, *Report of the General Executive Board to the 17th Biennial Convention of the International Ladies' Garment Workers' Union* (New York: ILGWU, 1924): 226–27.

37. Transcript of interview with Israel Breslow by Henoch Mendelsund, March 2, 1982, p. 25.

38. Quoted in "Women's Union Decides that Men Must Conduct Their Affairs," *New York World,* January 29, 1922, 4.

39. Craton, "Working the Women Workers," 312.

40. Some of these activities were summarized in a 1922 pamphlet published by Local 25. See "Report of the Ladies' Waistmakers' Union Local 25," in *Report and Proceedings of the 16th Convention of the International Ladies' Garment Workers' Union* (1922): 3–5. The pattern was followed by Philadelphia's Local 15, described in 1920 by the General Executive Board as a "banner local." See *Report and Proceedings of the 15th Biennial Convention,* 29.

41. Louis Levine, *The Women's Garment Workers: A History of the International Ladies' Garment Workers' Union* (New York: B. W. Huebsch, 1924), 431.

42. "A Union Leader: Jennie Matyas," in *Women in the American Economy: A Documentary History, 1675–1929,* ed. W. Elliot Brownlee and Mary M. Brownlee (New Haven, Conn.: Yale University Press, 1976), 239–40.

43. *Report and Proceedings of the 15th Biennial Convention,* 29.

44. I. Weinzweig to Theresa Wolfson, May 9, 1922, in the possession of Peggy Frank. Quoted with permission.

45. A remarkable example of Cohn's humiliation exists in the following General Executive Board comment, which is here quoted from the GEB Minutes, June 11, 1923, in its entirety:

The trip to Europe made last year by Miss Fannia Cohn at the advice of her physician, the financial loss of which she had to bear herself, has made it impossible for her to straighten out her financial situation and she asked therefore to be reimbursed four weeks' pay. It was decided to grant this request and in the future on occasions of that kind, requests are to be made prior to the taking of vacations. While in Europe, Miss Cohn attended the First International Conference on Workers' Education as the delegate of the Workers' Education Bureau. (1796)

The effect of such treatment on the morale of female members of the ILGWU is illustrated by Rose Pesotta's outburst in an undated letter to David Dubinsky, box 134, file 2, David Dubinsky Collection, ILGWU Archives:

Fannia Cohn's service to our organization is only recognized by those on the outside who can dispassionately evaluate such unselfish efforts on the part of one person, for the cause of workers' education. But most of the credit is now the heritage of a director who has entered the field after the thorns were weeded out, the marshes dried, and all other obstacles removed. She remains a tragic figure amidst her own fellow workers, whom she helped to gain prestige with the outside educational world. Were she a man, it would have been entirely different.

46. "Report of the Ladies' Waistmakers' Union Local 25," 7. The pamphlet was signed by four delegates to the convention from Local 25. They were Miriam Levine, Lena Goodman, Ida Rothstein, and Rose Pasatta (*sic*). Only Ida Rothstein was an avowed communist. Pesotta was an anarchist, and both she and Levine opposed communist attempts to undermine the ILGWU. I have no information on Lena Goodman.

47. *Justice*, October 8, 1920, 2. Schlesinger continued, "We hope there are no such spirits in the Waist and Dressmakers Union. But should there appear any, we assure them that the International will know how to combat them."

48. *Report and Proceedings of the 16th Convention*, 114.

49. Abraham Baroff in the General Executive Board Minutes, October 17, 1923, p. 1833, ILGWU Archives.

50. *Advance*, September 3, 1926, 1.

51. *Advance*, October 8, 1926, 6.

52. *Advance*, May 6, 1927, 6, 7.

53. *Advance*, October 8, 1926, 6.

54. Fannia M. Cohn, "Do Sex Quarrels Help?" *Justice*, October 14, 1927, 186.

55. Nestor, "Experiences of a Pioneer Woman Trade Unionist," 932.

56. Helen Hamilton, "Women's Locals," *American Federationist* 36 (September 1929): 1061.

57. Ibid., 1060; Belle Trouland, "The Woman's Local," *American Federationist* 36 (September 1929): 970.

Chapter 5: Stratifying by Sex

1. See, for example, Valerie Kincaide Oppenheimer, *The Female Labor Force in the United States: Demographic and Economic Factors Governing Its Growth and Changing Composition* (Berkeley: University of California Press, 1970); James A. Sweet, *Women in the Labor Force* (New York: Seminar Press, 1973); John Shea, Ruth Spitz, Frederick

Zeller et al., *Dual Career: A Longitudinal Study of Labor Market Experience of Women* (Columbus: Ohio State University Press, 1970); and Juanita Kreps, *Sex in the Marketplace: American Women at Work* (Baltimore: Johns Hopkins University Press, 1971).

2. Eli Zaretsky, "Capitalism, the Family, and Personal Life," *Socialist Revolution* 3.3 (1973): 69–125. For an extended discussion of the implications of changes in household production, an issue only touched upon in this essay, see Wally Secombe, "The Housewife and Her Labor under Capitalism," *New Left Review* 83 (1974): 3–24.

3. Examples of those who raised these questions range from Ann Hutchinson in 1635 to Frances Wright in the nineteenth century, and Charlotte Perkins Gilman and Emma Goldman in the twentieth.

4. Edmund Morgan, *The Puritan Dilemma* (Boston: Little, Brown, 1958), 71; also see John Demos, *A Little Commonwealth: Family Life in Plymouth Colony* (New York: Oxford, 1970), 78.

5. Demos, *Little Commonwealth*, 186.

6. Arthur W. Calhoun, *A Social History of the American Family from Colonial Times to the Present* (New York: Barnes and Noble, 1945), 201.

7. Demos, *Little Commonwealth*, 89.

8. Edith Abbott, *Women in Industry* (New York: Appleton, 1910), 34.

9. Caroline T. Ware, *The Early New England Cotton Manufactures: A Study in Industrial Beginnings* (Boston: Houghton Mifflin, 1931), 198. Hannah Josephson, *The Golden Threads: New England's Mill Girls and Magnates* (New York: Duell, Sloan, and Pearce, 1949), 22; Oscar Handlin, *Boston's Immigrants: 1790–1880* (1941; reprint, New York: Atheneum, 1971), 74–76; Reinhard Bendix, *Work and Authority in Industry: Ideologies of Management* (New York: Wiley, 1956), 39.

10. Josephson, *Golden Threads*, 63 and 23. See also John Kasson, "Civilizing the Machine: Technology, Aesthetics, and Society in Nineteenth-Century American Thought" (Ph.D. diss., Yale University, 1972); and Holland Thompson, *From the Cotton Field to the Cotton Mill: A Study of the Industrial Transition in North Carolina* (1906; reprint, New York: Books for Libraries Press, 1971), 52, for a similar example of paternal employment in the South. About one-half of the employees in the New England textile mills were recruited in this way. That an undetermined number of the women who worked in the mills were self-supporting or responsible for families of their own fails to undermine the rationale.

11. Kasson, "Civilizing the Machine," 41.

12. Ibid., 53–55.

13. John B. Andrews and W. D. P. Bliss, *History of Women in Trade Unions*, vol. 10 of the Report on the Condition of Women and Child Wage Earners in the United States, Senate Doc. 645, 61st Cong., 2d Sess. (Washington, D.C.: Government Printing Office, 1911), 12 (hereafter "Report").

14. Ware, *Early New England Cotton Manufactures*, 231.

15. Ibid., 234.

16. Quoted in Constance McLaughlin Green, *Holyoke, Massachusetts: A Case History of the Industrial Revolution in America* (New Haven, Conn.: Yale University Press, 1939), 31n.

17. Abbott, *Women in Industry*, 90.

18. Bernard Wishy, *The Child and the Republic* (Philadelphia: University of Pennsylvania Press, 1972), 28.

19. Ruth Miller Elson, *Guardians of Tradition: American Schoolbooks of the Nineteenth Century* (Lincoln: University of Nebraska Press, 1964), 309; Siegfried Giedion, *Mechanization Takes Command: A Contribution to Anonymous History* (1948; reprint, New York: Norton, 1969), 514. For discussions of the nineteenth-century woman, see also Barbara Welter, "The Cult of True Womanhood, 1820–1860," *American Quarterly* 18 (Summer 1966): 151–74; and Glenda Gates Riley, "The Subtle Subversion: Changes in the Traditionalist Image of the American Woman," *Historian* 32 (February 1970): 210–24.

20. See Michael B. Katz, *The Irony of Early School Reform: Educational Innovation in Mid-Nineteenth-Century Massachusetts* (Boston: Beacon Press, 1968), for a general discussion of schools in this period. Arguments for domestic education for women are widespread, but see especially any of Catharine Beecher's numerous works; Elson, *Guardians of Tradition*, 309; and Gerda Lerner, "Women's Rights and American Feminism," *American Scholar* 40 (Spring 1971): 238.

21. Aileen Kraditor, *Up from the Pedestal* (Chicago: Quadrangle, 1968), 13. Kraditor continues: "The home was the bulwark against social disorder, and woman was the creator of the home . . . she occupied a desperately necessary place as symbol and center of the one institution that prevented society from flying apart."

22. Quoted in Elson, *Guardians of Tradition*, 309.

23. Andrews and Bliss, *History of Women in Trade Unions*, 118.

24. See Green, *Holyoke*, for example. Helen Sumner, *History of Women in Industry in the United States*, "Report," vol. 9, 28, notes that the *Workingman's Advocate* in 1868 complained that women only got one-quarter of men's wages.

25. John R. Commons et al., eds., *A Documentary History of American Industrial Society*, vol. 6, *The Labor Movement* (Cleveland: A. H. Clark, 1910), 195; Emilie Josephine Hutchinson, *Women's Wages: A Study of the Wages of Industrial Women and Measures Suggested to Increase Them* (Providence, R.I.: American Mathematical Society, 1968), 24–25. Handlin, *Boston's Immigrants*, 81, notes that women earned an average of $1.50 to $3.00 per week, while men earned from $4.50 to $5.50.

26. *Wage-Earning Women in Stores and Factories*, "Report," vol. 5, 13, 22; Commons, *Documentary History*, 210.

27. Commons, *Documentary History*, 282, 284.

28. Andrews and Bliss, *History of Women in Trade Unions*, 48.

29. Elizabeth F. Baker, *Technology and Women's Work* (New York: Columbia University Press, 1964), 17. See also Sumner, *History of Women in Industry*, 51, who indicates that the number of women dropped to 40.6 percent in 1900.

30. Katz, *Irony of Early School Reform*, 12. There is a discrepancy in the figures Katz presents in the appendix (224) and in the text. I have used the more conservative figures here. See also Hutchinson, *Women's Wages*, 34 and 158.

31. Quoted in Sumner, *History of Women in Industry*, 29.

32. Andrews and Bliss, *History of Women in Trade Unions*, 104.

33. *The Silk Industry*, "Report," vol. 4, 40, 41.

34. Andrews and Bliss, *Women in Trade Unions*, 122.

35. Hutchinson, *Women's Wages,* 159–60; Andrews and Bliss, *History of Women in Trade Unions,* 10, 151; also see p. 179 for the cigar industry. The report attributes the decline in membership that occurred among women after 1902 to deliberate hostility by employers.

36. Andrews and Bliss, *History of Women in Trade Unions,* 39, 41, 46, 47, 57; and Sumner, *History of Women in Industry,* 61n.

37. Commons, *Documentary History,* 9, 205; Andrews and Bliss, *History of Women in Trade Unions,* 17.

38. Boone, *Women's Trade Union League,* 166–67; Margaret Rankin to Mrs. Raymond Robins, March 30, 1919, Margaret Dreier Robins Collection, University of Florida, Gainesville.

39. Andrews and Bliss, *History of Women in Trade Unions,* 103, 94.

40. Quoted in Sumner, *History of Women in Industry,* 26.

41. The same moral code seems to have had a better impact on middle-class women, for whom it not only provided justification for opening up educational institutions to them but also provided a basis for the suffrage argument at the end of the nineteenth century.

42. These figures are for females over sixteen. See Joseph A. Hill, *Women in Gainful Occupations: 1870–1920,* Census Monographs 9 (Washington, D.C.: Government Printing Office, 1929), 19. Oppenheimer, *Female Labor Force in the United States,* 2–6, has an excellent discussion of the debate over the increase after that date.

43. Hill, *Women in Gainful Occupations,* 40.

44. Sumner, *History of Women in Industry,* 59, 60. See Carroll D. Wright, *The Working Girls of Boston* (1889; reprint, New York: Arno Press, 1969), for a breakdown of women in manufacturing in Boston in 1880.

45. *Relation of Occupation and Criminality among Women,* "Report," vol. 15, p. 93, 34, 70. Department-store owners were defensive about the question of morality. One, for example, insisted of his employees that "the majority must be good girls from sheer physical necessity. They cannot live a fast life after 6 o'clock for successive days and weeks and be in proper condition to do their work in the store. If they are busy at night when they should be taking their rest they are soon in such shape that they cannot attend to business and are discharged." *Wage-Earning Women in Stores and Factories,* "Report," vol. 5, 32.

46. Among those who worked, 12.1 percent were married in 1890, and 19.8 percent in 1910. The percentage of married women who worked increased from 3.3 in 1890 to 6.8 percent in 1910. Donald Lescohier, "Working Conditions," in *History of Labor in the United States, 1896–1932,* ed. John Commons, vol. 3 (New York: Macmillan, 1918), 37; and Hill, *Women in Gainful Occupations,* 76–77.

47. Caroline Manning, *The Immigrant Woman and Her Job* (1930; reprint, New York: Arno Press, 1970). See also Barbara Klazynska, "Why Women Work: A Theory for Comparison of Ethnic Groups," Paper delivered at the American Studies Association Meeting, San Francisco, October 18–20, 1973. The Strasser quote is from the *Cigar Maker's Journal,* September 15, 1879, 22.

48. Hill, *Women in Gainful Occupations,* 101–2, 94. Part of this pattern can be

explained by population shifts. The proportion of immigrants and their children in the population as a whole increased slightly until 1910. But the proportion of foreign-born women who were working outpaced it. Between 1910 and 1920, the proportion of immigrants in the population dropped slightly, but the decline in the relative proportion of working women who were foreign-born far exceeded it. See table accompanying n.51 below; U.S. Census Office, *11th Census of Populations*, pt. 2 (Washington, D.C.: Government Printing Office, 1890); U.S. Census Office, *14th Census of Populations*, vol. 3 (Washington, D.C.: Government Printing Office, 1920), 15.

49. The work of Carroll Smith-Rosenberg is important in illuminating the problems of middle-class women in the nineteenth century. See, for example, Carroll Smith-Rosenberg and Charles Rosenberg, "The Female Animal: Medical and Biological Views of Women in Nineteenth-Century America," *Journal of American History* 60 (September 1973): 332–56. Good perspectives on the forces driving the late nineteenth-century middle-class woman can be obtained from a number of autobiographies and biographies, including Vida Scudder, *On Journey* (New York: Dutton, 1937); Mary Kingsbury Simkhovitch, *Neighborhood: My Story of Greenwich House* (New York: Norton, 1938); Josephine Goldmark, *Impatient Crusader: Florence Kelley's Life Story* (Urbana: University of Illinois Press, 1953); and Allen F. Davis, *American Heroine: The Life and Legend of Jane Addams* (New York: Oxford University Press, 1973).

50. Allen F. Davis, *Spearheads for Reform: The Social Settlements and the Progressive Movement, 1890–1914* (New York: Oxford University Press, 1967), describes the work of some of these people. The results of their efforts are found in such books as Helen Campbell, *Prisoners of Poverty: Women Wage Workers, Their Trades, and Their Lives* (1887; reprint, New York: Garrett Press, 1970); Elizabeth Butler, *Women and the Trades: Pittsburgh, 1907–1908* (New York: Charities Publication Committee, 1909); and Elizabeth Butler, *Saleswomen in Mercantile Stores: Baltimore, 1909* (New York: Russell Sage, 1912).

51. The shift occurred largely at the expense of African American and immigrant women, as the following table indicates.

Comparison of Working Women in Each Group, by Percentages, with Their Proportion in the Population as a Whole, 1890–1920

	Proportion of each group engaged in gainful occupations				Proportion of each group in total population			
Year	Native-born of native-born parents	Native-born of foreign parents	Foreign-born	Negro	Native-born of native-born parents	Native-born of foreign parents	Foreign-born	Negro
1890	35.3	20.9	20.4	23.4	55.03	18.37	14.4	12.2
1900	36.7	22.6	17.4	23.2	53.9	20.6	13.4	11.6
1910	38.3	22.0	16.1	23.9	53.8	20.5	14.5	10.7
1920	43.8	24.9	13.4	17.6	55.3	21.4	13.09	9.9

Source: Hill, pp. 85, 94, 102, 110 and U.S. Census, 11th Census 1890, clx; 14th Census 1920, 15. Orientals and Indians excluded.

52. Hill, *Women in Gainful Occupations,* 90, 96, 39–41. See also Margery Davies, "Woman's Place Is at the Typewriter: The Feminization of the Clerical Labor Force," in *Labor-Market Segmentation,* ed. Richard Edwards, Michael Reich, and David Gordon (Lexington, Mass.: D. C. Heath, 1975), 279–96.

53. Good descriptions of this ferment can be found in William Chafe, *The American Woman: Her Changing Social, Economic, and Political Roles, 1920–1970* (New York: Oxford University Press, 1972); and Eleanor Flexner, *Century of Struggle: The Woman's Rights Movement in the United States* (1959; reprint, New York: Atheneum, 1970).

54. John R. Commons and John B. Andrews, *Principles of Labor Legislation,* rev. ed. (New York: Harper, 1927), 30, has a statement of the general principles of protective legislation. Elizabeth Faulkner Baker, *Protective Labor Legislation,* vol. 66 of *Studies in History, Economics, and Public Law* (New York: Columbia University, 1925), contains a summary of laws and court decisions to 1925.

55. See Edwards, Reich, and Gordon, eds., *Labor Market Segmentation,* chap. 1, for a description and analysis of this process.

56. Hutchinson, *Women's Wages,* 81.

57. Commons and Andrews, *Principles of Labor Legislation,* 69, 30.

58. Hutchinson, *Women's Wages,* 161.

59. After an extensive study, based on an investigation that threatened to split the Women's Bureau itself, the bureau issued a bulletin in 1928 entitled *The Effects of Labor Legislation in the Employment Opportunities of Women.* Much of the debate was chronicled by the press in reporting the meetings of the Women's Industrial Conference in January 1926. See especially the *New York Times,* January 20, 1926; *Boston Globe,* January 20, 1926; *Washington Evening Star,* January 21, 1926; and *New York Herald Tribune,* January 27, 1926.

60. The following difficulties recorded by a Women's Bureau interviewer of her conversation with a California can manufacturer are typical of the negative comments expressed by employers affected by protective legislation: "In the lithograph department several years ago a rush order was received from raisin growers for a large quantity of cans. Most of the press feeders were girls and it was necessary to work overtime to get orders out. Requested permission to work girls overtime and it was refused. . . . Men were put on press feeders for overtime and as the girl press feeders have left or been transferred men have been given their jobs as there is always a chance of potential overtime on rush orders and a 'busy time is not a time when you want to put men workers for a few days.' However none of the women were discharged because they were not able to work overtime but it led to a change in policy of filling press feeding jobs." Long Day Hour Schedule, Record Group 86, Accession no. 51A101, box 12, Women's Bureau Collection, California, National Archives, Washington, D.C. A more forceful statement came from the representative of a Massachusetts employer group who indicated that "in an industry where women constitute less than 25 percent of the working force, it will not pay to change the hours for the whole plant nor to keep the women and have two sets of hours, therefore the women will be dismissed." Individual Interviews, Record Group 86, Accession no. 51A101, box 40, Bulletin 15, Women's Bureau Collection, Massachusetts, National Archives, Washington, D.C.

61. Oppenheimer, *Female Labor Force*, 3–5; Janet M. Hooks, *Women's Occupations through Seven Decades*, Women's Bureau Bulletin no. 218 (Washington, D.C.: Government Printing Office, 1947), 34; Chafe, *American Woman*, 54–55. I have not attempted to estimate how much these changes were affected by increased affluence or by the withdrawal of immigrant women from the labor market. For an account of the effect of minimum wages on the most disadvantaged group of workers, see Elizabeth Ross Haynes, "Two Million Women at Work," in *Black Women in White America: A Documentary History*, ed. Gerda Lerner (New York: Pantheon, 1972), 256–57. Haynes writes: "With the fixing of the minimum wage in the hotels, restaurants, etc., at $16.50 for a 48 hour week, and the increasing number of available white women, Negro women were to a very large extent displaced. Wages for domestic service for the rank and file have fallen in the past twelve months from $10.00 a week without any laundry work to $7 and $8 with laundry work. . . . The numbers driven into domestic work are very large."

62. A good description of this conflict is in J. Stanley Lemons, *The Woman Citizen: Social Feminism in the 1920s* (Urbana: University of Illinois Press, 1973), esp. chap. 7.

63. Quoted in Mary Van Kleeck to Mary Anderson, February 21, 1923, Mary Van Kleeck Papers, unsorted, Sophia Smith Collection, Smith College, Northampton, Mass.

64. Mary Anderson to Mary Van Kleeck, May 28, 1927, Mary Van Kleeck Papers, unsorted, Sophia Smith Collection, Smith College, Northampton, Mass.

65. Rose Schneiderman with Lucy Goldthwaite, *All for One* (New York: Paul Erickson, 1967), 43. This is in sharp contrast to the early years of the New England textile industry, when mill workers might become teachers for several months each year.

66. *Wage-Earning Women in Stores and Factories*, "Report," vol. 5, 193.

67. Schneiderman and Goldthwaite, *All for One*, 97; Rose Pesotta, *Bread upon the Waters* (New York: Dodd, Mead, 1944), 19.

68. Emma L. Shields, "The Tobacco Workers," in *Black Women in White America: A Documentary History*, ed. Gerda Lerner (New York: Pantheon, 1972), 253; and Klaezynska, "Why Women Work," n.47.

69. *Wage-Earning Women in Stores and Factories*, "Report," vol. 5, 98.

70. For example, women had been 81.8 percent of all teachers in 1930 and dropped to 75.3 percent of the total in 1940. Nurses dropped from 98.1 percent of the total to 97.8 percent; librarians from 91.4 to 89.5 percent. In the clothing trade, women reversed a thirty-year trend to substitute men for women and climbed from 64.4 percent of all clothing workers in 1930 to 74 percent in 1940. The 1930s, statistically, continued a trend for married women to enter the labor force. By 1940, 35.5 percent of all women workers were married, as compared to 28.8 percent in 1930 and 22.8 percent in 1920. Hook, *Women's Occupations through Seven Decades*, 160, 163, 170, 115, 39.

71. The following quote is illustrative: "A first general step towards the problem of rehabilitating women (and through women, children of both sexes and adults of the next generation) would be public recognition in substantial ways of the powerful role and special importance of mothers as transmitting agents, good or bad, of feelings, personality, and character. This would pave the way for over-all action by national and local governments and by private organizations." Ferdinand Lundberg and Marynia Farnham, *Modern Woman: The Lost Sex* (New York: Harper and Brothers, 1947), 356.

72. For an extended discussion of these issues, see Alice Kessler-Harris and Bertram Silverman, "Women in Advanced Capitalism," *Social Policy* (July–August 1973): 16–22.

73. Richard Nixon's veto of the Comprehensive Child Development Act as reported in the *New York Times,* December 10, 1971, 20, is an example of official policy. For disaffection, see *Work in America,* Report of a Special Task Force to the Secretary of Health, Education, and Welfare (Boston: Massachusetts Institute of Technology, 1973). And for some startling differences between middle- and working-class women, see "Widening Gap Is Registered between College and Non-College Women," *New York Times,* May 22, 1974, 45.

74. An extended discussion of these shifts can be found in Daniel Bell, *The Coming of Post-Industrial Society* (New York: Basic Books, 1973); John Kenneth Galbraith, *The New Industrial State* (Boston: Houghton Mifflin, 1967); and Victor Fuchs, *The Service Economy* (Washington, D.C.: National Bureau of Economic Research, 1968).

75. Valerie Kincaide Oppenheimer, "Demographic Influence on Female Employment and the Status of Women," *American Journal of Sociology* 78 (January 1973): 946–61.

76. See Juanita Kreps, *Sex in the Marketplace;* and Oppenheimer, *Female Labor Force,* for details. These figures have changed since this essay first appeared: 47 percent of the paid labor force is now female, and 60 percent of mothers of small children earn wages. For an update and discussion of recent trends, see Alice Kessler-Harris, Epilogue to *Out to Work: A History of Wage-Earning Women in the United States,* 20th Anniversary Ed. (New York: Oxford University Press, 2003).

77. The wage gap has now narrowed from fifty-nine cents to seventy-six cents to the dollar, largely as a result of declining male wages. A good illustration is Gertrude Ezorsky, "Fight over University Women," *New York Review of Books* May 16, 1974, 32–39.

78. Katherine Ellis and Rosalind Petchesky, "Children of the Corporate Dream: An Analysis of Day Care as a Political Issue under Capitalism," *Socialist Revolution* 2.6 (1972): 8–28.

Chapter 6: Independence and Virtue in the Lives of Wage-Earning Women in the United States, 1870–1930

1. *Daily Evening Voice,* June 12, 1865.

2. *Daily Evening Voice,* April 7, 1865.

3. *New York Times,* October 17 , 1869, 3. The *New York World,* December 1, 1863, 4, estimated the number at three hundred thousand.

4. *Daily Evening Voice,* January 7, 1865, 2.

5. *Fincher's Trades Review,* June 6, 1863, 2; "Two Heads or One," *Workingman's Advocate,* May 7, 1870, 4; *Workingman's Advocate,* April 9, 1870, 1. See also "A Wife's Power," *Workingman's Advocate,* March 11, 1876, 1; *Workingman's Advocate,* November 13, 1869, 4; and "A Perfect Wife," *Workingman's Advocate,* March 19, 1870, 1.

6. Ellen Butler, "Women and Work," *Daily Evening Voice,* January 12, 1865, 1.

7. "The Wail of the Women," *Workingman's Advocate,* April 24, 1869, 1.

8. See Leslie Tentler, *Wage-Earning Women: Industrial Work and Family Life in the United States, 1900–1930* (New York: Oxford University Press, 1979). Carolyn Dall,

Women's Right to Labor (Boston: Walker, Wise, and Co., 1860), 72, provides a particularly clear statement: "How we rate an idle boy! How we bear with a dawdling girl! That father grows impatient whose son does not rise early, or show some desire for employment; but the same man keeps his daughters in Berlin wool and yellow novels, and looks to marriage as their salvation, even when he blushes to be told of it."

9. Mary Van Kleeck, *Artificial Flower Makers* (New York: Survey Associates, 1913), 38; Mary Kenney O'Sullivan, "Autobiography," p. 28, in Mary Kenney O'Sullivan Collection, Schlesinger Library, Cambridge, Mass.

10. Quoted in Daniel Walkowitz, "Working-Class Women in the Gilded Age: Factory, Community, and Family Life among Cohoes, N.Y., Cotton Workers," *Journal of Social History* 5 (Summer 1972): 476.

11. Clippings from the *Utica Daily Press,* March 29, 1899, box 8, file 85, Leonora O'Reilly Collection, Schlesinger Library, Cambridge, Mass.

12. Rose Schneiderman with Lucy Goldthwaite, *All for One* (New York: Paul Erickson, 1967), 43.

13. *Wage-Earning Women in Stores and Factories,* vol. 5 of the Report on the Condition of Women and Child Wage Earners, Senate Doc. 645, 61st Cong., 2d Sess. (Washington, D.C.: Government Printing Office, 1911), 134–35.

14. Ibid., 193, 199.

15. Elizabeth Butler, *Saleswomen in Mercantile Stores: Baltimore, 1909* (New York: Russell Sage, 1912), 144, 121.

16. Ella Wolff interview, typescript in Amerikaner Yiddish Geshichte Bel-Pe, December 27, 1963, p. 3, YIVO Archive, New York.

17. Eleanor Gilbert, lecture manuscript, "Office Work as Training for Executive Positions," October 25, 1915, box 1, file 7, Bureau of Vocational Information, Schlesinger Library, Cambridge, Mass. (hereafter BVI).

18. Edward Woods, "Selling Life Insurance: A Vocation for Girls," *The Scholastic,* February 9, 1924, 9. See also Ida White Parker, "Women in the Insurance Fields," *The Businesswoman* (January 1923): 17–18; Eugenia Wallace, "Filing, a Stepping Stone," *The Spotlight* (February 1918): 4; clipping from the *New York Times,* February 29, 1924, box 4, file 63, BVI; Mrs. Crocker, "Women in Civil Service," March 28, 1916, box 1, file 23, BVI.

19. Interviews of February 11, 1919, and February 27, 1919, in Philadelphia Candy Study Home Visits, box 40, Women's Bureau papers, National Archives, Washington, D.C.

20. Interview, November 28, 1921, in South Carolina Home Visits, box 43, Women's Bureau, National Archives, Washington, D.C.

21. Ella V. Price of the Narrow Fabric Company, Reading, Pennsylvania, April 12, 1918, box 14, file 179, BVI.

22. "Training Women for a New Occupation," *School Life,* clipping (1922), box 4, file 63, BVI. "For example," the article continued, "the withdrawal of an account gives indication of possible distress in a household. In such a case, the home service director may investigate the circumstances, and often she can suggest methods of retrenchment that will enable the family to continue saving."

23. Clipping from unidentified paper about Mrs. E. M. Abernathy of Lexington, Oklahoma, March 20, 1923, box 1, file 23, BVI.

24. Unidentified clipping, March 9, 1925, box 4, file 69, BVI.

25. *New York Herald,* July 3, 1925, 3.

Chapter 7: A New Agenda for American Labor History

1. Michael Frisch, "Sixty Characters in Search of Authority: The Northern Illinois University NEH Conference," *International Labor and Working-Class History* 27 (September 1985): 101.

2. Eric Foner, "Labor Historians Seek Useful Past," *In These Times,* December 12–18, 1984, 11.

3. A good summary of this position can be found in Ira Berlin, "Introduction: Herbert Gutman and the American Working Class," in *Power and Culture: Essays on the American Working Class,* by Herbert G. Gutman (New York: Pantheon Books, 1987), 3–69.

4. See David Gordon, Richard Edwards, and Michael Reich, *Segmented Work, Divided Workers: The Historical Transformation of Labor in the United States* (Cambridge: Cambridge University Press, 1982).

5. Troublesome issues surrounding social history were raised by Herbert Gutman, "The Missing Synthesis: Whatever Happened to History?" *The Nation* 233 (November 21, 1981): 521, 553–54. For full-scale critiques, see Eugene Genovese and Elizabeth Fox-Genovese, "The Political Crisis of Social History: A Marxian Perspective," *Journal of Social History* 10 (Winter 1976): 205–20; Gertrude Himmelfarb, *The New History and the Old* (Cambridge, Mass.: Belknap Press of Harvard University Press, 1987), esp. chap. 1; and Theodore S. Hamerow, *Reflections on History and Historians* (Madison: University of Wisconsin Press, 1987).

6. Sean Wilentz, *Chants Democratic: New York City and the Rise of the American Working Class, 1788–1850* (New York: Oxford University Press, 1984). See also the critique by John Patrick Diggins, "Comrades and Citizens: New Mythologies in American Historiography," *American Historical Review* 90 (June 1985): 614–38; Leon Fink, "The New Labor History and the Powers of Historical Pessimism: Consensus, Hegemony, and the Case of the Knights of Labor," *Journal of American History* 75 (June 1988): 115–36; and the roundtable that follows, particularly John P. Diggins, "The Misuses of Gramsci," *Journal of American History* 75 (June 1988): 141–45.

7. These progressive unions include Local 1199 of the National Health and Hospital Workers Union; the American Federation of State, County, and Municipal Employees; and District 65, now a national local of the United Auto Workers.

8. Herbert Gutman's absence from the meeting was crucial. Had he been present, we would not, I think, have been permitted to take the concept for granted.

9. E. P. Thompson, *The Making of the English Working Class* (New York: Vintage Books, 1963), 11.

10. A point made by Eric Hobsbawm at the meetings.

11. Foner, "Labor Historians Seek Useful Past."

12. For an elaboration of the usefulness of gender analysis, see Joan Scott, "Gender: A Useful Category of Historical Analysis," *American Historical Review* 91 (December 1986): 1053–75. See also Sally Alexander, "Women, Class, and Sexual Difference," *History Workshop* 17 (Spring 1984): 125–49; and Ava Baron, "Gender and Labor History:

Notes towards a New Historical Look at Women, Men, and Work," unpublished essay in the author's possession.

13. I have borrowed the notion of a meaning system from Frank Parkin, *Marxism and Class Theory: A Bourgeois Critique* (New York: Columbia University Press, 1979), 44–46.

14. Thompson, *Making of the English Working Class*, 9.

15. Mary Blewett, *Men, Women, and Work: Class, Gender, and Protest in the New England Shoe Industry, 1790–1910* (Urbana: University of Illinois Press, 1988), 320. Blewett's interpretation should be contrasted with that of Alan Dawley, *Class and Community: The Industrial Revolution in Lynn* (Cambridge, Mass.: Harvard University Press, 1976). See also Susan Porter Benson, *Counter Cultures: Saleswomen, Managers, and Customers in American Department Stores, 1890–1940* (Urbana: University of Illinois Press, 1986); and Sallie Westwood, *All Day, Every Day: Factory and Family in the Making of Women's Lives* (Urbana: University of Illinois Press, 1985).

16. For example, I find inadequate the caveat offered by Ira Katznelson and Aristide Zolberg, *Working-Class Formation: Nineteenth-Century Patterns in Western Europe and the United States* (Princeton, N.J.: Princeton University Press, 1986), 4. Although the authors apologize for omitting a discussion of the consequences of industrial transformation for women, they fail to acknowledge that to appreciate the process of transformation requires an understanding of gender.

17. Wilentz, *Chants Democratic*, chap. 2; Linda Kerber, *Women of the Republic: Intellect and Ideology in Revolutionary America* (Chapel Hill: University of North Carolina Press, 1980).

18. Susan Levine, *Labor's True Woman: Carpet Weavers, Industrialization, and Labor Reform in the Gilded Age* (Philadelphia: Temple University Press, 1984). On the idea of free labor, see William E. Forbath, "The Ambiguities of Free Labor: Labor and the Law in the Gilded Age," *Wisconsin Law Review* (July/August 1984): 767–817.

19. The idea is best developed in David Montgomery, *Workers' Control in America: Studies in the History of Work, Technology, and Labor Struggles* (New York: Cambridge University Press, 1979), chap. 1. See also Nick Salvatore, *Eugene V. Debs: Citizen and Socialist* (Urbana: University of Illinois Press, 1982).

20. Patricia A. Cooper, *Once a Cigar Maker: Men, Women, and Work Culture in American Cigar Factories, 1900–1919* (Urbana: University of Illinois Press, 1987), 156.

21. See Ruth Milkman, *Gender at Work: The Dynamics of Job Segregation by Sex during World War II* (Urbana: University of Illinois Press, 1987); Ruth Roach Pierson, *"They're Still Women After All": The Second World War and Canadian Womanhood* (Toronto: McClelland and Stewart, 1986).

22. Christine Stansell, *City of Women: Sex and Class in New York, 1789–1860* (Urbana: University of Illinois Press, 1987).

23. The best illustration here is Rebecca Harding Davis's novel, *Life in the Iron Mills* (Old Westbury, Conn.: Feminist Press, 1972). And see also the animal-like representations of workers reproduced in the film *The Grand Army of Starvation*, produced by the American Social History Project (directed by Stephen Brier; VHS, 1987).

24. Heidi Hartmann, "The Unhappy Marriage of Marxism and Feminism: Towards a More Progressive Union," *Capital and Class* 8 (Summer 1979): 1–43.

25. A parallel argument was made for the history of race and racism by Barbara Fields at the meeting. Fields suggested that in addition to looking at the history of race as the history of black people, we also need to ask what it tells us about the development of an economy based on relations between black and white people.

Chapter 8: Treating the Male as "Other"

1. Quoted in Theresa Wolfson, *The Woman Worker and the Trade Unions* (New York: International Publishers, 1926), 77–78.

2. Richard Oestreicher, "Separate Tribes? Working-Class and Women's History," *Reviews in American History* 19 (1991): 228.

3. Ibid., 229.

4. For examples of how this has happened, see Ava Baron, "Gender and Labor History: Learning from the Past, Looking to the Future," in *Work Engendered: Toward a New History of American Labor,* ed. Ava Baron (Ithaca, N.Y.: Cornell University Press, 1991), 1–46; and Sonya Rose, *Limited Livelihoods: Gender and Class in Nineteenth-Century England* (Berkeley: University of California Press, 1992).

5. See the report of this conference and some of the papers in J. Carroll Moody and Alice Kessler-Harris, eds., *Perspectives on American Labor History: Towards a New Synthesis* (DeKalb: Northern Illinois University Press, 1987).

6. One could as easily engage in the same exploration around race. I focus on gender here because that is my charge, but as I have come to many of these formulations by reading the literature on racism, I hope that many of the conclusions I reach here will speak to issues of race as well as gender.

7. The clearest articulation of standpoint theory is in Sandra Harding, *Whose Science? Whose Knowledge? Thinking from Women's Lives* (Ithaca, N.Y.: Cornell University Press, 1990). See also Patricia Hill Collins, "Learning from the 'Outsider Within': The Sociological Significance of Black Feminist Thought," *Social Problems* 33 (1986): 14–32; Patricia Hill Collins, *Black Feminist Thought: Knowledge, Consciousness, and the Politics of Empowerment* (New York: Routledge, 1991), chap. 10; and Nancy Hartsock, *Money, Sex, and Power: Toward a Feminist Historical Materialism* (New York: Longman, 1983), chap. 10.

8. Harding, *Whose Science?* 123.

9. Joan W. Scott, "Women and the Making of the English Working Class," in *Gender and the Politics of History* (New York: Columbia University Press, 1988), 89.

10. Even when the workplace is female-centered, we debate whether it can be the source of female identity. For example, Leslie Tentler takes an extreme position on the importance of a narrowly circumscribed domesticity in *Wage-Earning Women: Industrial Work and Family Life in the United States, 1900–1930* (New York: Oxford University Press, 1979). Other sources that focus on women's relation to wage work as a product of domestic life include Louise Lamphere, *From Working Daughters to Working Mothers: Immigrant Women in a New England Community* (Ithaca, N.Y.: Cornell University Press, 1987); and Sallie Westwood, *All Day, Every Day: Factory and Family in the Making of Women's Lives* (Urbana: University of Illinois Press, 1985).

11. Earl Lewis, *In Their Own Interests: Race, Class, and Power in Twentieth-Century Norfolk, Virginia* (Berkeley: University of California Press, 1991), 1–7.

12. Henry Ford understood this fully when he adopted the five-dollar day and conditioned it on the respectable home lives of his employees. See Stephen Meyer, *The Five-Dollar Day: Labor Management and Social Control in the Ford Motor Company, 1908–1921* (Albany: State University of New York Press, 1981), 124–47.

13. David Roediger, *The Wages of Whiteness: Race and the Making of the American Working Class* (London: Verso, 1991). See also Barbara J. Fields, "Ideology and Race in American History," in *Region, Race, and Reconstruction: Essays in Honor of C. Vann Woodward,* ed. J. Morgan Kousser and James M. McPherson (New York: Oxford University Press, 1982), 143–77.

14. Several historians have explored how the workplace constructs gender. See especially Ava Baron, "Questions of Gender: Deskilling and Demasculinization in the U.S. Printing Industry, 1830–1915," *Gender and History* 1 (1989): 178–99; and Cynthia Cockburn, *Brothers: Male Dominance, and Technological Change* (London: Pluto, 1983). This is a useful but partial response to the question I raise here, for it continues the separation of class and gender. Rather, I want to suggest that our project is to explore how class is constructed in the household.

15. This view is informed by Jurgen Habermas's notions of public space as described in *The Structural Transformation of the Public Sphere: An Inquiry into a Category of Bourgeois Society* (Cambridge: Massachusetts Institute of Technology Press, 1989), pt. 5, and the difficulty of locating spaces in which women are enabled to shape public opinion. Historians are only beginning to come to grips with how women exercised their public voices. See especially Joan B. Landes, *Women and the Public Sphere in the Age of the French Revolution* (Ithaca, N.Y.: Cornell University Press, 1988); and Mary Ryan, *Women in Public: Between Banners and Ballots, 1825–1880* (Baltimore: Johns Hopkins University Press, 1990).

16. P. D. Anthony, *The Ideology of Work* (London: Tavistock, 1977), traces the history of workers' relationship to work; Alice Kessler-Harris and Bertram Silverman, "Beyond Industrial Unionism," *Dissent* (Winter 1992): 61–67, summarizes arguments about the contemporary transition in attitudes towards work and suggests its relationship to changing trade-union practices; Juliet B. Schor, *The Overworked American: The Unexpected Decline of Leisure* (New York: Basic Books, 1991), discusses the effects of the desire for increased consumption.

17. For a superb illustration of the uses of early twentieth-century consumption to reconcile issues of workplace exploitation and immigrant adaptation, see Andrew J. Heinze, *Adapting to Abundance: Jewish Immigrants, Mass Consumption, and the Search for American Identity* (New York: Columbia University Press, 1990).

18. Jeanne Boydston, *Home and Work: Housework, Wages, and the Ideology of Labor in the Early Republic* (New York: Oxford University Press, 1990).

19. Joan Jensen, *Loosening the Bonds: Mid-Atlantic Farm Women, 1750–1850* (New Haven, Conn.: Yale University Press, 1986).

20. For the language of republicanism as invoked by women workers, see Thomas Dublin, *Women at Work: The Transformation of Work and Community in Lowell, Massachusetts, 1826–1860* (New York: Columbia University Press, 1979); and Mary Blewett, *Men, Women, and Work: Class, Gender, and Protest in the New England Shoe Industry, 1780–1910* (Urbana: University of Illinois Press, 1988).

21. Christine Stansell, *City of Women: Sex and Class in New York, 1789–1860* (Urbana: University of Illinois Press, 1987); and Ryan, *Women in Public.*

22. Elliott J. Gorn, *The Manly Art: Bare Knuckles Prize Fighting in America* (Ithaca, N.Y.: Cornell University Press, 1986); Joe William Trotter, *Black Milwaukee: The Making of an Industrial Proletariat, 1915–45* (Urbana: University of Illinois Press, 1988).

23. See the pioneering work of Tamara Hareven, *Family Time and Industrial Time: The Relationship between the Family and Work in a New England Industrial Community* (Cambridge: Cambridge University Press, 1982).

24. Carole Turbin, *Working Women of Collar City: Gender, Class, and Community in Troy, 1864–86* (Urbana: University of Illinois Press, 1992); Ardis Cameron, *Radicals of the Worst Sort: The Laboring Women of Lawrence, Massachusetts, 1860–1912* (Urbana: University of Illinois Press, 1993).

25. Elizabeth Faue, *Community of Suffering and Struggle: Women, Men, and the Labor Movement in Minneapolis, 1915–1945* (Chapel Hill: University of North Carolina Press, 1991).

26. Lizabeth Cohen, *Making a New Deal: Industrial Workers in Chicago, 1919–1939* (Cambridge: Cambridge University Press, 1990).

27. David Montgomery, *Workers' Control in America: Studies in the History of Work, Technology, and Labor Struggles* (Cambridge: Cambridge University Press, 1979).

28. Ava Baron, "Acquiring Manly Competence: The Demise of Apprenticeship and the Remasculinization of Printers' Work," in *Meanings for Manhood: Constructions of Masculinity in Victorian America,* ed. Mark C. Carnes and Clyde Griffen (Chicago: University of Chicago Press, 1990), 152–63; Ava Baron, "The Masculinization of Production: The Gendering of Work and Skill in U.S. Newspaper Printing, 1850–1920," in *Gendered Domains: Rethinking Public and Private in Women's History,* ed. Dorothy O. Helly and Susan M. Reverby (Ithaca, N.Y.: Cornell University Press, 1992), 277–88. See also David Bensman, *The Practice of Solidarity: American Hat Finishers in the Nineteenth Century* (Urbana: University of Illinois Press, 1985); and Patricia Cooper, *Once a Cigar Maker: Men, Women, and Work Culture in American Cigar Factories, 1900–1919* (Urbana: University of Illinois Press, 1987).

29. Heidi Hartman, "Capitalism, Patriarchy, and Job Segregation by Sex," *Signs* 1 (1976): 137–69; Mary Ann Clawson, *Constructing Brotherhood: Class, Gender, and Fraternalism* (Princeton, N.J.: Princeton University Press, 1989).

30. See Amy Dru Stanley, "Conjugal Bonds and Wage Labor: Rights of Contract in the Age of Emancipation," *Journal of American History* 75 (1988): 471–500; Susan Levine, *Labor's True Woman: Carpet Weavers, Industrialization, and Labor Reform in the Gilded Age* (Philadelphia: Temple University Press, 1984).

31. Nick Salvatore, *Eugene V. Debs: Citizen and Socialist* (Urbana: University of Illinois Press, 1982); Faue, *Community of Suffering and Struggle,* chap. 3.

32. Mary Blewett, "Manhood and the Market: The Politics of Gender and Class among the Textile Workers of Fall River, Massachusetts, 1870–1880," in *Work Engendered: Toward a New History of American Labor,* ed. Ava Baron (Ithaca, N.Y.: Cornell University Press, 1991), 92–113.

33. The work of Cynthia Cockburn is useful here, especially "The Material of Male

Power," *Feminist Review* 9 (October 1981): 41–58. See also Rosemary Pringle, *Secretaries Talk: Sexuality, Power, and Work* (London: Verso, 1989).

34. Kathy Peiss, *Cheap Amusements: Working Women and Leisure in Turn-of-the-Century New York* (Philadelphia: Temple University Press, 1988).

35. Dorothy Sue Cobble, *Dishing It Out: Waitresses and Their Unions in the Twentieth Century* (Urbana: University of Illinois Press, 1991). The importance of the positions of women within households is also emphasized by Mary Blewett, *Men, Women, and Work.*

36. Alice Kessler-Harris, *A Woman's Wage: Historical Meanings and Social Consequences* (Lexington: University of Kentucky Press, 1990).

37. Larry Glickman, "Inventing the 'American Standard of Living': Gender, Race, and Working-Class Identity," *Labor History* 34 (Spring 1993): 256–73.

Chapter 9: Reconfiguring the Private

1. Technical Branch, Employee interview no. 300, June 19, 1930, Microfiche 186, Western Electric, Hawthorne Studies, Baker Library, Harvard University (hereafter Hawthorne Microfiche).

2. Frank B. Gilbreth, *Primer of Scientific Management* (New York: D. Van Nostrand Co., 1912), 62. On scientific management in general, see Frederick Winslow Taylor, *Scientific Management: Comprising Shop Management, the Principles of Scientific Management, Testimony before the Special House Committee* (New York: Harper and Brothers, 1947); Robert Franklin Hoxie, *Scientific Management and Labor* (1915; reprint, New York: Augustus M. Kelley, 1966); Milton J. Nadworny, *Scientific Management and the Unions, 1900–1932: A Historical Analysis* (Cambridge, Mass.: Harvard University Press, 1955); and Samuel Haber, *Efficiency and Uplift: Scientific Management in the Progressive Era, 1880–1920* (Chicago: University of Chicago Press, 1964).

3. Harry Braverman, *Labor and Monopoly Capital: The Degradation of Work in the Twentieth Century* (New York: Monthly Review Press, 1974); Margery Davis, *A Woman's Place Is at the Typewriter: Office Work and Office Workers, 1870–1930* (Philadelphia: Temple University Press, 1982); Elyce J. Rotella, *From Home to Office: United States Women at Work, 1870–1930* (Ann Arbor, Mich.: UMI Research Press, 1981); Lisa M. Fine, *The Souls of the Skyscraper: Female Clerical Workers in Chicago, 1870–1930* (Philadelphia: Temple University Press, 1990).

4. See Andrea Tone, *The Business of Benevolence: Industrial Paternalism in Progressive America* (Ithaca, N.Y.: Cornell University Press, 1997); Gerald Zahavi, *Workers, Managers, and Welfare Capitalism: The Shoeworkers and Tanners of Endicott Johnson, 1890–1950* (Urbana: University of Illinois Press, 1988); and Sanford Jacoby, *Employing Bureaucracy: Managers, Unions, and the Transformation of Work in American Industry, 1900–1945* (New York: Columbia University Press, 1985).

5. The best summary of these programs is Stuart Brandes, *American Welfare Capitalism, 1880–1940* (Chicago: University of Chicago Press, 1976). Brandes notes that a third of companies with pension programs in the 1920s required thirty years of continuous service; 87 percent required twenty years of service, in addition to an age requirement (108). Such conditions were impossible for most women to meet, even when they were

formally eligible. See Daniel Nelson and Stuart Campbell, "Taylorism versus Welfare Work in American Industry: H. L. Gantt and the Bancrofts," *Business History Review* 46 (Spring 1972): 1–16, for a discussion of initial conflicts between the two systems.

6. Ronald Schatz, *The Electrical Workers: A History of Labor at General Electric and Westinghouse, 1923–1960* (Urbana: University of Illinois Press, 1983), 20–21.

7. Stephen Meyer, *The Five-Dollar Day: Labor Management and Social Control in the Ford Motor Company, 1908–1921* (Albany: State University of New York Press, 1981), 117. The profit-sharing system fell apart in 1920, partly as a result of worker resentment against intrusive investigations into their domestic arrangements, and partly out of the inflationary pressures that increased wages and cut into profits. Wayne A. Lewchuk, "Men and Monotony: Fraternalism as a Managerial Strategy at the Ford Motor Company," *Journal of Economic History* 53 (December 1993): 824–56; Martha May, "The Historical Problem of the Family Wage: The Ford Motor Company and the Five-Dollar Day," *Feminist Studies* 8 (Summer 1982): 399–424.

8. Brandes, *American Welfare Capitalism*, 5, 35.

9. For an overview of the Western Electric Company and its personnel policies, see Stephen B. Adams and Orville R. Butler, *Manufacturing the Future: A History of Western Electric* (Cambridge: Cambridge University Press, 1999), chap. 4. I am indebted to John Howell Harris for calling this source to my attention. For the research program, see F. J. Roethlisberger and William J. Dickson, *Management and the Worker: An Account of a Research Program Conducted by the Western Electric Company, Hawthorne Works, Chicago* (1939; reprint, Cambridge, Mass.: Harvard University Press, 1964); and Richard Gillespie, *Manufacturing Knowledge: A History of the Hawthorne Experiments* (New York: Cambridge University Press, 1991).

10. Roethlisberger and Dickson, *Management and the Worker*, 185.

11. Gillespie, *Manufacturing Knowledge*, chap. 1.

12. The fullest discussion of the RATR is in ibid., chap. 2.

13. Two of the original women in the RATR were returned to their regular jobs after nine months in the experiment. Managers accused them of not cooperating, of talking too much in the test room, and noted that their production was falling. They also cited the complaints (never adequately documented) of co-workers. Good friends, both insisted that they were merely following the experimenters' directives to work as they felt. When they were let go, the room adjusted quickly, and one of the two replacements, Julia, became by all accounts its leader. Richard Gillespie suggests that the two women were fired because they were outspoken, and managers did not like taking suggestions from teenage girls.

14. Bank Wiring Test, Record of Interview, March 17, 1932, box 9, p. 8, Westinghouse Electric, Hawthorne Studies, Baker Library, Harvard University (hereafter Bank Wiring Test).

15. Roethlisberger and Dickson, *Management and the Worker*, 560–61.

16. Ibid. See also Henry A. Landsberger, *Hawthorne Revisited: Management and the Worker, Its Critics, and Developments in Human Relations Industry* (Ithaca, N.Y.: Cornell University Press, 1958), 74–75.

17. This point is also made by Gillespie, *Manufacturing Knowledge*, 81, 94. And see

Martha Banta, *Taylored Lives: Narrative Productions in the Age of Taylor, Veblen, and Ford* (Chicago: University of Chicago Press, 1993).

18. Roethlisberger and Dickson, *Management and the Worker,* 560.

19. February 27, 1929, box 3, Hawthorne Studies, Baker Library, Harvard University, p. 2.

20. RATR Operators' Comments, 1927–30, Operator 2, May 8, 1929, box 3, Hawthorne Studies, Baker Library, Harvard University. Ronald Schatz confirms these findings. He concludes that as a result of the social solidarity encouraged in particular jobs, some women workers "who ordinarily manifested little interest in unions, proved to be the most tenacious fighters in shop-floor disputes and strikes." Schatz also comments that women's sociability and solidarity at work helped to restrict their output. Schatz, *Electrical Workers,* 33.

21. Interesting Interviews, vol. 2, box 20, no. 94, p. 4, Mayo Collection, Baker Library, Harvard University, Cambridge, Mass.

22. Interview 300, June 19, 1930, p. 5, Technical Branch, Hawthorne Microfiche 186.

23. This contrasts with arguments of some officials in the Women's Bureau of the Department of Labor who insisted that women did not want to work at night. See Mary Anderson, "Should There Be Labor Laws for Women? Yes," *Good Housekeeping* 81 (September 1925): 4–5.

24. Mica Splitting Test Room Studies, Operator 5, February 12, 1930, p. 5, Hawthorne Microfiche 65.

25. RATR Operators' Comments, 1927–30, Operator 5, May 2, 1928, and Operator 3, March 27, 1928, box 3, Hawthorne Studies, Baker Library, Harvard University.

26. Employee Interview 11, November 22, 1929, p. 27, Operating Branch, Hawthorne Microfiche 163.

27. Employee Interview, October 16, 1929, box 4, file 1, p. 2, Hawthorne Microfiche 6.

28. Employee Interview 96, January 13, 1932, p. 96, Bank Wiring Test Room Study, Hawthorne Microfiche 76.

29. Interview 300, June 19, 1930, p. 1, Technical Branch, Hawthorne Microfiche 186.

30. Employee Interview 142, June 27, 1929, p. 2, Operating Branch, Hawthorne Microfiche 167.

31. Employee Interview 131, May 27, 1929, p. 3, Operating Branch, Hawthorne Microfiche 167.

32. Interesting Interviews, September 17, 1930, Specialty Products Branch, vol. 1, box 20, p. 4, Mayo Collection, Baker Library, Harvard University.

33. Interesting Interviews, Interview 105, n.d., Inspection Branch, vol. 2, box 20, p. 3, Mayo Collection, Baker Library, Harvard University.

34. Employee Interview, October 15, 1929, Operating Branch, Hawthorne Microfiche 163.

35. Interview, March 17, 1932, p. 8, Bank Wiring Test Room Study, Hawthorne Microfiche 76.

36. Interesting Interviews, Interview 81, October 30, 1930, Technical Branch, vol. 1, box 20, Mayo Collection, Baker Library, Harvard University, Cambridge, Mass.

37. Banta, *Taylored Lives,* 166. Apparently women (widows, overeducated women)

who evaded or transcended the claims of family were granted some of the status of "real boys," though hardly that of men.

38. Meyer, *Five-Dollar Day*, 117, 140.

39. Mary Barnett Gilson, *What's Past Is Prologue* (New York: Harper, 1940), 98–99, 186, 290.

40. Ida Tarbell, "The New Place of Women in Industry—V: The Forewomen," *Industrial Management* 61 (February 1, 1921), 135.

41. Interesting Interviews, Interview 104, November 11, 1930, vol. 2, box 20, p. 4, Mayo Collection, Baker Library, Harvard University, Cambridge, Mass.

42. RATR, Operator Comments, 1927–30, Operator 2, September 11, 1930, and August 6, 1930, box 3, Hawthorne Studies, Baker Library, Harvard University. Julia had given up the idea of working in an office because it would not pay enough for her family to subsist on.

43. Interview 287, November 11, 1930, Technical Branch, p. 9, Hawthorne Microfiche 184.

44. Ibid., p. 15.

45. Interview 211, October 27, 1971, pp. 4–5, Operating Branch, Hawthorne Microfiche 174.

46. Zahavi, *Workers, Managers, and Welfare Capitalism*, 74. See also Alice Kessler-Harris, "Gender Ideology in Historical Reconstruction," *Gender and History* 1 (Spring 1989): 39.

47. Interview 49, August 21, 1929, p. 1, Operating Branch, Hawthorne Microfiche 164.

48. RATR, Operators Comments, 1927–30, Operator 2, May 15, 1930, box 3, p. 3, Hawthorne Studies, Baker Library, Harvard University.

49. Employee Interview 7, August 27, 1929, p. 1, Operating Branch, Hawthorne Microfiche 163.

50. RATR, Operators Comments, 1927–30, April 23, 1930, May 8, 1930, and May 29, 1930, vol. 2, box 3, Hawthorne Studies, Baker Library, Harvard University.

51. RATR, Operators Comments, 1927–30, May 8, 1930, vol. 2, box 3, Hawthorne Studies, Baker Library, Harvard University. See also Employee Interview 287, November 11, 1930, p. 18, Technical Branch, Hawthorne Microfiche 184.

52. Operator 4, March 1, 1931, p. 2, Mica Splitting Test Room Studies, Hawthorne Microfiche.

53. "Resumé of Methods, Practices, Employee Interviewing Program," April 17, 1929, p. 2, Operating Branch, Hawthorne Microfiche 104.

54. Interview 52, June 3, 1929, p. 1, Operating Branch, Hawthorne Microfiche 164.

Chapter 10: The Just Price, the Free Market, and the Value of Women

1. Brief of the American Civil Liberties Union et al., amici curiae, in *California Federal Savings and Loan Association v. Mark Guerra et al.*, 85–494 U.S. 12–14 (1986); and Brief of Equal Rights Advocates et al., amici curiae, in *California Federal Savings and Loan Association v. Mark Guerra*, 85–494 U.S. 7–9 (1986).

2. In *U.S. Steelworkers v. Weber,* 443 U.S. 193 (1979), the court sustained a voluntary and temporary affirmative action plan to redress past grievances suffered by a specific group. Quotations are from the decision as it appeared in the *Daily Labor Report,* March 20, 1987, D16.

3. "Comparable Worth: An Interview with Heidi Hartmann and June O'Neill," *New Perspectives* 17 (September 1985): 29.

4. Donald J. Treiman and Heidi Hartmann, eds., *Women, Work, and Wages: Equal Pay for Jobs of Equal Value* (Washington, D.C.: National Academy Press, 1981), 28, ix.

5. Barbara R. Bergmann, "Pay Equity—Surprising Answers to Hard Questions," *Challenge* 30 (May–June 1987): 47. See also Helen Remick, ed., *Comparable Worth and Wage Discrimination: Technical Possibilities and Political Realities* (Philadelphia: Temple University Press, 1984), for essays generally favorable to comparable worth.

6. Michael Levin, "Comparable Worth: The Feminist Road to Socialism," *Commentary* 79 (September 1984): 13–19. See also E. Robert Livernash, ed., *Comparable Worth: Issues and Alternatives* (Washington, D.C.: Equal Employment Advisory Council, 1984), for essays generally opposed to comparable worth.

7. Raymond de Roover, "The Concept of the Just Price: Theory and Economic Policy," in *Economic Thought: A Historical Anthology,* ed. James Gherity (New York: Random House, 1969), 23.

8. John Dunlop, "Wage Contours," in *Unemployment and Inflation: Institutional and Structural Views,* ed. Michael Piore (White Plains, N.Y.: M. E. Sharpe, 1979), 66.

9. Arthur M. Ross, *Trade Union Wage Policy* (Berkeley: University of California Press, 1948), 49.

10. Ibid., 50–51 (emphasis mine).

11. Michael J. Piore, "Unemployment and Inflation: An Alternative View," in *Unemployment and Inflation: Institutional and Structural Views,* ed. Michael Piore (White Plains, N.Y.: M. E. Sharpe, 1979), 6.

12. Eileen Power, *Medieval Women* (London: Cambridge University Press, 1975), 60.

13. William Bielby and James Baron, "Undoing Discrimination: Job Integration and Comparable Worth," in *Ingredients for Women's Employment Policy,* ed. Christine Bose and Glenna Spitz (Albany: State University of New York Press, 1987), 218.

14. "Corporate Women: They're About to Break Through to the Top," *Business Week,* June 22, 1987, 74.

15. Edward Hallett Carr, *What Is History?* (New York: Knopf, 1962), 105–6.

16. Quoted in Mary Heen, "A Review of Federal Court Decisions under Title VII of the Civil Rights Act of 1964," in *Comparable Worth and Wage Discrimination: Technical Possibilities and Political Realities,* ed. Helen Remick (Philadelphia: Temple University Press, 1984), 217.

17. The Sears case pitted the EEOC's accusations of discrimination against the company's defense of practices that assigned women to jobs of their choice. See Ruth Milkman, "Women's History and the Sears Case," *Feminist Studies* 12 (Summer 1986): 375–400; and Alice Kessler-Harris, "Equal Employment Opportunity Commission v. Sears Roebuck and Company: A Personal Account," *Radical History Review* 35 (April 1986): 57–79.

18. Judith Long Laws, "Work Aspiration of Women: False Leads and New Starts," in *Women and the Workplace: The Implications of Occupational Segregation,* ed. Martha Blaxall and Barbara Reagan (Chicago: University of Chicago Press, 1976), 33–49.

19. Carole Turbin, "Reconceptualizing Family, Work, and Labor Organizing: Working Women in Troy, 1860–90," *Review of Radical Political Economy* 16 (Spring 1984): 1–16; Mary Blewett, *Men, Women, and Work: Class, Gender, and Protest in the New England Shoe Industry, 1780–1910* (Urbana: University of Illinois Press, 1988).

20. Audre Lorde, "The Master's Tools Will Never Dismantle the Master's House," in *This Bridge Called My Back: Writings by Radical Women of Color,* ed. Cherrie Moraga and Gloria Anzaldua (New York: Kitchen Table/Women of Color Press, 1983), 99.

21. Lillian Breslow Rubin, *Worlds of Pain: Life in the Working-Class Family* (New York: Basic Books, 1976), 176.

22. Brigitte Berger and Peter L. Berger, *The War over the Family: Capturing the Middle Ground* (Garden City, N.Y.: Anchor Press, Doubleday, 1983), 205.

Chapter 11: The Debate over Equality for Women in the Workplace

1. Long before Carol Gilligan articulated the differences between men and women in terms of their moral stance, historians spoke of a socialization process that yielded differentiated male and female stances towards the world. See, for example, Barbara Welter's classic "The Cult of True Womanhood: 1820–1860" *American Quarterly* 17 (1966): 151–74. For a discussion of the uses of these different relationships in the workforce, see chapter 5 in this volume. Gilligan's work sustains these earlier notions but is not necessary to it. Carol Gilligan, *In a Different Voice: Psychological Theory and Women's Development* (Cambridge, Mass.: Harvard University Press, 1982); Marguerite Thibert, "The Economic Depression and the Employment of Women: II." *International Labor Review* 27 (1933): 621.

2. Carl Degler, *At Odds: Women and the Family in America from the Revolution to the Present* (New York: Oxford University Press, 1980), 452–53.

3. Michael Piore, "Fragments of a 'Sociological' Theory of Wages" in *Unemployment and Inflation: Institutional and Structuralist Views,* ed. Michael Piore (White Plains, N.Y.: M. E. Sharpe, 1979), 135.

4. Kessler-Harris, "Stratifying by Sex"; Natalie Sokoloff, *Between Money and Love: the Dialectics of Women's Home and Market Work* (New York: Praeger, 1980); Cynthia Fuchs Epstein, *Woman's Place: Options and Limits in Professional Careers* (Berkeley: University of California Press, 1971); Rosabeth Moss Kanter, *Men and Women of the Corporation* (New York: Basic Books, 1977).

5. Iris Young, "Humanism, Gynocentrism, and Feminist Politics" in *Hypatia Reborn: Essays in Feminist Philosophy,* ed. Azizah Y. al-Hibri and Margaret A. Simons (Indianapolis: Indiana University Press, 1990), 231–48.

6. This is the theory offered by Mary Wollstonecraft in her classic *Vindication of the Rights of Woman,* first published in 1792 and now available in many editions. Margaret Fuller, *Woman in the Nineteenth Century* (New York: W. W. Norton, 1977).

7. Nancy Woloch, *Women and the American Experience* (New York: Alfred A. Knopf, 1984), 383.

8. Mary Ryan, *Womanhood in America: From Colonial Times to the Present* (New York: Franklin Watts, 1983); Carroll Smith-Rosenberg, "Beauty, the Beast, and the Militant Woman: A Case Study in Sex Roles and Social Stress in Jacksonian America," *American Quarterly* 23 (1971): 562–84.

9. Elizabeth F. Baker, *Protective Labor Legislation: With Special Reference to Women in the State of New York* (New York: AMS Press, 1969).

10. M. Shuler, "Industrial Women Confer," *The Woman Citizen,* January 27, 1923, 12.

11. Judith A. Baer, *The Chains of Protection: The Judicial Response to Women's Labor Legislation* (Westport, Conn.: Greenwood Press, 1978); Elizabeth F. Baker, *Technology and Women's Work* (New York: Columbia University Press, 1964); Ann C. Hill, "Protection of Women Workers and the Courts: A Legal Case History," *Feminist Studies* 5 (1979): 271; Alice Kessler-Harris, *Out to Work: A History of Wage-Earning Women in the United States* (New York: Oxford University Press, 1982).

12. Mary Anderson, "Should There Be Labor Laws for Women? Yes," *Good Housekeeping* 81 (September 1925): 4.

13. Eleanor Roosevelt, *It's Up to the Women* (New York: Franklin A. Stokes, 1933), 145.

14. Kessler-Harris, *Out to Work,* chap. 8; Ruth Milkman, "Women's Work and the Economic Crisis: Some Lessons from the Great Depression," *Review of Radical Political Economics* 8 (1976): 73–97.

15. Julia K. Blackwelder, *Women of the Depression: Caste and Culture in San Antonio, 1929–1939* (College Station: Texas A&M University Press, 1983), chaps. 4 and 5.

16. Anderson, "Should There be Labor Laws for Women?"

17. Susan D. Becker, *The Origins of the Equal Rights Amendment: American Feminism between the Wars* (Westport, Conn.: Greenwood Press, 1981).

18. Quoted in ibid., 180.

19. Quoted in ibid., 179.

20. Eleanor Roosevelt, Personal communication to Rose Schneiderman, April 13, 1944, Eleanor Roosevelt Collection, Franklin Delano Roosevelt Library, Hyde Park, N.Y.

21. Alice Hamilton, Personal communication to Miss Magee, May 15, 1953, Wayne State University Archives in Labor History and Urban Affairs, Detroit.

22. "Reasons for Opposing the Equal Rights Amendment," n.d., p. 8, Wayne State University Archives in Labor History and Urban Affairs, Detroit.

23. Nancy Pratt, "When Women Work," *American Federationist* 64 (1957): 7–9, 25.

24. Evidence on this point is ambiguous. In her concluding remarks to a recent survey and evaluation of occupational segregation, Francine Blau notes rather pessimistically that "sex segregation in employment remains a pervasive feature of the labor market and a major cause of women's lower earnings." Francine Blau, "Concluding Remarks," in *Sex Segregation in the Work Place: Trends, Explanations, and Remedies,* ed. Barbara F. Reskin (Washington, D.C.: National Academies Press, 1984), 313. She reaches this conclusion despite the relatively optimistic account of Andrea H. Beller and Rachel A. Rosenfeld in the same volume and in view of research findings by William T. Bielby and James N. Baron, also in the same volume (note also the comments

of Pamela Stone Cain on this issue). Thanks to Louise Tilly for drawing this volume to my attention. Francine Blau, "Occupational Segregation and Labor Market Discrimination" (in *Sex Segregation in the Work Place*, 117–43), suggests that a modest decline in the rate of occupational segregation in the 1970s may be due to the shifting priorities of younger women vis-à-vis paid work and home work. If this is so, then some way of narrowing the separation between home and work becomes ever more crucial as this generation confronts conflicts between home and work in the future.

25. Marcia Greenberger cites lack of federal enforcement as well as the inadequacy of some of the laws themselves as responsible for slow progress. Marcia Greenberger, "The Effectiveness of Federal Laws Prohibiting Sex Discrimination in Employment in the United States," in *Equal Employment Policy for Women: Strategies for Implementation in the United States, Canada, and Western Europe*, ed. Ronnie Steinberg Ratner (Philadelphia: Temple University Press, 1980), 108–27.

26. For unemployment figures, see the U.S. Department of Labor, Bureau of Labor Statistics (Washington, D.C.: Government Printing Office, 1983). Despite the generally higher ratio of female unemployment to male, during the recession of the early 1980s, women's level of unemployment dropped below that of men, indicating their persistence in occupationally segregated areas that were less vulnerable in this downturn. For female earnings and the level of poverty among wage-earning women, see U.S. Department of Labor, Bureau of Labor Statistics, *Report Number 663* (Washington, D.C.: Government Printing Office, 1981), 644, which indicates that the median earnings of female household heads were less than half those of male household heads.

27. Sokoloff, *Between Money and Love.*

28. Charlotte Perkins Gilman, *Women and Economics* (Boston: Small and Maynard, 1898).

29. Dolores Hayden, *The Grand Domestic Revolution: A History of Feminist Designs for American Homes, Neighborhoods, and Cities* (Cambridge: Massachusetts Institute of Technology Press, 1981); Dolores Hayden, *Redesigning the American Dream: The Future of Housing, Work, and Family Life* (New York: W. W. Norton, 1984).

30. Contrast this with the New Right position that, still wedded to the old notion of difference, reasserts the importance of the work/family dichotomy by implying that women will be returned to the home. See Sara Ruddick, "Maternal Thinking," *Feminist Studies* 6 (1980): 342–67.

Chapter 12: Gendered Interventions

1. Daniel T. Rodgers, "Republicanism: The Career of a Concept," *Journal of American History* 79 (June 1992): 11–38; Rogers M. Smith, "One United People: Second-Class Female Citizenship and the American Quest for Community," *Yale Journal of Law and Humanities* 1 (1989): 236–39; J. R. Pole, *The Pursuit of Equality in American History* (Berkeley: University of California Press, 1978), 36–37.

2. Smith, "One United People," 234.

3. David Thelen, Introduction to "Part II: Rights Consciousness in American History," *Journal of American History* 74 (December 1987): 797.

4. Lawrence Friedman, *A History of American Law* (New York: Simon and Schuster,

1973), chap. 4; Joan Hoff, *Law, Gender, and Injustice: A Legal History of U.S. Women* (New York: New York University Press, 1991), chap. 4; Linda Kerber, "The Legal Status of Women in the Early Nineteenth Century," *Human Rights* 6 (Winter 1977): 115–24.

5. Contrast, for example, Mary Blewett, *Men, Women, and Work: Class, Gender, and Protest in the New England Shoe Industry, 1780–1910* (Urbana: University of Illinois Press, 1988), with Alan Dawley, *Class and Community: The Industrial Revolution in Lynn* (Cambridge, Mass.: Harvard University Press, 1976).

6. Marjorie S. Turner, *The Early American Labor Conspiracy Cases: Their Place in Labor Law* (San Diego: San Diego State College Press, 1967), chaps. 2–4; Sean Wilentz, *Chants Democratic: New York City and the Rise of the American Working Class, 1788–1850* (New York: Oxford University Press, 1984), 97–99.

7. For an extended discussion of these cases, see Christopher Tomlins, *Law, Labor, and Ideology in the Early American Republic* (New York: Cambridge University Press, 1993), 128–52. See also John R. Commons et al., eds., *A Documentary History of American Industrial Society*, vol. 3 (Cleveland: A. H. Clark Co., 1910), 251–385.

8. For the pre–Civil War notion, see Eric Foner, *Free Soil, Free Labor, Free Men: The Ideology of the Republican Party before the Civil War* (New York: Oxford University Press, 1970); for legal development in the Gilded Age, see William Forbath, "The Ambiguities of Free Labor: Labor and the Law in the Gilded Age," *Wisconsin Law Review* 4 (July/August 1985): 767–817.

9. As Sean Wilentz notes, the transition to independence was constrained by a sense of the "community's good." Wilentz, *Chants Democratic*, 76–77, 92–93.

10. The patriarchal assumptions of free labor have yet to be fully explored, but for a start, see Jonathan A. Glickstein, *Concepts of Free Labor in Antebellum America* (New Haven, Conn.: Yale University Press, 1991), 11–16.

11. These ideas are developed in Alice Kessler-Harris, *A Woman's Wage: Historical Meaning and Social Consequences* (Lexington: University Press of Kentucky, 1990), chap. 2. See also Amy Dru Stanley, "Conjugal Bonds and Wage Labor: Rights of Contract in the Age of Emancipation," *Journal of American History* 75 (September 1988): 471–500; and Smith, "One United People."

12. Wendy Gamber, "A Precarious Independence: Milliners and Dressmakers in Boston, 1860–1890," *Journal of Women's History* 4 (Spring 1992): 60–88.

13. Linda Kerber, *Women of the Republic: Intellect and Ideology in Revolutionary America* (Chapel Hill: University of North Carolina Press, 1980); Norma Basch, *In the Eyes of the Law: Women, Marriage, and Property in Nineteenth-Century America* (Ithaca, N.Y.: Cornell University Press, 1982), 26–27.

14. Michael Grossberg, *Governing the Hearth: Law and the Family in Nineteenth-Century America* (Chapel Hill: University of North Carolina Press, 1985), 300–302.

15. Basch, *In the Eyes of the Law*, 30. Basch continues: "Nevertheless they did not effect an enormous, radical change in . . . the family."

16. Friedman, *History of American Law*, 186.

17. Additional evidence that poor women looked to the state comes from their efforts to persuade it to provide housing. See Alice Kessler-Harris, *Out to Work: A History of Wage-Earning Women in the United States* (New York: Oxford University Press, 1982), 80–81.

18. The phrase is from David L. Kirp, Mark G. Yudof, and Marlene Strong Franks, *Gender Justice* (Chicago: University of Chicago Press, 1986), 224.

19. This allegiance has now been contested, especially as historians have come to question the existence of boundaries between the private and public. For access to the debate, see especially Christine Stansell, *City of Women: Sex and Class in New York, 1789–1860* (Urbana: University of Illinois Press, 1987); Mary P. Ryan, *Women in Public: Between Banners and Ballots, 1825–1880* (Baltimore: Johns Hopkins University Press, 1990); Nancy A. Hewitt, "Beyond the Search for Sisterhood: American Women's History in the 1980s," *Social History* 10 (October 1985): 299–321.

20. In *Bradwell v. Illinois*, 83 U.S. 130 (1873), the Court decided that the Constitution does not prohibit states from restricting the occupations in which women could engage. In *Minor v. Hapersett*, 88 U.S. 162 (1875), the Supreme Court refused to confront the issue of whether a classification by sex violated the equal protection clause of the amendment and thus tacitly sanctioned the assumption that women constituted a legal "class." Finally, in *In re Lockwood*, 154 U.S. 116 (1894), the Court turned down Belva Lockwood's efforts to be admitted to the Virginia Bar on the ground that states had the right to define a "person" and could, if they wished, define the word as male. For some discussion of these cases, see Nancy S. Erickson, "*Muller v. Oregon* Reconsidered: The Origins of a Sex-Based Doctrine of Liberty of Contract," *Labor History* 30 (Spring 1989): 230–31; Hoff, *Law, Gender, and Injustice*, 183–84; Michael Grossberg, "Institutionalizing Masculinity: The Law as a Masculine Profession," in *Meanings for Manhood: Constructions of Masculinity in Victorian America*, ed. Mark C. Carnes and Clyde Griffen (Chicago: University of Chicago Press, 1990), 133–51; and Kirp, Yudof, and Franks, *Gender Justice*, 225.

21. For the expansion of women's individual rights with relation to the family as a consequence of judicial discretion, see Grossberg, *Governing the Hearth*, 300–301. For a succinct summary of the legal changes, see Eileen Boris and Peter Bardaglio, "The Transformation of Patriarchy: The Historic Role of the State," in *Families, Politics, and Public Policy: A Feminist Dialogue on Women and the State*, ed. Irene Diamond (New York: Longman, 1983), 70–93.

22. See, for example, the *Slaughter-House Cases*, 16 Wall 36 (1983), and *Commonwealth v. Hamilton Mfg. Co.*, 120 Mass. 383 (1876); as well as *Bradwell v. Illinois* and *Minor v. Hapersett*, cited above. See also the discussion in Kirp, Yudof, and Franks, *Gender Justice*, 85–87, 225, who point out that these decisions about women contrasted sharply with the Court's insistence that classifications by race were not "protected."

23. The struggle is chronicled in such books as Leon Fink, *Workingmen's Democracy: The Knights of Labor and American Politics* (Urbana: University of Illinois Press, 1983); and Brian Greenberg, *Worker and Community: Response to Industrialization in a Nineteenth-Century American City, Albany, New York, 1850–1884* (Albany: State University of New York Press, 1985).

24. See Christopher L. Tomlins, *The State and the Unions: Labor Relations, Law, and the Organized Labor Movement in America, 1880–1960* (New York: Cambridge University Press, 1985), 61–63, for elaboration of this argument.

25. Exceptions to a worker's right to freedom of contract generally included only

such occupations as railroad workers, miners, and seamen, where public health and safety was at risk. Where private health was concerned, as in the case of bakers and cigar makers, courts generally refused to support state intervention.

26. Martha May, "Bread before Roses: American Workingmen, Labor Unions, and the Family Wage," in *Women, Work, and Protest: A Century of U.S. Women's Labor History,* ed. Ruth Milkman (Boston: Routledge and Kegan Paul, 1985), 1–21; Kessler-Harris, *Woman's Wage,* chap. 1.

27. Stanley, "Conjugal Bonds and Wage Labor," 471–500. Between 1860 and 1880, women's demands for equal rights shifted their rationale from an insistence on workplace rights to their 1880s focus on the home. See Blewett, *Men, Women, and Work;* and Susan Levine, *Labor's True Woman: Carpet Weavers, Industrialization, and Labor Reform in the Gilded Age* (Philadelphia: Temple University Press, 1984).

28. Joy Parr, *The Gender of Breadwinners: Women, Men, and Change in Two Industrial Towns, 1880–1950* (Toronto: University of Toronto Press, 1990), 150. See also Jeanne Boydston's formulation of the relationship between economic independence and citizenship in *Home and Work: Housework, Wages, and Ideology of Labor in the Early Republic* (New York: Oxford University Press, 1990), 43.

29. David Montgomery, *Workers' Control in America: Studies in the History of Work, Technology, and Labor Struggles* (New York: Cambridge University Press, 1979), chap. 1.

30. Ava Baron, "Acquiring Manly Competence: The Demise of Apprenticeship and the Remasculinization of Printers' Work," in *Meanings for Manhood: Constructions of Masculinity in Victorian America,* ed. Mark C. Carnes and Clyde Griffen (Chicago: University of Chicago Press, 1990), 152–63.

31. Quoted in Linda Schneider, "The Citizen Striker: Workers' Ideology in the Homestead Strike of 1892," *Labor History* 23 (Winter 1982): 52.

32. Theresa Wolfson, *The Woman Worker and the Trade Unions* (New York: International Publishers, 1926), 76.

33. Quoted in Tomlins, *State and the Unions,* 63.

34. Only five states (Massachusetts, Pennsylvania, Nebraska, Washington, and Oregon) had successfully passed laws regulating women's working hours and condition before 1908. An Illinois law, upheld by the state, was overturned at the federal level.

35. Evelyn Brooks Higginbotham, "African-American Women's History and the Metalanguage of Race," *Signs* 17 (Winter 1992): 251–74.

36. This point is made by Eileen Boris, "The Power of Motherhood: Black and White Activist Women Redefine the 'Political,'" *Yale Journal of Law and Feminism* 2 (Fall 1989): 35.

37. See especially William Forbath, *Law and the Shaping of the American Labor Movement* (Cambridge, Mass.: Harvard University Press, 1991), chap. 5.

38. Robyn Muncy, *Creating a Female Dominion in American Reform, 1890–1935* (New York: Oxford University Press, 1991); Kathryn Kish Sklar, "Hull House as a Community of Women Reformers in the 1890s," *Signs* 10 (1985): 657–77; Linda Gordon, "Social Insurance and Public Assistance: The Influence of Gender in Welfare Thought in the United States, 1890–1935," *Journal of American History* 97 (February 1992): 19–54.

39. Much of the current literature attributes the origins of the American welfare

state to "maternalist" legislation promoted and promulgated by networks of women. One interpretation suggests that where states are weak, the role of women in the form of strong, organized movements has been enhanced. But the literature attributes the sources of this legislation to structures of organization and is contradictory as to its ultimate effect. See, for example, Sonya Michel and Seth Koven, "Womanly Duties: Maternalist Politics and the Origins of Welfare States in France, Germany, Great Britain, and the United States, 1880–1920," *American Historical Review* 95 (October 1990): 1076–1108; Ann Shola Orloff, "Gender in Early U.S. Social Policy," *Journal of Policy Issues* 3.3 (1991): 249–81; and Theda Skocpol, *Protecting Soldiers and Mothers: The Political Origins of Social Policy in the United States* (Cambridge, Mass.: Harvard University Press, 1992).

40. See chapter 13 of this volume. There still exists a lively debate as to whether protective labor legislation for women had long-term harmful effects for women. See Kessler-Harris, *Out to Work,* chap. 7; and Kathryn Kish Sklar, "'The Greater Part of the Petitioners Are Female': The Reduction of Women's Working Hours in the Paid Labor Force, 1840–1917," in *Worktime and Industrialization: An International History,* ed. Gary Cross (Philadelphia: Temple University Press, 1989), 103–34. Molly Ladd-Taylor, *Mother-Work: Women, Child Welfare, and the State, 1890–1940* (Urbana: University of Illinois Press, 1994), argues that mothers' pensions effectively discriminated against women of color and those who violated traditional family norms. Muncy, *Creating a Female Dominion,* focuses on the positive consequences of this legislation.

41. For an excellent discussion of how this was stymied in Germany, see Sabine Schmitt, "Protective Labor Legislation for Women in Germany: 1878–1914," in *Comparative Studies in Protective Labor Legislation,* ed. Ulla Wikander (Urbana: University of Illinois Press, 1995), 125–49.

42. Quoted in Beatrix Hoffman, *The Wages of Sickness: The Politics of Health Insurance in Progressive America* (Chapel Hill: University of North Carolina Press, 2001).

43. The argument here sustains part of Heidi Hartmann's in "Capitalism, Patriarchy, and Job Segregation by Sex," *Signs* 1 (1976): 137–69.

Chapter 13: The Paradox of Motherhood

1. Joanne Goodwin, "An American Experiment in Paid Motherhood: The Implementation of Mothers' Pensions in Early Twentieth-Century Chicago," *Gender and History* 4 (Autumn 1992): 323–42; Molly Ladd-Taylor, *Raising a Baby the Government Way: Mothers' Letters to the Children's Bureau, 1915–1932* (New Brunswick, N.J.: Rutgers University Press, 1986); Molly Ladd-Taylor, *Mother-Work: Women, Child Welfare, and the State, 1890–1930* (Urbana: University of Illinois Press, 1994); Theda Skocpol, *Protecting Soldiers and Mothers: The Political Origins of Social Policy in the United States* (Cambridge, Mass.: Harvard University Press, 1993).

2. New York State provides perhaps the only exception to this. For a discussion of the New York legislative debates of 1917–19, when a maternity benefit proposal went down to defeat, see Beatrix Hoffman, *The Wages of Sickness: The Politics of Health Insurance in Progressive America* (Chapel Hill: University of North Carolina Press, 2001).

3. *Lochner v. New York,* 198 U.S. 45 (1905). A good discussion of law in relation to American workers can be found in William Forbath, *Law and the Shaping of the American Labor Movement* (Cambridge, Mass.: Harvard University Press, 1991). The standard discussion of law in relation to gender is in Leo Kanowitz, *Sex Roles in Law and Society: Cases and Materials* (Albuquerque: University of New Mexico Press, 1973).

4. A summary and discussion of this legislation can be found in Alice Kessler-Harris, *Out to Work: A History of Wage-Earning Women in the United States* (New York: Oxford University Press, 1982), chap. 7. See also Judith Baer, *The Chains of Protection: The Judicial Response to Women's Labor Legislation* (Westport, Conn.: Greenwood Press, 1978).

5. *Muller v. Oregon,* 208 U.S. 412 (1908).

6. Skocpol, *Protecting Soldiers and Mothers;* Kathryn Kish Sklar, *Florence Kelley and the Nation's Work: The Rise of Women's Political Culture, 1830–1900* (New Haven, Conn.: Yale University Press, 1995).

7. Vivien Hart, *Bound by Our Constitution: Women, Workers, and the Minimum Wage* (Princeton, N.J.: Princeton University Press, 1994), suggests that the shaping strategy was a desire to avoid the constraints of rigid judicial interpretation of the Constitution.

8. Michael Grossberg, *Governing the Hearth: Law and the Family in Nineteenth-Century America* (Chapel Hill: University of North Carolina Press, 1985), 300.

9. See, for example, discussions of New York and Massachusetts in Clara M. Beyer, *History of Labor Legislation for Women in Three States,* Women's Bureau Bulletin no. 66 (Washington, D.C.: Government Printing Office, 1929); and Elizabeth Faulkner Baker, *Protective Labor Legislation, with Special Reference to Women in the State of New York* (New York: Columbia University Press, 1925), 236.

10. These were Massachusetts (1890), Indiana (1894), Nebraska (1898), and New York (1903). See Mary D. Hopkins, *The Employment of Women at Night,* Women's Bureau Bulletin no. 64 (Washington, D.C.: Government Printing Office, 1928), 2.

11. There is certainly evidence, however, that American reformers and legislators were aware of it. For example, when the New York State law came under judicial scrutiny in 1913–14, *The Survey,* an important outlet for the reform community, reported that in drafting the original law, members of a Factory Investigation Commission had "availed themselves of the recorded experience of the fourteen European nations who in 1906 met in Bern, Switzerland, to sign an international treaty prohibiting night work for women in industrial establishments." "Progress of the New York Women's Night Work Case," *The Survey* 32 (June 12, 1914): 169. The 1906 Bern Convention shows up frequently in the literature of reformers, who refer to it as a mark of civilization. For example, *The Survey* frequently compared the lack of night-work laws in the United States with those in Europe: "This tardy progress is in striking contrast to the action of the fourteen civilized countries of Europe which have, since 1906, by international treaty prohibited the night work of women." "Night Work Law Tested in New York State," *The Survey* 31 (December 24, 1913): 343. Similar references can be found in the editorial pages of *The Charities and the Commons,* for example, contrasting "the European movement towards total prohibition of women's nightwork in industrial estab-

lishments—representatives of all the civilized governments, having met twice during the past two years to draw up international agreements on the subject—and the indifference to such protection in this country." "Night Work: Women and the New York Courts," *The Charities and the Commons* 17 (December 1906): 183.

12. Nancy Erickson sees this decision as less dramatic than is typically the case. "*Muller v. Oregon* Reconsidered: The Origins of a Sex-Based Doctrine of Liberty of Contract," *Labor History* 30 (Spring 1989): 230–31.

13. *State Laws Affecting Working Women,* Women's Bureau Bulletin no. 40 (Washington, D.C.: Government Printing Office, 1924), 5.

14. Hopkins, *Employment of Women at Night,* 4.

15. *State Laws Affecting Working Women,* 5.

16. "Regulation of Women's Working Hours in the United States," *American Labor Legislation Review* 8 (December 1918): 345–54.

17. *State Laws Affecting Working Women,* 5.

18. Hopkins, *Employment of Women at Night,* 6, acknowledges the possibility of an undercount.

19. Ibid., 10.

20. Agnes de Lima, *Night Working Mothers in Textile Mills: Passaic, New Jersey* (n.p.: National Consumer's League and the Consumer's League of New Jersey, 1920), 8. Another study of forty-six women revealed that forty-two of them were under school age. See Mary E. McDowell, "Mothers and Night Work," *The Survey* 39 (December 22, 1917): 335.

21. African American women are a significant exception. Since the vast majority of them were excluded from industrial work and were occupied in domestic service and agricultural work, they would, in any event, not have been covered by this legislation. See U.S. Department of Labor, *Negro Women in Industry,* Women's Bureau Bulletin no. 20 (Washington, D.C.: Government Printing Office, 1922).

22. Charles Iffland, "Reasons Why Night Work Should Be Abolished in Bakeries," *American Federationist* 26 (May 1919): 408.

23. Josephine Goldmark, *Fatigue and Efficiency: A Study in Industry* (New York: Charities Publication Committee, 1912), 266.

24. Emery Hayhurst, M.D., "Medical Argument against Night Work Especially for Women Employees," *American Journal of Public Health* 9 (1919): 367.

25. 155 Ill. 98 (1895), 105.

26. 15 Pa. Superior Court, 5 (1900), 17. See also *People v. Williams,* 184 N.Y. 131 (1907).

27. Baker, *Protective Labor Legislation,* 236–37. Part of the difficulty here was the insistence of the courts on dealing with "women and children" as if they had unified interests and needs.

28. *People v. Schweinler Press,* 214 N.Y. 395 (1915), 400, 409.

29. Ibid., 401–2.

30. Francis Perkins, "Do Women in Industry Need Special Protection?" *The Survey* 55 (February 15, 1926): 531.

31. "A Summary of the 'Facts of Knowledge' Submitted on Behalf of the People,"

in National Consumer's League, *The Case against Night Work for Women* (New York: National Consumer's League, 1914), A10.

32. *People v. Schweinler Press,* 403.

33. Elizabeth Faulkner Baker, "Do Women in Industry Need Special Protection?" *The Survey* 55 (February 15, 1926): 583.

34. "A Summary of the 'Facts of Knowledge,'" A10.

35. De Lima, *Night Working Mothers in Textile Mills,* 5.

36. *The Cotton Textile Industry,* vol. 1 of the Report on the Condition of Women and Child Wage Earners in the United States, Senate Doc. 645, 61st Cong., 2d Sess. (Washington, D.C.: Government Printing Office, 1910), 289, 293.

37. Goldmark, *Fatigue and Efficiency,* 275.

38. Ibid., 267.

39. De Lima, *Night Working Mothers in Textile Mills,* 5; *Wage-Earning Women in Stores and Factories,* vol. 5 of the Report on the Condition of Women and Child Wage Earners in the United States, Senate Doc. 645, 61st Cong., 2d Sess. (Washington, D.C.: Government Printing Office, 1910), 214; Goldmark, *Fatigue and Efficiency,* 275.

40. "Night Work Law Tested in New York State," 343.

41. *Annual Report of the Consumers' League of New York* (1906) quoted in Baker, "Do Women in Industry Need Special Protection?" 239.

42. "Progress of the New York Women's Night Work Case," 169.

43. *Summary: The Effects of Labor Legislation on the Employment Opportunities of Women,* Women's Bureau Bulletin no. 68 (Washington, D.C.: Government Printing Office, 1928), 15.

44. See Hopkins, *Employment of Women at Night,* 57. For a discussion of glass workers and decent women, see "Fighting Women's Night Work in Rhode Island," *The Survey* 36 (February 13, 1916): 48.

45. Rheta Childe Dorr, "Should There Be Labor Laws for Women? No," *Good Housekeeping* 81 (September 1925): 52–54.

46. Baker, "Do Women in Industry Need Special Protection?" 531.

47. "Night Work: Women and the New York Courts," 183.

48. Perkins, "Do Women in Industry Need Special Protection?" 530.

49. Ibid., 532; Beyer, *History of Labor Legislation far Women.*

50. De Lima, *Night Working Mothers in Textile Mills,* 16.

Chapter 14: Measures for Masculinity

1. These policies have sometimes been identified as the products of a two-channel state that assigned most women and men of color to means-tested policies. See, for example, Barbara J. Nelson, "The Origins of the Two-Channel Welfare State: Workmen's Compensation and Mothers' Aid," in *Women, the State, and Welfare,* ed. Linda Gordon (Madison: University of Wisconsin Press, 1990), 123–51; and Gwendolyn Mink, *The Wages of Motherhood: Inequality in the Welfare State, 1917–1942* (Ithaca, N.Y.: Cornell University Press, 1995). They were also the product of shared assumptions about wage work, as is argued by Linda Gordon, *Pitied but Not Entitled: Single Mothers and*

the History of Welfare, 1890–1935 (New York: Free Press, 1994). See also Joanne Goodwin, *Gender and the Politics of Welfare Reform: Mothers' Pensions in Chicago, 1911–1929* (Chicago: University of Chicago Press, 1997); and Theda Skocpol, *Protecting Soldiers and Mothers: The Political Origins of Social Policy in the United States* (Cambridge, Mass.: Harvard University Press, 1992).

2. On the history of voluntarism in the 1930s, see George Gilmary Higgins, *Voluntarism in Organized Labor in the United States, 1930–1940* (1944; reprint, New York: Arno Press and the New York Times, 1969).

3. Samuel Gompers, "Labor vs. Its Barnacles," *American Federationist* 23 (April 1916): 270.

4. Beatrix Hoffman, *Health Insurance and the Making of the American Welfare State, 1915–1920* (Chapel Hill: University of North Carolina Press, 1999); Patricia Brito, "Protective Labor Legislation in Ohio: The Interwar Years," *Ohio History* 88 (Spring 1979): 178–97.

5. Louis Reed, *The Labor Philosophy of Samuel Gompers* (New York: Columbia University Press, 1930), 126.

6. *Report of the Proceedings of the 52nd Annual Convention of the American Federation of Labor,* Cincinnati, 1932, AFL records, Sanford, N.C.: pt. 2, reels 58–144, 245 (hereafter *Proceedings of the AFL*). Records held by the State Historical Society of Wisconsin, edited by Harold L. Miller.

7. Ibid., 245–46.

8. Ibid., 246.

9. Ibid. (the general discussion is on 244–47; the quotes are on 246–47). Andrew Furuseth's comments continued: "I cannot see any reason why we should follow some of the mad ideas of Europe when they set out from an entirely different point of view in dealing with governmental and social questions than we do" (246).

10. Ibid., 292–93. See also David R. Roediger and Philip S. Foner, *Our Own Time: A History of American Labor and the Working Day* (New York: Greenwood Press, 1989), 246–47.

11. U.S. Congress, *Hearings before a Subcommittee of the Committee on the Judiciary,* 72d Cong., 2d Sess., January 1933, "Thirty-Hour Work Week," 1 (hereafter *Senate Hearings,* "Thirty-Hour Work Week"). I found this story in Stanley Vittoz, *New Deal Labor Policy and the American Industrial Economy* (Chapel Hill: University of North Carolina Press, 1987), 83–85.

12. *Senate Hearings,* "Thirty-Hour Work Week," 426.

13. Ibid. He continued: "During a depression, who can estimate the number of people who have become reconciled to charity, professional pensioners on the public bounty or professional hobos and criminals?"

14. This sense was fueled by the fact that some of the same people who sought a thirty-hour week to expand employment and maintain citizenship attacked the rights of married women to work. One rank and filer, Louis Draudt, wrote to William Green that he thought it would be a "God-send" if the AFL could "get a 30 hour week for all wage-earners." He then urged "a national law passed eliminating all married women working where their husbands are working." Louis Draudt to William Green, October

16, 1933, AFL-CIO Papers, RG21, box 44, file 46, George Meany Memorial Archives, Silver Springs, Maryland.

15. For more on the larger debate, see Benjamin Kline Hunnicutt, *Work without End: Abandoning Shorter Hours for the Right to Work* (Philadelphia: Temple University Press, 1988), 154, and discussion, 153–63. For the following discussion, see Grant Farr, *Origins of Recent Labor Policy* (Boulder: University of Colorado Press, 1959), 63–64, 99–101.

16. "President Limits 30–Hour Week Bill," *New York Times,* April 13, 1933, 2; Hunicutt, *Work without End,* 153.

17. These two groups are frequently conflated under the "social insurance" rubric to distinguish their proposals from those of the champions of assistance to the needy. See, for example, Linda Gordon, "Social Insurance and Public Assistance: The Influence of Gender and Welfare Thought in the United States, 1890–1935," *American Historical Review* 97 (February 1992): 19–54. Despite their overlapping concerns, I've sharpened the distinctions for the purposes of examining the sources of the employment legislation.

18. John Commons, *History of Labor in the United States,* vol. 3 (New York: Macmillan, 1935), xix.

19. Ibid., xxvii.

20. John R. Commons, "The Right to Work," *The Arena* 21 (February 1899): 134.

21. Roy Lubove, *The Struggle for Social Security, 1900–1935* (Cambridge, Mass.: Harvard University Press, 1968), 172; Daniel Nelson, *Unemployment Insurance: The American Experience, 1915–1935* (Madison: University of Wisconsin Press, 1969), 152n. Within a year, by January 1934, the plan had been considered by the legislatures of seventeen states. It would soon be adopted not only by Ohio but, in modified version, by New York.

22. Quoted in Kenneth Casebeer, "The Workers' Unemployment Insurance Bill: American Social Wage, Labor Organization, and Legal Ideology," in *Labor Law in America: Historical and Critical Essays,* ed. Christopher Tomlins and Andrew King (Baltimore: Johns Hopkins University Press, 1992), 232.

23. *Proceedings of the AFL,* 1931, 397.

24. AFL vice president Mathew Woll, speaking at the convention, *Proceedings of the AFL,* 1931, 370.

25. Boston AFL Convention, 1930, quoted in ibid., 369–70.

26. Quoted in Casebeer, "Worker's Unemployment Insurance Bill," 232. This is, of course, exactly what protective labor legislation did to women. Gompers continued, "The whole of our activity organized to assert and to live our own lives would be subject to every petty or high official . . . according to the government's conception of what is and what is not voluntary employment."

27. Woll, *Proceedings of the AFL,* 1931, 369.

28. Quoted in ibid.

29. Ibid.

30. Ibid., 394.

31. Ibid., 372.

32. Ibid., 373.

33. Ibid., 374. See also Florence Hanson, of the Teachers Union, who states: "I believe

... unemployment insurance will increase the freedom of the worker and his self-respect, and that unemployment insurance will be of great strength to trade unionists." Ibid., 383.

34. *Proceedings of the AFL,* 1932, 339.

35. Ibid., 336.

36. Ibid., 40–41.

37. Ibid., 346.

38. Ibid., 39, 43.

39. Ibid., 43.

40. Ibid., 10.

41. Edwin Witte, "Organized Labor and Social Security," in *Labor and the New Deal,* ed. Milton Derber and Edwin Young (Madison: University of Wisconsin Press, 1961), 252–53.

42. William Green, testimony at U.S. Congress, *Hearings before a Subcommittee of the House Committee on Ways and Means on H.R. 7659,* 73d Cong., 2d Sess., March 24, 1934, 256.

43. J. Douglas Brown recalls a conversation with Green during which Green told him, "We will go along with you on joint contributions for old-age insurance, but we will not make contributions to the unemployment insurance." J. Douglas Brown, interview by Peter Corning, February 6, 1965, p. 4, Columbia Oral History Project, New York.

44. U.S. Congress, *Hearings before the Senate Committee on Finance, on S. 1130, Economic Security Act,* 74th Cong., 1st Sess., January 22 to February 20, 1935, 167–73. Green had remained a reluctant supporter until the very end—a reluctance that undermined his influence. For example, in the Wagner-Lewis hearings the year before, he testified to his wish that such unemployment insurance were not necessary but claimed that he would support it to protect the purchasing power of families. "We have always believed that it would be far better for our social and economic order if employment could be furnished workers so that they could earn their living as decent, upstanding American citizens. We prefer that." The male content of work and citizenship is apparent as the statement continues: "We believe a man will maintain his independence and his manhood better if he is permitted to earn a living, but we have found from experience that we have not yet mastered our economic forces, so that we can maintain an economic order which will guarantee and grant to the workers of this country even limited opportunities to earn a living" (256–57).

Chapter 15: In Pursuit of Economic Citizenship

1. Quoted in Alice Kessler-Harris, *In Pursuit of Equity: Women, Men, and the Quest for Economic Citizenship in Twentieth-Century America* (New York: Oxford University Press, 2001), 273.

2. I mean something more than the criterion put forward by Barbara Hobson and Ann Orloff of the ability to establish an independent household. In addition, I would include the capacity to make choices about how to earn one's living. Barbara Hobson, "No Exit, No Voice: Women's Economic Dependency and the Welfare State," *Acta Sociologica* 33 (1990): 235–50; Ann Orloff, "Gender and the Social Rights in Citizenship:

The Comparative Analysis of Gender Relations and Welfare States," *American Sociological Review* 58 (1993): 303–28.

3. T. H. Marshall, *Citizenship and Social Class and Other Essays* (Cambridge: Cambridge University Press, 1950).

4. Nancy Fraser, *Unruly Practices: Power, Discourse, and Gender in Contemporary Social Theory* (Minneapolis: University of Minnesota Press, 1989); Helga Hernes, *Welfare State and Woman Power: Essays in State Feminism* (Oslo: Norwegian University Press, 1987); Hobson, "No Exit, No Voice"; Walter Korpi, "Faces of Inequality: Gender, Class, and Patterns of Inequalities in Different Types of Welfare States," *Social Politics* 7.2 (2000): 127–91; Arnlaug Leira, *Welfare States and Working Mothers* (Cambridge: Cambridge University Press, 1992); Jane Lewis, "Gender and the Development of Welfare Regimes," *Journal of European Social Policy* 2 (1992): 159–73; Ruth Lister, *Citizenship: Feminist Perspectives* (London: Macmillan, 1997); Julia O'Connor, "Gender, Class, and Citizenship in the Comparative Analysis of Welfare State Regimes," *British Journal of Sociology* 44 (1993): 501–18; Carol Pateman, "The Patriarchal Welfare State," in *Democracy and the Welfare State*, ed. Amy Gutman (Princeton, N.J.: Princeton University Press, 1988), 231–60.

5. Marshall, *Citizenship and Social Class*, 10.

6. Jon Elster, "Is There (or Should There Be) a Right to Work?" in *Democracy and the Welfare State*, ed. Amy Gutman (Princeton, N.J.: Princeton University Press, 1988), 56.

7. Korpi, "Faces of Inequality," 140.

8. Hernes, *Welfare State and Woman Power*.

9. Vicki Schultz, "Life's Work," *Columbia Law Review* 100 (2000): 1881–1964.

10. Nancy Folbre, *Invisible Heart: Economics and Family Values* (New York: New Press, 2001).

11. Marshall, *Citizenship and Social Class*, 15.

12. Carol Pateman, *The Sexual Contract* (Stanford, Calif.: Stanford University Press, 1988); Susan James, "The Good-Enough Citizen: Citizenship and Independence," in *Beyond Equality and Difference: Citizenship, Feminist Politics, Female Subjectivity*, ed. Gisela Bock and Susan James (New York: Routledge, 1992), 48–65.

13. Clara Bingham and Laura Leedy Gansler, *Class Action: The Story of Lois Jenson and the Landmark Case That Changed Sexual Harassment Law* (New York: Doubleday, 2002).

14. Kessler-Harris, *In Pursuit of Equity*.

15. *Truax v. Raich*, 239 U.S. 33 (1915), 41.

16. From a speech he made before Congress on December 30, 1930, at the U.S. Congress, *Hearings before a Subcommittee of the Committee on Banking and Currency on Full Employment Act of 1945*, Senate Doc. 380, 79th Cong., 1st Sess., July 30–September 1, 1945 (Washington, D.C.: Government Printing Office), 1–2.

17. Björn Wittrock and Peter Wagner, "Social Science and the Building of the Early Welfare State: Toward a Comparison of Statist and Non-Statist Western Societies," in *States, Social Knowledge, and the Origins of Modern Social Policies*, ed. Dietrich Rueschemeyer and Theda Skocpol (Princeton, N.J.: Princeton University Press, 1996).

18. Marshall, *Citizenship and Social Class*, 28.

19. Ibid., 8, 33.

20. Kessler-Harris, *In Pursuit of Equity;* Ann Shola Orloff, "Gender in Early U.S. Social Policy," *Journal of Policy History* 3.3 (1991): 249–81.

21. Barbara Nelson, "The Origins of the Two-Channel Welfare State: Workmen's Compensation and Mother's Aid," in *Women, the State, and Welfare,* ed. Linda Gordon (Madison: University of Wisconsin Press, 1990), 123–51.

22. Mary Lynn Stewart, *Women, Work, and the French State: Labour Protection and Social Patriarchy, 1879–1919* (Montreal: McGill-Queens University Press, 1989); Ulla Wikander, Alice Kessler-Harris, and Jane Lewis, eds., *Protecting Women: Labor Legislation in Europe, the United States, and Australia* (Urbana: University of Illinois Press, 1995).

23. *Muller v. Oregon,* 208 U.S. 412 (1908).

24. Kessler-Harris, *In Pursuit of Equity.* This approach was not reversed until the 1970s. See *Reed v. Reed,* 404 U.S. 71 (1971); and *Weinberger v. Wiesenfeld,* 420 U.S. 636 (1975).

25. Gwendolyn Mink, *Welfare's End* (Ithaca, N.Y.: Cornell University Press, 1998).

26. Eva Feder Kittay, "From Welfare to a Public Ethic of Care," and Joan Tronto, "Who Cares? Public and Private Caring and the Rethinking of Citizenship," in *Women Welfare: Theory and Practice in the United States and Europe,* ed. Nancy J. Hirschmann and Ulrike Liebert (New Brunswick, N.J.: Rutgers University Press, 2001), 38–64, 65–83.

27. Diane Sainsbury, *Gender, Equality, and Welfare States* (Cambridge: Cambridge University Press, 1996).

28. Judith Shklar, *American Citizenship: The Quest for Inclusion* (Cambridge, Mass.: Harvard University Press, 1991).

29. In the United States, many of the most valuable prerogatives of social citizenship have been manipulated to reserve economic autonomy to men. Examples of this include the granting of old-age benefits to the husbands of wives; the assignment to widows of only a portion of their husband's benefit; provision of child care as a function of the need for women in the labor force; and restriction of unemployment benefits so that they effectively discriminate against wives. Social rights offered as a benefit of earning and attached to the contributions made by individuals—old-age pensions and unemployment insurance in the United States fall into this category—are available as a matter of "right." Those acquired without access to "rights to earn" may be called "entitlements," but they are encumbered with restrictions as to the morality and behavior of the recipient, threatening to reduce rather than enhance self-respect.

30. Mink, *Welfare's End;* Ann Orloff, "Ending the Entitlements of Poor Single Mothers: Changing Social Policies, Women's Employment, and Caregiving in the Contemporary United States," in *Women Welfare: Theory and Practice in the United States and Europe,* ed. Nancy J. Hirschmann and Ulrike Liebert (New Brunswick, N.J.: Rutgers University Press, 2001), 133–59.

31. Korpi, "Faces of Inequality"; Hernes, *Welfare State and Woman Power;* Sainsbury, *Gender, Equality, and Welfare States.*

32. Shklar, *American Citizenship,* 98–99.

33. Kessler-Harris, *In Pursuit of Equity,* 272.

34. Eileen Applebaum, "U.S. Lags Behind in Family Friendly Work Policies," *Wom-*

en's Enews, January 2002 (www.womensenews.org/article.cfm/dyn/aid/792/context/archive; accessed May 13, 2006).

35. Arlie Hochschild, *The Time Bind* (New York: Henry Holt, 1997).

36. Hernes, *Welfare State and Woman Power.*

37. Korpi, "Faces of Inequality."

38. Marga Bruyn-Hundt, "Scenarios for the Distribution of Unpaid Work in the Netherlands," *Feminist Economics* 2 (1996): 127–41.

39. *Nevada Department of Human Resources v. Hibbs,* 538 U.S. 2 (May 27, 2003).

Chapter 16: Reframing the History of Women's Wage Labor

1. Antoinette Burton, *At the Heart of Empire: Indians and the Colonial Encounter in Late Victorian Britain* (Berkeley: University of California Press, 1998); Ann Laura Stoler, *Race and the Education of Desire: Foucault's 'History of Sexuality' and the Colonial Order of Things* (Durham, N.C.: Duke University Press, 1995); Kumari Jayawardena, *Feminism and Nationalism in the Third World* (London: Zed Books, 1939), introduction.

2. Ann Garrols, reporting for National Public Radio, December 4, 2001.

3. It is impossible to provide all the pertinent examples here, but a small selection would include Barbara Hanawalt, ed., *Women and Work in Pre-Industrial Europe* (Bloomington: Indiana University Press, 1986); Emily Honig, *Sisters and Strangers: Women in the Shanghai Cotton Mills, 1919–1949* (Stanford, Calif.: Stanford University Press, 1986); Alice Kessler-Harris, *Out to Work: A History of Wage-Earning Women in the United States* (New York: Oxford University Press, 1982); Tessie P. Liu, *The Weaver's Knot: The Contradictions of Class Struggle and Family Solidarity in Western France, 1750–1914* (Ithaca, N.Y.: Cornell University Press, 1994); Louise Tilly and Joan Scott, *Women, Work, and Family* (New York: Holt, Reinhart and Winston, 1978); and Deborah Valenze, *The First Industrial Woman* (New York: Oxford University Press, 1995).

4. See especially Kathleen Canning, *Languages of Labor and Gender: Female Factory Work in Germany, 1850–1914* (Ithaca, N.Y.: Cornell University Press, 1996); and Carole Turbin, *Working Women of Collar City: Gender, Class, and Community in Troy, 1864–86* (Urbana: University of Illinois Press, 1992).

5. Examples include Theresa L. Amott and Julie A. Matthaie, *Race, Gender, and Work: A Multicultural Economic History of Women in the United States* (Boston: South End Press, 1991); Leonore Davidoff and Catherine Hall, *Family Fortunes* (Chicago: Chicago University Press, 1987); and Bonnie Smith, *Ladies of the Leisure Class* (Princeton, N.J.: Princeton University Press, 1981).

6. Examples include Catherine Hall, ed., *Cultures of Empire: Colonizers in Britain and the Empire in the Nineteenth and Twentieth Centuries, a Reader* (Manchester: Manchester University Press, 2000); Donna Guy, *Sex and Danger in Buenos Aires: Prostitution, Family, and Nation in Argentina* (Lincoln: University of Nebraska Press, 1990); Helen Safa, *The Myth of the Male Breadwinner: Women and Industrialization in the Carribbean* (Boulder, Colo.: Westview Press, 1995); Patricia E. Tsurumi, *Factory Girls: Women in the Thread Mills of Meiji Japan* (Princeton, N.J.: Princeton University Press, 1990); and Joel Wolfe, *Working Women, Working Men: Sao Paolo and the Rise of Brazil's Industrial Working Class, 1900–1955* (Durham, N.C.: Duke University Press, 1993).

7. The best examples come from South Asia: Nirmala Banerjee, "Working Women in Colonial Bengal: Modernization and Marginalization," in *Recasting Women: Essays in Indian Colonial History,* ed. Kumkum Sangaria and Sudesh Vaid (New Brunswick, N.J.: Rutgers University Press, 1990), 269–301; Antoinette Burton, *Burdens of History: British Feminists, Indian Women, and Imperial Culture, 1865–1915* (Chapel Hill: University of North Carolina Press, 1994); and Mrinalini Sinha, *Colonial Masculinity: The 'Manly Englishman' and the 'Effeminate Bengali' in the Late Nineteenth Century* (Manchester: University of Manchester Press, 1995).

8. Leela Fernandes, *Producing Workers: The Politics of Gender, Class, and Culture in the Calcutta Jute Mills* (Philadelphia: University of Pennsylvania Press, 1997); William E. French, "Prostitutes and Guardian Angels: Women, Work, and the Family in Porfirian Mexico," *Hispanic American Historical Review* 72 (November 1992): 529–53.

9. Karen Tranberg Hansen, *Distant Companions: Servants and Employers in Zambia, 1900–1945* (Ithaca, N.Y.: Cornell University Press, 1989); Luise White, *The Comforts of Home: Prostitution in Colonial Nairobi* (Chicago: University of Chicago Press, 1990).

10. See the essays in Judith Bennett et al., eds., *Sisters and Workers in the Middle Ages* (Chicago: University of Chicago Press, 1989); Hanawalt, *Women and Work in Pre-Industrial Europe;* and Martha Howell, *Women, Production, and Patriarchy in Late Medieval Cities* (Chicago: University of Chicago Press, 1986).

11. Joy Parr, *The Gender of Breadwinners: Women, Men, and Change in Two Industrial Towns, 1880–1950* (Toronto: University of Toronto Press, 1990); Lena Sommestad, "Welfare State Attitudes to the Male Breadwinning System: The United States and Sweden in Comparative Perspective," *International Review of Social History* 42.5 (1997): 153–74.

12. Tilly and Scott, *Women, Work, and Family;* Leslie Woodcock Tentler, *Wage-Earning Women: Industrial Work and Family Life in the United States, 1900–1930* (New York: Oxford University Press, 1979); Tera Hunter, *To 'Joy My Freedom: Southern Black Women's Lives and Labors after the Civil War* (Cambridge, Mass.: Harvard University Press, 1993); Eileen Boris, "Homework and Women's Rights: The Case of the Vermont Knitters, 1980–85," in *Homework: Historical and Contemporary Perspectives on Paid Labor at Home,* ed. Eileen Boris and Cynthia R. Daniels (Urbana: University of Illinois Press, 1989), 123–57.

13. Alice Kessler-Harris, "In the Nation's Image: The Gendered Limits of Social Citizenship in the Depression Era," *Journal of American History* 86 (December 1999): 1251–79.

14. Among many sources, see Barbara Hobson, ed., *Gender and Citizenship in Transition* (New York: Routledge, 2000); Alice Kessler-Harris, *In Pursuit of Equity: Women, Men, and the Quest for Economic Citizenship in Twentieth-Century America* (New York: Oxford University Press, 2001); Jane Lewis, "Gender and the Development of Welfare Regimes," *Journal of European Social Policy* 2 (1992): 159–73; Ann Shola Orloff, "Gender and the Social Rights in Citizenship: The Comparative Analysis of Gender Relations and Welfare States," *American Sociological Review* 58 (1993): 303–28; Ann Shola Orloff, *The Politics of Pensions: A Comparative Analysis of Britain, Canada, and the United States, 1890–1940* (Madison: University of Wisconsin Press, 1993); and Ulla Wikander, Alice Kessler-Harris, and Jane Lewis, eds., *Protecting Women: Labor Legislation in*

Europe, Australia and the United States, 1880–1920 (Urbana: University of Illinois Press, 1995).

15. Except in sub-Saharan Africa, where their already high rates of participation declined slightly. United Nations, *The World's Women, 1995: Trends and Statistics* (New York: United Nations Publication, 1995), xviii–xix, xxii.

16. Susan Schaefer Davis, "Working Women in a Moroccan Village," in *Women in the Muslim World,* ed. Lois Beck and Nikki Keddie (Cambridge, Mass.: Harvard University Press), 419–20.

17. Ester Boserup, *Women's Role in Economic Development* (New York: St. Martin's, 1970), chap. 2; Philippe Antoine and Jeanne Nanitelamio, "Can Polygyny Be Avoided in Dakar?" in *Courtyards, Markets, and City Streets: Urban Women in Africa,* ed. Kathleen Sheldon (Boulder, Colo.: Westview Press, 1996), 129–52; Sharon Stichter, "Women, Employment, and the Family: Current Debates," in *Women, Employment, and the Family in the International Division of Labour,* ed. Sharon Stichter and Jane L. Parpart (London: Macmillan, 1990), 60.

18. Ursula Sharma, "Women and Work in India," in *Women, Employment, and the Family in the International Division of Labour,* ed. Sharon Stichter and Jane L. Parpart (London: Macmillan, 1990), 233–35.

19. Susan Mann, *Precious Records: Women in China's Long Eighteenth Century* (Stanford, Calif.: Stanford University Press, 1997).

20. Stichter, "Women, Employment, and the Family"; Sylvia Arrom, *The Women of Mexico City, 1790–1857* (Stanford, Calif.: Stanford University Press, 1985).

21. Altagracia Ortiz, "Puerto Rican Women Workers in the Twentieth Century: A Historical Appraisal of the Literature," in *Puerto Rican Women's History: New Perspectives,* ed. Felix V. Matos-Rodriguez and Linda C. Delgado (Armonk, N.Y.: M. E. Sharpe, 1998). For China, see Susan Mann, "Household Handicrafts and State Policy in Qing Times," in *To Achieve Security and Wealth: The Qing Imperial State and the Economy, 1644–1911,* ed. Jane Kate Leonard and John Watt (Ithaca, N.Y.: Cornell University Press, 1992).

22. David Landes, *The Wealth and Poverty of Nations: Why Some Are So Rich and Others Are So Poor* (New York: Norton, 1999), 413; Jayawardena, *Feminism and Nationalism in the Third World,* 8.

23. Richard Anker, *Gender and Jobs: Sex Segregation of Occupations in the World* (Geneva: International Labor Office, 1998), 245, 289; Nadia Hijab, *Womanpower: The Arab Debate on Women at Work* (Cambridge: Cambridge University Press, 1988).

24. Catherine Hall, *Civilizing Subjects: Metropole and Colony in the English Imagination, 1830–1867* (Chicago: University of Chicago Press, 2002); Jayawardena, *Feminism and Nationalism in the Third World.*

25. Maxine Berg, "What Difference Did Women's Work Make to the Industrial Revolution?" in *Women's Work: The English Experience, 1650–1914,* ed. Pamela Sharpe (London: Arnold, 1998), 149–71.

26. Emily Honig, *Sisters and Strangers: Women in the Shanghai Cotton Mills, 1919–1949* (Stanford, Calif.: Stanford University Press, 1986), 3.

27. Francesca Bray, *Technology and Gender: Fabrics of Power in Late Imperial China* (Berkeley: University of California Press, 1997), chap. 5.

28. Tsurumi, *Factory Girls.*

29. Elizabeth Prügl, "Home Based Producers in Development Discourse," in *Home-workers in Global Perspective: Invisible No More,* ed. Eileen Boris and Elizabeth Prügl (New York: Routledge, 1996), 39–61.

30. Anker, *Gender and Jobs,* 403.

31. Ann Stoler, "Cultivating Bourgeois Bodies and Racial Selves," in *Cultures of Empire: Colonizers in Britain and the Empire in the Nineteenth and Twentieth Centuries, a Reader,* ed. Catherine Hall (Manchester: Manchester University Press, 2000), 87–119; Sinha, *Colonial Masculinity.*

32. Fernandes, *Producing Workers.*

33. Wikander, Kessler-Harris, and Lewis, *Protecting Women,* introduction.

34. Karen Tranberg Hansen, *Distant Companions: Servants and Employers in Zambia, 1900–1945* (Ithaca, N.Y.: Cornell University Press, 1989), 5.

35. White, *Comforts of Home.*

36. Donna Guy, *Sex and Danger in Buenos Aires.*

37. Lin Lean Lim, ed., *The Sex Sector: The Economic and Social Bases of Prostitution in Southeast Asia* (Geneva: International Labor Office, 1998): 209–11.

38. Gail Hershatter, *Dangerous Pleasures: Prostitution and Modernity in Twentieth-Century Shanghai* (Berkeley: University of California Press, 1997); Tsurumi, *Factory Girls.*

39. Helen Safa, "Female Employment in the Puerto Rican Working Class," in *Women and Change in Latin America,* ed. Helen Safa and June Nash (South Hadley, Mass.: Bergin and Garvey, 1986), chap. 6.

40. Barbara Ehrenreich and Alrie Russell Hochschild, eds., *Global Woman: Nannies, Maids, and Sex Workers in the New Economy* (New York: Metropolitan Books, 2003).

41. Edna Bonacich, "The Garment Industry, National Development, and Labor Organizing," in *Global Production: The Apparel Industry in the Pacific Rim,* ed. Edna Bonacich et al. (Philadelphia: Temple University Press, 1994), 371.

42. Diane Lauren Wolf, *Factory Daughters: Gender, Household Dynamics, and Rural Industrialization in Java* (Berkeley: University of California Press, 1992).

43. Vanessa Maher, "Work, Consumption, and Authority within the Household: A Moroccan Case," in *Of Marriage and the Market: Women's Subordination Internationally and Its Lessons,* ed. Kate Young, Carol Wolkowitz, and Roslyn McCullagh (London: Routledge, 1980), 117–35.

44. Marcia Wright, "Technology, Marriage, and Women's Work in the History of Maize-Growers in Mazubuka, Zambie: A Reconnaissance," *Journal of South African Studies* 10 (1983): 71–85.

Chapter 17: "History Is Public or Nothing"

1. Warren I. Susman, *Culture as History: The Transformation of American Society in the Twentieth Century* (New York: Pantheon, 1984), xii.

2. Ibid., 7.

3. William H. Whyte, *The Organization Man* (New York: Simon and Schuster, 1972); David Riesman with Reuel Denney and Nathan Glazer, *The Lonely Crowd: A Study of the Changing American Character* (New Haven, Conn.: Yale University Press, 1950).

4. Karl Mannheim, *Ideology and Utopia: An Introduction to the Sociology of Knowledge* (London: Routledge, 1991).

5. E. P. Thompson, interview by Mike Merrill, in *Visions of History,* ed. Henry Abelove, Betsy Blackmar, Peter Dimock, and Jonathan Schneer (New York: Pantheon Books, 1983), 5–25.

6. Karl Marx, "Excerpt from *Toward the Critique of Hegel's Philosophy of Right,*" in *Karl Marx and Friedrich Engels' Basic Writings on Politics and Philosophy,* ed. Lewis S. Feuer (1844; reprint, New York: Doubleday, 1959), 263.

7. Richard Hoggart, *Uses of Literacy: Changing Patterns in English Mass Culture* (Fair Lawn, N.J.: Essential Books, 1957).

8. Herbert Marcuse, *One-Dimensional Man: Studies in the Ideology of Advanced Industrial Society* (Boston: Beacon Press, 1971); Antonio Gramsci, *Prison Notebooks,* ed. Joseph A. Buttigieg (New York: Columbia University Press, 1992).

9. Natalie Zemon Davis, interview by Rob Harding and Judy Coffin, in *Visions of History,* ed. Henry Abelove, Betsy Blackmar, Peter Dimock, and Jonathan Schneer (New York: Pantheon Books, 1983), 99–122.

10. Lewis A. Ehrenberg, *Steppin' Out: New York Nightlife and the Transformation of American Culture, 1890–1930* (Westport, Conn.: Greenwood Press, 1981); Kathy Peiss, *Cheap Amusements: Working Women and Leisure in Turn-of-the-Century New York* (Philadelphia: Temple University Press, 1986); Roy Rosenzweig, *Eight Hours for What We Will: Workers and Leisure in an Industrial City, 1870–1920* (New York: Cambridge University Press, 1983); Herbert George Gutman, *Work, Culture, and Society in Industrializing America: Essays in American Working-Class and Social History* (New York: Knopf, 1976).

11. Selig Perlman, *A History of Trade Unionism in the United States* (New York: Macmillan, 1922).

12. Philip Taft, "Theories of the Labor Movement," in *Interpreting the Labor Movement,* Industrial Relations Research Association (Madison, Wisc.: Industrial Relations Research Association, 1952), 31, 35, 37.

13. C. Wright Mills, *The Sociological Imagination* (New York: Oxford University Press, 1959).

14. Daniel Bell, "The Capitalism of the Proletariat: A Theory of American Trade Unionism," in *The End of Ideology: On the Exhaustion of Political Ideas in the Fifties* (New York: Free Press, 1960), 208–21.

15. John J. Sweeney, "Time for a New Contract," *Dissent* 44 (Winter 1997): 35.

16. Allen Ginsberg, "Wales Visitation," in *Planet News, 1961–1967* (San Francisco: City Lights Books, 1968), 140–41.

17. Raymond Williams, "Base and Superstructure in Marxist Cultural Theory," *New Left Review* 82 (1973): 3–16.

18. Raymond Williams, "The Welsh Industrial Novel," in *Problems in Materialism and Culture: Selected Essays* (London: Verso, 1980), 223.

19. Raymond Williams, *Border Country* (New York: Horizon Press, 1962), 284.

Index

Abbott, Edith, 19, 99
ACLU (American Civil Liberties Union), 203–4
ACWA (Amalgamated Clothing Workers of America), 31, 54, 67–68, 85, 305n2. See also *Advance* (ACWA)
Advance (ACWA), 57, 67–68
affirmative action: comparable worth juxtaposed to, 184; limited effects of, 203; male entitlement vs., 259; Supreme Court on, 180–81, 336n2
Afghanistan: U.S. war on, 270–71
AFL-CIO, 180. *See also* American Federation of Labor (AFL)
Africa: family wealth in, 275; labor migration in, 282; slavery in, 281; women's domestic power in, 284
African Americans: excluded in unemployment insurance proposals, 244–45; history of, 2–3, 329n25; "home sphere" and, 150. *See also* race
African American women workers: excluded from "woman" category, 218; minimum-wage laws and, 324n61; night-work debate and, 232, 345n21; number and occupations of, 107, 124, 305n3, 322n51
African American working men: as union members, 29, 238
agency, 149, 290
Alabama: night work in, 227
Albertus Magnus (saint), 182–83
Alexander, Sally, 253
Amalgamated Clothing Workers of America

(ACWA), 31, 54, 67–68, 85, 305n2. See also *Advance* (ACWA)
Amalgamated Streetcar Workers Union, 30
American Civil Liberties Union (ACLU), 203–4
American Civil War, 119–22
American Federationist (AFL): on equal rights, 201; on organizing women, 28; on protective legislation, 31; on women's displacement of male workers, 24, 26; on women's place, 27, 61
American Federation of Labor (AFL): ambivalence about organizing women, 21–22, 53–54, 82; attitudes of, 25–27; CIO split from, 87–88; criticism of, 80–81; dual closure of, 60–61; on equal pay, 25, 27; goals of, 60, 74; on governmental intervention, 238–41, 245; incentive for organizing women, 27–28; liberty conception of, 246; protective legislation and, 30–32, 84, 224, 239–40; on social insurance, 242–43; on Social Security, 248–49; unemployment insurance campaign and, 243–44; women organizers of, 27, 28, 29–30; women workers as threat to, 24, 26, 90; WTUL's relationship with, 61, 82, 85, 87–89. *See also* AFL-CIO; *American Federationist* (AFL); masculinity
American Federation of State, County, and Municipal Employees, 327n7
American Historical Association, 253–54
Americanization, 109
American Journal of Public Health, 229

ALICE KESSLER-HARRIS is the R. Gordon Hoxie Professor of American History at Columbia University. Her books include *Women Have Always Worked: A Historical Overview, Out to Work: A History of Wage-Earning Women in the United States, A Woman's Wage: Historical Meanings and Social Consequences,* and *In Pursuit of Equity: How Gender Shaped American Economic Citizenship,* which won the Joan Kelly, Phillip Taft, Herbert Hoover, and Bancroft Prizes.

The University of Illinois Press
is a founding member of the
Association of American University Presses.

Composed in 10.5/13 Adobe Minion
with Meta display
by Jim Proefrock
at the University of Illinois Press
Designed by Copenhaver Cumpston
Manufactured by Sheridan Books, Inc.

University of Illinois Press
1325 South Oak Street
Champaign, IL 61820-6903
www.press.uillinois.edu